Journal of the Early Book Society
for the study of manuscripts and printing history

Edited by Martha W. Driver
Volume 13, 2010

ISBN: 1-935625-0-39
ISBN-13: 978-1935625-0-32 (pbk: alk.ppr.)
ISSN: 1525-6790

Member

Council of Editors of Learned Journals

™ The paper used in this publication meets the minimum requirements
of American National Standard for information Sciences—Permanence of
Paper for printed Library Materials,
ANSI Z39.48—1984.

The *Journal of the Early Book Society* is published annually. JEBS invites longer articles on manuscripts and/or printed books produced between 1350 and 1550. Special consideration will be given to essays exploring the period of transition from manuscript to print. Articles should not exceed 8000 words or thirty typed pages. Authors are asked to employ American spelling and punctuation conventions, and to follow *The Chicago Manual of Style*. A Works Cited list at the end of the text should include city, publisher, and date. Manuscripts are to be sent, in triplicate, along with an abstract of up to 150 words, to Martha Driver, Early Book Society, Department of English, Pace University, 41 Park Row, New York, New York 10038. Only materials accompanied by a self-addressed, stamped envelope (or international reply coupon) will be returned. Members of the Early Book Society who are recent authors may send review books for consideration to Susan Powell, Reviews Editor, School of English, Sociology, Politics and Contemporary History (ESPaCH), University of Salford, Salford M5 4WT UK. Brief notes on recent discoveries, highlighting little-known or recently uncovered texts and/or images, may be sent to Linne R. Mooney, Centre for Medieval Studies, King's Manor, University of York, York YO1 2EP UK. Subscription information may be obtained from Martha Driver or from Pace University Press.

Those interested in joining the Early Book Society or with editorial inquiries may contact Martha Driver by post or e-mail (MDriver@Pace.edu). Information may also be found at <www.nyu.edu/projects/EBS>. For ordering information, call Pace University Press at 212-346-1405, email PaceUP@Pace.edu, or visit http://www.pace.edu/press. Institutions and libraries may purchase copies directly from Ingram Library Services (1-800-937-5300).

The editor wishes to thank Gill Kent, as well as Beth Scorzato and Mark Hussey of Pace University Press, for their help and advice on this issue.

Journal of the Early Book Society
For the Study of Manuscripts and Printing History

Editor
Martha W. Driver, *Pace University*

Associate Editors
Emily Butler, *University of Toronto*
Linne R. Mooney, *University of York*
Susan Powell, *University of Salford*

Editorial Board
Matthew Balensuela, *DePauw University*
Julia Boffey, *Queen Mary, University of London*
Cynthia J. Brown, *University of California, Santa Barbara*
Richard F. M. Byrn, *University of Leeds*
James Carley, *York University*
Joyce Coleman, *University of Oklahoma*
Margaret Connolly, *University of St Andrews*
Susanna Fein, *Kent State University*
Alexandra Gillespie, *University of Toronto*
Vincent Gillespie, *Lady Margaret Hall, Oxford University*
Stanley S. Hussey, *Lancaster University*
Ann M. Hutchison, *Pontifical Institute of Mediaeval Studies and York University*
William Marx, *University of Wales, Lampeter*
Carol M. Meale, *Bristol University*
Charlotte C. Morse, *Virginia Commonwealth University*
Daniel W. Mosser, *Virginia Polytechnic Institute and State University*
Ann Eljenholm Nichols, *Winona State University*
Judy Oliver, *Colgate University*
Michael Orr, *Lawrence University*
Steven Partridge, *University of British Columbia*
Derek Pearsall, *Harvard University*
Pamela Sheingorn, *The City University of New York Graduate School and University Center*
Alison Smith, *Wagner College*
Toshiyuki Takamiya, *Keio University*
Andrew Taylor, *University of Ottawa*
John Thompson, *Queen's University, Belfast*
Ronald Waldron, *King's College, University of London*
Edward Wheatley, *Loyola University*
Mary Beth Winn, *SUNY Albany*

Contents

Articles

**Nota Bene: Brief Notes on Manuscripts and Early Printed Books
Highlighting Little-Known or Recently Uncovered Items or Related Issues**

The *Romanz* Psalter in England and Northern France in the Twelfth Century: Production, *Mise-en-page*, and Circulation

GEOFF RECTOR

Prior to the emergence of romance as a genre in the 1160s and 1170s, the translation of the Psalms into *romanz* was the single most comprehensive vernacular literary impulse in the Anglo-Norman world.[1] As many as five separate, complete *romanz* translations of the Psalms, in both its Gallican and Hebrew forms, were made in England and northern France in the twelfth century.[2] Around these massive projects of translation, we find a constellation of associated texts: prayers on the Psalms, Penitential Psalms, Canticles, as well as a series of related and yet more massive vernacular Psalter Commentaries. The prominence of the Psalms in the broader emergence of the new vernacular literary culture is also witnessed in the material record. As Tony Hunt has recently observed, "about half of the surviving twelfth-century manuscripts containing French come from English Benedictine houses and almost half of these are Psalters."[3] Among these texts are two of the very oldest extant works of Anglo-Norman literature: the 'Cambridge Psalter' (*ca.* 1125-1140), an interlinear translation of the Hebrew version now extant in the luxurious Eadwine Psalter (Cambridge, Trinity College, MS R.17.1), and the 'Oxford Psalter' (*ca.* 1100-1115), a complete prose translation of the Gallican Psalms extant in the Montebourg Psalter (Oxford, Bodleian Library, MS Douce 320). In size and in breadth of circulation, these projects dwarf all other *romanz* works produced in the first half of the twelfth century.[4] These works must then be placed at the very center of the emerging Anglo-Norman literary culture.

Here they would stay for the next three centuries, in which time the Oxford Psalter became among the most widely read and widely distributed of all Anglo-Norman literary works.

Since the publication in 1860 of Francisque Michel's edition of the Oxford Psalter, philologists have assigned these Psalter translations a prominent place in the history of the language, but the Psalters have not taken a comparable place in literary histories, possibly as a result of the lingering habit of separating the devotional and the pedagogical from the domain of the literary.[5] But, as we see below, the Psalms were every bit as poetic as they were devotional in the period, and the bustling energies that gave us these translations were inseparable from the new, courtly vernacular literary culture. These *romanz* Psalters emerged from the same social contexts as other literary works of this early period, sharing similar reading practices, as well as material and even rhetorical forms. As I will argue, just as the "'Englishing,' of the biblical Psalms" would do in "sixteenth- and seventeenth-century England," so the 'romancing' of the Psalms "substantially shaped the |literary| culture" of twelfth-century England and northern France.[6]

Most narrowly, this paper examines the production, *mise-en-page* and circulation of *romanz* Psalters in twelfth-century England and northern France. Its primary goal is to describe this vibrant and insufficiently historicized movement in early *romanz* literature in its basic material, practical and social contexts. It will move chronologically and formally: from the Psalter translations of the early century and their widespread circulation and adaptation, to the vernacular Psalter Commentaries of the last third of the century. As we trace the circulation of these texts and the history of their material forms, we can see how the *romanz* Psalter operated within broader vernacular literary developments. The chronological movement through the century will reveal three processes shaping both the *romanz* Psalter and that larger literary culture: first, an early engagement, both imitative and competitive, with the literary traditions of Anglo-Saxon England; second, the adoption of monastic reading practices and the texts appropriate to them by vernacular reading audiences; and, third an intense engagement—in material form, in genre and in style—between the devotional and the courtly. These last two points are particularly crucial. On the one hand, they speak to the social networks within which these Psalters were produced and circulated, where we systematically see the interaction of the aristocratic court and the cloister. On the other, the interaction of the vernacular Psalms with courtly discourses confirms again the point that the literary cannot be separated in this period from other, more 'interested'—devotional, meditational, pedagogical—discursive forms. Even in their most meditational and monastic expressions, the vernacular Psalms are literary and exercised a powerfully shaping influence within the emerging vernacular literary culture.

The Sauter de romance in the twelfth century

At the very dawn of francophone literature in England, we find two distinct translations of the Psalter, extant in two very different material forms. The one is a translation of the Hebrew Psalms extant in the Eadwine Psalter, a deluxe *psalterium triplex* that contains Anglo-Saxon and Anglo-Norman glosses to two of its three Psalters (the Romanum and Hebrew versions respectively); the other is the so-called Oxford Psalter, a prose translation of the entire Gallican Psalter whose earliest, and in this context most important, witness is the rather humble Oxford, Bodleian MS Douce 320 (the Montebourg Psalter).[7] In this manuscript, the *romanz* Psalms are presented alone, without the traditional apparatus and decoration used to frame the reading of liturgical or exegetical Psalters, and still more strikingly, without any accompanying Latin text whatsoever. Although very different in form, these two *romanz* Psalters speak to a coherent set of impulses driving the larger emergence of *romanz* literature in post-conquest England.

Of these two early Anglo-Norman Psalters, the translation found in the Eadwine Psalter (Cambridge, Trinity College, MS R.17.1) most clearly illustrates the response to the precedent of Anglo-Saxon literary culture, in this case the traditions of the Old English Psalter. The Eadwine Psalter is a *psalterium triplex* produced at Canterbury (*ca.* 1155), whose complex scriptorial engineering is matched only by the splendor of its pictorial programme.[8] Famous for its portrait of Eadwine, 'prince of scribes,' the Eadwine Psalter contains "one hundred and sixty-six colored outline drawings," derived from the drawings of the Utrecht Psalter (Utrecht, University Library, MS script. eccl. 484), illustrating the Psalms, Canticles and Creeds.[9] Below these illustrations, which occupy the upper register, we find the Latin text of the Gallican Psalms in a central textual column surrounded by marginal Latin glosses. Towards the gutter, we find two smaller columns: the first presenting the Romanum Psalms with an interlinear Old English translation, and the second, closest to the gutter, the Hebrew Psalms with an interlineal Anglo-Norman translation— the only translation of the Hebrew Psalms made in any medieval French dialect.[10] As Dominique Markey shows, this translation, the Cambridge Psalter, clearly predates the manuscript itself, placing it back into the cradle of *romanz* literature in England.[11] The triplex format of the Eadwine Psalter is not itself unique, but its integral trilinguality is, making the manuscript an eloquent witness to the sociolinguistic dynamics that framed the mid-twelfth-century emergence of Anglo-Norman literature.[12]

Anglo-Norman literature emerges against the backdrop and precedent of Old English literature. Continuities with that past are most tangible here in the Old English gloss. The Romanum Psalms text that it accompanies was the "Psalter *par excellence* of the Anglo-Saxon Church from the seventh to the mid-tenth century."[13] As F. G. Berghaus has shown, the Eadwine Psalter's Old

English glosses "belong to the mainstream of Old English Psalter glosses," showing a composite derivation from several Old English gloss types.[14] Yet the text and *mise-en-page* of the Old English glosses speak as much to rupture and the displacement of English literary traditions as they do to their continuity. In the course of the monastic reforms of the tenth and eleventh centuries, the Romanum Psalter had already been almost entirely superseded in England by the Gallican Psalter, so that even this Psalter text and its Old English glosses look back to a tradition long outdated. Moreover, the Old English glosses of the Eadwine Psalter are a "linguistic gallimaufry" of forms cobbled together from "several periods and dialects," including a brief use of the Old English Metrical Psalms from Psalm 90.15 to 95.2.[15] The Old English text is peppered with scribal errors that testify to the scribes' difficulties with the archaic English of their source, as well as with "peculiar spellings" that reveal the influence of both "contemporary Middle English" and Anglo-Norman.[16]

The Anglo-Norman gloss to the Hebrew Psalter shows the same mix of continuity and discontinuity that we see in the Old English gloss. Patrick O'Neill notes that, at first glance, "the English and the French gloss" seem to be "so similar in their interlinear form and glossarial function that to explain the presence of one should cast light on the presence of the other."[17] This would suggest that the French translation—entirely unprecedented—and its *mise-en-page* may have been modeled on its more established, venerable Old English companion. In this respect, the Anglo-Norman text would represent an imitative continuity with Anglo-Saxon traditions. And yet, "even here" O'Neill continues, "there is evidence that the French gloss was regarded as the more important of the two."[18] First, wherever "the English and the French vie for space," the Old English gloss is "sacrificed by being omitted" to maintain the material and discursive integrity of the French text.[19] Second, the effort to maintain that integrity is reiterated in the textual form of the Anglo-Norman gloss. In comparison to the cobbled discontinuities of the inherited Old English gloss, the Anglo-Norman text is written in a syntactically coherent and continuous prose. However, translations are lacking for Psalms 125 to 130, 149 and 150, which effectively divides the Anglo-Norman text into two unequal groups. Dominique Markey, confirming the work of Walter Schumann, concludes that the gloss to Psalms 1-124 is a copy of a preexistent (and probably complete) Anglo-Norman translation of the Hebrew Psalter, while the text of Psalms 131-148 is the work of a second "single author... who avoids repetition and Latinisms in favour of a more varied" and rhetorically innovative vocabulary.[20] Where Schumann concludes that this second translator was a member of the Eadwine Psalter's scribal team, supplementing a faulty original, Markey suspects, on the basis of paleographic and linguistic evidence, the prior existence of yet another *romanz* Hebrew Psalter translation.[21]

Regardless of whether we are dealing with one original or two, the central facts remain: the manuscript is evidence of a vast project of literary vernacularization, undertaken well before 1155, that is discursively continuous, rhetorically innovative and, in many important ways, entirely new. This is the only Old French translation of the Hebrew Psalter, and neither is there a prior tradition of Old English glosses to the Hebrew Psalter from which it could take precedent.[22] These characteristics suggest that the Anglo-Norman text was not only preferred in relation to the Old English, but also that it was opportune, newly useful in this moment for a specific kind of reading. In O'Neill's assessment, the Old English gloss ought to be understood, not "as a text to be read and studied in its own right," but "as a formal parallel to the French" translation and a sign of cultural continuity.[23] This suggests, of course, that the French text *was* designed "to be read and studied in its own right." What this use might have been is suggested by the fact that, unlike the Gallican and Romanum Psalters, the Hebrew Psalter never found common use in liturgical or devotional practices, but was valued primarily as "a hermeneutic instrument" in the context of study and exegesis.[24] Its Anglo-Norman gloss, in turn, "reflects the desire to establish a good vernacular translation" that would aid in the study of the Latin text.[25] Yet the drive to maintain the material integrity and discursive continuity of the Anglo-Norman text, as well as the rhetorical innovations of the last eighteen Psalms, all suggest that the *romanz* text was something more than just a handmaiden to a Latin original, and rather, that it enjoyed pedagogical utility and literary value in and of itself. Thus, the Cambridge Psalter shows us that by mid-century *romanz* had acquired a precedence over Old English as Latin's principal handmaiden and in so doing had acquired a sociolinguistic prestige that it had not enjoyed prior to the Conquest. This new rhetorical elevation, in large part a sociolinguistic effect of the Conquest, made Anglo-Norman suitable to the texts, reading practices and social desires of education (very broadly imagined). In fact, it made the language literary.

More characteristic than the almost singular Cambridge Psalter—a very rarely copied translation of the relatively rare Hebrew text, tied to *sacra pagina* in an extraordinary manuscript—is a contemporaneous translation of the Gallican Psalms: the Oxford Psalter (*ca.* 1100-1115).[26] Not only is the Oxford Psalter the oldest work of biblical translation in French and quite possibly the oldest extant work of Anglo-Norman literature but, as we see below, it is also among the most widely circulated of all Anglo-Norman texts.[27] The widespread popularity of this translation may be a function of the Gallican's Psalter's pre-eminence in the Western liturgy but at least as important is the fact that the translation seems to have been designed to furnish meditational and devotional reading practices rather than exegesis. As we know from other contexts, devotional reading was one of the great engines of vernacularization on both sides of the Channel in the twelfth century. Yet we can also see in the wide course of its transmission and adaptation—again in stark contrast to the Cambridge Psalter—an increasing engagement of the Oxford Psalter and its devotional practices with the styles and forms of the new courtly aesthetic. We might argue that this engagement between meditative reading and courtly entertainment, between Psalms and romance, structures both the history of the vernacular Psalms and the broader field of *romanz* literature in the period of its emergence.

In another expression of the literary self-sufficiency that we see in the Cambridge Psalter, the Oxford Psalter is written in a continuous prose that conforms, not to Latin word order, but "à la syntaxe de la langue vulgaire |to the syntax of the vernacular language|."[28] It is an organic vernacular literary text, readable in and of itself, and not a word-by-word translation; as the *mises-en-page* of its subsequent manuscripts attest, it could not, as a result, easily service interlinear reading of any kind. In the six twelfth-century copies that come after Douce 320, the Oxford Psalter appears interlineally in only a single manuscript (London, British Library MS Harley 5102); however, the *romanz* text in this manuscript breaks off after the twenty-fifth Psalm—an indication of the difficulty of trying to align the two texts.[29] Given its antiquity, the material and poetic independence of the vernacular in this text is an extraordinary testament to the prestige of *romanz* in twelfth-century England. The *mise-en-page* of its earliest extant manuscript, the rather modest Montebourg Psalter (Oxford, Bodleian MS Douce 320b), confirms the vernacular text's independence in the simplest possible manner: the Oxford Psalms are presented in a single prose column, without any accompanying Latin text. It offers no prologue to justify or praise the benefits of vernacular, as we see in so many early *romanz* works, and most dramatically there is no accompanying Latin text of the Psalms in any form. Indeed, there is barely a word of Latin in the entire manuscript.

The inspiration for both the prose form and this particular *mise-en-page* may have come in part from Old English Psalter traditions. The connection is made particularly tantalizing if we accept Canterbury Cathedral Priory as the Oxford Psalter's provenance.[30] The only precedent for a prose Psalter in any European vernacular is the Old English Prose Psalter, prose itself being extremely rare in French in this period.[31] In his genealogy of French prose, Omer Jodogne cites the Montebourg copy of the Oxford Psalms as the earliest witness, but shows that prose composition did not really become common in any form until the last third of the twelfth century.[32] Moreover, the Old English Prose Psalter is "several… steps removed from the word-for-word cribs of the glossed psalter tradition," is typically arranged in parallel prose columns rather than as interlinear gloss, and exhibits "clear connections with… the prose and poetry of the period," despite its liturgical and devotional origins—all characteristics shared by our Oxford Psalter.[33] But in its material and literary independence from the Latin, the Oxford Psalter in its earliest witness also seems like a radical innovation in vernacular literary culture.

As a complete translation of all 150 Psalms of the Gallican Psalter, the Oxford Psalter is a vast project of literary vernacularization. In the Douce 320 manuscript, it takes up thirty-seven folios (fol. 37a-73a), or seventy-three pages, and is followed by six Anglo-Norman canticles (Isaiah, Ezechias, Anne, Moses, Abacuc and Moses to the Children of Israel), similarly written in prose and taking up another six folios (fol. 73b-78b). These 73 pages of prose text are, moreover, presented in a format that is relatively large for twelfth-century Anglo-Norman manuscripts. The manuscript page itself is typically 29.3 x 20.4 centimeters (or approximately 11.5 x 8 in.), and the *mise-en-page* leaves very little marginal space. The frame ruling presents the text as a single, wide prose column measuring, generally, 25 x 16.5 centimeters, leaving only a little more than 2 centimeters along the top and bottom, and a little less than 2 centimeters for lateral margins, almost filling the relatively large page (see fig. 1). The ruling provides forty lines per page, thus making a total of almost three-thousand long prose lines for the entire text. In comparison, the *Vie de saint Alexis*, a work of contemporary Anglo-Norman provenance, takes up six folios (fols. 29a-34b) in the St. Albans Psalter (Dombibliothek Hildesheim, MS St. Godehard 1) and, although written in verse, is arranged on the page as a single prose column measuring 21.6 x 14.4 centimeters.[34] The only early Anglo-Norman or Old French works of comparable scale are the massive mid-century chronicle-romances, Geffrei Gaimar's *Estoire des Engleis* (*ca.* 1140) and Wace's *Roman de Brut* (*ca.* 1155).[35] As a result of the scale and literary complexity of its source, the Oxford Psalter demanded a range of lexical and rhetorical invention that expanded both the written francophone lexicon, as philologists have shown, as well as vernacular literary practice.[36]

The question of how this prodigious, innovative vernacular literary text was conceived and read remains to be answered in full, but many partial answers can be gleaned from its *mise-en-page* in the Douce 320 manuscript. First and foremost, the Oxford Psalms do not seem to have been intended for liturgical performance or chant. This is suggested, most immediately, by the lack of a liturgical apparatus (antiphons, calendar, and so on) or any accompanying Latin text, if not by the fact of its vernacularity alone.[37] What we do see, however, in both the layout of the individual Psalms and the division of the Psalter into discrete groups, suggests that the Montebourg Psalter was designed to furnish a meditational or devotional reading of the Psalms of a kind first practised in the monastic *otium* and increasingly imitated and cultivated by lay readers of the period.[38] These reading practices, conducted outside the *opus* of the Divine Office in varying degrees of withdrawal, combined meditation and study with a leisure that was thought to refresh the reading mind.[39] As in all forms of monastic study, the Psalms were the principal text of *otium* reading, but the practice ideally included a "healthy alternation" of diverse, salutary works: Old Testament histories, saints' lives, the Fathers, even acceptable classical authors, such as Seneca and Livy.[40] Regardless of the text employed, *otium* reading demanded specific literary forms and textual arrangements: brief, "didactically compact, self-contained units" of text arranged in a sequence.[41] These qualities of brevity and sequentiality accommodated both the practical demands of an "economy of daily readings," by providing brief texts for each day's limited period of study, and the cognitive demands of meditative reading.[42]

First, we see evidence of meditational use in the layout of the individual Psalms as continuous prose paragraphs. The beginning of each Psalm is marked at the left-hand margin by *litterae notabiliores* that alternate red and green. Smaller colored *litterae notabiliores*, continuous within the prose paragraph of each Psalm and also alternating in color, mark off individual verses within the prose paragraph of each Psalm. This arrangement conforms to neither of the two *mise-en-page* systems developed to aid in the liturgical performance of the Psalms: neither to the older *per cola et commata* arrangement of the Psalms, where each element of a grammatical period is given a new line, nor to the later stichic verse arrangement, where each verse begins on a new line with a *littera notabilior*.[43] Where these patterns divide the Psalms into a series of grammatical or metrical units suitable to chant, the Douce 320 Psalter arranges each Psalm as a distinct, self-contained unit of continuous prose. This basic prose unit is thus disposed for a leisurely, continuous act of reading, what Samuel Berger describes as "la lecture courante": the slow, fluid, quiet reading of private meditations and entertainment, rather than the performance of a liturgy sung communally and aloud ("chant à haute voix").[44]

The impulse towards offering brief, self-contained units of reading can also be seen in Douce 320's division of the Psalms into groups. Traditional methods for organizing the Psalms, signaled by the enlargement and rubrication of *litterae notabiliores*, change according to the Psalter's intended use. So-called 'Biblical Psalters' typically enlarge the initials to Psalms 1, 51 and 101 so as to divide the Psalms into three groups (1-50, 51-100, 101-150) and are typically associated with exegesis and *sacra pagina*.[45] More common is the monastic division of the Psalms into eight groups or nocturns, which provided the sets of Psalms to be performed during the offices of each day of the week.[46] In this system, the initial of the first Psalm of each nocturn group is enlarged: 1, 26, 38, 52, 68, 80, 97 and 109.[47] Just as with its atypical presentation as prose paragraphs, so the Psalms in the Montebourg Psalter follow neither of these traditional systems. Rather, through a variety of means, planned and for the most part ruled in advance, the Montebourg Psalter enlarges the initials to Psalms 1, 26, 51, 80, 101, 109, and 118.[48] This arrangement inconsistently mixes both biblical and monastic divisions and, by offering a new division at Psalm 118 (119), introduces at least one very practical ad hoc innovation.[49]

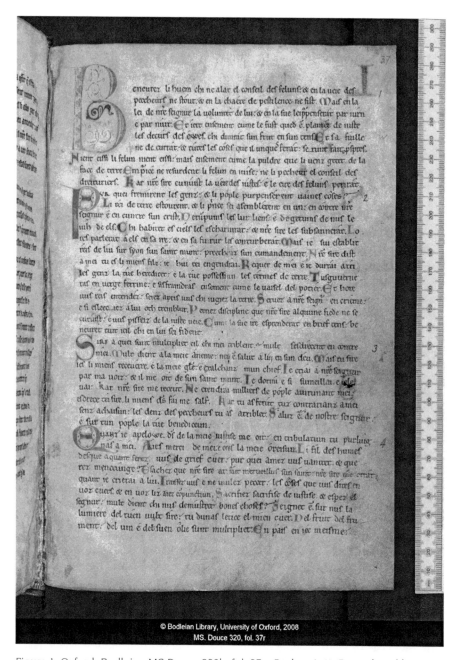

Figure 1: Oxford, Bodleian MS Douce 320b, fol. 37r., Psalms 1-4). Reproduced by permission of the Bodleian Library, University of Oxford.

Rather than the eightfold division of monastic traditions, this arrangement divides the Psalms into seven groups (1-25, 26-50, 51-79, 80-100, 101-108, 109-117, 118-150) of approximately the same length. This creates a sequence of manageable groups that could service a weekly "economy of daily readings," although not in any traditional liturgical form. The ad hoc and innovative arrangement is signaled in particular by the division at Psalm 118 (119), which accommodates that Psalm's unparalleled length and gives the final form of seven groups.[50] Interestingly, it is this very Psalm's own praise of a sevenfold division of Psalm reading —"Seven times a day I have given praise to thee, for the judgments of thy justice" (118: 164) —that was used to justify the Hours of the Day in the Benedictine Rule (chap. 16), with the eighth hour, Vigils, added onto the basic pattern on the authority of Psalm 118:62 ("I rose at midnight to give praise to thee"). By the twelfth century, the liturgical division of the Psalms into the eight groups had long been firmly codified, but in these same chapters on psalmody, Benedict invited other divisions of the Psalms to suit the demands of other practices; he writes, "Above all else we urge that it anyone finds this distribution of the psalms [into eight Hours] unsatisfactory, he should arrange whatever he judges better, provided that the full complement of one hundred and fifty psalms" be "carefully maintained every week."[51] Benedict here authorizes what would become a pattern in high and later medieval Psalm culture: the ad hoc re-organization of the Psalm divisions to suit non-liturgical, and particularly devotional and meditational, purposes.

The ultimate expression of this widespread desire for organized rounds of contemplative Psalm reading is the Book of Hours, which provides readings for the canonical hours of the day, most of which are principally comprised of Psalms: the Office of the Virgin (thirty-five complete psalms), the Penitential Psalms, and the Office of the Dead (twenty-one psalms).[52] After the late thirteenth century, Books of Hours are the most commonly privately owned books in England, and had a particular vogue among aristocratic families, especially women, as the guides to private contemplation, as symbols of a refined even courtly piety, and as primers for the instruction of children.[53] However, prior to the mid-thirteenth century, the Psalter itself was the preeminent text of private devotions, both for lay aristocrats and for the monks and canons whose reading practices they were studiously imitating. As Eamon Duffy has shown, by the late eleventh and early twelfth century, monks and canons were employing the Psalms in a round of private devotions that "were... arranged round the liturgical 'Hours,'" but remained outside the formal offices of the liturgy.[54] These private monastic devotions of the *otium* or *vacantes libros*, authorized by Benedict's permission to re-organize the Psalms to suit the occasion, had an effect on the form of Psalters, giving us the various "utilitarian collections" of the Psalms that are "the ultimate ancestors of... the Book of Hours."[55]

Lacking illumination, a colophon or any distinctive markings by which we could firmly locate its production, the Douce 320 Psalter cannot with any certainty be assigned to either monastic or lay readers. M. Dominica Legge has shown that monastic readers eagerly produced and consumed texts *en romanz* throughout the period, and by the fourteenth century, the manuscript was being held at the Norman monastery of Montebourg and had been bound with a late-thirteenth-century Norman prose version of the Benedictine Rule (fols. 1-36).[56] This Benedictine milieu is enticing because of the possible connection to Canterbury Cathedral, which we know from the Eadwine Psalter was a center of both Psalter production and vernacular innovation. However, given the prominence in the early twelfth century of lay-monastic literary sociabilities, which encouraged lay readers to imitate monastic reading practices and had a decisive influence on the development of vernacular literature, it is quite possible that the text could have been produced with a more fluid sense of the permeability between the two groups of readers.

Regardless of its intended audience, the Oxford Psalter in the innovative and ad hoc Douce 320 form is a remarkable and early witness of that evolution of the Psalter into "well-structured series of texts for private devotion" which ultimately produced the Book of Hours. Both in its decorative divisions and its *mise-en-page* as prose paragraphs, it furnishes the needs of a private, contemplative Psalter. It presents the Psalms as self-contained units of continuous prose, suited to leisurely, meditative reading, and it organizes them into a complete but extraliturgical sequence of daily readings. Just as important is the simple fact of its vernacularity. As Nicholas Watson and Jocelyn Wogan-Browne have argued, *romanz* would become the preeminent language of devotional reading in late medieval England.[57] The Oxford Psalter suggests that these developments were well rooted very early in the twelfth century.

Yet more broadly significant, the Oxford Psalter translation shows that by the first quarter of the twelfth century, *romanz* was already thought of as a linguistic medium sufficient to the high literary and spiritual refinements of the Psalms. This conclusion is as important to literary histories as it is to the history of devotional reading, not least of all because the Psalter was never just a devotional or liturgical text. As all great patristic and medieval Psalms commentaries will show, the Psalms were thought of as both a garden of all Christian belief and the medium of liturgical celebration, and a summa of poetry, a compendium of rhetorical tropes and literary forms, including verse history, lament, encomium, pastoral and love-song.[58] Thus the Psalms shaped medieval theories of genre and style, as well as models of poetic performance and authorship.[59] Although the facts of authorship may have vexed theologians, David's role as author of the Psalms was widely accepted in the medieval literary imagination. Looking back on a long tradition, Petrarch, for example, could refer to David as the very model of Christian poet: "Christianorum poetam," and particularly in the high Middle Ages, David is vividly imagined in both image and text as God's *jongleur* (*ioculator dei*), a courtly poet singing songs of praise and lament in specific historical circumstances.[60] Thus the translation of all 150 Psalms into a syntactic, discursively continuous prose so early in the development of literary *romanz* has to be understood as much as a literary event as a devotional one. The translation demanded literary innovations—in lexicon and grammar, as philological studies have shown, but also in style and genre—entirely without precedent in this vernacular.

The closer analysis of the specifically literary qualities of the individual Oxford Psalms lies beyond the scope of this paper, but there are ways in which we can document its literary character and significance. With surprising consistency, the Psalms provided the direct material and performative contexts for some of the earliest works of Old French and Anglo-Norman literature. The *Chanson de Sainte-Foy* (second half of eleventh century), for example, was produced at Conques as a narrative song to accompany a liturgical procession, while the *Jeu d'Adam* (*ca.* 1146), the "earliest surviving dramatic work in the French vernacular," is a "semiliturgical play" that contains seven "Gregorian chants…usually sung as part of Matins, the most substantial service in… the Divine Office," alternately quoting and alluding to the Psalms.[61] More typical, however, than these quasi-liturgical contexts are texts associated with the Psalter in its meditational and devotional forms. The most notable example is probably the *Vie de saint Alexis*, a saint's life, long seen as a proto-romance, that is one of the very earliest works of *romanz* literature. The earliest extant copy of the *Alexis* is found in the St. Albans Psalter (*ca.* 1125), one of a series of notable twelfth-century English Psalters produced "at monastic centers for clerical or lay patrons who were not members of the monastic community," in this case, for the recluse Christina of Markyate.[62] The *Vie de saint Alexis* appears in this manuscript between a cycle of forty full-page images (presenting a serial Christian history that focuses on the events of Christ's life) and the text of the Psalms, with the effect that the *Alexis* prologue (p. 57) faces the final of these full-page images, an image of David with his harp (p. 56) that is oddly out of its historical sequence.[63] Thus, not only is the *Alexis* paired with the Psalms for Christina's reading, but David in his role as *ioculator dei* presides over her reading of a narrative that is at once both an "estoire" and an "amiable cancun."[64] The 150 "amiable cancuns" of the Oxford Psalter might be thought of as the boldest early expression of this pattern of literary production that links new forms of vernacular literature and reading with the practices and sociabilities of monastic meditational reading.

Throughout the twelfth century, a remarkable concentration of cultural energy was devoted to the copying and adaptation of the Oxford Psalter. These texts and manuscripts, largely the product of monastic scriptoria, attest to the *romanz* Psalter's broad popularity as a devotional text. Yet they also show that the *romanz* Psalter maintained a very close and active engagement with secular and courtly literature. Ruth Dean counts no fewer than twelve complete extant copies of the Oxford Psalter that predate 1300, all of English provenance; seven of these date from the twelfth century, and to this list we must add dozens of partial or fragmentary texts from the same period.[65] In this first generation of transmission, we continue to see *romanz* Psalters emerging from institutions that had long-standing traditions of Old English composition, including Canterbury, Salisbury and Peterborough, suggesting a continuation of the kinds of interaction between Old English and Anglo-Norman that produced the Eadwine Psalter.[66]

The most prominent of these twelfth-century insular manuscripts comes from Winchester, another center of Anglo-Saxon Psalter production. The Winchester Psalter (London, BL Cotton Nero C.IV, *ca.* 1150-1160) was produced at St. Swithun's before it made its way later in the twelfth century to Shaftesbury Abbey. First produced for the great prince-bishop Henry of Blois, this is another of that series of prominent Psalters "made at monastic centers for clerical or lay patrons" which includes the St. Albans Psalter, as well as the *romanz* Psalter commentary produced at Durham later in the century for Hugh de Puiset (to which we will return).[67] Unlike the Montebourg Psalter, this is a deluxe Psalter conspicuous for its social, rhetorical, and material elevation— and indeed, in keeping with its patron, for its courtliness. As is signaled by its prayers, calendar and apparatus, as well by as its division into the standard nocturn groups, the Winchester Psalter was designed as a liturgical and, above all, a ceremonial manuscript. The Psalms are surrounded by a vast and luxurious visual program, which includes a prefatory cycle of thirty-eight full-page images (fols. 2-39) as well as inhabited initials for all 150 Psalms.[68] The kinds of elevation we see in the patronage, decoration and use of this manuscript are reiterated in the *mise-en-page* of the Psalms texts themselves, where we find a copy of the Oxford Psalter translation.

The Psalms are here laid out in parallel columns, carefully arranged so that the Latin and vernacular texts mirror one other. Each *littera notabilior* in the *romanz* text is presented in the same color and at the same position in the column as its corresponding Latin initial, thus making the prose French translation conform in decoration and form with the stichic verse arrangement of the Latin. The effect is to assert a horizontal equivalence between the two texts. The decorative programme similarly asserts a horizontal rather than hierarchical relationship between Latin and vernacular. For example, the 'B' initials of 'Beatus Vir' in Latin and 'Beonuret Barun [Blessed is the baron]' in *romanz* (fol. 46r) are of equal size and similar design; the only distinction—and it is indeed significant, since it associates David's voice with the Latin text—is found in the change from the leaf-scroll decoration of the French 'B' to the image of David as Psalmist that inhabits the bows of the Latin 'B'.[69] Similar decorative repetitions of initial letters can be seen at Psalms 80 (81) ('Exultate deo' and 'Esleecez a deu,' fol. 88v) and 109 (110) ('Dixit dominus' and 'Dist li sire,' fol. 105v), but the producers are equally happy to reproduce decorative patterns in different letters, as in the cases of Psalms 26 (27) ('Dominus illuminatio mea' and 'Li Sire,' fol. 57v) and 51 (52) ('Quid gloriaris' and 'Pur quei,' fol. 72r). Where the Montebourg Psalter had expressed the elevation and independence of the vernacular Psalms by material and textual means (e.g. the exclusion of any Latin text), the Winchester Psalter does so by arranging them as visual and textual metonyms. The vernacular in the Winchester Psalter is a sibling rather than a handmaiden to the parallel Latin text.

The Winchester Psalter also adapts its source text, shifting the register and lexicon of the vernacular text upwards, as it were, towards the courtly and the feudal. This shift is signaled from the very first words of the first Psalm. The Montebourg Psalter's first Psalm begins "Beneurez li huem chi ne alat el conseil des feluns" (fol. 37a), a translation that already casts the problem of virtue and sin into a familiar feudal lexicon of counsel and felony. The Winchester Psalter's text is still more comprehensively feudal and courtly. It begins:

> Beonuret Barun
> qui ne alat el cunseil des feluns
> et en la veie des pecheurs ne stout
> et en la chaere de pestilence ne sist.
> Mais en la lei de notre seignor la
> volunted e en la sue lei purpen-
> serat pur jurn e par nuit...
> Enpur ço ne surdent li felun en juise
> ne li pecheor el conseil des dreituriers
> Par nostre sire cunuist la vere des jus-
> tes e l'eire des feluns perirat[70]

> [Blessed is the baron who accepts not the counsel of felons, nor stands in the path of sinners, nor sits in the chair of pestilence. But whose will is in the law of our *seignor*, on whose law he meditates by day and by night... Because of this the felon will not rise again in justice, nor the sinner [in] the council (counsel) of the righteous. For our *sire* knows the path of the just, and that the *eire* [both path and eyre] of the felons will perish.]

"Beatus vir" has been transformed into a "Beonuret barun," announcing the relocation of the voice, the ethical drama and even the reading of the Psalms into the social, literary even legal domains of the feudal aristocracy. The first Psalm seems now to address "li baruns" directly, instructing them that aristocratic value is founded on the submission of "li felun [felons]" to justice and of the loyal to "la lei de notre seignor [the law of our *seignor*]," both of which are achieved through "el conseil des dreituriers [the counsel of those who act justly]."[71] Both the *ethos* of feudal justice and the voice of courtly instruction are characteristic of contemporary courtly literature, *chansons de geste* and courtly romances especially. An interesting parallel to this adaptation is found in London, British Library MS. Add. 35283, an early thirteenth-century bilingual Psalter, also associated with Durham, which adapts the opening of the Oxford Psalms to "Beneit seit li ber ki ne ala el conseil des feluns" (fol.7r) ("Blessed be the barons [or *chevaliers*] who do no follow the counsel of felons").[72] These patterns of stylistic adaptation, although (again) beyond the scope of this paper, make the Psalms themselves read as courtly lyrics or as 'romanced.' From mid-century, then, the generally literary qualities of the Oxford Psalter started to assume the literary features of the emerging courtly aesthetic.

Alongside the energetic circulation and adaptation of the Oxford Psalter, several other *romanz* Psalter translations were produced in the twelfth and thirteenth century. These other translations show both the centrality of the Psalter to vernacular literary culture in the period and its continuing engagement with more secular, courtly literary forms. Prior to 1170, three, and possibly four, other translations of the Gallican Psalter were made in England and northern France. There is, first, the fragmentary (but once complete) Orne Psalter (Paris, Archives Nationales AB xix, 1734), whose single remaining folio contains the Latin text of three Psalms with an interlinear prose Anglo-Norman translation distinct from the Oxford and Cambridge versions.[73] Both Charles Samaran and Yves Le Hir date this translation to the same era as the Cambridge and Oxford Psalters—that is "au commencement du XIIe siècle"—but also observe that it seems freer and less conservative ("moins traditionaliste") in its grammar and style.[74] Second is the Arundel (or sometimes London) Psalter (London, BL MS Arundel 230), a mid-century manuscript whose Calendar and Litany suggest connections to Croyland and Peterborough Abbeys respectively. Although seemingly related to the Oxford Psalter, the Arundel 230 translation of the Psalms (fols. 7-146) is a more literal, word-by-word rendering, apparently adapted to suit its role as an interlinear gloss on the Latin text.[75] The scribe of the original text, who wrote both the Latin and *romanz* texts, also wrote the first three verses of the Oxford translation in the right-hand margin of fol. 7, since damaged by the binder's knife.[76] This bilingual Psalter is accompanied by many other vernacular texts, including a poem on the Incarnation, as foretold to David (fol. 6), a table of unlucky days (fol. 6), a list of herb names (fol. 181), and much more significantly, Philippe de Thaon's *Comput* (fol. 1 and fol. 182r–fol. 194v), among the earliest Anglo-Norman literary works, and a now-fragmentary *Romance of Alexander*—a combination that speaks to the continuing convergence of the literary and the devotional in twelfth-century vernacular reading. Leena Löfstedt has recently drawn attention to the extensive quotation of the Psalms in the Old French translation of Gratian's *Decretals* (Brussels, Bibliothèque Royale MS 9084), which dates from the period 1164-1170 and seems to have had some connection to the coterie surrounding Thomas Beckett. She argues that the text for these *romanz* Psalms was drawn from another (third) independent translation of the Gallican Psalter that preexisted the *Decretals* translation.[77]

Arguably the most significant, and certainly the most monumental, of the independent twelfth-century translations is the one found within the body of a complete *romanz* Psalter commentary produced for Laurette d'Alsace (*ca.* 1165).[78] This text contains a complete translation of the Gallican Psalter up to Psalm 50 (51), with each verse presented *en romanz* at the head of its commentary (see fig. 2), and then a "loose translation" of the remaining Psalms "incorporated within the commentary as part of the exposition" that may have been produced at a slightly later date.[79] Gregory Stewart argues that this text, and especially the later, looser translation, is independent of "the |other| French translations of the twelfth century," although, echoes of the Oxford Psalter have long been observed.[80] The translation of the entire Psalter is itself a daunting task, but in this case the vernacular Psalter is embedded within a vast Old French Psalter Commentary. In its best copy, Durham Cathedral Library A.II.11-13, the commentary takes up three separate codices in a relatively large format, totaling 628 folios: a truly massive undertaking of vernacular composition and copying.[81] Here labor and material costs confirm cultural value: the production of a complete vernacular Psalter Commentary reveals the intensity of the desire to read the Psalter and to participate in its broader literary and devotional sociabilities through the vernacular. Fortunately, we know a fair bit about the intended audiences in this case; and as we will see, the Commentary, written for readers whose lives enact the engagement between court and cloister, itself engages directly with the aesthetics of courtly literature.

Laurette d'Alsace was the daughter of Thierry count of Flanders, and by the 1160s, she had been wife to no fewer than three prominent barons of north-eastern France: Iwan of Alost, Raoul I of Vermandois, and Henry the Blind of Namur (Count of Luxembourg), all of whom are named in the commentary on Psalm 36 (37). In the 1160s, Laurette retired to the convent of Forest-lez-Bruxelles, and as Stewart Gregory has shown, the Psalter Commentary seems to have been initiated from within her household to accompany this retirement from the aristocratic court to cloister.[82] Claiming in the commentary on Psalm 24:7 that ignorance of Scripture and of Latin is no "escusatiun |excuse|" for not knowing "que est biens |e| que est mals |that which is good and that which is evil|" the author asserts that "Se vos ne savez latin,

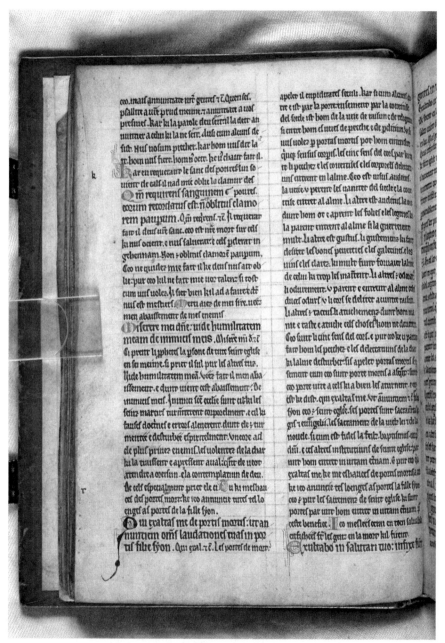

Figure 2: Durham Cathedral Library A.II.11, fol. 24. The commentary on Psalm 9:12-15.
Reproduced by permission of Durham Cathedral Library

vos saviez romanz u alvernaz. En teil language cum vos savez demandez, si
aprendez de vostre creanz que vos devez faire, que vos deveiz laier |If you do
not know Latin, you do know either *romanz* or *alvernaz*. In such language as you
know how to, ask, and so learn from your faith (or doctrine) what you ought to
do, what you ought to read|."[83] As in many *romanz* works of the twelfth century,
the vernacular Commentary is justified by the need to make the *biens* of the
Latin source, and the kinds of ethically formative, studious reading it carries,
available to a courtly audience that reads only "romanz u alvernaz," two forms
of the vernacular, most likely (as Gregory suggests), the northern *langue d'oil* or
the southern *langue d'oc*.[84]

This is a "complete |vernacular| commentary on the whole of the
Psalter," drawn principally from Gilbert de la Porrée's *Media Glossatura*,
to which, Gregory says, our author is "faithful in content rather than in
style."[85] The author liberally supplements the *Media Glossatura* with material
drawn from devotional works such as the *Homilies* of Gregory the Great and
Bernard of Clairvaux's *Sermons on the Song of Songs*. But the most significant
adaptations come in the increased use of narrative *exempla* and in what
Gregory describes as the author's "impassioned" style.[86] Significantly, both
of these changes are most evident in those places where the author praises
Laurette's rejection of the secular court.[87] The author repeatedly uses the
poles of Laurette's passage from court to cloister to frame the reading and
interpretation of the Psalms. Thus, Laurette's archetypically courtly life
becomes an essential part of the reading and even the 'story' of the Psalms,
and with it comes an intense engagement between the Psalms and the
courtly literary aesthetic.

The author's initial attempt to establish a clear opposition between court
and cloister, with each pole characterized by distinct values, styles and texts,
simply falls apart in the execution. His denunciation of worldly "vanities"
systematically and paradoxically confirms the value of the courtly life he rejects.
Denouncing the worldly "vanities" of Psalm 30:7, for example, he writes:

> Or le metons donques au *vacue* por ce que peu aide. Or
> prenduns cinc cens mars d'or fin, or prenduns tot l'or
> d'Arabie, toz les pailes d'Aumarie, le plus beel ami del
> siecle et le plus bele amie, le plus gentil dame del siecle,
> toz les castels de Lumbardie. Que valent a l'estroit
> besoi|n|g? Certes, nient.[88]

> |Now we shall therefore understand *vacue* as *that which aids
> little*. Let us take 500 marks of refined gold, let us take all
> the gold of Araby, all the silk of Almaría, the most beautiful
> lover in the world and the most beautiful beloved,

the most noble lady in the world, and all the castles
in Lombardy. What is it all worth to our true needs?
Certainly, nothing.|

Despite his final answer, these courtly desires retain their value for
the author. The repetition of superlative adjectives and the reiterative
accumulation of courtly *biens* suggests that the language and surplus value
of courtly desire has not been converted by the language of homily: "*tot* l'or
d'Arabie... et le *plus* bele amie, le *plus* gentil dame... toz les castels." Moreover,
these accumulating phrases are drawn directly from the lexical repertoire of
the courtly romance, where they typically occur in just this reiterative form.[89]
The effect appears again in the rejection of "la prosperité del siecle |worldly
prosperity|" in the commentary on Psalm 31:11, where the author hopes that
the powerful might distance themselves ("s'esleecent") from the objects of
courtly desire. But he again gets trapped, reiterating the most characteristic
tag phrasings of the courtly style: "l'or, l'argent, le vair et le gris, et les dames
et les beaus barons |the gold, the silver, the gray and the white miniver, and
the ladies and the *beaux* barons|."[90] The paradox of value leads to a series
of verbal paradoxes—"Ohi! Povre richoise, doleros deliz! |Oh! Impoverished
wealth, dolorous delights!|"—that not only confirm the value of secular wealth
and erotic love–"les povres deliz de la chambre |the impoverished delights of
the chamber|"—but which are characteristic or even, as Sarah Kay has recently
argued, generative of the courtly style.[91]

The reliance on the "impassioned" courtly style within the homiletic
commentary confirms the author's understanding of the genre of the Psalms.
Just as Jerome and his contemporaries imagined the Psalms as pastorals
and love songs, so our author here looks to contemporary poetic practice for
terminology to describe the Psalms as literary texts. In a telling commentary on
the "mirabilia" of Psalm 39:6 (40) ("Multa fecisti tu, Domine Deus meus, mirabilia
tua"), a term that by the early twelfth century had come to designate a type of
narrative (a *merveille*), the author condemns the "encantemenz |enchantments|"
of popular entertainments and encourages Laurette to read the Psalms instead.
But in praising the Psalms as poems, the author draws directly upon a courtly
literary terminology, imagining them as "plus beles miracles |more beautiful
miracles|" and "plus hautes aventures |greater adventures|," as "caroles" that
are in no way generically different from courtly songs, but are rather "mult
plus belement cante |much more beautifully sung|."[92] The author prefers the
Psalms, not as a wholly distinct mode of literature, but as more aesthetically
perfect—"*plus beles*" and "*plus hautes*"—forms of courtly song and narrative.

This passage echoes the more famous example of the prologue to Denis
Piramus's Vie *seint Edmund le rei* (ca. 1180), where, citing the courtly examples
of Hue de Rotelande's *Partenopeu de Blois* (ll. 25-31) and the "lais" of Marie de

France (ll. 35-48), Denis tries to turn an audience of courtly readers, "prince… courtur,/ cunte, baruns e vavasur |princes, courtiers, counts, barons and vavasours|" (ll. 5-7), away from the "cuntes, chanceuns e fables |stories, songs and fables|" (ll. 50-51) they love. Instead, he encourages them to read this vernacular saint's life, which he describes, not as a generically different form, but rather a "deduit," a common term for pleasurable, courtly narrative, "qui *mielz* valt asez |which is worth much *more*|" and which is "*plus* delitable a oïr |*more* delightful to hear|."[93] Clearly, for both authors, vernacular devotional texts, whether Psalms or saint's life, operate within the same generic field as vernacular "cuntes, chanceuns e fables." They cannot be distinguished by categorical definitions of style or form, but only qualitatively and aesthetically as *mielz* and *plus beles*.

Similarly, wherever the author situates Laurette's reading of the Psalms in relation to her other reading, similar effects can be seen. Although the commentary's exegesis clearly presumes the reader's knowledge of other biblical texts, the Gospels in particular, the author seems only to draw Laurette's direct attention to saints' lives (Dionysius and Maurice in Psalm 36 (37); and Cecilia, Lucie, and Agnes in Psalm 40 (41)); to classical authors, Ovid in particular stands out; and to legendary narratives like the story of "li set dormant," the Seven Sleepers of Ephesus, "cum vos bien avez oït dire |as you have certainly heard recited|."[94] These texts and genres populate the literary field within which the author measures and understands Laurette's reading of the Psalms–and they are all familiar sources of courtly, vernacular literature. Just as the "impassioned style" of Laurette's Psalter, with its paradoxes and its aestheticized catalogues of courtly *biens*, is produced by a close engagement between the devotional and the courtly, so in the larger context, the Oxford Psalter is not to be understood as a devotional text poised against a field of courtly literature, but one rather that competes for attention and value within a single constituency of readers and within a single vernacular literary field.

Where the text might take us away from our immediate geographical and social parameters, the earliest and best copy of Laurette's Commentary takes us directly back to twelfth-century Durham, and provides a concrete location for the engagement of the devotional and the courtly. Durham, Cathedral Library, A.II.11-13 was made and held at Durham Cathedral during the episcopacy of Hugh de Puiset (1153-1195). Hugh was nephew to King Stephen and had long served in the curia of Stephen's brother Henry of Blois, the patron, we recall, of the Winchester Psalter. De Puiset, also earl of Northumberland between 1189 and 1194, was a great prince-bishop who maintained his court in aristocratic splendor. This immense and costly copy of Laurette's Commentary was in all likelihood made for De Puiset himself. De Puiset's patronage of conspicuously luxurious books was very clearly a mechanism of social refinement and distinction, and this copy of Laurette's Psalter

Commentary should be thought of as part of the rich bequest of books that he left to his cathedral.[95] The Commentary receives the same kind of decoration and *mise-en-page* we see in other Latin Psalters and Psalter Commentaries from Durham, including those that so conspicuously count among De Puiset's bequests.[96] Thus, this manuscript belongs to a social environment very much like Laurette's own, where the impulses of the cloister and the aristocratic court converge. Not surprisingly, De Puiset's Durham was a major center for the production and reading of Anglo-Norman books, including some major works of courtly literature. Consider the example of Durham Cathedral Library C.IV.27, a manuscript produced in exactly this same period that contains the earliest and best witnesses of Wace's *Brut*, Geffrei Gaimar's *Estoire des Engleis*, Jordan Fantosme's *Chronicle*, the anonymous *Description of England*, and Helias's translation of the *Prophecies of Merlin*. The broader context of *romanz* reading at Durham would have brought this *romanz* Psalter Commentary into close contact with exactly the sorts of *aventures* and *deduits* that the author imagines.

While the best, and most, copies of Laurette's Psalter Commentary are Anglo-Norman, there is another avenue of transmission that is useful for reaffirming the broader conclusions of this paper. In the last decade of the twelfth century, Laurette's Commentary was copied and adapted at Troyes by the so-called Manerius atelier, a group of professional scribes and artisans working loosely together in the city of Troyes, and named after Manerius of Canterbury, a scribe who signed his name in a Latin Bible. The Manerius atelier produced a mixture of sacred and secular, Latin and vernacular, books for a network of local aristocratic readers that included members of the Champegnois court, including most prominently, Marie de Champagne.[97] Among these manuscripts are three separate copies of a *romanz* Psalter Commentary that, as Patricia Stirnemann observes, ultimately derive from Laurette's Commentary but have been adapted in a manner so consistent that they "form a separate textual family."[98] In the workshop of the Manerius atelier, and in the broader tastes of this aristocratic social network, these vernacular commentaries came into contact with some of the most important manuscripts of twelfth-century romance, including a copy of the *Roman de Troie* (London, BL Add. 30863); the Annonay fragments of Chrétien de Troyes; and the so-called Guiot manuscript (Paris, BnF 794). This last manuscript, "one of the most fetishized manuscripts of the entire French Middle Ages," is "an anthology of the works of Chrétien |de Troyes| and other romance authors arranged chronologically" and contains an inhabited initial (fol. 27) that "portrays Marie de Champagne" as an idealized reader of courtly romances.[99]

This portrait, along with the praise of Marie as reader and patron in the prologue to Chrétien de Troyes's *Chevalier de la Charette*, have encouraged us to see Marie as an idealized but also exemplary reader of courtly romance. But we must take account of the fact that Marie is praised in nearly identical terms in the prologue of Evrat's *Genèse*, a verse *romanz* translation of Genesis (1192) reputedly undertaken at the direct request of "ma dame de Chanpaigne."[100] (The manuscript containing Evrat's *Genèse*, Paris, BnF fr. 900, is also a product of the Manerius atelier.) Yet more directly pertinent is the E*ructavit cor meum*, a vernacular translation and adaptation of the Psalm 44 (45), produced by a monk at the abbey of St. Pierre-le-Vif in Sens (see ll. 769-786) for Marie, "ma dame de Champaigne" (l. 3).[101] In a direct allusion to the monastic meditational reading practices, the E*ructavit* author offers the "biaus saumes le roi David |beautiful Psalms of David|" (l. 2072) as a "Chançon de chambre" (l. 2075), a song of the bedchamber, in which she might "met son cuer a bon escole |set her heart to a good school|" (l. 2093). The Psalm translation, which appears to be entirely independent of the Oxford Psalter translation, is here embedded within a dream narrative in which David, in his role as God's *jongleur*—"'Juglerre sui,'" he says at line 235—finds himself presented before God and his barons (ll. 869-94) to sing at a wedding feast. This narrative, more courtly narrative than Psalms Commentary, is written in octosyllabic couplets, the romance's characteristic verse form, and is repeatedly described in terms familiar from Laurette's Commentary and the courtly idiom. It is a "chançonete" (l. 137) and a narrative "desduiz |or deduit|" (l. 236) sung before "barons et princes" (l. 27). In both its style and its circumstances of production, Marie's 44th Psalm, which was by tradition both royal Psalm and epithalamium, fully expresses the give-and-take between the courtly and the devotional that firmly places the vernacular Psalter at the center of the developing field of *romanz* reading.

The Circulation of the Romanz Psalter in the Thirteenth and Fourteenth Centuries

The broadest measurements of literary taste—book ownership and production—show not only the continuing popularity of *romanz* Psalters throughout the Middle Ages, but their systematic association with works of courtly literature, most particularly romances. In their "Liste Provisoire de Manuscripts du XIIe Siècle Contenant Des Textes en Langue Française," Brian Woledge and Ian Short identify 120 manuscripts definitively or possibly attributable to the twelfth century, nineteen (or 16%) of which contain Psalters or Psalter commentaries in French.[102] The Psalter is the most numerous of any individual text, rivaled numerically only by the total number of all romances (20), whole or fragmentary. This rough picture remains largely the same in Madeleine Blaess's catalogue of "French" manuscripts in medieval English monastic libraries. As she observes, wherever we can measure what medieval English monks were reading *en romanz*, biblical works and in particular Psalters "sont toujours en tête de liste |are always at the head of the list|."[103] Blaess's catalogue shows a great variety in the ways monks read their Psalters *en romanz:*, from the simple "Psalterium in gallico" to bilingual Psalters, such as the "Psalterium in latino et gallico" donated by a "Hugonis de Plukele" to Canterbury Cathedral, to numerous Psalters "glosata gallice" and "expositi in gallico."[104] Blaess observes that these same monastic institutions are also, like Durham, generously endowed with romances: typical in this respect would be the library of Canterbury Cathedral, which contained two Psalters *in latino et gallico*, as well as three vernacular *Brut* narratives ("Brutus gallice").[105]

Recent work by Christopher de Hamel, Jenny Stratford and Teresa Webber has also shown that, although relatively scarce, evidence of private and particularly aristocratic book collections (largely from inventories and wills) consistently shows high and late medieval audiences reading and inheriting the Psalter, frequently *en romanz*, alongside romances.[106] Perhaps most famous is the example of Guy de Beauchamp's donation of books to Bordesley Abbey (*ca.* 1305), where, among the first items, we find "Un sauter de Romaunce" lodged perfectly between "le premier livere de Launcelot |the first book of Lancelot|" and the "quatres principals Gestes de Charles |four principal *gestes* of Charlemagne|."[107] De Hamel cites the example of Joan Mortimer, Countess of March, who in 1322 held "a Psalter and four volumes of secular romances in Wigmore castle, Herefordshire... apparently the only books in this substantial house."[108] Similar evidence comes from the royal household. On the basis of the accounts left behind by John Flete, Keeper of the Privy Wardrobe between 1324 and 1341, Juliet Vale concludes that there was "in effect a royal library... within the privy wardrobe in the Tower" under the control of the Keeper.[109] The first recorded issue of books in Flete's tenure was in 1324, when "14 'romances' and a French Psalter" were sent to William Langley, Clerk of Edward II's Chamber, suggesting that these books may have been for "use in the King's household."[110] Flete's accounts also record the delivery of seven books in French to Queen Isabella in March 1327, including romances such as *Renard* and *Meraugys et Sado*.[111] Isabella was an assiduous reader of romances; at her death she owned a "liber Tristram & Isolda" and a "liber... de Perceual & Gauwayn," as well as a group of books that she kept in her chamber that included a bilingual French and Latin Psalter.[112] As Stratford and Webber note, this bilingual Psalter is in all probability the Psalter of Queen Isabella (Muniche, Bayerische Staatsbibliothek, Cod. Gall. 16), which contains a copy of the Oxford Psalter.[113]

Individual manuscripts localize and materialize these general trends. One vivid example is the Oscott Psalter (BL MS Add. 50000, *ca.* 1265-1270), a lavishly illustrated bilingual Psalter that is considered a masterpiece of the 'Court School' style and one of the "two finest illuminated manuscripts of the Early Gothic period in England."[114] The manuscript is famous for its full-page prefatory images, but just as striking is that the Anglo-Norman Psalms are, not in the prose of the Oxford Psalter, but in tail-rhyme stanzas, a verse form typically associated with Middle English romances. This tail-rhyme translation, also extant in London, British Library MS Harley 4070, consists of

2460 hexasyllabic sizains rhyming aab aab.[115]

Another important adaptation of the Oxford Psalter, many steps away from its original, is found in London, British Library MS Harley 273 (*ca.* 1314-1315), and with this text we come to the very heart of fourteenth-century English literary studies. The Psalter in Harley 273 has received scholarly attention in the reflected light of London, British Library MS Harley 2253—'*the* Harley manuscript'—a trilingual anthology, whose mix of poetry and narrative, romance and devotion, has placed it among the most important of all late medieval English literary manuscripts. The Harley scribe, who produced these two (Harley 273 and 2253) and one other extant manuscript (BL MS Royal 12.C.xii, *ca.* 1329-1340), worked in the area of Ludlow, copying legal documents and compiling literary manuscripts for a number of "local families of country-magnate status" who were tied together in a "network of social relationships."[116] Harley 2253 is famous for its Middle English lyrics and its fabliaux, but "numerically over half" of Harley 2253's contents are religious items, including three separate sets of instructions on prayer (items no. 101, 110, 111), all of which are exclusively focused on the use of the Psalms—once again documenting the affinities between secular poetry and the Psalms.[117]

The central feature of our Harley 273 is its *romanz* Psalter (fols. 8a-53b), which is here illuminated and combined with a *romanz* Hours of the Virgin (fols. 59c-67c). However, the Harley 273 Psalms are also bound, *inter alia*, with Nicholas Bozon's La *Plainte d'Amour* (fols. 199a-203b), written in six-line stanzas, and William of Waddington's *Le Manuel des Pechiez* (fols. 113a-190d), an "aid to confession" written in octosyllabic couplets, whose many *exempla* bear close affinities to secular narrative forms, including *fabliau*. Thus, in all three Harley manuscripts, we see contrapuntal engagements between the devotional and the courtly, the Psalms and popular *deduits*, in a manner that Carter Revard likens to the "oppositional thematics" of the *Canterbury Tales*.[118]

However, the most dramatic development in the later history of the *romanz* Psalms draws us back to the Oxford Psalter. In keeping with its largely devotional uses, the Oxford Psalter tends to circulate in the early period without the company of other biblical texts. But in the thirteenth century, it was incorporated into the larger context of French Bibles, giving the Oxford Psalter a circulation so vast that it would become, almost certainly, the most widely read of all Anglo-Norman texts. The first step in this process was its inclusion in the "Bible du XIIIe Siècle," compiled in Paris between 1225 and 1230; from there, it would become the base text for the Psalms in all great medieval French biblical translations, including Guyart de Moulins's *Bible historiale* and its later elaboration as the *Bible historiale completée*.[119] In this form the Oxford Psalms would remain in use as the standard French Psalms translation until the sixteenth century, and in the form of the Louvain Bibles until 1690.[120] Echoing Samuel Berger's reflections on its unprecedented longevity and "innombrables" copies in French Bibles, De Poerck and Van Deyck describe the Oxford Psalter as "un véritable texte reçu," a kind of *romanz* "vulgate" within "la littérature biblique en langue française."[121] And recalling its earliest engagements with English biblical translation, the Oxford Psalter rather than the Latin text of the Gallican Psalter itself, as Raymond St. Jacques has shown, served as the base text for the *Middle English Glossed Prose Psalter* (1325-1350).[122]

University of Ottawa

NOTES

1. I use 'romanz' to designate the francophone vernacular of northern France and England. If a *romanz* text was produced in England or Normandy, I will describe that text or manuscript as Anglo-Norman. The term 'Old French' anachronistically presumes modern national categories—as, in its way, 'Anglo-Norman' does. See Jocelyn Wogan Browne, "What's in a Name: the 'French' of 'England'," in *Language and Culture in Medieval Britain: The French of England, c. 1100-c.1500* (York: York Medieval Press, 2009), 1-16.
2. Jerome made three translations of the Psalms into Latin, all of which were available in varying degrees throughout the Middle Ages. They are, in order: the Romanum, the Gallican, which became the standard Latin Psalter of the liturgy and Vulgate Bible, and the Hebrew (so-called because of its Hebrew, rather than Greek, source text).
3. Tony Hunt, "The Anglo-Norman book," sec. 1, 367-379, of Tony Hunt, Julia Boffey, A.S.G. Edwards and Daniel Huws, "Vernacular Literature and its readership," in *The Cambridge History of the Book in Britain, Vol. II: 1100-1400* (Cambridge: Cambridge University Press, 2008), 367-379, 369.
4. Only Gaimar's *Estoire des Engleis* could compare in size, but it is extant in only four manuscripts.
5. Francisque Michel ed., *Libri Psalmorum versio antiqua gallica e cod. ms. in Bibl. Bodleiana* (Oxford: Oxford University Press, 1860).
6. Hannibal Hamlin, *Psalm Culture and Early Modern English Literature* (Cambridge: Cambridge University Press, 2004), 1.
7. I refer to the Douce 320b manuscript itself as the "Montebourg Psalter" and to the translation it contains as the "Oxford Psalter."
8. T.A. Heslop, "Decoration and Illustration," in *The Eadwine Psalter: Text, Image and Monastic Culture in Twelfth-Century Canterbury*, ed. Margaret Gibson, T. A. Heslop, and Richard W. Pfaff (London: Modern Humanities Research Association, 1992), 25–59, 25.
9. Ibid., 25.
10. Dominique Markey, "The Anglo-Norman Version," in *The Eadwine Psalter: Text, Image and Monastic Culture in Twelfth-Century Canterbury*, 139-156, 142.
11. On the Anglo-Norman text in the Eadwine Psalter generally, see Ibid., 139-156 *passim*.

12. Margaret Gibson, "Introduction," The Eadwine Psalter: Text, Image and Monastic Culture in Twelfth-Century Canterbury, 1-3.

13. Patrick P. O'Neill, "The English Version," in The Eadwine Psalter: Text, Image and Monastic Culture in Twelfth-Century Canterbury, 123-138, 124.

14. Ibid., 126 and 124. See F. G. Berghaus, Der Verwandtschaftsverhältnisse der altenglischen Interlinearversionen des Psalters und der Cantica, Palaestra 272 (Göttingen: Vandenhoeck & Ruprecht, 1979), 18-21, 44-64, 73-76.

15. S.H. Kuhn, "The Vespasian Psalter Gloss: Original or Copy," PMLA 74:3 (1959): 168. See also, O'Neill, "The English Version," 137.

16. O'Neill, "The English Version," 125 and 135.

17. Ibid., 136.

18. Ibid.,137, quoting H. Kuhn, "The Vespasian Psalter Gloss," 168.

19. O'Neill writes, "For example, in the first line of fol. 275 v. the French gloss Beneissiez vos tutes (Latin 'benedicite omnes') is sprawled across the supralinear space; the corresponding English gloss, Bletsige ealle, is parenthetically inserted between Beneissiez and vos tutes. On the same folio, at the top of column B, where the main illumination intrudes on the space allotted to the vernacular glosses, it is the English gloss which is sacrificed by being omitted." O'Neill, "The English Version," 137.

20. Markey, "The Anglo-Norman Version," 147. See Walter Schumann, Vocalismus und Konstantismus des Cambridger Psalters Mit einem Anhang: Nachträge zur Flexionslehre desselben Denkmals. (Heilbronn: Gegr. Henninger, 1883), 7-8.

21. Ibid., 151-154.

22. Ibid., 142 and 142.n.15.

23. O'Neill, "The English Version," 137.

24. D. Markey, "The Anglo-Norman Version," 152 and 139; and Charles M. Cooper, "Jerome's 'Hebrew Psalter' and the New Latin Version," Journal of Biblical Literature, 69:3 (1950), 233-244.

25. D. Markey, "The Anglo-Norman Version," 152.

26. The Eadwine Psalter's Cambridge translation seems only to have been reproduced once, in the 'Paris Psalter' (Paris, BN, MS lat. 8846), which is in effect an incomplete copy of the Eadwine Psalter. For the dating of the Oxford Psalter, I follow Brian Merrilees, who writes, "The Oxford Psalter is considered by some scholars to be oldest surviving Anglo-Norman text, and may date from as early as 1100," "Oxford Psalter," in The Dictionary of the Middle Ages, ed., Joseph R. Strayer (New York, 1982-1989) vol. 9, 319-320, at 319. Ruth Dean follows this dating in her Anglo-Norman Literature: A Guide to Texts and Manuscripts (London: Anglo-Norman Text Society, 1999), 239-242. The Montebourg Psalter is certainly a copy of an earlier text, giving us a terminus ante quem of c. 1115-20.

27. See Jean Bonnard, Les Traductions de la Bible en vers français au Moyen Âge (Geneva: Slatkine Reprints, 1967), 130-149; Samuel Berger, La Bible Française au Moyen Age: Étude sur Les Plus Anciennes Versions de la Bible Écrites en Prose de Langue d'Oil (Paris: Champion, 1884; Geneva: Slatkine Reprints, 1967), 3-4 and 16-17; and the introductory materials in F. Michel, ed., Libri Psalmorum versio

antiqua gallica e cod. ms. in Bibl. Bodleiana (Oxford: Oxford University Press, 1860), as well as No. 445-457 in Ruth Dean, *Anglo-Norman Literature: A Guide to Texts and Manuscripts*, 239-249. On the unprecedented scale of its dissemination, see Guy de Poerck and Rika van Deyck, "La Bible et l'activité traductrice dans le pays romane avant 1300," in *Grundriss der romanischen Literaturen des Mittelalters* (GRLMA), (Heidelberg: Carl Winter, 1968) vol. 6:1, 21-57, 26.

28. De Poerck and van Deyck, "La Bible et l'activité traductrice," GRLMA vol. 6:1, 26.

29. In London, British Library MS Cotton Vitellius E.ix, each complete verse of the *romanz* text is written below its complete corresponding Latin verse, suggesting that equivalence could only be established on the scale of larger discursive units. In the remaining four manuscripts (Cambridge, Clare College MS Kk.3.6; London, BL MS Cotton Nero C.IV; Paris, BN Latin 768; and Paris, BN nouv. acq. lat 1670), the Oxford Psalter text appears in parallel, facing columns. This arrangement establishes an equivalence between Latin and *romanz* at the level of the individual Psalm and presumes a self-sufficiency of the vernacular on yet a larger scale.

30. The claim for a Canterbury provenance is more commonly made than explained, but it does have prominent supporters; e.g. Hunt, "The Anglo-Norman Book," 372.

31. The only other prior tradition of vernacular Psalms translation comes from Germany. See G. W. H. Lampe, "Germany and Low Countries," sec. 4 of "The Vernacular Scriptures," in *The Cambridge History of the Bible* (Cambridge: Cambridge University Press, 1963–1970), 2:423.

32. Omer Jodogne, "La naissance de la prose française." *Bulletin de la Classe des Lettres et des Sciences Morales et Politiques*, Académie Royale de Belgique, 5th ser., 49 (1963): 296-308, 297.

33. M. J. Toswell, "The translation techniques of the old English metrical psalter, with special reference to Psalm 136." *English Studies* 75:5 (1994): 393–407, 393. See also M. J. Toswell, "The Late Anglo-Saxon Psalter: Ancestor of the Book of Hours?" *Florilegium* 14 (1995-96): 1-24; George Philip Krapp, *The Paris Psalter and the Meters of Boethius* (New York: Columbia University Press, 1932), x-xi.

34. The codicological description of the *Vie de saint Alexis* and its quire is available at the University of Aberdeen's St. Albans Psalter website: http://www.abdn. ac.uk/stalbanspsalter/english/essays/codicology.shtml#rulingandvellum.

35. Wace's *Brut*, which consists of 14866 lines in octosyllabic couplets, takes up 95 folios (fols. 1a-94a) in its best copy, Durham Cathedral Library C.IV.27. Here the text is set out in two columns per page, with the ruled space of each column measuring 19 x 5.3 centimeters. Gaimar's *Estoire des Engleis*, whose best copy is found in the very same manuscript, takes up 45 folios (fols. 94b-138d) in two columns measuring 18.5 x 6.1 centimeters.

36. Since the publication of J. H. Meister's *Die Flexion im Oxforder Psalter* (Halle, Germany: M. Niemeyer, 1877), the earliest critical assessment of Francisque Michel's 1860 edition, by far the greatest amount of work on the Oxford Psalter has been philological. Even the most cursory search for the citations of the

Oxford Psalter in the *Anglo-Norman Dictionary*, ed. Louise W. Stone and William Rothwell (London: Modern Humanities Research Association, 1977-1992), in which there are 730 separate citations; or standard Old French Dictionaries will confirm its extraordinary place in French lexical and philological history.

37. Vernacularity itself is insufficient to rule out liturgical use; there were many common paraliturgical uses of the vernacular, particularly in prayers and hagiographical readings, and some were willing to allow the vernacular within the liturgy itself. Jean Leclercq cites both Peter of Poitiers and the Franciscan Bertrand de la Tour justifying the use of the vernacular in the liturgy—an allowance that would demand *romanz* translations of the Psalms. Jean Leclercq, "Les Traductions de la Bible et la Spiritualité Médiévale," in *The Bible and Medieval Culture*, ed. W. Lourdaux and D. Verhelst (Leuven: Leuven University Press, 1979), 263–277, 265, n.12 and n. 13.

38. On the secular imitation of *otium* reading in the twelfth century, see Geoff Rector "*En sa chambre sovent le lit*: Literary Leisure and the Sociabilities of Early *Romanz* Literature (*ca.* 1100-1150)," forthcoming.

39. The standard work on medieval notions of *otium* and its classical heritage is Jean Leclercq, *Otia Monastica: Études sur le vocabulaire de la contemplation au moyen age*, Studia Anselmiana 51 (Rome: Herder, 1963).

40. Ibid., 77-78.

41. R.D. Ray, "Medieval Historiography Through the Twelfth Century," *Viator* 5 (1974), 33–59, 41.

42. Ibid., 41. On brevity and division, see Mary Carruthers, *The Book of Memory: A Study of Memory in Medieval Culture* (Cambridge: Cambridge University Press, 1990), 81-85. On the cognitive demands of meditative reading see also Carruthers, *The Craft of Thought: Meditation, Rhetoric and the Making of Images 400-1200* (Cambridge: Cambridge University Press, 1998).

43. Malcolm Parkes, *Pause and Effect: An Introduction to the History of Punctuation in the West* (Berkeley: University of California Press, 1993), 35-38.

44. Berger, *La Bible Française au Moyen Âge*, 16.

45. The threefold division of the Psalter not only accommodated exegesis, but became in turn a common subject of twelfth-century exegesis, typically involving number symbolism as a way of solving the Psalms' "mosaic of mysteries"; see A.J. Minnis, *Medieval Theory of Authorship: Scholastic Literary Attitudes in the Later Middle Ages* (London Scolar Press, 1984), 151.

46. The eighth group, of Psalms 109-150, was spread out over days of the week at Evensong.

47. V. Leroquais, *Les Psautiers Manuscrits Latins des Bibliothèques Publiques de France* (Mâcon: Protat Frères, 1940), I, xliv-lvii.

48. The typical space left for the rubrication of Psalm initials in the Montebourg Psalter is two lines. This provides a standard against which to measure the enlargement of other *litterae notabiliores*. First, the 'B' (fol. 37r) of Psalm 1 is afforded six lines, while the initials of Psalms 51 (fol. 48v) and 101 (fol. 61v) are given each four lines. This arrangement draws on the tradition of the Biblical

Psalter. Three lines are given for the initials of Psalms 80 (fol. 56r) and 109 (fol. 64v), which are divisions within the liturgical system, but also to the initial of Psalm 118 (fol. 66v), which is not a traditional division in either one. The only other Psalm to receive a decorative attention that draws it out from the standard two-line enlargement is Psalm 26 (fol. 42r). The original ruling provided only the standard two lines, but the decorator wrote the first two words entirely in red capitals, as "LI SIRE," a decoration not repeated in any other Psalm.

49. I follow the numbering of the Latin Vulgate Psalter, since this is the numbering system followed in virtually all medieval European Psalters. This numbering system is still followed in the modern Douay-Rheims version, which I will use as the source of my English translations. Wherever the article discusses the text of a specific Psalm, the Hebrew Psalms numbers, generally employed in post-Reformation Bibles and familiar from the King James and NAB versions, will be indicated in parentheses. The divergence between the two systems occurs at Psalm 9, which becomes Psalms 9 and 10 in the Hebrew numbering system.

50. The Benedictine Rule makes its own special arrangements to deal with Psalm 118's unwieldy length, dividing its verses among the Hours of Sunday and Monday; see Benedict of Nursia, *The Rule of St. Benedict in English*, ed. and trans. Timothy Fry (Collegeville, MN: Liturgical Press, 1982), chapter 18: 2 and 7-8.

51. Fry, *The Rule of St. Benedict in English*, chap. 18.22-23, 47.

52. Christopher de Hamel, "Books of Hours: Imaging the Word," in *The Cambridge History of the Book in Britain, vol. II, 1100–1400*, ed. Lotte Hellinga and J. B. Trapp (Cambridge: Cambridge University Press, 2008), 3–21, 13–14.

53. Ibid., 13-14.

54. Eamon Duffy, *Marking the Hours: English People and Their Prayers 1240-1570* (New Haven, CT, and London: Yale University Press, 2006), 6.

55. Ibid., 5-6.

56. Legge, *Anglo-Norman in the Cloisters: The Influence of the Orders upon Anglo-Norman Literature* (Edinburgh: Edinburgh University Press, 1950).

57. Nicholas Watson and Jocelyn Wogan-Browne, "The French of England: the *Compileison, Ancrene Wisse*, and the Idea of Anglo-Norman." *The Journal of Romance Studies* 4:3 (Winter 2004): 35-59.

58. Pierre Riché, *Education and Culture in the Barbarian West: Sixth through Eighth Centuries*, trans. John J. Contreni (Columbia: University of South Carolina Press, 1976), 167; J.M. Cortes, "Figures et tropes dans le psautier de Cassiodore," *Revue des études latines* xlii (1964): 361-375. The opinion was frequently authorized by reference to Jerome; Paula and Eustochium, in a letter to Marcella that circulated among and *as* one of Jerome's letters, describe the Psalms as "love songs |amatoriae cantiones|" sung by reapers and shepherds—literally "pastorales"—working in a bucolic Palestine. *Sancti Eusebii Hieronymi Epistulae*, ed. Isidorus Hilberg, 3 vols. (New York: Johnson, 1970; repr. Vienna: F. Tempsky, 1910-18), epistle 46.

59. See A.J. Minnis, *Medieval Theory of Authorship*, 42-50. See also, Michael Kuczynski, *Prophetic Song: The Psalms as Moral Discourse in Late Medieval England* (Philadelphia: University of Pennsylvania Press, 1995), esp. chap. 4, "The Psalms as Models for Middle English Poetry," 120-148.

60. Petrarch, *Lettres Familières* VIII-XI (*Reum familiarium* VIII-XI). Ed. Pierre Laurens and trans. André Longpré. Les Classiques de L'Humanisme (Paris: Les Belles Lettres, 2003), X.4, 280. On David's role as *ioculator dei*, see Jean Leclercq, "'Ioculator et saltator': S. Bernard et l'image du jongleur dans les manuscrits," in *Translatio studii: Manuscript and Library Studies Honoring Oliver L. Kapsner, O.S.B.*, ed. Julian G. Plante (Collegeville, Minn.: St John's University Press, 1973), 24-48.

61. On the *Chanson de Sainte-Foy*, see Michel Zink, *Littérature française du Moyen Âge* (Paris: Presses Universitaires de France, 2001), 32. Charles T. Downey, "Ad imaginem suam: Regional Chant Variants and the Origins of the *Jeu d'Adam*." *Comparative Drama* 36:3/4 (*Fall-Winter* 2002), 359. See also the remarks of *Le Jeu d'Adam*'s editors, Willem Noomen, *Le jeu d'Adam* (*Ordo representacionis Ade*) (Paris: Champion, 1971), 7 and Wolfgang van Emden, ed. and trans. *Le jeu d'Adam* (Edinburgh: British Rencesvals Publications, 1996), iv.

62. Nigel Morgan, "Books for the liturgy and private prayer," in *The Cambridge History of the Book in Britain, vol. II*, 1100–1400 (Cambridge: Cambridge University Press, 2008), 291-316, 312. This group also includes the Winchester Psalter, London, British Library, Cotton Nero C.IV, a manuscript, which we will return to shortly, that contains another early copy of the Oxford Psalms.

63. Since the nineteenth century, when page numbers were added in arabic numerals in the top right hand corner of every recto, the editorial convention has been to refer to page rather than folio numbers in the St Albans Psalter.

64. The effect of these two facing pages can be seen at the University of Aberdeen's St. Albans Psalter website: http://www.abdn.ac.uk/stalbanspsalter/images/bifolios/pages56_57.html.

65. Dean, *Anglo-Norman Literature*, no. 445, 239-240; for the list of fragmentary texts, see Brian Woledge and H.P. Clive, *Répertoire des plus anciens textes en prose française: depuis 842 jusqu'aux premières années du XIIIe siècle* (Geneva: Droz, 1964), 97.

66. Like the Eadwine and Montebourg Psalters, Paris BnF nouv. acq. lat. 1670, another late twelfth-century copy of the Oxford Psalter, seems to have been composed at Christ Church, Canterbury. Similarly, two copies produced early in the thirteenth century, the Corbie Psalter (Paris, BnF lat. 768) and Cambridge, Clare College MS Kk.3.6, have associations with Salisbury and Peterborough, respectively. Woledge and Clive, *Répertoire des plus anciens textes*, 98.

67. Nigel Morgan, "Books for the liturgy and private prayer," 312.

68. For a description of the manuscript, with numerous plates, see Francis Wormald, *The Winchester Psalter* (London: Harvey Miller and Medcalf, 1973).

69. An image of fol. 46r appears as fig. 95 in Wormald's *The Winchester Psalter*, 92

70. London, British Library, Cotton Nero C.IV, fol. 46r.

71. "Dreituriers," "those who act justly," is difficult to translate because of its many social and legal connotations. Like the other terms in this passage,

it associates "the just" with a specific social class: those who exercise and deliver justice. With equal accuracy, we might even have translated "dreiturier" as "justiciar."

72. I suspect there is a direct connection between these manuscripts, since the *mise-en-page* of the British Library Add. 35283 Psalter is identical to that of London, British Library, Cotton Nero C.IV. The Latin and *romanz* texts are presented in parallel columns, the two B initials in nearly identical leaf-scroll decoration, and each *littera notabilior* in the *romanz* text presented in the same color and at the same position in the column as its corresponding Latin initial.

73. Dean, *Anglo-Norman Literature*, No. 447, 242. Woledge and Clive, *Répertoire des plus anciens textes*, no.41, 97 and 14; Yves Le Hir, "Sur des traductions en prose française du Psautier," *Revue de Linguistique Romane* 25 (1961), 324-28. Charles Samaran demonstrates the independence of the Orne Psalter from the earlier Oxford and Cambridge versions. Charles Samaran "Fragment d'une traduction en prose française du Psautier," *Romania* 55 (1929), 161-173.

74. Samaran, "Fragment d'une traduction," 173; Le Hir, "Sur des traductions en prose française du Psautier," 324-38.

75. Ruth Dean, *Anglo-Norman Literature*, no. 446, 242; Woledge and Clive, *Répertoire des plus anciens textes*, no. 39, 94; Guy de Poerck, Rika van Deyck, "La Bible et l'activité traductrice," GRLMA vol. 6:2, no.1864, 94. See also the partial diplomatic edition of Arundel 230 in A. Beyer, "Die Londoner Psalterhandschrift Arundel 230," in *Zeitschrift für romanische Philologie* 11 (1887): 513–534, and 12 (1888): 1–56.

76. Interestingly, the text of the first folio's interlinear *romanz* translation has been replaced, due to either fading or erasure. A seventeenth-century note says that the text was replaced with another *romanz* translation taken from a manuscript held, due to its beauty and antiquity, at Trinity College, Cambridge—almost certainly the Eadwine Psalter.

77. Leena Löfstedt, "Le Psautier en Ancien Français," *Neuphilologische Mitteilungen*, 100:4 (1999), 421-432.

78. Durham, Cathedral Library, A.II.11-13. S. Gregory, ed. *The Twelfth-Century Psalter Commentary in French for Laurette d'Alsace : an Edition of Psalms I-L.* (London: Modern Humanities Research Association, 1990), vol. 1, 6-7.

79. Gregory, *The Twelfth-Century Psalter Commentary*, vol. 1, 6.

80. Following the convention set by Michel, Berger, Beyer and others, Guy de Poerck and Rika van Deyck state that the Oxford Psalter "à servi de base" for Laurette's commentary. de Poerck and van Deyck, "La Bible et l'activité traductrice," GRLMA vol. 6:2, no. 1480, 63.

81. The first two codices, A.II.11 and 12, are contemporaneous and were produced at Durham at the end of the twelfth century; the third codex, A.II.13, is of later Durham production, possibly as late as the mid-thirteenth century. A.II.11 and 12 measure 33.5 x 23.5 centimeters, while A.II.13 measures 36.2 x 25.5 centimeters.

82. On the dedication to Laurette, her marital history and the occasion of her retirement to Forest-lez-Bruxelles, see Gregory, *The Twelfth-Century Psalter Commentary*, vol. 1, 18-19.

83. Gregory, *The Twelfth-Century Psalter Commentary*, (24.165-170), vol. 1, 277-278.

84. Ibid., vol. 2, 655.n.171.

85. Ibid., vol. 1, 6 and 11-12.

86. Ibid., vol. 1, 12.

87. Ibid., vol. 1, 11-12; and Gregory, "The Twelfth-Century Psalter Commentary in French Attributed to Simon of Tournai," *Romania* 100 (1979), 289-340.

88. Gregory, *The Twelfth-Century Psalter Commentary* (30. 199-216), vol. 1, 322.

89. "Pailes d'Aumarie," for example, is a tag phrase repeated throughout all the branches of the *Roman d'Alexandre* and "Aumarie" occurs as a place name in Chrétien de Troyes' *Cligès*, l. 6248. For the "pailes d'Aumarie," the legendary silks of Spanish Almería, see *Roman d'Alexandre* Branch I, ll. 162, 1122, 2437; Branch IV, l. 1146, as well *Les Enfances Guillaume* l. 1766. For an example of rhetorical reiteration in the description of wealth, see the description of the markets of Carthage in the *Roman d'Eneas*: "la vendoit an lo vair, lo gris/ coltes de paile, covertors,/ porpres, pailles, dras de color,/ pierres, epices et vaiselle;/ marcheandie riche e bele/ i pooit l'an toz tenz trover," ll. 450-455. *Eneas: Roman du XIIe siècle.* Ed. J. J. Salvedra de Grave (Paris: Champion, 1985), 14-15.

90. Gregory, *The Twelfth-Century Psalter Commentary* (31.333-45), vol. 1, 341.

91. Ibid., vol. 1, 341. See Sarah Kay, *Courtly Contradictions: The Emergence of the Literary Object in the Twelfth Century* (Stanford: Stanford University Press, 2001).

92. Gregory, *The Twelfth-Century Psalter Commentary* (39.136-149), vol. 2, 427-428 and 459.

93. Denis Piramus, *La Vie Seint Edmund le Rei*, ed. H. Kjellman (Göteborg: Göteborg Kungl. Vetenskaps-och Vitterhets-Samhälles Handlingar, 1935; Geneva: Slatkine Reprints, 1974).

94. The author cites Ovid, for example, in commenting on Psalm 23.1; Ovid is here cited beside Moses as an authority on Creation. Gregory, *The Twelfth-Century Psalter Commentary* (23.25), vol. 1, 269. Juvenal (*Satires*, X.276) is quoted, but not named, in the commentary on Psalm 33 (33.373-74), vol. 1, 360. The Seven Sleepers appear in the commentary on Psalm 43:13 (43.235), vol. 2, 459.

95. The list is preserved in Durham, Muniments of the Dean and Chapter, Misc. Charter 2622, printed in *Catalogi Veteres Librorum Ecclesiae Cathedralis Dunelm: Catalogues of the Library of Durham Cathedral*, Ed. James Raine. Publications of the Surtees Society, (London: J. B. Nichols and Son, 1838), 7:118-119, and described in part by R. A. B Mynors in *Durham Cathedral Manuscripts to the End of the Twelfth Century* (Oxford: Oxford University Press, 1939).

96. For example, the script of A.II.11 and 12 is closely related to the script of Durham Cathedral Library A.II.2, a Latin Bible that belonged to de Puiset, and as Stewart Gregory observes, it is thus "reasonable to assume that they too were made for de Puiset in the Durham scriptorium." Gregory, *The Twelfth-Century Psalter Commentary*, vol. 1, 1.

97. Patricia Stirnemann, "Some Champenois Vernacular Manuscripts and the Manerius Style of Illumination," in *The Manuscripts of Chrétien de Troyes*, ed. Keith Busby et al. (Amsterdam: Rodopi, 1993), vol. 1, 195-226, 197, 201-202 and 204; see also Keith Busby, *Codex and Context: Reading Old French Verse Narrative in Manuscript* (Amsterdam: Rodopi, 2002), 2: 571.

98. Stirnemann, "Some Champenois Vernacular Manuscripts," 197 and 201-202.

99. Ibid., 204. See also Busby, *Codex and Context*, 2: 572.

100. Stirnemann, "Some Champenois Vernacular Manuscripts," 197.

101. *Eructavit*, T. Atkinson Jenkins ed. (Dresden: Gesellschaft fur Romanische Literatur, 1909); George Fitch McKibben, *The Eructavit, an Old French Poem: the Author's Environment, his Argument and Materials* (Baltimore: J.H. Furst, 1907).

102. Brian Woledge and Ian Short, "Liste Provisoire de Manuscrits du XIIe Siècle Contenant Des Textes en Langue Française," *Romania* 102 (1981), 1-17, 17.

103. Blaess, "Les manuscrits français dans les monastères anglais au Moyen Âge," *Romania* 94 (1973), 321–358, 324.

104. Ibid., 330, 356, 335 and 328.

105. Ibid., 324-25, 330-331, and 356-57.

106. de Hamel, "Books and Society," at 14-17; Jenny Stratford and Teresa Webber, "Bishops and kings: private book collections in medieval England," in *Cambridge History of Libraries in Britain and Ireland* (Cambridge: Cambridge University Press, 2006), 178-217. Both of these studies make use of S. H. Cavanaugh, "A Study of books privately owned in England 1300-1450," unpublished PhD thesis, University of Pennsylvania, 1980.

107. Madeleine Blaess, 'L'Abbaye de Bordesley et les livres de Guy de Beauchamp,' *Romania* 78 (1957): 513.

108. de Hamel, "Books and Society," 14.

109. Juliet Vale, *Edward III and Chivalry: Chivalric Society and its Context, 1270-1350* (Woodbridge, UK: Boydell and Brewer, 1982), 49-50 and appendix 9.

110. Jenny Stratford, "The early royal collections and the Royal Library to 1461," in *The Cambridge History of the Book in Britain, Vol. 3: 1400-1557*, ed. Lotte Hellinga and J.B. Trapp (Cambridge: Cambridge University Press, 1999), 255-266, 257-58.

111. London, British Library, Add. MS 60584, fol. 27v. Stratford and Webber, "Bishops and kings," 202.

112. Edith Rickert, "King Richard's Books, *Library*, 4th ser., 13 (1932), 145; and Stratford and Webber, "Bishops and kings," 203.

113. Stratford and Webber, "Bishops and kings," 203.

114. D.H. Turner, *Early Gothic Illuminated Manuscripts in England* (London, 1965), 25.

115. See Jean Bonnard, *Les Traductions de la Bible en vers français au Moyen Âge*, 130-131.

116. Carter Revard, "Four Fabliaux from London, BL MS Harley 2253, Translated into English Verse," *The Chaucer Review* 40.2 (2005), 22-23.

117. Michael P. Kuczynski, "'An Electric Stream': The Religious Contents," in *Studies in the Harley Manuscript: the Scribes, Contents, and Social Contexts of British Library MS Harley 2253*, ed. Susanna Fein (Kalamazoo, Mich., 2000), 123-161, 124 and 148.

118. Revard, "Scribe and Provenance," in *Studies in the Harley Manuscript: The Scribes, Contents, and Social Contexts of British Library* MS Harley 2253, ed. Susanna Fein (Kalamazoo, MI: Medieval Institute Publications, Western Michigan University, 2000), 111–140, 111.
119. de Poerck and van Deyck, "Bible et l'activité traductrice," vol. 6:1, 29–30; vol. 6:2, no. 1416, 57–58.
120. Ibid., vol. 6:1, 26; vol. 6:2, no. 1480, 62–64.
121. Ibid., vol. 6:1, 26. See Samuel Berger, *La Bible Française ay Moyen Age: Étude sur Les Plus Anciennes Versions de la Bible Écrites en Prose de Langue d'Oïl* (Paris: Champion, 1884), 3-4 and 16-17.
122. Raymond St. Jacques, "The *Middle English Glossed Prose Psalter* and its French Source," in *Medieval Translators and their Craft*, ed. Jeanette Beer (Kalamazoo, MI: Medieval Institute Publications, Western Michigan University, 1999), 135-154.

WORKS CITED

Atkinson Jenkins, T., ed. *Eructavit*. Dresden, Germany: Gedruckt für die Gesellschaft für Romanische Literatur, 1909.

Benedict of Nursia. *The Rule of St. Benedict in English*, ed. and trans. Timothy Fry. Collegeville, MN.: Liturgical Press, 1981.

Berger, Samuel. *La Bible Française au Moyen Âge: Étude sur Les Plus Anciennes Versions de la Bible Écrites en Prose de Langue d'Oïl.* Paris: Champion, 1884; Geneva: Slatkine Reprints, 1967.

Berghaus, F. G. *Der Verwandtschaftsverhältnisse der altenglischen Interlinearversionen des Psalters und der Cantica*, Palaestra 272. Göttingen: Vandenhoeck & Ruprecht, 1979.

Beyer, A. "Die Londoner Psalterhandschrift Arundel 230." *Zeitschrift für romanische Philologie* 11(1887): 513-34 and 12 (1888): 1-56.

Blaess, Madeleine. "Les manuscrits français dans les monastères anglais au moyen age." *Romania* 94 (1973): 321-358.

Bonnard, Jean. *Les Traductions de la Bible en vers français au Moyen Âge.* Genève: Slatkine Reprints, 1967.

Busby, Keith. *Codex and Context: Reading Old French Verse Narrative in Manuscript.* Amsterdam: Rodopi, 2002.

Carruthers, Mary. *The Book of Memory: A Study of Memory in Medieval Culture.* Cambridge Studies in Medieval Literature 34. Cambridge, UK: Cambridge University Press, 1990.

——. *The Craft of Thought: Meditation, Rhetoric and the Making of Images 400-1200.* Cambridge, UK: Cambridge University Press, 1998.

Cavanaugh, S. H. "A Study of books privately owned in England 1300-1450." Unpublished PhD thesis, University of Pennsylvania, 1980.

Cooper, Charles M. "Jerome's 'Hebrew Psalter' and the New Latin Version." *Journal of Biblical Literature*, 69.3 (1950): 233-244.

Cortes, J. M. "Figures et tropes dans le psautier de Cassiodore." *Revue des études latines* xlii (1964): 361-375.

Dean, Ruth, with Maureen B. M. Boulton. *Anglo-Norman Literature: A Guide to Texts and Manuscripts*. Anglo-Norman Text Society Occasional Publications Series 3. London: Anglo-Norman Text Society, 1999.

De Hamel, Christopher. "Books and Society." In *The Cambridge History of the Book in Britain, Vol. II*: 1100-1400. Ed. Lotte Hellinga and J.B. Trapp. Cambridge, UK: Cambridge University Press, 2008. 3-21.

De Hamel, Christopher. "Books of Hours: Imaging the Word." In *The Bible as Book: The Manuscript Tradition*. Ed. John L. Sharpe III and Kimberly Van Kampen. London: British Library; New Castle, DE: Oak Knoll Press, 1998. 137–144.

De Poerck, Guy and Rika van Deyck, "La Bible et l'activité traductrice dans le pays romane avant 1300," *Grundriss der romanischen Literaturen des Mittelalters* (GRLMA), vol. 6:1, 21-57. Heidelberg: Carl Winter, 1968, vol. 6:1, 21–57.

Downey, Charles T. "*Ad imaginem suam*: Regional Chant Variants and the Origins of the *Jeu d'Adam*." *Comparative Drama*, 36. 3/4 (2003): 359-390.

Duffy, Eamon. *Marking the Hours: English People and Their Prayers* 1240-1570. New Haven, CT: Yale University Press, 2006.

Gibson, Margaret. "Introduction," in *The Eadwine Psalter: Text, Image and Monastic Culture in Twelfth-Century Canterbury*. ed. Margaret Gibson, T.A. Heslop, and Richard W. Pfaff. London: Modern Humanities Research Association, 1992. 1–3.

Gregory, Stewart, ed. *The Twelfth-Century Psalter Commentary in French for Laurette d'Alsace: an Edition of Psalms I-L*. London: Modern Humanities Research Association, 1990.

Hamlin, Hannibal. *Psalm Culture and Early Modern English Literature*. Cambridge, UK: Cambridge University Press, 2004.

Heslop, T. A. "Decoration and Illustration." In *The Eadwine Psalter: Text, Image and Monastic Culture in Twelfth-Century Canterbury*. ed. Margaret Gibson, T.A. Heslop, and Richard W. Pfaff. London: Modern Humanities Research Association, 1992, 25–59.

Hilberg, Isidorus, ed. *Sancti Eusebii Hieronymi Epistulae*, 3 vols. New York: Johnson, 1970; repr. Vienna: F. Tempsky, 1910-18.

Hunt, Tony. "The Anglo-Norman Book." Section 1 of Tony Hunt, Julia Boffey, A. S. G. Edwards, and Daniel Huws, "Vernacular Literature and Its Readership." In *The Cambridge History of the Book in Britain, Vol. II*: 1100-1400. Ed. Lotte Hellinga and J.B. Trapp. Cambridge, UK: Cambridge University Press, 2008, 367-396.

Jodogne, Omer. "La naissance de la prose française." *Bulletin de la Classe des Lettres et des Sciences Morales et Politiques, Académie Royale de Belgique*, 5th ser., 49 (1963): 296-308.

Krapp, George Philip, ed. *The Paris Psalter and the Meters of Boethius*. New York: Columbia University Press, 1932.

Kuczynski, Michael P. "'An Electric Stream': The Religious Contents." In *Studies in the Harley Manuscript: the Scribes, Contents, and Social Contexts of British Library* MS Harley 2253. Ed. Susanna Fein. Kalamazoo, Mich.: Medieval Institute Publications, 2000. 123-161.

———. *Prophetic Song: The Psalms as Moral Discourse in Late Medieval England.* Philadelphia: University of Pennsylvania Press, 1995.

Kuhn, H. "The Vespasian Psalter Gloss: Original or Copy." PMLA 74.3 (1959): 161-77.

Lampe, G. W. H. "Germany and Low Countries." Section 4 of "The Vernacular Scriptures." In *The Cambridge History of the Bible*, vol. 2. Cambridge, UK: Cambridge University Press, 1963-70.

Leclercq, Jean. "'Ioculator et saltator': S. Bernard et l'image du jongleur dans les manuscrits." In *Translatio studii: Manuscript and Library Studies Honoring Oliver L. Kapsner, O.S.B.*, ed. Julian G. Plante, 24-48. Collegeville, Minn.: St John's University Press, 1973. 24–48.

———. "Les Traductions de la Bible et la Spiritualité Médiévale." In *The Bible and Medieval Culture.* Ed. W. Lourdaux and D. Verhelst, 263-277. Leuven, Belgium: Leuven University Press, 1979. 263–277.

———. *Otia Monastica: Études sur le vocabulaire de la contemplation au moyen âge.* Studia Anselmiana 51. Rome: Herder, 1963.

Legge, M. Dominica. *Anglo-Norman in the Cloisters: The Influence of the Orders upon Anglo-Norman Literature.* Edinburgh: Edinburgh University Press, 1950.

Le Hir, Yves. "Sur des traductions en prose française du Psautier." *Revue de Linguistique Romane* 25 (1961): 324-28.

Leroquais, V. *Les Psautiers Manuscrits Latins des Bibliothèques Publiques de France.* Macon: Protat, 1940-1941.

Löfstedt, Leena. "Le Psautier en Ancien Français." *Neuphilologische Mitteilungen*, 100.4 (1999): 421-432.

Markey, Dominique. "The Anglo-Norman Version." In *The Eadwine Psalter: Text, Image and Monastic Culture in Twelfth-Century Canterbury.* Ed. Margaret Gibson, T. A. Heslop, and Richard W. Pfaff. London: Modern Humanities Research Association, 1992. 139–156.

McKibben, George Fitch. *The Eructavit, an Old French Poem: the Author's Environment, his Argument and Materials.* Baltimore, MD: J. H. Furst, 1907.

Meister, J. H. *Die Flexion im Oxforder Psalter.* Halle, Germany: M. Niemeyer, 1877.

Merrilees, Brian. "Oxford Psalter." In *The Dictionary of the Middle Ages*, vol. 9. Ed. Joseph R. Strayer. New York: American Council of Learned Societies, 1982-1989.

Michel, Francisque, ed., *Libri Psalmorum versio antiqua gallica e cod. ms. in Bibl. Bodleiana.* Oxford: Oxford University Press, 1860.

Minnis, J. *Medieval Theory of Authorship: Scholastic Literary Attitudes in the Later Middle Ages.* London: Scolar Press, 1984.

Morgan, Nigel. "Books for the Liturgy and Private Prayer." In *The Cambridge History of the Book in Britain, vol.* II, 1100–1400. Ed. Lotte Hellinga and J. B. Trapp. Cambridge: Cambridge University Press, 2008. 291–316.

Mynors, R. A. B. *Durham Cathedral Manuscripts to the End of the Twelfth Century.* Oxford: Oxford University Press, 1939.

Noomen, Willem, ed. *Le jeu d'Adam (Ordo representacionis Ade).* Paris: H. Champion, 1971.

O'Neill, Patrick P. "The English Version." In *The Eadwine Psalter: Text, Image and Monastic Culture in Twelfth-Century Canterbury.* Ed. Margaret Gibson, T. A. Heslop, and Richard W. Pfaff. London: Modern Humanities Research Association, 1992. 123–138.

Parkes, Malcolm. *Pause and Effect: An Introduction to the History of Punctuation in the West.* Berkeley: University of California Press, 1993.

Petrarch. *Lettres familières VIII–XI (Rerum familiarium VIII–XI).* Ed. Pierre Laurens. Trans. André Longpré. Les Classiques de L'Humanisme. Paris: Les Belles Lettres, 2003.

Piramus, Denis. *La Vie Seint Edmund le Rei.* Ed. H. Kjellman. Göteborg: Göteborg Kungl. Vetenskaps-och Vitterhets-Samhälles Handlingar, 1935; Geneva: Slatkine Reprints, 1974.

Raine, James, ed. *Catalogi veteres librorum ecclesiae cathedralis Dunelm: Catalogues of the Library of Durham Cathedral,* vol. 7. Publications of the Surtees Society. London: J. B. Nichols and Son, 1838.

Ray, R. D. "Medieval Historiography through the Twelfth Century." *Viator* 5 (1974): 33–59.

Revard, Carter. "Scribe and Provenance." In *Studies in the Harley Manuscript: The Scribes, Contents, and Social Contexts of British Library MS Harley 2253.* Ed. Susanna Fein. Kalamazoo, MI: Medieval Institute Publications, Western Michigan University, 2000. 111–140.

Riché, Pierre. *Education and Culture in the Barbarian West: Sixth through Eighth Centuries.* Trans. John J. Contreni. Columbia: University of South Carolina Press, 1976.

Rickert, Edith. "King Richard's Books." *Library* 4th ser., 13 (1932): 144–147.

St.-Jacques, Raymond. "The *Middle English Glossed Prose Psalter* and Its French Source." In *Medieval Translators and Their Craft.* Ed. Jeanette Beer. Kalamazoo, MI: Medieval Institute Publications, Western Michigan University, 1999. 135–154.

Salverda de Grave, J. J. ed. *Eneas: Roman du XIIe siècle.* Paris: Champion, 1985.

Samaran, Charles. "Fragment d'une traduction en prose française du Psautier," *Romania* 55 (1929): 161-173.

Stirnemann, Patricia. "Some Champenois Vernacular Manuscripts and the Manerius Style of Illumination." In *The Manuscripts of Chrétien de Troyes,* vol. 1. Ed. Keith Busby, Terry Nixon, Alison Stones, and Lori Walters. Amsterdam and Atlanta, GA: Rodopi, 1993. 195–226.

Stratford, Jenny. "The early royal collections and the Royal Library to 1461." In *The Cambridge History of the Book in Britain*, Vol. 3: 1400-1557. Ed. Lotte Hellinga and J.B. Trapp. Cambridge: Cambridge University Press, 1999. 255-266.

Stratford, Jenny, and Teresa Webber. "Bishops and Kings: Private Book Collections in Medieval England." In *The Cambridge History of Libraries in Britain and Ireland*, vol. 1. Ed. Elisabeth Leedham-Green and Teresa Webber. Cambridge: Cambridge University Press, 2006. 178–217.

Toswell, M. J. "The Late Anglo-Saxon Psalter: Ancestor of the Book of Hours?" *Florilegium* 14 (1995-96): 1-24.

——. "The translation techniques of the old English metrical psalter, with special reference to Psalm 136." *English Studies* 75.5 (1994): 393–407.

Turner, D. H. *Early Gothic Illuminated Manuscripts in England*. London: Trustees of the British Museum, 1965.

Vale, Juliet. *Edward III and Chivalry: Chivalric Society and its Context, 1270-1350*. Woodbridge, UK: The Boydell Press, 1982.

van Emden, Wolfgang, ed. and trans. *Le jeu d'Adam*. London: Anglo-Norman Texts Society, 1996.

Watson, Nicholas and Jocelyn Wogan-Browne. "The French of England: the *Compileison, Ancrene Wisse*, and the Idea of Anglo-Norman." *The Journal of Romance Studies* 4.3 (Winter 2004): 35-59.

Woledge, Brian and H. P. Clive. *Répertoire des plus anciens textes en prose française: depuis 842 jusqu'aux premières années du XIIIe siècle*. Genève: Droz, 1964.

Wormald, Francis. *The Winchester Psalter*. London: London, Harvey Miller and Medcalf, 1973.

Zink, Michel. *Littérature française du Moyen Age*. Paris: Presses universitaires de France, 2001.

What's in a Paraph?
A New Methodology and Its
Implications for the Auchinleck
Manuscript

HELEN MARSHALL

By the end of the fourteenth century, the process by which multiple craftsmen came together to collaborate on the production of vernacular books had undergone major changes. These changes included an increasing demand for specifically English texts, the emergence of a community of book producers within London and other major centers of the book trade, and the increased interface between authors and professional scribes. As the demand for books rose, book producers began to form networks through guild association, parish affiliation, and proximity. *The Directory of London Stationers and Book Artisans: 1300–1500* locates 136 stationers and craftsmen within the immediate area of St. Paul's Cathedral.[1] These developing networks became the basis for collaboration on major projects, allowing multiple scribes to participate in ad hoc arrangements and likewise facilitating the exchange of exemplars or small textual units that could be employed within the production of major codices.

The study of these textual networks has benefited greatly from work conducted by Linne Mooney, Estelle Stubbs, and Simon Horobin in their Arts and Humanities Research Council (AHRC) funded project to identify the scribes involved in major late-medieval English manuscripts. In 2000 Mooney laid the groundwork for the subfield of scribal identification as a new direction in medieval manuscript studies.[2] Six years later, her identification of Adam Pinkhurst as Doyle and Parkes's Scribe B, the primary scribe of the Hengwrt and Ellesmere manuscripts, concretely demonstrated the need for inquiry into the makers of manuscripts.[3] For the first time, it seems possible to understand the London literary milieu as a community of *people*, and by identifying those people it is possible to assess more accurately the nature of their production arrangements.

Unarguably, this work is an important step in developing a new social and literary history of late-medieval book production. However, little has been done to address features of the text that potentially represent a further stage of production and therefore a further stage of collaboration—features such as the paraph.[4] My purpose, then, is to address the nature of the paraph as a textual object, one capable of being scrutinized with the same rigor applied to scribal hands of the period.

National Library of Scotland, Advocates MS 19.2.1
(the Auchinleck Manuscript)

Production of the Manuscript

Produced some time between 1330 and 1340, the Auchinleck manuscript has gained a place within the critical gaze of pre-Chaucerian scholars, who have mined it as a source for scholarly editions of many Middle English texts and have performed close analyses of its codicological breakdown. The current manuscript is made up of 331 folios and fourteen stubs, while an additional ten folios have been located detached from the manuscript. The book currently contains forty-four items, including romances, hagiographical texts, chronicles, and the like. Alison Wiggins's computer analysis of scribal habits confirms the early work of Timothy Shonk and A. J. Bliss, determining that we can distinguish six scribes who often share tasks within the booklets.[5] All of the scribes are anonymous and none of them has been identified as having worked on another manuscript.

Studies of the Auchinleck manuscript provide several models for book production in the early fourteenth century. The scholarship discussing the Auchinleck manuscript's production has been contentious, beginning with Laura Hibbard Loomis's groundbreaking article in the 1940s.[6] Adapting the model of the monastic scriptorium to a commercial venture, Hibbard Loomis proposes that the manuscript was created in what she calls a "lay scriptorium" or "bookshop."[7] This need not have been an *actual* shop; rather she proposes the idea of a lay center "where went on, whether under one roof or not, the necessarily unified and directed work of compiling, copying, illuminating, and binding any book."[8]

This model persisted for some time and was altered slightly by Pamela Robinson thirty years later in her Oxford dissertation.[9] While Robinson accepts the model of the bookshop, she argues that the manuscript was assembled from twelve fascicles—smaller booklets containing a number of completed texts that could have either circulated independently or been bound together to create a larger book. Her analysis implies that fascicles were part of a process of speculative production in which a buyer could select from a number of premade fascicles.

Shonk, however, proposes an alternate model in which the product was commissioned by a buyer from a *stationarius* who worked as both scribe and editor on the project. Specifically, he puts forward Scribe 1 as an editor of sorts, copying the bulk of the material, overseeing the various stages of construction, and coordinating between the buyer and the other scribes.[10] Shonk argues that Scribe 1 wrote all of the extant catchwords that determine the order in which the booklets were arranged and was likely responsible for the numbering of the items and the addition of titles after the manuscript had been decorated. The assumption of these duties suggests that Scribe 1 was employed for more than just copying; rather, he was an editor who determined the general layout of the page and the final order of the items within the book. Within this model, copying need not have been localized to a physical "shop" where all scribes were present. Rather, material could be farmed out to scribes within the city on an ad hoc basis. This arrangement has been accepted and expanded upon by Wiggins and Ralph Hanna, both of whom emphasize the nature of London's literary culture as a necessary milieu for textual information to be shared between scribes.[11]

The current production model favored by scholars clearly hinges upon the role played by Scribe 1 in the creation of the manuscript; Scribe 2, however, plays an equally interesting role. In her study, Wiggins compellingly suggests that the Worcestershire/Gloucestershire dialects of Scribe 2 and his fellow West Midlander, Scribe 6, could be a clue to uncovering the textual communities that gave rise to this important manuscript. She describes a model of production for the manuscript that would depend upon "the existence of sustained, long-standing professional relationships between scribes who moved between different regions and exchanged texts, exemplars, and readymade booklets as and when required."[12]

Scribe 2 remains the key to understanding such a model, representing an underexamined figure within the manuscript and within fourteenth-century book production—the "professional shape changer."[13] He collaborated on booklets with multiple scribes in addition to completing at least one on his own, but his habits of ruling and decoration often diverge from those maintained throughout the rest of the manuscript. Furthermore, I detect similarities in layout, aspect, and decoration between the stints of Scribe 2 and those of the scribe of Egerton 1993.[14] In particular, in an observation that would later prompt this paper, I noticed a strong resemblance between the distinctive paraphs of the Wavy Top (b) parapher—who, I suggest, is Scribe 2—and those of Egerton 1993, *despite* differences in the text hands.

Paraphs in the Auchinleck Manuscript

At his keynote address at the London Old and Middle English Research Seminar on the Auchinleck manuscript in June 2008, Shonk identified four styles of paraphs that appear within the manuscript.[15] He labeled these the Flat paraph, the Wavy Top paraph, the Upcurl paraph, and the Long Descender paraph, each of which takes its name from a prominent distinguishing feature (see Figs. 1.1, 1.2, 1.3, and 1.4). His work convincingly demonstrates that features of paraphs could be distinct enough for multiple styles of paraphs to be detected in a single manuscript.[16] I argue for the presence of a fifth paraph with a shape similar to that of Wavy Top (a) but distinct enough to be recognized as a separate hand (see Fig. 1.5). The second hand, Wavy Top (b), appears in the first text of Booklet 2 (fols. 39r–48r) and again in Booklet 12 (fols. 328r–334v). It is this delineation between two paraphs with the same distinctive feature that serves as the basis for the first part of my case study.

I have found four features by which I can distinguish between the Wavy Top (a) paraphs and the Wavy Top (b) paraphs: length and shape of top stroke, length and shape of descender, shape of bowl and fill stroke, and finally, length and shape of bottom stroke. I divide these features correspondingly into descriptive and measurable categories as shown in Figures 2.1 and 2.2.[17] When the paraph stints are compared according to descriptive categories, several features become apparent. Firstly, Wavy Top (a) and Wavy Top (b) differ in their primary usages in two descriptive categories: shape of bottom stroke and shape of descender. Wavy Top (a) tends to employ an upward hook in the bottom stroke of the paraph, while Wavy Top (b) never includes a bottom stroke. Furthermore, Wavy Top (a) primarily uses a straight descender whereas Wavy Top (b) uses a descender with a left lean.

Differences between the paraphs are further evident when the measurements are likewise analyzed, contributing to a very different "aspect" to each paraph. Although the bowl heights are approximately the same for both paraph sets, the bowl width of Wavy Top (a) is close to 1 millimeter narrower than that of Wavy Top (b). The lengths of the top strokes and the descenders are equally revealing. The scribe of Wavy Top (a) draws his top strokes about 2 millimeters longer than those of Wavy Top (b) while drawing his descenders up to 5 millimeters longer than those of Wavy Top (b). The differences in these measurements give Wavy Top (a) a much more compressed aspect that tends to produce tall, narrow paraphs. Wavy Top (b), on the other hand, tends to produce paraphs that are more regular in shape, with a boxlike appearance.

The differences in shape and measurement patterns between Wavy Top (a) and Wavy Top (b) lead me to conclude that they represent two distinct paraphing hands. I would like to advance a further argument that the Wavy Top (b) paraphs were, in fact, written by Scribe 2, in whose text stints they appear. Here I follow Ian Cunningham, who states in the introduction to the facsimile that Scribe 2 was responsible for his own red paragraph signs in the aforementioned booklets.[18] Cunningham's reasons for this are not well documented, so I provide evidence on several grounds.

Codicological Divisions

Scribe 2 appears in the Auchinleck manuscript at three points. First, he wrote the "Speculum Gy" (fols. 39r–48r), which appears at the beginning of Booklet 2. The rest of this booklet was completed by Scribe 1 (fols. 48r–59v). Second, Scribe 2 wrote the "Sayings of the Four Philosophers" (fol. 105r), which appears near the end of Booklet 3. Third, he wrote the "Simony" (fols. 328r–334v), which makes up the twelfth and final booklet of the collection. In the entire manuscript, Wavy Top (b) paraphs occur only in the first and last stint of Scribe 2 and nowhere else. Furthermore, the only break in a paraph stint that does *not* correspond to the end of a quire occurs at folio 48r, when the scribal hand changes from Scribe 2 to Scribe 1. This suggests that the change in scribal hands and the change in paraphing hands were connected.

Paraph Guide Marks

In folios 39r to 48r of Booklet 2, paraph guide marks are particularly scarce. On folio 39r, one marker is visible in the lower left-hand corner in a shape that is difficult to distinguish (see Fig. 3.1). To my knowledge, this is the only such case within this booklet. The paraphs that occur in this section are narrative markers rather than formal ones, so their occurrence could not be easily predicted on the basis of stanza length. Therefore it seems likely that whoever supplied the paraphs must have been familiar with the text. Likewise, in folios 328r to 334v of Booklet 12, only two paraphs guide marks are visible, both occurring at the top of folio 328v and both likewise in the shape of an extended "a" (see Fig. 3.2). Elsewhere throughout this text, a small punctus is used when text is positioned along the right-hand margin of the page. When this occurs, a paraph also marks the separated text. Throughout both booklets, paraph guide marks are exceptionally rare and typically occur on the first folio of the booklet only.

In Booklet 3, folio 105r, where Scribe 2 has a very brief stint (see below), paraph guide marks are included regularly, but the paraphs are identifiable as belonging to the flat top and long descender varieties that occur elsewhere within this manuscript. The lack of regular guide marks in the sections in which Wavy Top (b) paraphs occur suggests that these paraphs were provided by the scribe himself, whereas the presence of guide marks elsewhere suggests that they were for the benefit of other paraphers.

Booklet 3

Booklet 3 represents something of an anomaly within the manuscript in that it is the only booklet in which more than two scribes' hands are present. Scribe 3 wrote six texts from folios 70r to 104v, apparently leaving several folios ruled but unfilled at the end of the final quire. Scribe 2 supplied "The Sayings of the Four Philosophers" on folio 105r (see Fig. 4.1). He wrote this text to conform to the ruling that had already been provided by Scribe 3, cramping his otherwise tall textualis to fit into the forty-four lines provided rather than the typical twenty-four that appear in his other stints. After this short stint, Scribe 4 reruled the remaining folios into three columns in order to accommodate "The Battle Abbey Roll" on folios 105v to 107v.

As mentioned above, throughout Scribe 2's stint only flat top and long descender paraphs are evident. It seems to me that in this particular stint, Scribe 2 was called upon to copy text after the booklet had already been started, and as a result, Booklet 3 conforms to Scribe 1's layout and paraphing system rather than the alternate layout and paraphing system in Booklets 2 and 12. The fact that Scribe 2 includes paraph marks at this point—when the paraphs do not correspond with those that, I suggest, are his own—may be a further indicator that his stints in Booklet 2 and 12 represent unique moments in the production of the manuscript.

Aspect and Ink Color

The aspect of the paraphs in Booklets 2 and 12 corresponds to the aspect of the text, particularly in terms of the width of the pen strokes and the length and shape of the descenders. The leftward curve of the descenders matches a similar curve in the descenders of the capital "f" and the lowercase thorn. Furthermore, only red paraphs appear in Booklets 2 and 12, whereas red and blue paraphs alternate throughout the rest of the manuscript. The shade of the red ink, a slightly washed-out orange-red, differentiated from the crisper cherry red of the other paraphs, matches the rubricated Latin on folio 40v in Booklet 2, written in Scribe 2's distinctive textualis (see Fig. 5.1). This shade of ink further matches the two-line block initial "h" that appears on folio 40r in Booklet 2 (see Fig. 5.2). This initial, consisting of a block letter outlined in red dots, is the only one of its kind throughout the manuscript. These similarities in ink color suggest that Scribe 2 wrote, rubricated, and even began the initial stage of decoration within Booklet 2. During this process, he used the same red ink to complete the paraphs.

Conclusions and Implications

If we accept that Scribe 2 was responsible for the Wavy Top (b) paraphs and that these paraphs are indeed distinct from the Wavy Top (a) paraphs, what broader conclusions can we draw? At the very least, this identification allows us to localize Scribe 2's involvement in the book with more accuracy. His stints in Booklets 2 and 12 are important because they follow a layout different from the other booklets in the manuscript, a manuscript noted for its layout coherence despite the collaboration of so many scribes.[19] These stints also begin their respective booklets, lending evidence to Wiggins's assertion that Scribe 2 may have started the booklets either before the project was initiated or apart from the compiler's decorative model.

In assessing the consistency in color and design of miniatures, initials capitals, and paraphs, Shonk asserts that these features may have been added by several craftsmen working in a single atelier during a separate stage of production: "Thus, it appears that the volume was decorated as a unit after the completion of the writing, and no segment of it appears to have been designed for independent circulation."[20] Such an atelier is also proposed by Kathleen Scott, who identifies the style of the miniatures as the same as that used in the Queen Mary Psalter.[21]

If the manuscript was completed in an atelier, how, then, can we accommodate the lack of miniatures, the aberrant initials, and the distinctive red paraphs that occur in the stints of Scribe 2? The most likely solution is that Scribe 2 began both Booklet 2 and Booklet 12 outside his collaboration with Scribe 1. He copied the text, included paraphs, and potentially began his own scheme of initials. These codicological packets were then obtained by Scribe 1, after which he completed his own stint in Booklet 2, consisting of "Amis and Amiloun," "The Life of St. Mary Magdalene," and "The Nativity and Early Life of Mary" (fols. 48r–69v). After Scribe 1 completed his stint, the material was sent to the atelier for decoration of the latter portions.

If we view these booklets as being at their inception outside the original plan of the Auchinleck manuscript, then we must reevaluate the production model established for the book as a whole, a production model that focuses primarily upon Scribe 1 as an organizer and controlling figure parceling out portions of the writing when necessary. Instead, the model must emphasize the improvisational nature of the production of the manuscript—how Scribe 1 may have taken partially completed booklets and adapted them for his own work. I do not wish to suggest that the manuscript may have been compiled from preproduced booklets according to the model of speculative book production advanced by Pamela Robinson and Derek Pearsall.[22] Instead, I put forward an intermediary model in which some booklets were "bespoke" while others—created in advance or, at the least, created outside Scribe 1's planning—were incorporated into the codex as whole units or as the basis for booklets in which further scribal stints were added.

London, British Library MS Egerton 1993

The Manuscript

The second part of my test case assesses whether the Wavy Top (b) paraphs can be convincingly identified as the same as those of a South English Legendary (SEL) manuscript, London, British Library MS Egerton 1993 (MS E). The manuscript is described by numerous scholars, including Carl Horstmann in *The Early South-English Legendary*[23] and Manfred Görlach in *The Textual Tradition of the South English Legendary*.[24] It consists of 238 parchment folios divided into three booklets that correspond to different textual units: the "Banna Sanctorum," the *temporale* material, and the *sanctorale* material. The book was written by one scribe in a regular, closely spaced textualis similar to but not identical with that of Scribe 2. Similarities can be found between the decorative initials of MS E and those in the West Midlands portions of the Auchinleck manuscript. MS E is the main representative of the "E" redaction of the South English Legendary, a redaction characterized by shorter lines and the inclusion of a great number of additional legends, many of which portray English saints such as Aetheldreda and Birin.[25]

Grounds for establishing a possible connection between these manuscripts can be determined on the basis of date and dialect. Horstmann dates MS E to 1320, though that is generally considered too early. Görlach advocates a date in the second quarter to mid-fourteenth century on the basis of script and layout. This makes the manuscript broadly contemporaneous with the date given for the Auchinleck manuscript. The *Linguistic Atlas of Late Medieval England* locates the dialect of the MS E scribe in northern Gloucestershire and that of Auchinleck Scribe 2 in the region near the Gloucester/Hereford border.[26] These similarities in date and dialect provide grounds for the reasonable comparison of the paraphs of these manuscripts.

The MS E Scribe

An analysis of the textualis of both scribes reveals enough differences at the level of both aspect and individual letter forms to refute the claim that the scribe who wrote the *text* of MS E was in fact Scribe 2 of the Auchinleck manuscript. For example, the MS E scribe utilizes a much more vertically and horizontally compressed hand, contributing to the "woven" appearance of the text. Scribe 2 tends to have a far more vertical hand with long ascenders and descenders. Furthermore, Scribe 2 employs a distinctive curved ascender and descender on his thorns, whereas the MS E scribe does not. Nevertheless, it is possible that the Wavy Top (b) parapher provided only the paraphs for the manuscript.

The MS E *Paraphs*

Paraphs occur frequently within MS E, corresponding with narrative breaks in the texts. The number of lines varies considerably between occurrences, with some sections of the text more sparsely decorated than others. The MS E scribe primarily uses two diagonal slashes in order to mark paraph placement, although at times he employs the extended "a" shape utilized by Scribe 2 in Booklet 3. Paraphs alternate between red and blue ink, and consistency in shape tends to be maintained best within color sets, suggesting that the parapher likely worked in stints to draw paraphs of one color at a time. Overall, the paraphs correspond in general aspect and shape to those of the Wavy Top (b) parapher. The pen strokes are of a similar thickness throughout, and the paraphs appear to be of similar proportions. The MS E paraphs demonstrate a slight general slant to the left, whereas the Wavy Top (b) paraphs tend to lean slightly to the right, but these features of their aspect are not consistent throughout (see Fig. 6.1).

In order to test the possible connection between these manuscripts, I employed a similar methodology to that of the first test case. Figures 7.1 and 7.2 contain the profiles for the Wavy Top (b) parapher and the MS E parapher. A comparison of descriptive features reveals that both sets of paraphs correspond in their primary usages for all four categories. The MS E parapher, however, shows much more variance in the kinds of shapes he employs throughout his paraphing stint. While the Wavy Top (b) parapher does not employ any secondary or tertiary usages, the MS E parapher uses secondary forms for the top stroke and for the descender, both of which tend to be straighter forms rather than the curved or wavy forms employed elsewhere. Furthermore, he employs tertiary forms for the bottom stroke and descender, although in both cases these are very rare.

Further differences are revealed when the measurement profiles are compared. Although the statistical data for the height of the paraph, the length of the top stroke, and the length of the bottom stroke are all quite close, the width of the bowl, the width of its shading, and the length of the descender all show statistically significant discrepancies. The MS E paraph bowls are about 0.5 millimeter wider than the Wavy Top (b) paraph bowls, and the overall bowl width is about 1 millimeter wider. The descender of the MS E paraphs tends to be about 2 millimeters longer on average, and its maximum length is up to 4 millimeters longer than that of the Wavy Top (b) paraphs. It is my opinion that the variations in the shapes of the paraph and the discrepancies in measurement do not contribute to a definite difference in aspect between the MS E paraphs and the Wavy Top (b) paraphs. Nevertheless, in comparing detailed profiles it becomes increasingly apparent that significant differences exist between the two hands that must be accounted for.

Assessing the Evidence

Comparisons within the Manuscript Corpus

In order to determine if the shape alone offers enough grounds to establish a plausible connected between the paraphs, I compared the descriptive profiles of both the Wavy Top (b) parapher and the MS E parapher to a database compiled from over one hundred manuscripts surveyed that had either dialectal or provenance evidence of having been produced by a West Midlands scribe in the fourteenth century. Latin manuscripts (approximately sixty of those surveyed) show a tendency toward regular, professional paraphs with far less variation in the potential shapes. These paraphs tend to have a D-shaped bowl with a flat top stroke, an upcurl bottom stroke, and no descender. Vernacular manuscripts tend to have the most variation in the styles of paraphs employed and therefore yield those hands most likely to be identifiable across manuscripts.

Within these vernacular manuscripts (approximately fifty of those surveyed), I recorded seven basic shapes for paraph top strokes: flat, upward slope, downward slope, wave, upcurl, flat with decorative tip, and no top stroke. Of these manuscripts, twenty-four paraphers employed a flat top stroke as their primary form, ten employed no top stroke, seven employed an upcurl top stroke, seven employed a wavy top stroke, five employed an upward top stroke, two a downward top stroke, and two a flat stroke with a decorative tip. Likewise, I found three primary shapes for the bottom stroke: none, upward-curved, and flat. Of these manuscripts, thirty-six had no bottom stroke, twelve had an upward-curved bottom stroke, and one had a flat bottom stroke. Finally, I found eight primary shapes for the descender: straight, left curl, left hook, left lean, right curl, right hook, right lean, and none. Of the manuscripts, twenty-three had straight descenders, six had no descenders, five had left-curling descenders, five had right-hooking descenders, four had left-hooking descenders, three had left-curling descenders, two had left-leaning descenders, and one had a right-leaning descender.

Of the vernacular and Latin manuscripts surveyed, only one matched the descriptive profile of the Wavy Top (b) parapher in all four points: London, British Library MS Harley 2398. This collection of Middle English sermons has been dated to the late fourteenth century and therefore is unlikely to be genuinely connected to either parapher.[27] The scarcity of matches corresponding to the descriptive shape profile suggests that when shape alone is analyzed, a positive identification can be made.

Paraph Consistency

In order to assess the effectiveness of my comparison of measurement data, it is necessary to establish a sense of the consistency of the parapher. The accurate analysis of measurement data is difficult because changes occur within the stint of a parapher and within separate stints, based on external influences such as the size of the text line, the position of the paraph within the text, at a side margin, or at the top or bottom of a page, and the size of the quill. Furthermore, as is the case with scribal hands, some paraphing hands tend to develop new forms or change their practice over time. For example, Oxford, Bodleian Library MS Rawlinson B.171 contains paraphs that tend to develop a curled tip on their top strokes. The most common changes in paraph consistency tend to be the loss or addition of decorative elements such as curls and hooks over time and a change in either the size of the body of the paraph or the size of ascenders and top strokes.

In order to establish a sense of the consistency of the Wavy Top (b) parapher across codicological breaks, I compared the data taken from the paraphs in Booklet 2 and the data generated from the first fifty paraphs of Booklet 12. In particular, this was useful to determine whether the measurement data was in fact a good representative of the Wavy Top (b) parapher's habits in general. Figure 8.1 shows the results of the comparison, demonstrating a close grouping of score—consistently with less than 0.5 millimeters variation—in all cases except the length of the top stroke, which appeared about 1 to 1.5 millimeters shorter in the second stint than in the first stint. This is not entirely surprising, as the length of the top stroke is one of the features most likely to vary within a scribe's stint, as evidenced by the fact that both the Wavy Top (b) parapher and the MS E parapher have larger ranges for this category than any other.

Conclusions

Although a great similarity exists between the stints of the MS E parapher and the Wavy Top (b) parapher, there is not enough evidence to prove beyond a reasonable doubt that they are the same hand. The fact that the Wavy Top (b) paraphs have closely grouped scores while the MS E paraphs have scores that do not fit the pattern is a stumbling block for any positive identification. It is possible that these deviations could be explained by a change in habit over time or by factors of the mise-en-page such as line height and margin width. If we accept an early date for MS E, then its paraphing stints may well fall in the early part of the scribe's career. This might account for the variation in the shape of the paraph within the manuscript. A second possibility may be that the general shape of these paraphs represents a regional style, thus explaining the similarity in the dialects of scribes of the two manuscripts but accounting for the variation between stints. A more focused study comparing paraphs found in West Midlands manuscripts to those from other regions in England is beyond the scope of this paper but could nevertheless reveal trends useful to the dating and localization of manuscripts.

Methodological Applications

The methods employed for this project have broader implications for the field of paleographical analysis beyond a codicological reevaluation of the Auchinleck manuscript. The studies undertaken by Horobin, Stubbs, and Mooney raise a number of methodological questions about the extent to which one can construct an accurate scribal profile sustainable across a number of manuscripts and comparable to potential matches beyond the established "canon." I argue that such profiles are likewise employable for other graph-based aspects of *ordinatio* such as the paraph. The study of the paraph adds a potential aspect to profiling that has been fairly unmanageable within paleographical studies—that is, the close scrutiny of a single character over time. It would be entirely improbable and unlikely for a scholar to take the time to measure every instance of the "w" within a manuscript, but this kind of detailed, focused analysis is made possible precisely by the scarcity of measurable data for the paraph.

My paper uses detailed analysis of paraph profiles in order to indicate some of the differences between positive identifications and merely plausible identifications. It is only through increasingly focused analysis of a variety of details—here I think of Wiggins's use of the whole-data analysis of electronic texts—that we can begin to develop the kinds of profiles that make the line between positive and plausible identifications clearer. In the case of the material I present here, a number of key features separate Wavy Top (a) paraphs from Wavy Top (b) paraphs: length and shape of top stroke, length and shape of descender, shape of bowl and fill stroke, length and shape of bottom stroke, and finally ink pigmentation. The comparison relies upon both descriptive characteristics and numeric characteristics that can be tracked across a stint, compared to a second stint, and then compared against a broader assemblage of data on paraphs in West Midlands manuscripts. The second case proves that substantial similarities exist between the Wavy Top (b) parapher and the MS E parapher, but not enough to push the identification beyond reasonable doubt. Thus, at this time, the data is sufficient at most to establish a plausible identification but not a positive one. The question remains unresolved.

Although the analysis of paraphs is not always capable of making positive identifications without further information, it nevertheless provides a useful starting point for further inquiry. Expanding the range of paraphs compared and the sophistication with which data is collected could lead to further conclusions about the development of regional styles of decoration, the differences in the mise-en-page of Latin and vernacular manuscripts, and the influence of page layout on scribal hands. Furthermore, the identification of paraph hands within a manuscript and across manuscripts can offer us a better understanding of the collaboration of tradesmen in book production, the stages of manuscript production, and the importance of decorative features in the developing aesthetic of the book. Were paraphs typically provided by a manuscript's scribe, by an outside craftsman, or by the rubricator? Were they included on a quire-by-quire basis or according to other codicological units? What do changes in paraph hands tells us about breaks in productions? My paper, I hope, demonstrates that the answer to these questions lies within our grasp through careful study of the paraph.

Centre for Medieval Studies, University of Toronto

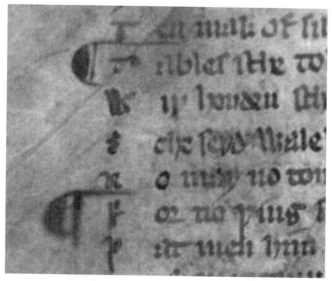

Figure 1.1: Flat paraph (fol. 1v).[28]

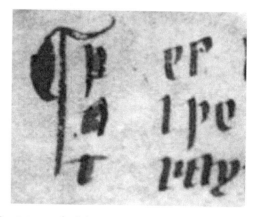

Figure 1.2: Wavy Top (a) paraph (fol. 169r).

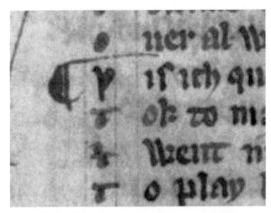

Figure 1.3: Upcurl paraph (fol. 300r).

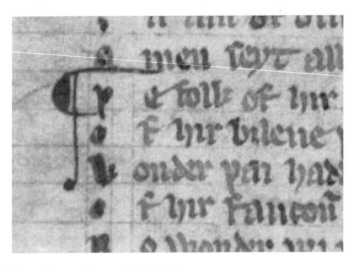

Figure 1.4: Long Descender paraph (fol. 62v).

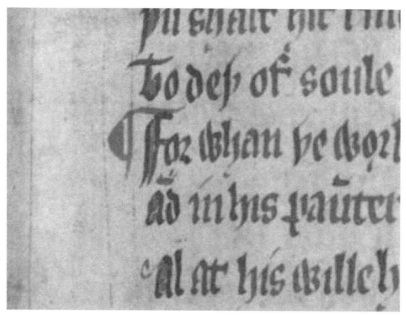

Figure 1.5: Wavy Top (b) paraph (fol. 39r).

	Wavy Top (a) Parapher	Wavy Top (b) Parapher
Shape of Bowl:	D	D
Shape of Top Stroke:	Wave	Wave
Shape of Bottom Stroke:	Upward hook ((none))	None
Shape of Descender:	Straight (left lean) ((left hook))	Left lean

Figure 2.1: Paraph descriptive shape profile for Wavy Top (a) and Wavy Top (b).

	Bowl Shading	Bowl Height	Bowl Width	Top Stroke	Bottom Stroke	Descender
Wavy Top (a) f. 169r-175v						
Average	1.64	4.89	2.34	4.32	1.47	5.83
Mode	1.5	5	2	4	1	7
Range	1 to 2	4 to 6	2 to 3	3.5 to 5.5	0 to 3	0 to 9
Wavy Top (b) f. 39r-42r						
Average	1.79	4.74	3.1	6.73	0	2.4
Mode	1.5	5	3	6	0	2
Range	1 to 3	3.5 to 6	2 to 4.5	4 to 10	0	.5 to 4

Figure 2.2: Paraph measurement profile (mm) for Wavy Top (a) and Wavy Top (b).

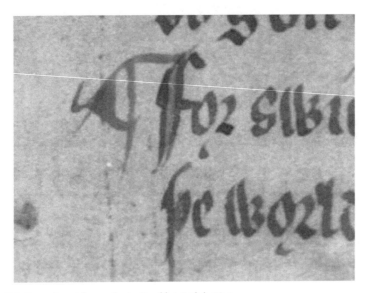

Figure 3.1: Paraph guide marks in Booklet 2 (fol. 39r).

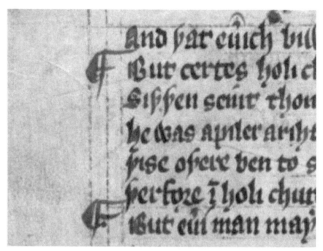

Figure 3.2: Paraph guide marks in Booklet 12 (fol. 328v).

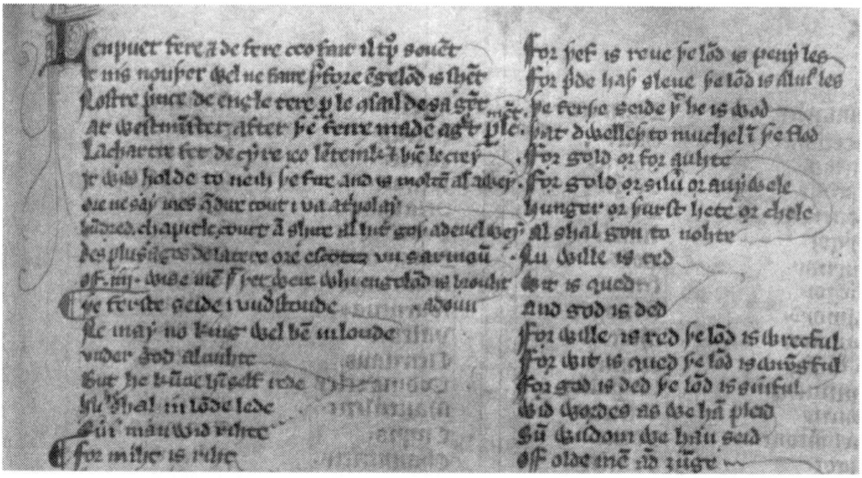

Figure 4.1: Scribe 2's stint in Booklet 3 (fol. 105r).

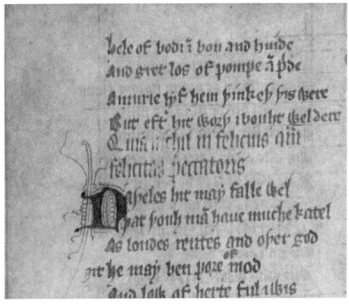

Figure 5.1: Rubricated Latin in Booklet 2 (fol. 40v).

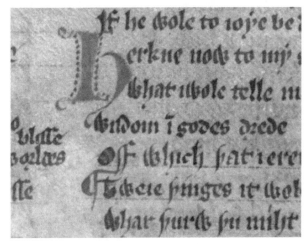

Figure 5.2: Red Block initial in Booklet 2 (fol. 40r).

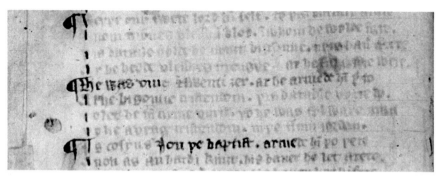

Figure 6.1: Paraphs in Egerton 1993 (fol. 41v). [29]

	Wavy Top (B) Parapher	Egerton 1993 Parapher
Shape of Bowl	D	D
Shape of Top Stroke	Wave	Wave (Flat)
Shape of Bottom Stroke	None	None ((Upward Curve))
Shape of Descender	Left Lean	Left Lean (Straight) ((Right Lean))

Figure 7.1: Descriptive profile for Wavy Top (b) and Egerton 1993.

	Bowl Shading	Bowl Height	Bowl Width	Top Stroke	Bottom Stroke	Descender
Egerton 1993 f. 5r-12v						
Average	2.12	4.48	3.96	6.33	0	4.16
Mode	2	4	4	6	0	4
Range	1.5 to 3.5	3 to 6	3 to 6	3 to 10	0 to .5	2.5 to 8
Wavy Top (b) f. 39r-42r						
Average	1.79	4.74	3.1	6.73	0	2.4
Mode	1.5	5	3	6	0	2
Range	1 to 3	3.5 to 6	2 to 4.5	4 to 10	0	.5 to 4

Figure 7.2: Paraph measurement profile (mm) for Wavy Top (b) and Egerton 1993.

	Bowl Shading	Bowl Height	Bowl Width	Top Stroke	Bottom Stroke	Descender
Wavy Top (b) f. 39r-42r						
Average	1.79	4.74	3.1	6.73	0	2.4
Mode	1.5	5	3	6	0	2
Range	1 to 3	3.5 to 6	2 to 4.5	4 to 10	0	.5 to 4
Wavy Top (b) f. 328r-328v						
Average	1.5	4.45	3.06	4.88	0	2.12
Mode	1.5	4	3	5	0	2
Range	1.5 to 3	4 to 6	2 to 4	3 to 7	0	1 to 5

Figure 8.1: Paraph measurement profile (mm) for Wavy Top (b) in Booklets 2 and 12.

NOTES

1. Of these, 119 could be found in seven parishes whose churches were in close proximity to the cathedral: St. Faith the Virgin, St. Augustine, St. Michael le Querne, St. Botolph without Aldersgate, St. Nicholas at the Shambles, St. Sepulchre without Newgate, and St. Bride. C. Paul Christianson, A *Directory of London Stationers and Book Artisans: 1300–1500* (New York: Bibliographical Society of America, 1990), 32–33.
2. Linne Mooney, "Professional Scribes? Identifying English Scribes Who Had a Hand in More Than One Manuscript," in *New Directions in Later Medieval Manuscript Studies: Essays from the 1998 Harvard Conference*, ed. Derek Pearsall (Woodbridge, UK, and Rochester, NY: York Medieval Press in association with Boydell Press, 2000), 131–141.
3. See Linne Mooney, "Chaucer's Scribe", *Speculum* 81 (2006): 97–138.
4. Joel Fredell, who champions the cause of the "lowly paraf," demonstrates that the graph was an integral textual marker in late-medieval manuscripts, dividing up narrative portions in the text, signaling poetic form, and marking important notes in the text. Fredell's work on the *Canterbury Tales* demonstrates the importance of the paraph as a feature of textual history and literary construction, simultaneously revealing trends in the punctuation and copying of manuscripts even as it offers a glimpse into two very different modes of reading. Fredell's work has been useful in drawing critical attention to the literary relevance of paraphs and their transmission across manuscripts. To my knowledge, this is the only scholarly work to date that has taken the paraph as its primary subject. See Joel Fredell, "The Lowly Paraf: Transmitting Manuscript Design in *The Canterbury Tales*," *Studies in the Age of Chaucer* (2000): 213–280.

5. Wiggins, "Are Auchinleck Manuscript Scribes." A. J. Bliss first identified six scribes in an early article, "Notes on the Auchinleck Manuscript," *Speculum* 26 (1951): 652–658. This work was later confirmed in a paleographical and codicological study of the manuscript, Timothy Shonk, "A Study of the Auchinleck Manuscript: Bookmen and Bookmaking in the Early Fourteenth Century," *Speculum* 60 (1985): 71–91.

6. Laura Hibbard Loomis, "The Auchinleck Manuscript and a Possible London Bookshop of 1330–1340," PMLA 57 (1942): 595–627.

7. Ibid., 597, 599.

8. Ibid., 597.

9. See Pamela Robinson, "A Study of Some Aspects of the Transmission of English Verse Texts in Late Mediaeval Manuscripts," B.Litt. diss., Oxford University, 1972.

10. Shonk states, "He copied most of the material himself, farmed out other pieces to independent scribes, and then completed the work needed to put the book into its final form. . . . He served as 'editor' of the manuscript and did much of the writing, but some of the work he subcontracted to other scribes and rubricators." Shonk, "Study of the Auchinleck Manuscript," 73.

11. See, respectively, Alison Wiggins, "Guy of Warwick: Study and Transcription," Ph.D. diss., University of Sheffield, 2000; and Ralph Hanna III, "Reconsidering the Auchinleck Manuscript," in *New Directions in Later Medieval Manuscript Studies: Essays From the 1998 Harvard Conference*, ed. D. Pearsall (Woodbridge, UK, and Rochester, NY: York Medieval Press in association with Boydell Press, 2000), 91–102.

12. Wiggins, "Are Auchinleck Manuscript Scribes," 18.

13. Ibid.

14. I would like to thank Orietta Da Rold, who also pointed out similarities between the layout and decoration of these two manuscripts in her paper "Dismantling the Paradigms of Manuscript Production, 1200–1400," presented at the New Chaucer Society in Swansea on July 21, 2008.

15. Timothy Shonk, "Paraphs, Piecework, and Presentation: The Production Methods of the Auchinleck Revisited," paper presented at the London Old and Middle English Research Seminar: Studies in the Auchinleck Manuscript, London, UK, June 20, 2008.

16. This work modified his early conclusions for the presence of three paraphers in the manuscript. See Shonk, "Study of the Auchinleck Manuscript," 78.

17. The descriptive categories have been modeled upon the dialect profiles found in A. McIntosh, M. L. Samuels, and M. Benskin, A *Linguistic Atlas of Late Middle English*, 4 vols. (Aberdeen, UK: Aberdeen University Press, 1986). Terms appearing without brackets show the primary usage of the scribe. Terms appearing with one set of brackets show the secondary usage of the scribe, showing shapes that appear less than 40 percent of the time. Terms appearing with two sets of brackets show the tertiary usage of the scribe,

showing shapes that appear less than 15 percent of the time. Both charts are based upon data taken from fifty paraphs that occur in a single stint.

18. Derek Pearsall and Ian Cunningham, eds., *The Auchinleck Manuscript* (London: Scolar Press, 1977), xv. This position was also supported by Dan Embree and Elizabeth Urquhart, eds., *The Simonie: A Parallel-Text Edition*, Middle English Texts 24 (Heidelberg, Germany: Winter, 1991), 9.

19. Shonk, in particular, argues that the appearance of unity across the work of so many scribes raises "the possibility of a predetermined design"; see Shonk, "Study of the Auchinleck Manuscript," 77.

20. Ibid., 78.

21. See Kathleen L. Scott, "A Mid-Fifteenth Century English Illuminating Shop and Its Customers," *Journal of the Warburg and Courtauld Institutes* 31 (1968): 195.

22. See Pearsall and Cunningham, "Auchinleck Manuscript"; and Robinson, "A Study of Some Aspects of the Transmission of English Verse Texts."

23. Carl Horstmann, *The Early South-English Legendary, or, Lives of Saints: MS Laud 108* (Millwood, NY: Kraus Reprint, 1973), xviii.

24. Manfred Görlach, *The Textual Tradition of the South English Legendary* (Leeds, UK: Scolar Press, 1974), 80–81.

25. The "E" redaction was first addressed by Görlach when he drew attention to the number and nature of "additional" legends that it includes. He presumed a source located near Hereford. See ibid., 17. Several editions of the marginal "E" legends have been published separately from the main text. See Laurel Braswell, "St. Edburga of Winchester: A Study of Her Cult A.D. 950–1500, with an Edition of the Fourteenth-Century Middle English and Latin Lives," *Medieval Studies* 33 (1971): 292–333; and Michael S. Nagy, "Saint Aeþelberht of East Anglia in the South English Legendary," *Chaucer Review* 37 (2002): 159–172.

26. See, respectively, LP 7130 for MS E and LP 6940 for Auchinleck Scribe 2 in McIntosh, Samuels, and Benskin, *Linguistic Atlas*, 3: 133, 144. I recognize that the dialect of the MS E scribe in this case does not necessarily correspond to the dialect of the MS E parapher. It does, however, establish grounds for the production of the manuscript in the area or by at least one book producer trained in the area.

27. For a discussion of this manuscript, see R. H. Bremmer, ed., *The Fyve Wyttes: A Late Middle English Devotional Treatise* (Amsterdam: Rodopi, 1987), i–xii.

28. All images of Edinburgh, National Library of Scotland, MS Advocates 19.2.1 are used with permission of the Trustees of the National Library of Scotland.

29. All images of London, British Library MS Egerton 1993 are used with permission from the British Library.

WORKS CITED

Bliss, A. J. "Notes on the Auchinleck Manuscript." *Speculum* 26 (1951): 652-658.

Braswell, Laurel. "St Edburga of Winchester; a Study of her Cult A.D. 950-1500, with an edition of the fourteenth-century Middle English and Latin lives." *Medieval Studies* 33 (1971): 292-333.

Bremmer, R. H. ed. *The Fyve Wyttes: A Late Middle English Devotional Treatise*. Amsterdam: Rodopi, 1987.

Christianson, C. Paul. *A Directory of London Stationers and Book Artisans: 1300-1500*. New York: The Bibliographical Society of America, 1990.

Embree, Dan and Elizabeth Urquhart, eds. *The Simonie: A Parallel-Text Editio.*, Middle English Texts 24. Heidelberg: Winter, 1991.

Fredell, Joel. "The Lowly Paraf: Transmitting Manuscript Design in *The Canterbury Tales*." *Studies in the Age of Chaucer* (2000): 213-280.

Görlach, Manfred. *The Textual Tradition of the South English Legendary*. Leeds: Scolar Press, 1974.

Hanna III, Ralph. "Reconsidering the Auchinleck Manuscript." In *New Directions in Later Medieval Manuscript Studies: Essays From the 1998 Harvard Conference*. Ed. D. Pearsall. Woodbridge: Boydell and Brewer. 91-102.

Hibbard Loomis, Laura. "The Auchinleck Manuscript and a Possible London Bookshop of 1330-1340." PMLA 57 (1942): 595-627.

Horstmann, Carl. *The Early South-English Legendary*. Millwood, NY: Kraus Reprint Co., 1973.

McIntosh, Angus, M. L. Samuels, and M. Benskin, eds. *A Linguistic Atlas of Late Middle English*. 4 vols. Aberdeen: Aberdeen University Press, 1986.

Mooney, Linne. "Professional Scribes? Identifying English Scribes who had a Hand in more than one Manuscript." In *New Directions in Later Medieval Manuscript studies: Essays from the 1998 Harvard Conference*. Ed. Derek Pearsall. Cambridge: Brewer, 2000. 131-142.

Nagy, Michael S. "Saint AEþelberht of East Anglia in the South English Legendary." *The Chaucer Review* 37 (2002), 159-172.

Pearsall, Derek and Ian Cunningham, eds. *The Auchinleck Manuscript*. London: Scolar Press, 1977.

Robinson, Pamela. "A Study of Some Aspects of the Transmission of English Verse Texts in Late Mediaeval Manuscripts." B.Litt. diss: Oxford University, 1972.

Scott, Kathleen L. "A Mid-Fifteenth Century English illuminating Shop and its Customers." *Journal of the Warburg and Courtault Institutes* 31 (1968): 195.

Shonk, Timothy. "Paraphs, Piecework, and Presentation: The Production Methods of the Auchinleck Revisited." Presented at *The London Old and Middle English Research Seminar: Studies in the Auchinleck Manuscript*. June 20, 2008.

———. "A Study of the Auchinleck Manuscript: Bookmen and Bookmaking in the Early Fourteenth Century." *Speculum* 60 (1985), 71-91.

Wiggins, Alison. "Are Auchinleck Manuscript Scribes 1 and 6 the same Scribe? The Advantages of Whole-Data Analysis and Electronic Texts." *Medium Aevum* (2004): 1-10.

———. "Guy of Warwick: Study and Transcription." Ph. D diss., U of Sheffield, 2000.

The Paper Stocks of the Beryn Scribe

DANIEL W. MOSSER

I have previously argued that the physical evidence provided by paper and the principle of symmetry that governs the distribution of watermarks in medieval manuscripts and incunabula allow us to reconstruct seemingly impossible collations. Paper evidence also allows us to construct a production sequence in the *oeuvres* of scribes working on multiple paper manuscripts.[1] The confidence with which one can accomplish the dating and sequencing of a scribe's work is increased when "runs" of the same paper are employed and when identical or near-identical dated examples are available. This is premised on two assumptions: that a given mold used for the production of a paper stock had a working life of one to two years; and that a scribe or stationer would not be motivated to hoard materials for any length of time and thus would consume the bulk of a purchase of paper within a fairly short time after its acquisition. "Remnant" paper stocks—single or relatively few sheets of a paper—can be dated far less confidently, as these are probably survivors of an earlier project and might be consumed over a lengthier period of time.

In what follows, I make reference to four primary resources of dated watermarks: the published album of Charles Moïse Briquet (shorthand reference=Briquet); the unpublished archive of tracings at the Bibliothèque de Genève (shorthand reference=Briquet Archive); the print volumes of Gerhard Piccard (cited by volume); and the online database of the Piccard collection (=Piccard Online). It is customary to refer to the published Briquet images by number, with place of use (when known) and date in parentheses. Briquet published the tracings with their accompanying number separately from his discussion of them (including information about papermaker, place of manufacture, place of use, range of dated examples, citation of variants). When reference is made to the Briquet text, the citation will include page numbers.

The present study focuses on the surviving output of a single scribe (who does collaborate, however, in some instances, though probably in a supervisory capacity), the "Beryn Scribe," so-called because his is the hand responsible for the only surviving copy of the *Tale of Beryn* in Northumberland MS 455. He has been identified at work in ten manuscripts, and it would not be surprising to find still more examples.[2] Of these, six are copied in whole or in part on paper. Oxford, St John's College, MS 57; Cambridge University Library MS Kk.1.3 (10); University of Michigan MS 225; and Oxford, Bodleian Library, Tanner MS 11 share a pool of paper stocks, while the paper portion of Princeton MS 100 (formerly the "Helmingham Manuscript"; Paper, fols. 1-165, 203-215; parchment, fols. 166-202) and Oxford, Bodleian Library, Rawlinson MS C.901 are entirely on paper stocks that do not come from that pool. The paper stock with the latest date is found in three of these manuscripts and carries a Dragon/*Basilic*[3] mark (see figs. 1–2); Briquet dates this stock to 1457 and 1460 and identifies it as of Italian manufacture.[4] Briquet records only two examples of this mark and notes that this paper is *"probablement d'un battoir piémontais."*[5]

Since the Dragon-marked paper in the Beryn Scribe's manuscripts is mixed with runs of other paper dating to the mid-1440s, these paper stocks with the Dragon mark must be earlier than the examples collected and dated by Briquet and probably even earlier than the closest example recorded by Piccard, which dates from 1455.[6] In the St. John's manuscript, the Dragon paper stock occurs only in two booklets, one containing a London chronicle, "ending in 1431/2 (cf. IPMEP 365E)"[7] and one containing the *Parliament of Fowls* (fols. 138–240). The form of the Dragon watermark in MS Kk.1.3 is rather different (see fig. 3).[8]

The St. John's manuscript contains a paper stock that does not occur in any other Beryn Scribe manuscript. The watermark, which is found only in the *Prick of Conscience* (fols. 1–135), is a Scales/*Balance*/*Waage*, associated by Ralph Hanna with an example in "Piccard V 5, nos. 258–319, 382–4, in common use 1441 x 1499; and Briquet's no. 2446 (1443)" (see fig. 4).[9] Compare this with Briquet 2467, variants dating from 1446 to 1477. The watermark, unlike any of the Briquet examples, is sewn on two chain lines rather than being bisected by one.

A third stock, a Bull's Head/*Tête de Boeuf*, can be found in three of the Beryn Scribe's manuscripts: Tanner MS 11 (see fig. 5), Cambridge MS Kk.1.3 (10) (see fig. 6),[10] and Michigan MS 225. This mark is very similar to an example found in the Briquet Archive (Mütingen 1443; see fig. 7).[11] The processes of paper manufacture employed a pair of molds, thus producing a pair of watermarks—twins—for each paper stock. The Bull's Head twin has a somewhat narrower muzzle and shorter face. In the Michigan manuscript, the Bull's Head mark occurs in the sixth and seventh gatherings, with the rest of the manuscript made up of the Dragon paper stock. In Tanner MS 11, the mark occurs only in folios 133 to 211, the section copied by Hand C.

In Tanner MS 11, a fourth stock occurs, bearing a watermark consisting of a Star with Cross Tipped by Circles/*Étoile à Cinq Rayons* (see fig. 8), which is very similar to an example in the Briquet Archive (dated to 1443; see fig. 9), the latest variant of Briquet's published examples 6009 and 6010.[12] Perhaps one explanation for runs of the same paper stock being mixed with runs of other papers in these manuscripts is that here the Beryn Scribe was collaborating with other scribes, and so the production of these manuscripts was carried out simultaneously.

While Princeton MS 100 employs none of these stocks, one of its papers is quite similar to but not identical with one of the Rawlinson MS C.901 papers, a Bull/*Boeuf* that is itself very similar to Piccard's *Ochse* 1004, dated to 1444: folios 1 to 91, 203 and 210 (see the MS 100 Bull in fig. 10).[13] The most satisfying match to this mark is again found in the Briquet Archive in an example from Grenoble (dated to 1438, see fig. 11).[14] The twin has a somewhat different morphology and a distinctive head (see fig. 12). It corresponds fairly closely to a Briquet Archive tracing of a document used in Silly (dated to 1442; see fig. 13). The form of the Bull appearing in Rawlinson MS C.901 is in many respects different from either of these but clearly belongs in the same family of paper stocks and is probably from the same or very similar source (see fig. 14).[15] This mark is similar to Briquet 2774 (Colmar 1423) but more closely matches one of the variants for this mark found in the Briquet Archive (Bretagne 1455–1456; see fig. 15).

The Princeton manuscript also has a run of paper bearing a Tulip/*Fleur en Forme de Tulipe* mark (folios 92 to 145; see fig. 16), which is similar in structure to Briquet 6645 (Lucques/Lucca 1445, with variants to 1449) but larger (5 cm tall) and bisected by a chainline 2.8 to 3 centimeters from the ones to the right and left.[16] A better analogue, from the Briquet Archive, was used in Siena in 1443 and 1444 (see fig. 17).[17]

The final mark in the Princeton manuscript is of Two Unicorns' Heads/ *Deux Têtes de Licorne* (see fig. 18), which is most similar to an example in the Briquet Archive dated to 1441 (see fig. 19; this is a variant of the published examples, numbers 15,841–2). It appears on folios 204 to 209 and 211 to 215 of the Princeton manuscript.[18] Note the near-horizontal alignment of both horns. See also the Piccard example of an *"Einhorn Doppelkopf"* (used in Segewalde in 1436).[19]

In addition to the Bull-marked paper (fig. 14), three other paper stocks occur in Rawlinson MS C.901. One contains a Crescent/*Croissant* mark (see fig. 20) that is most similar to Briquet 5291 (Grenoble 1443; variants to 1457), and is mixed with the Bull-marked paper stock. Perhaps the closest match to the Rawlinson Crescent is one in the Briquet Archive that was used in Grenoble in 1448 (see fig. 21).[20] Note that one of the circles on the horizontal part of the cross is pointed upward, while the one on the other side is pointed somewhat downward. A gathering that appears between those signed "k" and "L" contains a Grapevine/*Vigne* mark (see fig. 22). Briquet provides one published example of this mark, number 13,053 (Catane 1449). There is also one example in the Briquet Archive that is very close to the Rawlinson MS C.901 mark: Perpignan 1449 (see fig. 23).[21] Mixed with the Bull mark in gatherings "i," "k," and "L" is a Bishop's Hat with Lily/*Mitre* (see fig. 24), for which the closest analogues are found in Piccard's online site, with dates ranging from 1448 to 1455 and perhaps later.[22]

In Cambridge MS Kk.1.3, the text that follows the Beryn Scribe's *Life of Our Lady* (Part 10), Hoccleve's *De regimine*, or *Regiment of Princes* in Part 11, is copied on paper from one of the stocks used frequently by the Beryn Scribe and found in the MS Kk.1.3 *Life of Our Lady*: the Bull's Head—marked paper described above (see fig. 25).[23] The hand that produced the *Regiment* appears on paleographical grounds to be congruent with Hand B in the Oxford, Bodleian Library, Hatton MS 50 copy of the *Brut*.

Conclusions

A tabular summary of the findings presented here reveals a probable range for the Beryn Scribe's paper manuscripts from the late 1430s to perhaps 1455, though I am inclined to think that 1450 is a more probable *terminus ad quem*, given the collocation of paper stocks prior to that date with those for which recorded examples range beyond that date. The paper portion of Princeton MS 100 ("Helmingham") would seem to mark the earliest surviving example of the scribe's resorting to paper. St. John's MS 57, Oxford Tanner MS 11, and Michigan MS 225[24] would all seem to be from the early to mid-1440s, with Rawlinson MS C.901 perhaps marking the end of the scribe's production. It is notable in this regard that Lister Matheson places Rawlinson MS C.901 at the end of the development of the textual group (AV–1419:B) to which he assigns Michigan MS 225, Oxford Tanner MS 11, and the Beryn Scribe's parchment *Brut* manuscripts, Hatton MS 50, London, British Library, Harley MS 1337, and London, British Library, Harley MS 6251.[25] MS Kk.1.3 (10) is difficult to place because no clear match for its form of the Dragon has yet been located, though it would seem to be of the same origin as the form that has analogues in the late 1450s.

Most, if not all, of the papers associated with the Beryn Scribe's manuscripts are of Italian manufacture, specifically from the Piedmont region, though some may originate in the adjacent South of France. The Bishop's Hat—marked paper is plausibly Italian, but I cannot claim it to be so with certainty. That all of the papers seem to share origins in closely proximate locations suggests a common supplier who specialized in paper of Italian manufacture.

The precision of the dates and the sequence proposed below are possible because the scribe employed paper and because it is possible to match those paper stocks with examples in dated documents. When more dated examples are made available—and more readily accessible—it is likely we will see a marked improvement in our ability to perform this kind of analysis. Paleographical analysis can rarely produce the same kinds of precision as analysis of paper stocks, and while parchment may provide similar structural evidence (though the evidence is rarely as transparent), that material is not particularly useful in the dating of artifacts.

We still know far too little about the acquisition and distribution of paper in England in this early period, and this, unfortunately, prevents me from saying with certainty that the presence of these papers of Italian manufacture in manuscripts produced by the Beryn Scribe point to a particular locus for his production of vernacular literary manuscripts. The apparent ready access to supplies of paper and the copiousness of his output suggest London and its environs as the likely place of his employment, but that is only a best guess at this point.

Virginia Tech

Acknowledgments

I would like to thank the Leverhulme Trust for funding my visiting professorship at the Center for Medieval Studies at the University of York in the fall of 2007 and 2008, during which the research for this project was initiated.

Paper Stock	Manuscript	Range	Date
Bull 1 (twins)	Princeton 100 (figs. 10, 12)	fols. 1–99, 203+210	1438–1442
Two Unicorns' Heads	Princeton 100 (fig. 18)	fols. 146–165, 204–209, 211–215	1441
Scales	St. John's 57 (fig. 4)	fols. 1–137	1441–1449
Bull's Head	Kk.1.3 (10) (fig. 6)	fols. 2–40, 43+46, 49+56	1443
	Tanner 11 (fig. 5)	pp. 17–112, 157–211	1443
	Michigan 225	fols. 40–63	1443
	[Kk.1.3 (11) (fig. 25)	throughout	1443][27]
Star	Tanner 11 (fig. 8)	pp. 1–15	1443
Tulip	Princeton 100 (fig. 16)	fols. 92–145	1443–1444
Crescent	Rawlinson C.901 (fig. 20)	fols. 15–35	1448
Grapevine	Rawlinson C.901 (fig. 22)	fols. 106–120	1449
Bishop's Hat with Lily	Rawlinson C.901 (fig. 24)	fols. 105, 125, 127, 129	1448–1455
Bull 2	Rawlinson C.901 (fig. 14)	fols. 1–12, 36–130[28]	1455–1456
Dragon 1	St. John's 57 (fig. 1)	fols. 138–236	1455–1460
	Michigan 225	fols. 1–39, 64–135	1455–1460
Dragon 2	Kk.1.3 (10) (fig. 3)	fols. 41–93[29]	1455–1460

Table 1: Dates and Distribution of the Beryn Scribe's Paper Stocks[26]

NOTES

1. For an example of the use of paper evidence to reconstruct problematic collations, see Daniel W. Mosser, "Corrective Notes on the Structures and Paper Stocks of Four MSS Containing Extracts from Chaucer's *Canterbury Tales*," *Studies in Bibliography* 52 (1999): 97–114; see also R. J. Lyall, "Material: The Paper Revolution," in *Book Production and Publishing in Britain 1375–1475*, ed. J.

Griffiths and D. Pearsall (Cambridge, UK: Cambridge University Press, 1989), 11–29, esp. 21–26. For the dating and sequencing of a scribe's work in multiple paper manuscripts, see Daniel W. Mosser, "Dating the Manuscripts of the 'Hammond Scribe': What the Paper Evidence Tells Us," *Journal of the Early Book Society* 10 (2007): 31–70; see also Lyall "Material," 15–21. [I would like to take this opportunity to correct some typographical errors in Mosser, "Corrective Notes": 98, 2 ll. up: for "cordicologist," read "codicologist"; 100, 14 ll. up: for "*10*.2.10.11," read "*10*.2.*10*.11" (i.e., italicized "10"); 101, l. 14: for "149.145," read "149.154"; 103, l. 7: for "reco," read "recto"; 105, l. 17: for "Picard," read "Piccard"; 105, l. 22: for "pp. 228–290," read "pp. 225–290"; 107, l. 11: for "CW on 12ᵛ," read "CW on 12" (MS is paginated); 108, l. 5: for "195/196.205/506," read "195/196.205/206"; 109, l. 6: for "pp. 291–306," read "pp. 291–318"; l. 14: for "pp. 310–338," read "316–354"; 111, 2 up: for "5.15," read "5.16".]

2. The "Beryn Scribe" has been identified at work in the following MSS:

Alnwick Castle, Duke of Northumberland, MS 455 *Canterbury Tales* (with *Tale of Beryn*)

Ann Arbor, MI, University of Michigan Library, MS 225, fols. 1–29, 108 (ll. 22)–135 (Linne R. Mooney and Lister M. Matheson, "The Beryn Scribe and His Texts: Evidence for Multiple-Copy Production of Manuscripts in Fifteenth-Century England," *The Library* 7th ser., 4 (2003): 347–370)
Prose *Brut*

Cambridge University Library MS Kk.1.3 (10) (Mooney and Matheson, "Beryn Scribe")
Lydgate, *Life of Our Lady*

London, British Library, Harley MS 1337 (Mooney and Matheson, "Beryn Scribe")
Prose *Brut*

London, British Library, Harley MS 6251 (Mooney and Matheson, "Beryn Scribe")
Prose *Brut*

Oxford, Bodleian Library, Hatton MS 50), fols. 2–17v, 84v (l. 21)–107v, 119 (l. 7)–130v (Mooney and Matheson, "Beryn Scribe")
Prose *Brut*

Oxford, Bodleian Library, Rawlinson C.901 (Daniel W. Mosser and Linne R. Mooney, "More Manuscripts by the '*Beryn* Scribe' and His Cohorts," in preparation)
Prose *Brut*

Oxford, Bodleian Library, Tanner MS 11, pp. 1–116, 140 (l. 19)–163, 164 (ll. 27–31), 196 (corrected catchword), 205 (l. 4)–209 (l. 3) (Mooney and Matheson, "Beryn Scribe")
Prose *Brut*

Oxford, St. John's College MS 57 (Mooney and Matheson, "Beryn Scribe")
Prick of Conscience, London Chronicle, *Parliament of Fowls*

Princeton MS 100 ("Helmingham") (Simon Horobin, "The Scribe of the Helmingham and Northumberland Manuscripts of the *Canterbury Tales*," *Neophilologus* 84 (2000): 457–465 |identifying the scribe of the parchment "core" as the Beryn Scribe|; Mosser and Mooney, "More Manuscripts" |identifying the scribe of the paper "surround" as also the Beryn Scribe|)
Canterbury Tales

3. Secondary and tertiary signifiers in italics refer to the names employed by Briquet (French) and Piccard (German).

4. Briquet 2691; (text, p. 193). Cf. Ralph Hanna III, *A Descriptive Catalogue of the Western Manuscripts of St John's College, Oxford* (Oxford: Oxford University Press, 2002), 75, who suggests "Briquet, no. 2692 (1460)." It is possible that numbers 2691 and 2692 are the same paper stock, perhaps twins (from the pair of molds that produced a pair of watermarks for each paper stock; see Allan H. Stevenson, "Watermarks Are Twins," *Studies in Bibliography* 4 (1951–1952): 57–91), but I detected no examples of Briquet 2692, though conditions for examining the details of watermarks in the St. John's Library are not ideal.

5. Briquet, p. 193.

6. Gerhard Piccard, ed., *Digital Publication of the "Piccard" Collection of Watermarks*. Landesarchiv Baden-Württemberg, 2004–, number 124053, *Drache*, Nürnberg 1455, available at http://www.piccard-online.de/?nr=124053.

7. Hanna, *Descriptive Catalogue*, 76.

8. See also Michael C. Seymour, "The Manuscripts of Hoccleve's *Regiment of Princes*," *Edinburgh Bibliographical Society Transactions* 6 (1974): 255–297, at 282. Seymour identifies the Dragon mark as Briquet 2691, as do I.

9. Hanna, *Descriptive Catalogue*, 75. Briquet identifies his example as being of Venetian manufacture (p. 179).

10. See Seymour, "Manuscripts," 282: "Briquet 15089" (Soleure 1488).

11. This Bull's Head mark is recorded by Briquet as a "|v|ar du groupe 15.045 à 15.090" (p. 756), with the entire group of variants being produced and consumed over a span of eighty years and originating in the South of France ("le Midi") or the Piedmont region of Italy ("Piémont"; p. 750).

12. Although Star-marked paper is for the most part Italian, Briquet believes these two types belong to the south of France (p. 346).

13. Gerhard Piccard, ed., *Wasserzeichen Vierfüsser*, vol. XV.3 of *Die Wasserzeichen Piccard im Haupstaatsarchiv Stuttgart* (Stuttgart, Germany: Verlag W. Kohlhammer, 1987), number 1004.

14. This example is a variant of Briquet's number 2776, characterized by a head that is large in proportion to the body. The manufacture is Italian, probably emulating the arms of Turin (Briquet, *Les filigranes*, 195–196).

15. Turin is also the probable location for the papermaker(s) of this mark. Briquet suggests that the common use of these papers in the west of France ("Bordeaux, Poitiers, Châteaudun et Caen") might suggest an alternative (p. 196).

16. Cf. Gerhard Piccard, ed., *Wasserzeichen Blatt, Blume, Baum*, vol. XII of *Die Wasserzeichen Piccard im Haupstaatsarchiv Stuttgart* (Stuttgart, Germany: Verlag W. Kohlhammer, 1982), numbers 1510 (1473) and 1511 (1466).

17. Listed by Briquet as a variant of his number 6650 (Florence 1442–1447). The Tulip mark is exclusively Italian. Briquet, *Les filigranes*, 376.

18. Once again, Briquet expresses no doubt in assigning the production of this paper to Italy (p. 794).

19. Piccard, *Digital Publication*, number 125007, available at http://www.piccard-online.de/?nr=125007.

20. This is a variant of Briquet's number 5291 (Grenoble 1443). Paper with this watermark comes from the South of France or the Piedmont region of Italy. Briquet, *Les filigranes*, 308.

21. This paper originates in the Piedmont region of Italy (Briquet, *Les filigranes*, 646).

22. See Piccard, *Digital Publication*, number 031866, dated 1455, available at http://www.piccard-online.de/?nr=031866, and number 031868, dated 1448, available at http://www.piccard-online.de/?nr=031868.

23. See Seymour, "Manuscripts," 282: "Briquet 15089" (Soleure 1488).

24. The rubric on page 36 of Brie's edition reads "How king Westmer 3af to Beringer an lland forlete; and þere þis Beringer made þe toune of Berwik. *Capitulo* xlj." See Friedrich W. D. Brie, ed., *The Brut or The Chronicles of England: Edited from MS. Rawl. B 171, Bodleian Library, &c.*, Part I. EETS o.s. 131 (London: Kegan Paul, Trench, Trübner & Co., Ltd., 1906). In Michigan MS 225, the corresponding rubric reads "Of kyng Westmere þa gaff Berwick to Beryn" (fol. 12). To my knowledge, none of the other Beryn Scribe *Brut* manuscripts have this rendering, raising the possibility that the Michigan *Brut* was copied after the parchment Northumberland MS 455, thus situating the copying of the *Beryn* text between that of the Helmingham and Michigan manuscripts or at least before, say, 1443.

25. Lister M. Matheson, *The Prose Brut: The Development of a Middle English Chronicle* (Tempe, AZ: Medieval and Renaissance Texts & Studies, 1998), 226.

26. Note that these dates are based on those of the closest analogues discovered so far.

27. Not by the Beryn Scribe, but probably by one of his collaborators in Hatton MS 50.

28. Mixed with the Bishop's Hat and Grapevine marks.

29. Mixed with the Bull's Head, which occurs on fols. 43+46, 49+56.

WORKS CITED

Brie, Friedrich W. D., ed. *The Brut, or The Chronicles of England: Edited from MS. Rawl. B 171, Bodleian Library, &c.* Part I. EETS o.s. 131. London: Kegan Paul, Trench, Trübner & Co., Ltd., 1906.

Briquet, Charles Moïse. *Les filigranes: Dictionnaire historique des marques du papier dès leur apparition vers 1282 jusqu'en 1600.* Edited by Allan Stevenson. 4 vols. Amsterdam: Paper Publications Society, 1968. (Facsimile of the 1907 edition with supplementary material contributed by a number of scholars.)

——. "The Briquet Archive." The unpublished tracings and papers of Charles Moïse Briquet. Bibliothèque de Genève, Ms Briquet xxx. (For a translation of the French descriptions of the materials, see Daniel W. Mosser, "The Papers of Charles Moïse Briquet," at http://wiz2.cath. vt.edu:8200/briquet/briqeng.html.)

Hanna, Ralph III. *A Descriptive Catalogue of the Western Manuscripts of St John's College, Oxford. Using material collected by the late Jeremy J. Griffiths.* Oxford: Oxford University Press, 2002.

Horobin, Simon. "The Scribe of the Helmingham and Northumberland Manuscripts of the *Canterbury Tales.*" *Neophilologus* 84 (2000): 457–465.

Lyall, R. J. "Material: The Paper Revolution." In *Book Production and Publishing in Britain 1375–1475,* edited by J. Griffiths and D. Pearsall. Cambridge, UK: Cambridge University Press, 1989, 11–29.

Matheson, Lister M. *The Prose Brut: The Development of a Middle English Chronicle.* Tempe, AZ: Medieval and Renaissance Texts & Studies, 1998.

Mooney, Linne R., and Lister M. Matheson. "The Beryn Scribe and His Texts: Evidence for Multiple-Copy Production of Manuscripts in Fifteenth-Century England." *The Library* 7th ser., 4 (2003): 347–370.

Mosser, Daniel W. "Corrective Notes on the Structures and Paper Stocks of Four MSS Containing Extracts from Chaucer's *Canterbury Tales.*" *Studies in Bibliography* 52 (1999): 97–114.

——. "Dating the Manuscripts of the 'Hammond Scribe': What the Paper Evidence Tells Us." *Journal of the Early Book Society* 10 (2007): 31–70.

Mosser, Daniel W., and Linne R. Mooney. "More Manuscripts by the 'Beryn Scribe' and His Cohorts." In preparation.

Piccard, Gerhard, ed. *Wasserzeichen Waage.* Vol. V of *Die Wasserzeichen Piccard im Haupstaatsarchiv Stuttgart.* Stuttgart, Germany: Verlag W. Kohlhammer, 1978.

——. *Wasserzeichen Fabeltiere,* Vol. X of *Die Wasserzeichen Piccard im Haupstaatsarchiv Stuttgart.* Stuttgart, Germany: Verlag W. Kohlhammer, 1980.

——. *Wasserzeichen Blatt, Blume, Baum.* Vol. XII of *Die Wasserzeichen Piccard im Haupstaatsarchiv Stuttgart.* Stuttgart, Germany: Verlag W. Kohlhammer, 1982.

————. *Wasserzeichen Vierfüsser*. Vol. XV.3 of *Die Wasserzeichen Piccard im Haupstaatsarchiv Stuttgart*. Stuttgart, Germany: Verlag W. Kohlhammer, 1987.

————. *Digital Publication of the "Piccard" Collection of Watermarks*. Landesarchiv Baden-Württemberg, 2004–, at http://www.piccard-online.de/start.php. (The complete "Piccard" watermark collection, including both published and unpublished items.)

Seymour, Michael C. "The Manuscripts of Hoccleve's *Regiment of Princes*." *Edinburgh Bibliographical Society Transactions* 6 (1974): 255–297.

Stevenson, Allan H. "Watermarks Are Twins." *Studies in Bibliography* 4 (1951–1952): 57–91.

Figure 1: Oxford, St. John's College, MS 57, fol. 236v. Beta-radiograph. By permission of the President and Scholars of Saint John Baptist College in the University of Oxford.

Figure 2: Bibliothèque de Genève, Ms Briquet xxx ("Briquet Archive"). Grenoble 1460. Tracing.

Figure 3: Cambridge University Library MS Kk.1.3 (10), fol. 41v. Transmitted light. Reproduced by kind permission of the Syndics of Cambridge University Library.

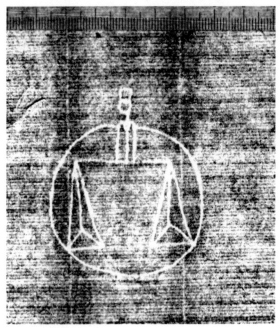

Figure 4: Oxford, St. John's College, MS 57, fol. 137v. Beta-radiograph. By permission of the President and Scholars of Saint John Baptist College in the University of Oxford.

Figure 5: Oxford, Bodleian Library, Tanner MS 11, fol. 211v. Beta-radiograph. The Bodleian Library, University of Oxford.

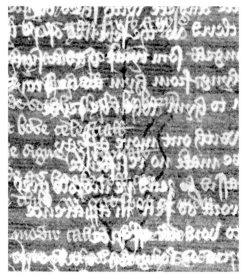

Figure 6: Cambridge University Library MS Kk.1.3 (10), fol. 3v, *Life of Our Lady*. Transmitted light. Reproduced by kind permission of the Syndics of Cambridge University Library.

Figure 7: Bibliothèque de Genève, Ms Briquet xxx ("Briquet Archive"). Mütingen 1443.

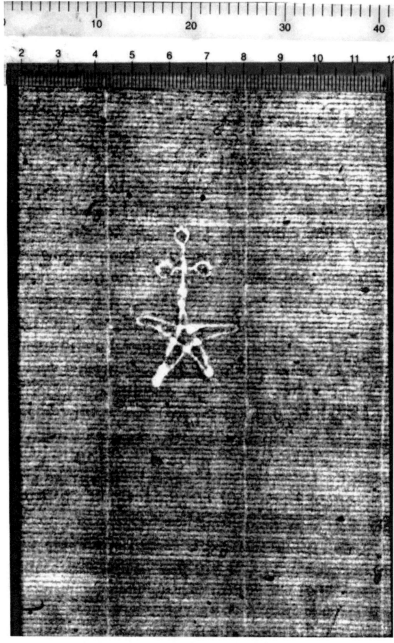

Figure 8: Oxford, Bodleian Library, Tanner MS 11, fol. 3r. Beta-radiograph. The Bodleian Library, University of Oxford.

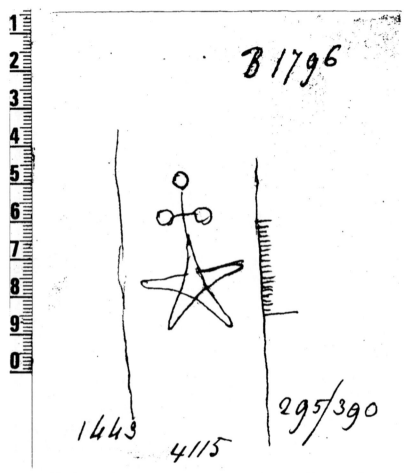

Figure 9: Bibliothèque de Genève, Ms Briquet xxx ("Briquet Archive"). 1443.

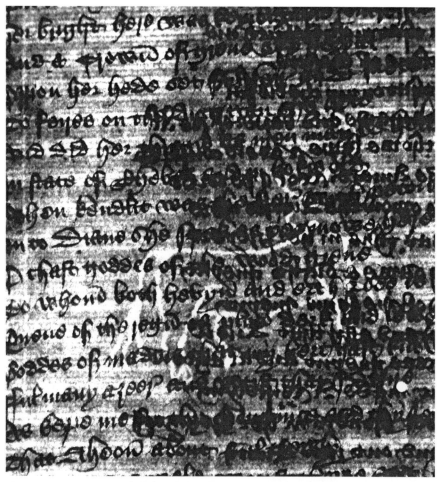

Figure 10: Princeton Medieval and Renaissance Manuscript No. 100 ("Helmingham"), fol. 5. Transmitted light. Manuscripts Division, Department of Rare Books and Special Collections, Princeton University Library.

Figure 11: Bibliothèque de Genève, Ms Briquet xxx ("Briquet Archive"). Grenoble 1438.

Figure 12: Princeton Medieval and Renaissance Manuscript No. 100 ("Helmingham"),
fol. 203. Transmitted light. Manuscripts Division, Department of Rare Books and Special
Collections, Princeton University Library.

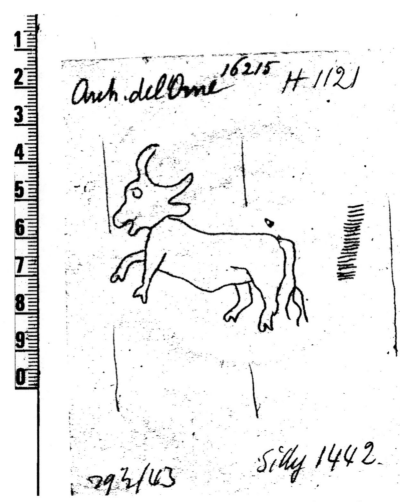

Figure 13: Bibliothèque de Genève, Ms Briquet xxx ("Briquet Archive"). Silly 1442.

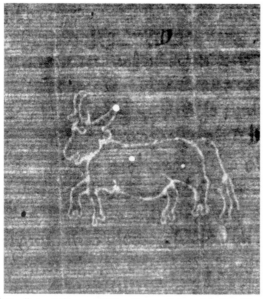

Figure 14: Oxford, Bodleian Library, MS Rawlinson C.901, fol. 130. The Bodleian Library,
University of Oxford.

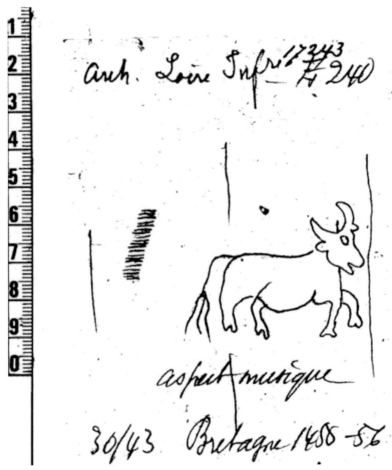

Figure 15: Bibliothèque de Genève, Ms Briquet xxx ("Briquet Archive"). Bretagne 1455–1456.

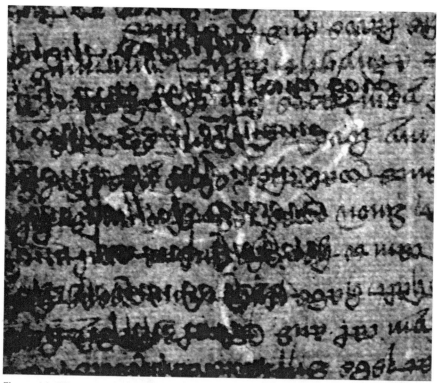

Figure 16: Princeton Medieval and Renaissance Manuscript No. 100 ("Helmingham"), fol. 145. Transmitted light. Manuscripts Division, Department of Rare Books and Special Collections, Princeton University Library.

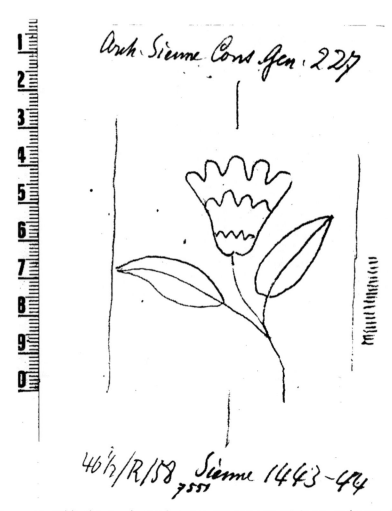

Figure 17: Bibliothèque de Genève, Ms Briquet xxx ("Briquet Archive"). Sienne 1443–1444.

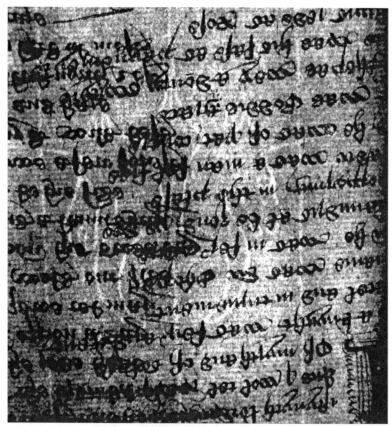

Figure 18: Princeton Medieval and Renaissance Manuscript No. 100 ("Helmingham"), fol. 158 Transmitted light. Manuscripts Division, Department of Rare Books and Special Collections, Princeton University Library.

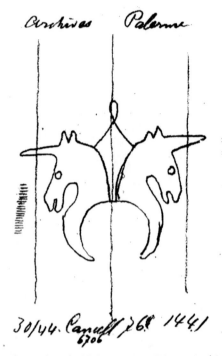

Figure 19: Bibliothèque de Genève, Ms Briquet xxx ("Briquet Archive"). 1441.

Figure 20: Oxford, Bodleian Library, MS Rawlinson C.901, fol. 32. The Bodleian Library, University of Oxford.

Figure 21: Bibliothèque de Genève, Ms Briquet xxx ("Briquet Archive"). Grenoble 1448.

Figure 22: Oxford, Bodleian Library, MS Rawlinson C.901, fol. 114. The Bodleian Library, University of Oxford.

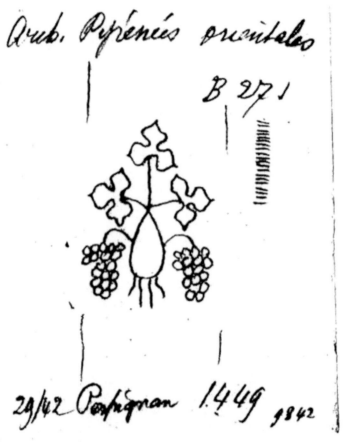

Figure 23: Bibliothèque de Genève, Ms Briquet xxx ("Briquet Archive"). Perpignan 1449.

Figure 24: Oxford, Bodleian Library, MS Rawlinson C.901, fol. 129. The Bodleian Library, University of Oxford.

Figure 25: Cambridge University Library, MS Kk.1.3 (11), fol. 79v, *Regiment of Princes*. Transmitted light. Reproduced by kind permission of the Syndics of Cambridge University Library.

An Unpublished Lollard Psalms *Catena* in Huntington Library MS HM 501[1]

MICHAEL P. KUCZYNSKI

Lollard attitudes toward the Old Testament have not received the scholarly attention they deserve. The four Gospels, the Acts of the Apostles, the Pauline epistles, and to a lesser extent, the Apocalypse, all figure prominently in the writings of John Wyclif and his followers, and therefore, appropriately enough, in modern accounts of Lollardy. Wyclif's honorific, Doctor Evangelicus,[2] acknowledges the priority of the New Testament in his thought. It would be difficult to undervalue the importance to Wycliffism of a text such as the *Glossed Gospels*, for instance, with its sustained coordination of the narratives of Christ's ministry and the pastoral activity of Lollardy itself in the form of commentaries assembled from the best exegetical authorities and translated into the vernacular.[3]

At the same time, however, a movement based in the ideology of *sola Scriptura* could hardly neglect Old Testament writing—and in fact Lollard authors concentrate on and emphasize the Old Testament in many important ways. For example, key features of Lollard critiques of secular authority derive from the Book of Kings: "This prosces |argument| of the .iij. book of Kingis schulde stire |incite| kingis and lordis to be mersyful and pytouse on her sugetis that trespasen aȝens hem, and in alle thingis eschewe |reject| ydilnesse, leccherie, tresoun, ydolatrie, and false counceilouris."[4] Many Lollard ideas about the veneration of images and the character of true and false oaths, major themes of the popular arm of the movement, evolved from Wycliffite readings of a number of Old Testament texts.[5] According to the medieval practice of typological exegesis, certain events or "types" of the Old Testament (e.g., the Deluge) are linked not only chronologically but prophetically with the New Testament, in which they have their "antitypes" or fulfillment (e.g., the baptism of Christ).[6]

While Lollardy was suspicious of overly ingenious allegorizing, which it dismissed as self-serving (one thinks of the glossing Friar in Chaucer's "Summoner's Tale"), it accepted and even valorized a disciplined application of this hermeneutic.[7] Wyclif's remark in his treatise *De ecclesia* that "in all of Scripture there is not a syllable without meaning" (*in tota scriptura non ponitur vel una sillaba sine sensu*),[8] applies of course to the Old Testament as well as to the New and encouraged among Wycliffites a close and persistent interpretation of both scriptures independently and in relation to each other.

In this essay I discuss Lollard attitudes toward an especially important Old Testament book, the Psalms, in connection with an unpublished and apparently unique abridgement of the Wycliffite Psalter (Later Version) that survives in Huntington Library MS HM 501, a compendium of selections from across the Wycliffite Old Testament.[9] The Huntington Psalms abridgement is presented by its anonymous compiler as a *catena*, a linked series of extracts from twenty-three psalms, one of these used twice, without any intervening expository matter (Figure 1). Despite the lack of exposition, I argue that the text may have been intended as a kind of sermon, perhaps an experiment in the almost exclusively Scripture-based homiletics that the Lollards preferred to formal, scholastic sermonizing as practiced by the friars.[10]

My discussion falls into three parts: an introduction to Lollard regard for the Psalms as a preeminent biblical book, a description of the *catena* as an underappreciated medieval literary form, and in light of these remarks and two Latin psalm commentaries especially favored by the Lollards, Augustine's *Enarrationes in Psalmos* and the Psalms section of Nicholas of Lyra's *Postilla perpetua*, an analysis of the Huntington Psalms *catena*. I then offer a critical edition of the Huntington *catena* collated against Forshall and Madden's edition of the Wycliffite Bible and arranged to reflect the rhetorical structure and argumentative patterns implicit in the text.

I. Lollard Regard for the Psalms

The Lollards valued the Psalms highly among Old Testament writings for a number of reasons, several of which are explored in four Psalter prologues (the first two of these are Jerome's and the other two are derived from the prologue to Richard Rolle's *English Psalter*) copied out in HM 501 before the Huntington Psalms *catena*.[11]

First, the Psalter was the prayer book of the Church, adapted by early Christians from the Jewish temple service: "Also it is to be notid," the first HM 501 prologue explains, "þis scriptur<e oft ben vsid in hooli chir>chis seruyse mor than other" (fol. 21r). Indeed, in some Wycliffite Bible manuscripts, this distinction of the Psalter among biblical writings is mentioned by way of an introductory rubric, as in Bodleian Library, Oxford, MS Bodley 296: *Here bigynneþ þe Sauter, which is red comynly in chirchis. Þe firste salm* (fol. 177rb). As communal prayers, the Psalms, even in Latin, provided medieval congregants with a unique connection to the primitive Church, Lollardy's template for its own reformist project.[12] Likewise, as the common property of the faithful, the Psalter apparently escaped, at least until the promulgation in 1409 of Arundel's *Constitutions*, normal prohibitions imposed on the translation of Scripture into the vernacular.[13]

Another dimension of the Psalter's uniqueness, according to several commentators, is that the Psalms are a digest of all Scripture, a kind of Bible *in parvo*, "the fulle ending |fulfillment| of <the hole boc of Goddis> word" (Prologue 1, fol. 21r). This point connects Lollardy's special regard for the Psalms with the priority of the New Testament in Wyclif's writings, because the Psalter encompasses and anticipates the Gospels by prophesying, in a unique and direct way, the passion, death, and resurrection of Christ. To quote from another of the Psalms prologues in HM 501:

> This book comprehendiþ <al þe oolde and newe> testament and techiþ pleyn<li |openly| þe mysteries> of þe trynytee and of Cristis incarnacio<un, passioun,> risynge aȝen, and stiynge |ascension| into heuene; and sendyng doun of þe hooly goost and prechynge of þe gospel; and þe comyng of Antecrist; and þe general doom of Crist, and þe glorie of chosun men to blisse and þe peynes of hem þat schulen be dampned in helle; and ofte rehersiþ þe stories of þe oolde testament and bryngiþ in |discusses or encourages| þe kepyng of Goddis heestis |commandments| and loue of enemyes. (Prologue 3, fols. 22r–v)

Wycliffite preachers sometimes take the comprehensiveness of the Psalter for granted, invoking the Christological authority of certain psalm verses without even quoting them directly. In speaking of the proverbial "stone which the builders rejected; the same that is become the head of the corner |i.e., cornerstone|" (*lapidem quem reprobaverunt aedificantes hic factus est in caput anguli*, Ps. 117:22), one Lollard preacher notes simply that David prophesies how this figure stands for Christ ("þat Dauid telliþ") and thus "it is knowen to cristen men þat þis stoon is Crist in figure, and hed and heelþ of holy chirche, as þe salm seiþ."[14] Possibly implied here is the congregation's prior instruction in the Psalter's literal and figurative senses by means of a vernacular translation of the book and some elementary glosses.

That the last prologue quoted above derives from a Middle English Psalms translation and commentary by the Yorkshire contemplative Richard

Rolle (d. 1349) also testifies to Lollard respect for the Psalter's preeminence among Old Testament writings. Rolle's *English Psalter*, adapted from a Latin textbook by Peter Lombard, was revised and amplified extensively by Wyclif's followers.[15] While these Wycliffite versions of Rolle (there are three distinct manuscript traditions) are not strictly analogous to the *Glossed Gospels*, they might be described as a parallel textual enterprise—a sustained commentary on a key biblical book that makes available in the vernacular the insights of the best Latin exegetes, in this case Peter Lombard, with additional matter taken perhaps directly from Augustine and Cassiodorus.[16] Unlike the *Glossed Gospels*, many Wycliffite revisions of Rolle contain a large measure of obvious polemic. Their rhetoric can be at times as ideological as it is scholarly.

This polemical character itself, however, reflects the vitality of the Psalter in Lollard texts and society. For the Wycliffite, the Psalmist's voice speaks in an unmediated way, moving in some of the Rolle revisions from literal translation of the Latin biblical verse to an almost conversational exegetical idiom that realizes Paul's utopian vision in his Letter to the Ephesians of Christians "Speaking amongst |themselves| in psalms and hymns and spiritual songs" (Eph. 5:19). For instance:

> *Reges eos in virga ferrea; et tanquam vas figuli confringes eos* |Ps. 2:9|; "Thou schalt gouerne hem in ȝerde of iren; and as vessel of a potter, þou schalt breke hem." Þese wordis þe fadir of heuen spekiþ to his sone Ihesu Crist, in þe verse bifore seiynge þus, "I schal ȝiue to þe men" |Ps. 2:8|, and þou schalt not be to hem tiraunte, to pile |rob| and to spuyl hem, as wickid princes don, þat ben worldly lordis, but þou schalt be þeir trewe kyng in gouernynge hem in ȝerde of iren, þat is a stable and vnfailyng riȝtwisnesse, and kynges pousté |power|. And in þis riȝtwise ȝerde, not britil ne faylynge, but stalworþ and lastynge, þou schalt hem breke, þat is, þu schalt distroie in hem þorouȝ verrei penaunce, erþeli couetise and synne and foule lustis, so þat þei hate to lyue flescheli and loue to lyue goostli. Þerfore seiþ he, "as vessel of þe potter," þat is, as in as mikil as þei ben foule, þei ben britil.[17]

Much of this, remarkably, is in Rolle's original.[18] The Lollards appreciated and expanded in their adaptations of the *English Psalter* its sense of immediacy, the contemplative's awareness that the Latin text was worth translating only if it could be moved into the realm of homiletics—moral instruction (including political discourse) based on Scripture.[19] The reviser drops in an important adjective: Rolle's reference to "penaunce" becomes *"verrei penaunce"* (my emphasis), an almost casual but pointed reminder of the Wycliffite rejection of the need for auricular confession. And he concludes the passage with some simple emotional parallelism, "*hate* to lyue flescheli . . . *loue* to lyue goostli" (my emphasis), that makes Rolle's flaccid sense—"Sinners stop being carnal and become spiritual" (*thai leue to be fleschly and lif gastly*)—more memorable. Finally, the Lollard reviser repeats at the end of this passage, with reference to those sinners broken by God's righteousness, the adjective "britil," transferring to the Psalmist's *figura* of the sinner/pot the fragility that the divine rod, according to Rolle's original exposition, does not have. This is a strategic rhetorical improvement on Rolle, who writes baldly that "in as much as the covetous are clay (*layre*), that is vile and sinful, . . . they must be broken in hell." Psalm commentary and conversation for the Lollards was not arid and academic. It straddled successfully the line between private devotion and public morality, liturgy and the ethical life. Like the Book of Psalms itself, the energy of Rolle's *English Psalter* engaged the sympathies and provoked the evangelical passions of its Lollard readers and revisers.

In Lollard writings, as elsewhere in Middle English religious verse and prose, the Psalms are models for devotion and the basis for a language of moral instruction that is at once traditional (an elaborate network of *topoi* or clichés) and innovative stylistically. If the Psalter was a digest of Old and New Testament Christology, it was also, as Peter Lombard points out, an ethical *summa* or comprehensive handbook of morality. To quote Rolle's amplification of the Lombard, which appears in HM 501:

> <Thare in>ne ben discryued þe medis |rewards| <of goed men, the pynes |punishments|> of yuel men, þe teching<of penaunce, the wax>inge |growth| in riȝtwise lyf, <the perfeccioun of haly men, the whi>che passen to heuene, þe <lyf of actyf men,> þe meditacioun of hem þat ben <contemplatifs, and> þe greete ioie of contemplacioun, <the heghest that may> be in man lyuynge in body and feland |feeling|. (Prologue 4, fols. 23r–v)[20]

The Psalmist himself, King David, is a compelling ethical exemplar whose paradoxical Old Testament designations as a man "beloved of God" (*Amabilis Domino*, 2 Sam. 12:25) and as a murderer and adulterer were understood to be linked. David teaches through the Psalms, not only by his words but also by example. The seven penitential psalms in particular, a devotional subset popular perhaps as early as the sixth century, implicitly sanction the expression of powerful emotions—even profound spiritual uncertainty and doubt—in the service of humility.[21] Moreover, the Psalms endorse the practice of moral reproof, an activity that is at the heart of the Lollard agenda of social and ecclesiastical reform. The trajectory of David's personal sins and penance, as charted in the Psalter, entails a new prophetic responsibility: he must now teach other sinners God's ways.[22]

Many of the Psalms take up, almost obsessively, themes that become important to later Lollards, who suffered as the blade was brought down by Arundel and his agents. These include the inescapable affliction of the righteous by their enemies, the corresponding need for perseverance in the face of persecution, and the reality both of God's wrath and his loving protection of his faithful servants. (All of these themes turn up repeatedly in the Huntington *catena*.) The Psalmist's discourse emphasizes dichotomies between different moral types that are commonplaces in Lollard ethical and polemical texts and especially in the Huntington *catena*: the faithless versus the faithful man; *vir malignus* versus *Beatus vir*; the unjust versus the just; and the rich versus the poor, these economic categories being elided in Lollard thought with the moral antithesis of unrighteousness versus righteousness. The turbulent vision of life that the Lollards extrapolated from David's poetry may have given rise to what Anne Hudson has called a self-conscious Lollard "sect vocabulary," which recycled in numerous literary and polemical contexts the moral discourse of the Psalms.[23]

When preparing their translation of the entire Bible into Middle English, Wyclif's followers wrestled with the special problems posed by the divergent textual traditions of the Psalter as represented in the three Latin translations by Jerome, the so-called Roman, Gallican, and Hebrew versions, and older and even more unstable texts still in circulation throughout the Middle Ages (by way of, for example, Augustine's *Enarrationes in Psalmos*), collectively called by scholars the *vetus Latina*.[24] The anonymous author of the General Prologue to the Wycliffite Bible observes, in a passage that ultimately praises the special virtue of the Psalms if they are regarded accurately and attentively, that:

> Noo book in the eld testament is hardere to vndirstonding to vs Latyns, for oure lettre [text] discordith [disagrees] myche fro the Ebreu, and many doctouris taken litel heede to the lettre, but al to the goostly vndirstonding [i.e., neglect the literal sense in favor of spiritual or allegorical interpretation]. Wel were him that koude wel vndirstonde the Sautir, and kepe [follow] it in his lyuyng, and seie [recite] it deuoutly, and conuicte [confute] Jewis therbi; for manye men that seyn it vndeuoutly, and [but] lyuen out of charite, lyuen foule on hemself to God, and blasfemen hym, whanne thei crien it ful loude to mennis eeris in the chirche.[25]

Textual, interpretive, and ethical approaches to the Psalter are always interrelated for the Lollards. Translation problems encouraged an especially focused and powerful engagement with the Latin texts and with the long exegetical tradition surrounding them, the very basis of moral reading and reflection. Evidence of this relationship survives in a strong commentary on the Psalms, nearly 1,500 discrete but cohesive glosses preserved uniquely in Bodleian Library, Oxford, MS Bodley 554.[26] Here minute textual criticism and analysis of the Psalter, much of this derived from Nicholas of Lyra (ca. 1270–1349), gets coordinated with the moralizing tradition of Psalms interpretation, particularly as it was developed by Augustine in his monumental *Enarrationes*, a commentary that originated in homiletic circumstances as separate sermons on each of the psalms.[27] In Lollard biblical scholarship and homiletics, philology and moral theology were finally not dissociable. Reading the Psalter with accuracy and living it in faith were complementary and potentially even identical practices.

Unsurprisingly, then, many Wycliffite writings quote the Psalms heavily as authorities. The authors of Lollard sermons, treatises, and longer polemical works such as *The Lanterne of Liȝt* often organize their arguments around a key psalm verse and sometimes groups of verses from the Psalter. In chapter 9 of *Lanterne*, for example, its anonymous author describes the efforts of "Studiars |especially attentive scholars| in Cristis chirche," who "studien |apply themselves diligently| dai and nyȝt in the lawe of þe lord." The author then alludes to and translates at length from the first psalm (*Beatus vir*):

> In lege Domini fuit voluntas eius; et in lege eius meditabitur die ac nocte, etc. |Ps. 1:2|. Þat is to seie, "Blessid be þat man, þat haþ his wille in þe lawe of þe Lord, and schal þink in his lawe, boþe nyȝt and day. For he schal be as a tree, þat is wiȷsli plauntid biside þe rendels |streams| of watris, þat schal ȝyue his fruyte in his due tyme, and his leef (þat is, his vertu) schal not falle awey, but alle þingis þat he schal do, in grace schullen be welþi |prosperous|. Wel is him þat so may studie to fynde þese preciouse fruytis, to make faire her owne soule wiþ flouris |rhetorical adornments| of holi writ. Þanne Crist wole take his resting place in þe chaumbre of her conscience.[28]

A passage such as this one goes beyond mere citation of a scriptural authority. Instead, it quotes a Latin psalm verse as the basis for an extended ethical process that begins with vernacular translation, involves in that context the glossing or explicit interpretation of *figurae* in the translated matter—for example, "leef (þat is, his vertu)"—and concludes with moral, psalm-based conversation conducted in an almost colloquial idiom: "Wel is him þat so may studie." The Latin verse has prominence but not structural autonomy in the text: it makes sense only as part of the writer's continuous discourse.

A Lollard tract on Bible study, *The holi prophete Dauid seith*, opens with the same kind of appeal to the Psalmist's prophetic authority as does the Huntington Psalms *catena* and, at least in its initial section, quotes the Psalter densely with only perfunctory exposition:

> The holi prophete Dauid seith in the persone of a iust man |cf. "God seiþ bi his profete," HM 501|: Lord, how swete ben thi spechis to my chekis |Ps. 118:103|; that is, to myn vndirstondyng and loue; and the prophete answerith and seith: *Tho ben swettere than hony to my mowth* |Ps. 118:103|. Eft the same prophet seith in the persone of a iust man: *Lord I was glad of thine spechis as he that fyndith many spoilis either praies* |Ps. 118:162|. Eft the same prophete seith: *The domes of the Lord ben trewe and iustified in hem silf; tho ben more desireable than gold and precious stones, and swettere than hony and hony comb; ffor whi? thi servant kepith tho, and moche rewarde is to kepe hem* |Ps. 18:11|. Therfor he seith: *Moche pees is to hem that louen thi lawe: and to hem is no sclander* |Ps. 118:165|.[29]

The passage continues, quoting from across the Psalter five more times. The author's range is wider than it appears: he uses only three psalms, but the one he quotes most frequently and variously is Psalm 118, the longest, which runs to 176 verses.

The text's first theme is the righteous man's reward for virtue and next the moral enlightenment that results from embracing divine truth:

> Ffor, as the same prophete seith: *Lord, thi word is a lanterne to my fet* (that ys, to rule myne affections and myne werkis), *and thi word is ligt to my pathis* (that is, myn thowttis and myne counceilis) |Ps. 118:105|. And eft he seith: *The comaundement of the Lord is ligtful, and ligtneth iyes of the sowle*, that is, resoun and will |Ps. 18:9|.[30]

The verses are held together by the author's concordantial approach, which associates across Psalm 118's considerable length and between three different psalms nouns such as "spechis" and images such as "hony" and "ligt." This concatenating of psalm verses into a continuous argument is, excepting the author's repeated transitional phrases ("And eft he seith"), the same technique used in the Huntington *catena*. The rationale behind it—that the Psalms as a theological and ethical *summa* might be almost infinitely excerpted and their verses creatively rearranged—demonstrates another truth about the Psalter that entered the commentary tradition via Peter Lombard (*ca.* 1100-1160): the

Psalms are not many poems or several books but a composite text, one long, structurally complex poem, the parts of which are densely and meaningfully interrelated (*Incipit liber Hymnorum, vel Soliloquiorum Prophetae de Christo. Liber* dicit et non *libri*).[31]

II. The *Catena* as a Medieval Literary Form

The history of the *catena* (Lat. a chain) as a medieval literary form is obscure. Originally the word meant, in the phrase *catena patrum*, a collection of extracts from the Church Fathers akin to the anthology or *florilegium*, grouped and coordinated according to theme and idea and presented in a series as a *glossa continua*.[32] Depending on the amount of care that went into the construction of particular *catenae*, extracts from different authorities might cohere simply by their organization under the same lemma (a biblical word, phrase, or verse) or be more meticulously interlinked by repeated keywords and phrases. (Rarely, a *catena* might be constructed using similar techniques out of the works of a single commentator.) As such, *catenae* were derivative, not original commentaries, their character determined by their compilers' principles of selection and arrangement from established authorities.

Milton uses the term "catena" for the first time in this sense in English in *Areopagitica* (1644), while lampooning the biblical studies of a "parochial minister" who, instead of reading the Fathers in full and thinking for himself, "finish[es] his circuit in an English concordance and a topic folio . . . a harmony and a catena, treading the constant round of certain common doctrinal heads."[33] *Catenae*, in Milton's view, are CliffsNotes versions of the Fathers, adequate for lazy or elementary students but not for serious scholars of the Bible.

This is a distortion. While many *catenae* must have been assembled and used almost mechanically, some, such as that on the first eight books of the Bible by the Greek scholar Nicephorus (*ca.* 1256–*ca.* 1335), display epitomizing habits that are new and insightful and would have been appreciated as such by their readers.[34] The juxtaposition of extracts from various commentators responding to the same text could generate a sense not only of agreement among authorities but of subtle differences, too, and thus release a dialectical potential for original thought. The great age of the Latin *catena* was the eleventh through thirteenth centuries, culminating in the monumental *Catena aurea* ("Golden Catena") of Thomas Aquinas (*ca.* 1225–1274), composed between 1262 and 1267, an elegant commentary on the four Evangelists that draws on almost eighty known authorities and was perhaps used by the Wycliffites in assembling the *Glossed Gospels*.[35]

By the high Middle Ages, *catenae* served the important practical purpose of sifting and consolidating the unwieldy and uneven bulk of Greek and Latin commentary on the Bible, making it manageable for scholastic instruction and disputation. Peter Lombard assembled his groundbreaking Psalter *catena*,

Commentarium in Psalmos, for just this purpose, while at the same time using the Psalms and psalmic exegesis innovatively to generate theological *quaestiones*.[36] Such texts not only summarized past knowledge of Scripture but helped to advance it.

In this sense, the *catena* is like another consolidative medieval literary form, *cento*, which recycles fragments from one or more literary works by selecting and arranging them, collage-like, in new and different ways. A classical writer of *cento*, Ausonius (*ca.* 310–395), is self-deprecatory about the genre, calling it "a task for the memory only, which has to gather up scattered tags and fit these mangled scraps together into a whole |*integrare lacerata*|, and so is more likely to provoke your laughter than your praise."[37] (The same could be said, Milton might observe, of the less impressive exegetical *catenae*.) Other authors of *cento*, however, took the form more seriously, applying the ingenuity required to pull it off to superb rhetorical and argumentative effect. The best among these was Proba, a fourth-century Christian poet (*ca.* 322–*ca.* 370), who after her conversion composed a hexameter account of sacred history, including the life of Christ, using verses culled exclusively from the works of Virgil.[38] In its sophisticated allusive and linking strategies, such a text is akin to the kind of Psalms *catena* copied out in Huntington MS 501.

An important feature of *catena* that distinguishes it from much *cento* is its tone of authorial modesty. Because it suppresses literary self-expression, the rhetoric of *catena* is always inherently deferential: it underscores the prior and exclusive importance of the text or texts being quoted. This is especially true of *catenae* assembled directly from Scripture rather than from secondary works of exegesis, since the Bible's rhetorical authority was assumed in the Middle Ages to match or exceed that of even the greatest classical texts and certainly of individual scriptural commentators, who properly regarded themselves as serving rather than mastering Scripture's sense. For example, Thomas of Celano reports of the now-lost *Regula primitiva* of Francis of Assisi (1181-1226), assembled in 1210 and presented thereafter for endorsement to Pope Innocent III, that it was little more than selections from the Gospels extracted and linked together sequentially.[39] This, implies Thomas, was its strength as a rule: by its very form as a *catena*, it established both the absolute authority of Christ and the humility of its author (or more properly compiler), Francis himself.

Jean Leclercq notes a similar rhetoric of deference in the monastic technique of commenting on Scripture by way of Scripture rather than through personal, idiosyncratic expositions—a practice he calls "exegesis by concordance."[40] This technique, which contributed to the formulation of various medieval *catenae*, assumes that the Bible is ultimately an autoexegetical text, a self-explaining verbal system. The commentator's desire to expose the sense of a biblical passage while he meditates on it provokes reminiscences of and associations with other scriptures that use similar language. These mental habits generate an active and imaginative clustering of biblical *sententiae* (as, for example, in Gregory the Great's [*ca.* 540-604] *Moralia in Iob*), many of them drawn far from their original contexts and linked by what Leclercq calls "hook-words."[41] Properly read, reflected upon, and quoted from, the Bible reveals its own truths—a corrective to overly clever interpretive commentaries.

This kind of rhetorical deference operates implicitly in the Huntington Psalms *catena*, which is not compiled from works of Psalter exegesis but only from the Psalms. The Lollard compiler wants the Psalms to speak for themselves in the person of their author, who is named in the text's incipit: God's "profete" (prophet), King David. As Peter Lombard points out in his *Commentarium in Psalmos*, whenever "the Prophet" is referred to in medieval writing without further identification, he is to be understood as the Psalmist, just as "the Apostle" unqualified always refers to Paul, and the phrase "the City," to Rome.[42] A contemporary reader of the Huntington *catena*, therefore, would infer from the very start of the text that psalmic discourse was to follow and would bring to this *catena* an appreciation of the considerable authority David had throughout the Middle Ages as a moral teacher. Because its text consists entirely of psalm verses, with no intervening expository matter, David's authority speaks through the Huntington *catena* in an unmediated, especially forceful way.

The Huntington *catena* incorporates verses from twenty-three different psalms extracted and reconfigured as a continuous homiletic argument. Models for this kind of primary biblical *catena*, as opposed to the secondary exegetical type derided by Milton, were available to the Lollards directly from Scripture. In two of the Pauline epistles—Hebrews and Romans—verses from several different psalms (and a few other scriptures, such as Proverbs and Isaiah) are linked and presented as self-contained arguments with little or no added matter. In Hebrews 1:5–13, the argument concerns Christ's divinity; in Romans 3:10–18, the inveterate nature of human sinfulness. Here is the Romans *catena*, which consists almost entirely of psalm verses:

> 10 As it is written: *There is not any man just.*
> 11 *There is none that understandeth: there is none that seeketh after God.*
> 12 *All have turned out of the way: they are become unprofitable together: there is none that doth good, there is not so much as one* [Ps. 13:3].
> 13 *Their throat is an open sepulchre: with their tongues they have dealt deceitfully* [Ps. 5:11]. *The venom of asps is under their lips* [Ps. 139:4].
> 14 *Whose mouth is full of cursing and bitterness* [Ps. 9:7].
> 15 *Their feet swift to shed blood.*

16 *Destruction and misery in their ways:*
17 *And the way of peace they have not known* |Isa. 59:7|.
18 *There is no fear of God before their eyes* |Ps. 35:2|.[43]

Paul's *catena*, like Huntington, opens with a brief phrase that identifies the argument as authoritative, grounded in the *ipsissima verba* of Scripture: "As it is written." And as in Huntington, the Romans verses do not follow the regular order of the Psalter but are selected and rearranged according to the *modus tractandi* of Paul's argument. Again, these psalm verses, like Huntington's, follow on one another and read as continuous sense, linked by their specific verbal content (in Romans, a series of references to different parts of the body: throat/tongue/lips/mouth/feet/eyes; in Huntington, the motif of the "just" or "poor man," among others) instead of being connected with expository matter, even of a perfunctory sort. The Huntington compiler's method, in short, could have been inspired by or modeled on a Pauline *catena* such as this one from the third chapter of Romans. Biblical scholars call the linked verses in Paul's *catenae* "testimonies" (*testimoniae*), evidences or proof texts for the themes Paul is discussing, and each conflated text itself a "witness" (*testimonium*) or comprehensive argument demonstrating some spiritual truth.[44] A similar argumentative tone pervades the Huntington Psalms *catena*—a sense that the Psalter is being plundered for *sententiae* that, collectively and in a new order, will support a particular ethical case.

That the Psalms were used by the Wycliffites in just this way is suggested by Archbishop Arundel himself, as reported by the Lollard William Thorpe in his *Testimony* (1407), an autobiographical account of his interrogation by Arundel. While questioning Thorpe, Arundel observes: "Þou coueitist to haue aȝen þe Sauter þat I made |caused| to be taken fro þee at Cauntirbirie, forþi þat |because| þou woldist gadere out þereof and recorde scharpe verses aȝens vs."[45] Middle English "scharpe" here is equivalent to our modern adjective "pointed"—acute, incisive, or trenchant. Arundel repeats the word elsewhere during his questioning of Thorpe to suggest that Lollard principles of biblical argument are perverse because they involve quoting Scripture selectively.[46] Wyclif's followers distort perfectly orthodox authorities and bend them to their will, picking and choosing from the Bible particular texts that, out of their original contexts and in new associations with each other, seem to support heretical views.

Whether they were ever used to encourage heresy or not, two groups of psalms and psalm verses selected from the Wycliffite Psalter are copied out in Oxford, MS Laud Misc. 182 among other extracts from the Wycliffite Old and New Testaments (the entire manuscript, like HM 501, is a Lollard biblical compendium).[47] Unlike those in the Huntington *catena*, neither of these groups of verses displays a close internal coherence, in terms of either theme or repeated verbal motives. The first, however, opens and closes with a brief rubric suggesting that it may have had an independent textual life before being copied into Laud: *Here bigynneþ þe firste salme of þe sauter. . . . Here enden nyne salmes of þe sauter* (fols. 91r and 99r, respectively). The psalms copied here, each in full, are numbers 1, 2, 4, 5, 6, 36, 50, 70, and 98, Psalm 36 (fols. 93v–94r) being of special interest because it contains three marginal notes that agree with glosses in the Bodley 554 Lollard Psalms commentary mentioned above:

1. "Delite þou in þe lord; and he schal ȝyue to þee þe axyngis of þin herte" [Ps. 36:4]. Þe axingis of fleisch ben aboute þe helþe of fleisch, but þe axyngis of herte ben aboute euerelasting goodis. *Austyn here.*
2. "Nile þou sue him þat haþ prosperite in his weie, a man doynge vnriȝtfulnesse" [Ps. 36:7]. Þat is, haþ þe yuel þat he purposiþ. *Lire here.*
3. "And ȝit a litil, and a synnere schal not be; and þou schalt seke his place and schalt not fynde" [Ps. 36:10]. Þat is, to vse to purge goode men as he doiþ now, but he shal be in peyne wiþouten ende. *Lire here.*[48]

There is nothing the least bit controversial about these selections. This grouping of nine psalms from the Wycliffite Psalter, however, confirms the Lollard tradition of excerpting the Book of Psalms and perhaps, in the case of these three glossed verses, assembling extracts along with elementary exegetical material, in the interest of advancing an argumentative (or at least educative) rather than simply devout purpose.

The second group of Laudian psalm extracts occurs among briefer excerpts from the Wycliffite Bible assembled later in the manuscript (fols. 311r–312r):

Thou hatist alle þat worchen wickidnes; þou schalt lese hem alle þat speken lesynge. *Psalmus .v°.* [Ps. 5:7].

Myn yȝe is disturblid of woodnes; I haue wexid oold among alle myne enemyes. *Psalmus .vj.* [Ps. 6:8].[49]

Lord opene þou my lippis; and my mouþ schal telle þi preisinge. *Psalmus .l.* [Ps. 50:17].

For I kneew not lettrure, I schal entre into þe power of þe Lord; Lord I schal bi þenke on þi riȝtwiisnes aloone. *Psalmus .lxxj.* [Ps. 70:15–16].

Oonys I swoor in myn holy; I schal not lie to Dauiþ, his seede schal dwelle wiþouten eende. *Psalmus .lxxxviij.* [Ps. 88:36–37].

Alle þe goddis of heþene men ben feendis; but þe Lord made

heuenes. *Psalmus .lxxxxv.* |Ps. 95:5|.

I seide in my passinge; ech man is a liere. *Psalmus .Cxv.* |Ps. 115:11|.

Thou blamedist þe proude; þei ben cursid þat bowen awei fro þin heestis. *Psalmus .C&xviij.* |Ps. 118:21|.

Whidir schal I go fro þi spirit; and whidir schal I fle fro þi face? If I schal go doun into helle, þou art þere present. If I schal take my feþeris ful eerly; I schal dwelle in þe laste partis of þe see. And soþely þidur þin hond schal lede me forþ; and þi riȝthond schal holde me. *Psalmus .Cxxxviij.* |Ps. 138:7–10|.

Unlike the complete psalm texts assembled in *Nyne Salmes*, these are individual verses and groups of verses (Figure 2). They are identified by their compiler, as in the Huntington *catena*, by formal concluding attributions (although here not in red) and they cohere like the Huntington verses, albeit more loosely, around a contentious theme: the conflict between the wicked, who are both proud and untrustworthy, and the humbler virtuous man, who, despite his persecution, continues to praise God. They also have a loose structure that makes them read almost like continuous discourse, despite each verse being set off by what were intended to be larger initial capitals (not provided by the rubricator): beginning with a statement about God's hatred of the wicked, moving through the speaker's self-justification, and concluding with an assertion of his confidence in God's protection. Unlike the Huntington catenist, this compiler chooses to follow the regular order of the Psalter throughout his list. The reader gets the sense, however, as he does not from *Nyne Salmes*, of an argumentative organizing intelligence at work, someone interested in the same essential idea as the Huntington catenist—the perilous but finally secure place of the righteous man in an unrighteous world.

III. The Structure and Themes of the Huntington *Catena*

Nowhere in HM 501 is the text I edit below actually called a *catena*, nor indeed does the word ever seem to designate in medieval Latin a literary technique or genre.[50] *Catena* dates as a genre term only to the early modern period, the title of the formidable *Catena aurea* itself being postmedieval: Aquinas calls his text simply a *Glossa* or *Expositio continua in Matthaeum, Marcum, Lucam, et Iohannem.*[51] The Huntington text has, however, been described as an "abbreviated psalter," a label that associates it with another class of psalm selections from which it differs notably in purpose and design.[52] Some more precise term is needed. Given the linking strategies used to assemble the psalm verses in the Huntington text as continuous discourse, *catena* seems apt.

Abbreviated psalters—severe abridgements of the full run of 150 psalms—were intended in the Middle Ages primarily for devotional reading and meditation. The three best known, attributed to Jerome, Bernard of Clairvaux, and Bede (only this last attribution, however, is accurate), generally follow the regular sequence of Psalms and represent individual psalms by groups of verse extracts, or even single phrases, but rarely in full.[53] Sometimes, as in pseudo-Jerome, the Vulgate text is adjusted to make the grammatical drift of the extracts more fluent.[54] Abbreviated psalters are also often introduced in manuscript by rubrics that explain their circumstances of composition and devotional aims.

The most intriguing of these is the introduction to the so-called *Eight-Verse Psalter* of Bernard, which survives, like pseudo-Jerome, in both Latin and Middle English versions. It describes how Bernard tricked the devil into revealing to him "viij versus in the Sauter, tho wheche versus and a man sey hem wche |each| day, he schal never be dampnude."[55] The text that follows appeals to the superstitious medieval belief in psalm verses as talismans or charms that, if chanted or worn as amulets, will ward off evil.[56]

More liturgically substantial is the introductory rubric to pseudo-Jerome. This explains that the shortened Psalms text is intended for recitation by secular persons distracted by worldly responsibilities (e.g., in battle or traveling by sea), who are thus prevented from praying the entire Psalter straight through each week, the norm for monastic recitation.[57] The Middle English version of pseudo-Jerome that follows immediately on the Huntington *catena* in HM 501 (Figure 3) is introduced with a short rubric (*Here bigynneþ leroms Sautir*) and has a prose proem in the form of a generic prayer that declares its devotional purpose:

> Lord God almyȝty, vouchesaif to take up þese psalmes þat
> ben halowid to þee, which I synful and vnworþi desire to seie
> in worschip of þi name, and of þi modir oure ladi seint Marie,
> and of alle halowen |saints|. And Lord for me wrecche and
> vnworþi, and for alle my gode doers, and for my fadir and
> modir, and briþeren and sustren, and for alle my kinrede,
> and for alle my frendis and myn enemyes, and for alle trewe
> cristen peple boþe lyues and deþis. Graunte Lord Ihesu Crist
> and sauiour þat þese psalmes profite to us to helþe of bodi
> and of soule, and brynge us to euerlastinge lyf. Amen. (fol.
> 117r)

No such rubric or proem opens the Huntington *catena* itself, which begins abruptly with its brief introductory phrase ("God seiþ bi his profete") at the top of folio 113v of the manuscript. There is no reason to suppose that the

Huntington *catena* was modeled in any way on pseudo-Jerome,[58] although the two texts might have been intended for reading in sequence: the prayerful pseudo-Jerome would be an appropriate coda to the reformist message of the homiletic *catena*.

In fact, the Huntington scribe is careful to distinguish his two texts in terms of layout as entirely different kinds of Psalter abridgements. In pseudo-Jerome the start of the proem and each individual psalm is signaled by a large, blue initial capital with red vinet penwork; individual verses, in turn, are distinguished by smaller, alternating blue and red initial capitals. In the *catena*, by contrast, after a handsome four-line capital at the start of his text, the scribe asserts its continuity by his uninterrupted writing of psalm verses on the page, punctuated carefully but without colored initial capitals to mark divisions in the discourse. In pseudo-Jerome, the scribe provides no psalm numbers for the verses collected; they are presumably irrelevant to the text's devotional purpose. Conversely, in the *catena* he gives psalm numbers as glossarial-style attributions (*Psalmus .lxxvij.*, etc.) in red at the end of each selection, however brief (single verses) or protracted (entire psalms) these extracts are, perhaps so that an interested reader can consult the excerpted matter in its original Psalter contexts. The impression conveyed by the mise-en-page is of a continuous, running prose text, not a series of religious lyric prayers as in pseudo-Jerome.

The Huntington *catena* is, unlike *Ieroms Sautir*, explicitly didactic. It begins with an injunction to its audience, conflated from two psalms, to listen to and learn from God's "profete," King David: "Parseyue ȝe my lawe; bowe ȝoure eere into þe wordis of my mouþ"; "parseyue wiþ eeris" (Pss. 77:1–2 and 48:2–3 |a|).[59] (One can imagine the *catena* being read either aloud to a group or silently to oneself.) Three times the catenist reasserts the didactic character of his discourse: first, in |d|, when he narrows his target audience from "Alle ȝe folkis" in |a| to "kingis" ("Take ȝe lore; lest þe Lord be wrooþ sumtyme, and lest ȝe perische fro iust wey," Ps. 2:12); next, a third of the way into the *catena*, in |h|, when he encourages those who are blessed or holy in the Lord to learn how properly to fear him ("Come ȝe sones here ȝe me; and I schal teche ȝou þe drede of þe Lord," Ps. 33:12); and finally at the text's close, in |r|, when the catenist urges "vnwise men" and "foolis" to "vndirstonde; and . . . lerne sumtyme" (Ps. 93:8) the fear of God.

This final exhortation the catenist reinforces by a deft instance of moral sarcasm derived from the Psalms, a rhetorical question that underscores God's omniscient awareness of those crimes against widows and orphans that the powerful try vainly to hide: "Schal not he heere þat plauntide þe eere; eiþir biholdiþ not he þat made þe iȝe?" (Ps. 93:9). These are his last psalmic words to his audience, and they recall explicitly a categorical statement in |i| concerning God's attentiveness to those who are righteous: "The iȝen of þe

Lord ben on iust men; and his eeren ben to her preiers" (Ps. 33:16); as well as an even earlier verse in |e| concerning the Lord's attentiveness to the poor: "Hise iȝen biholden on a pore man; his iȝe liddis axen þe sones of men" (Ps. 10:6).

The entire *catena* text—142 verses, drawn from across the Psalter and reassembled out of their regular order but with a consistent sense—is held together by a network of verbal cross-associations. These establish clearly its major themes and amplify the ethical energy of phrases and imagery in particular psalms by linking them to similar phrases and imagery elsewhere in the Psalter.

Although there is no formal division to this effect in the manuscript, the *catena* seems to be organized into two roughly equal parts: the first half, consisting of approximately 1,500 words, runs from sections |a| through |l| in my edited version; the second, of nearly 1,700 words, runs from sections |m| through |r|. This structural analysis is necessarily hypothetical, since between folios 115v and 116r at least one leaf of the manuscript is missing. My surmise is that only a single leaf is lacking at this point, representing approximately 600 words, based on average word counts and lines per page elsewhere in the book (15 words/line, 20 lines/side of each folio). This total could accommodate the missing conclusion of Psalm 13 (four verses, Ps. 13:4–7), the third verse of which is acaudate at the end of folio 115v (*noon is til to oon. The þrote of . . .*, Ps. 13:3), and the long missing first part of Psalm 88 (forty verses, Ps. 88:2–42), the forty-third verse of which is acephalous at the beginning of folio 116r (*. . .-hond of men oppressynge him*, Ps. 88:43). My hypothesis assumes, therefore, that each of these psalms was copied out complete in the *catena*, as five other psalms are elsewhere in the text (nos. 1 |c|, 92 |j|, 14 |m|, 23 |m–n|, and 89 |p–q|).

In the *catena*'s first half, following the text's opening injunction to the audience to listen and learn from the Psalmist, there is a regular rhetorical movement back and forth between passages of declarative statements about God (these emphasize the integrity of his law and word and his roles as protector and defender of the oppressed) and moral imperatives directed in turn at kings especially; just, righteous, and holy men, who should praise God; and, most emphatically, in |l|, the "poor man," who must not despair of God's assistance. That is, across |a| through |l|, the catenist progressively narrows his stated audience until the text focuses finally in |k| and |l|, the *catena*'s midpoint, on the special status and difficulties of the "poor man," who encompasses and epitomizes within his archetypal person the traits of those who are just, righteous, and holy.

After the *catena*'s hortatory proem |a|, the catenist asserts immediately by way of Ps. 18:8–12 the absolute integrity of God's law ("The lawe of þe Lord is wiþouten wem |fault or blemish|," |b|) and then describes the nature of this law more extensively—including the blessedness it confers on its followers

and the fate of its detractors—by giving the full text of Psalm 1, *Beatus vir*, in
|c|. Hereby the catenist introduces a key theme of his text: the moral character
of the blessed (just, righteous, holy, poor) man, which distinguishes the
blessed man from his enemies and also establishes Psalm 1 at the beginning
of the catenist's discourse as a summary text for his argument, the equivalent
of the *thema* that begins a formal medieval sermon or homily. Jerome, in one
of his homiletic treatises on the Psalms, explains that the first psalm is the
"impressive doorway or foyer" to the "great house" of the entire Psalter, a digest
itself of the summary wisdom of the complete biblical book.[60] Quoted by the
Huntington catenist in full, Psalm 1 is the doorway or foyer to his meaning,
too, passage through which is necessary if the ethical force of the entire text to
follow is to be properly understood.

In his *English Psalter*, Rolle identifies *Beatus vir* in Psalm 1 with "Crist and
. . . his folowers," and (following Peter Lombard on this point) by extension
with all those who reject the world and live according to the Gospels.[61] The
Wycliffite Psalter commentary in Bodley 554, drawing on Nicholas of Lyra's
Postilla, is more pointed and ideological concerning the opposition between
those who achieve blessedness by meditating constantly on God's law and
their opponents, who sit down in the chair of pestilence. The wicked, whose
way or path *Beatus vir* avoids, are, according to Lyra, a *figura* for "þe false doctryn
of vnfeiþful men." Their way, moreover, not only is that "of synners," as the
text reads literally in HM 501, but, according to Jerome's retranslation of the
Psalter *iuxta Hebraicum* (his third, so-called Hebrew version), it is also the path
"*of scorneris* |detractors|, for þe techeris of weiward doctryn ben scorneris verili,
for þei techen errours vndur þe licnesse |appearance| of treuþe."[62]

For the Lollards, Psalm 1 establishes the essential dichotomy of the
moral life that persists throughout the Huntington Psalms *catena* as a major
theme: the opposition between those in authority, who ought to protect the
oppressed but do not, and those who, despite their lack of worldly power and
influence, espouse the cause of righteousness. When the catenist observes,
quoting Psalm 1:5, that "wickid men risen not aȝen in doom," an informed
Lollard listener or reader might have recalled Lyra's gloss—"Þat is, to her
saluacioun, but more to dampnacioun of bodi and soule." He might also
have understood that "þe counseil of iust men" mentioned in the catenist's
next verse is, according to Lyra, "in Ebreu |the Hebrew text| and in Ierom's
translacioun . . . *þe congregacioun of iust men* . . . in heuenli blisse." When David
concludes Psalm 1 by observing that the Lord knows the way of the just and
that the way of the wicked will perish, he was understood by the Lollards as
implicitly endorsing their communal desire to expose and amend vice: to
quote Lyra from the Bodley 554 commentary again, "God knowiþ bi knowing
of appreuyng |confirmation| þe wey of iust men; and bi knowing of repreuyng
|correction| þe weie of wickid men."[63]

Throughout the first half of the *catena*, the figure of the poor man gradually becomes the text's strongest motif. The catenist's thirteen references to the poor or the poor man, distributed across sections |a| through |l|, are cumulative in number and in rhetorical force: one in |a|, two each in |d| and |e|, one each in |f| and |g|, two in |k|, and four in |l|. The only reference to the poor in the *catena*'s second half is indirect (i.e., it does not use the adjective or noun "pore") but important in its singularity. It occurs in the catenist's closing exhortation against wicked men, who "killiden a widowe and a comelyng; and . . . han slayn fadirles children and modirles" (Ps. 93:6, |r|), a deliberate echo of the text's early moral challenge to kings in |d|: "Deeme ʒe to þe nedi and to þe modirles child; iustifie ʒe þe meke man and pore" (Ps. 81:3). The exhortation in |r| brings the argument of the *catena* full circle. Its didacticism concludes with a frustrated awareness that the wicked have not yet reformed: those in authority who are enjoined to do their duty to the poor throughout the first half of the discourse are obstinate in evil and may not repent and make amends. Nevertheless, God's message, as communicated by his moral prophet, is clear and unequivocal. The *catena*'s cycling back at its close to its hortatory proem is a structural means of confirming the steadfastness of the Psalmist's and the Lollard catenist's truth.

The figure of the poor man in this *catena* would have been understood by its audience in three related senses: literally, as representing those who are economically oppressed, who can neither satisfy their own basic needs for subsistence nor defend themselves from harm (e.g., widows and orphans); figuratively, as the "poor in spirit" (*pauperes spiritu*) valorized by Jesus in the Beatitudes (Matt. 5:3), who are blessed in their detachment—willing or enforced—from the things of this world but endure persecution because of their spiritual commitment; and polemically, as a surrogate for the text's fifteenth-century listener or reader, the persecuted Lollard who suffers for his theological and social beliefs and (as the second half of the *catena* makes clear) could fall prey to misgivings and even doubts concerning God's justice. In the second and third of these senses, then, the poor man is an ethical type related to *Beatus vir* in Psalm 1 in being apart from those who are slaves to the world in the form of either material possessions or false teaching.[64]

Anne Hudson shows how certain much-repeated phrases in Wycliffite writings, including "pore man," may have constituted a Lollard sect vocabulary, serving as a code whereby sympathetic recipients of Lollard writings might find their corporate identity defined and affirmed by an ideologically charged but simple lexicon. Lollards might refer to each other as "true" or "Bible men" in the same way that early Communists, for example, referred to each other as "comrades" (friends, colleagues, allies).[65] The phrase "pore man" could have been especially "obliquely self-naming" for Lollards, according to Hudson,[66] because it evokes the phrase "pore prest" used by Wyclif's followers to summarize the character of the ideal curate, who models his behavior on that of Christ and his followers by embracing apostolic poverty and devoting himself to preaching the Gospels with humility.[67]

Notwithstanding a possible association with Wyclif's "poor priests," poverty as it is described in Lollard texts in general and in the Huntington Psalms *catena* is not always or necessarily linked to material destitution, although Lollard writings do commonly see the image of Christ in "pore nedi men and wymmen" who are neglected by prelates and others who spend lavishly on the visual accoutrements of religion and empty devotional exercises such as pilgrimages.[68] In a wider sense, the "poor man" is blessed not only in his similarity to Christ, who was poor, but in being aware of himself as a contingent being, radically dependent upon God for the necessaries of both his corporeal and spiritual life. This man is to be understood in the Huntington *catena* as ultimately analogous to the just or righteous person ("ȝe iust men, haue fulli ioie in þe Lord; preisynge togidere bicomeþ riȝtful men," Ps. 32:1 [**f**]), someone who, as Augustine puts it in his *Enarrationes in Psalmos*, "opt[s] for poverty by loving nothing which either deserts a living person who loves it here on earth, or else is left behind at death."[69] Even the materially comfortable can possess a genuine poverty of spirit, according to Augustine in his explanation of one of the verses quoted in the Huntington *catena* ("This pore man criede, and þe Lord herde him," Ps. 33:7 [**g**]):

> *This poor man cried out, and the Lord hearkened.* Cry out in poverty, cry as a poor person, and the Lord will listen. "But how am I to cry out as a poor person?" Cry to him in such a way that even if you have possessions, you do not trust in your own resources, cry to him in a frame of mind that understands your need, cry to him in the knowledge that you will always be a pauper as long as you do not possess him who makes you rich.[70]

Physical destitution can certainly be a useful precondition to this spiritual state or attitude; in his commentary on Psalm 10, for example, Augustine remarks that the indigent are often, by virtue of their economic lack, "those who have been born anew by faith" and as such, are specially protected by God.[71] But lack of possessions is not a prerequisite to or guarantee of true spiritual poverty.

Neither Augustine nor his medieval followers, including the Lollards, were sentimental about material poverty. Rather than assuming that it should always compel our sympathy, they sometimes indicated its moral dangers, as Chaucer does in a passage from the "Man of Law's Tale" adapted from Innocent III's *De miseria conditionis humane* (1195), a blistering treatise on contempt for the world:

> Thow |the poor man| blamest Crist and seist ful bitterly
> He mysdeparteth |inequitably distributes| richesse
> temporal;
> Thy neighebor thou wytest |accuse| sinfully,
> And seist thou hast to lite and he hath al.[72]

The poor are tempted, in ways that the rich are not, to violate the two most important Gospel imperatives: to love God with one's entire being and to love one's neighbor as oneself (Mark 12:30–31). And, we might add, likewise the poor in spirit, those who suffer misery voluntarily by detaching themselves from the satisfactions of this world in the form of either material goods or the kind of earthly security provided by kings and prelates. Many Lollard texts instruct their sympathetic readers in purity of heart and humility as antidotes to pride. When the speaker notes, in section |**p**| of the *catena*, for example, the power of God and his chastisement of the human soul, he is not simply speaking about divine vengeance against his enemies. He also implicates himself:

> Oure ȝeeris schulen biþenke, as an ireyne |spider|; þe daies
> of oure ȝeeris ben in þo seuenty ȝeeris. Forsoþe if eiȝtetie
> ȝeeris ben in myȝty men; and þe more tyme of hem is traueile
> and sorewe. For myldenesse cam aboue; and we schulen be
> chastisid. Who knew þe power of þin ire; and durste noumbre
> þin ire for þi drede? Make þi riȝthond so knowun; and make
> men lerned in herte bi wisdom. (Ps. 89:9–11)

This wisdom consists, as another strong motif in the Huntington *catena* asserts, in fear of the Lord and a corresponding trust in his protection. Eight times across the text, fear of God is mentioned:

> |**b**| The holi drede of þe Lord dwelliþ into world of worlde;
> þe doomys of þe Lord ben trewe, iustified into hem silf. |Ps.
> 18:10|
> |**d**| Serue ȝe to þe Lord wiþ drede; and make ȝe ful ioie to
> him wiþ tremblyng. |Ps. 2:11|
> |**g**| Al erþe drede þe Lord; soþely alle men enhabitinge
> þe world ben moued of him. |Ps. 32:8|
> |**h**| Alle ȝe holy men of þe Lord drede him; for no nedynes
> is to men dredynge him. Men þat seken þe Lord; schulen not
> faile of al good. Come ȝe sones heere ȝe me; and I schal teche
> ȝou þe drede of þe Lord. |Ps. 33:10–12|
> |**m**| A wickid man is brouȝt to nouȝt in his siȝt; but he
> glorifieþ hem þat dreden þe Lord. |Ps. 14:4|

|**n**| Sorewe and cursidnesse is in þe weies of hem, and
þei knewen not þe weie of pees; þe drede of God is not bifor
her iȝen. |Ps. 13:3|

|**p**| Who knew þe power of þin ire; and durste noumbre
þin ire for þi drede? |Ps. 89:11|

The early instances here are either directed at the mighty or observe that the
"holi drede of þe Lord" (*timor Domini*) is a kind of ontological state, a condition
of the universe that holds it together and stable. The references in |**h**| through
|**p**|, however, represent pious fear as a higher form of knowledge that those
who are oppressed might learn and benefit from—indeed, a sensibility that
constitutes the beginning of their glorification or vindication. In explaining the
sense of Psalm 2:11–12, quoted in |**d**|, Lyra notes that the imperative "Serue
ȝe to þe Lord wiþ drede" means "bi deuocioun and reisyng of herte in to God,"
and that the Psalmist's subsequent parallel injunctions, "make ȝe ful ioie to
him wiþ trembling" and "Take ȝe lore; lest þe Lord be wrooþ sumtyme," might
be paraphrased, "make ȝe ȝou soget mekeli, to þe techyng of Crist."[73] In short,
the dread enjoined here, for rich and poor alike, is not fear of punishment
but proper awe before and deference to the Almighty, the foundation of true
humility.

That this attitude can be learned ("Come ȝe sones heere ȝe me; and I
schal teche ȝou þe drede of þe Lord," Ps. 33:12 |**h**|) establishes the purpose of
the second half of the catenist's discourse. Whereas the *catena*'s first half was
dominated by imperatives directed at the mighty, the second half begins on
a strong interrogative note with a quotation in full of Psalm 14 (*Domine quis
habitabit in tabernaculo?* "Lord, who schal dwelle in þi tabernacle; eiþer who schal
reste in þin holy hil?" |**m**|), and becomes increasingly introspective. Augustine
observes that the twin themes of this psalm are moral perfection (truth in
heart and mouth) and stability (persistence in living according to the truth).[74]
While such a gloss could be read by those under persecution as an implicit
endorsement of Lollardy's reformist agenda, this is too easy an analysis of the
tone of section |**m**|, which seems to imply by its questions that the *catena*'s
listeners or readers are in no position to presume on God's favor, any more
than their persecutors are.

The theme of divine wrath runs through many later Lollard texts, and
Lollards themselves, despite the swagger of a figure such as Thorpe before
Arundel, must have had misgivings about their enterprise. To maintain the
correctness of one's views against the institutional Church involved a continual
process of spiritual discernment—a frank confrontation with uncertainties.[75]
Following the catenist's quotation of Psalm 14 in full, he again enjoins princes
specifically to acknowledge God's preeminent kingship and authority (Ps.
23:10 |**n**|), but then immediately observes in |**o**|, by way of the despairing

tone of Psalm 88, God's apparent failure to vindicate the righteous man. In the face of persecution, Augustine notes concerning Psalm 88, it is easy and even understandable to ask, however erroneously, "What does it mean? That God really made insincere promises, or swore falsely? Why did he promise one thing and do something else?"[76] If the cause of reform is just, why are its proponents downcast and defeated? Why, to recall another of David's psalms of moral frustration, do the heathen rage (Ps. 2:1)?

The mood in the Huntington *catena* shifts markedly between |**p**| and |**q**|, from renewed confidence in God to denigration of the self (admission of personal wickedness, which presumably is the cause of the previously expressed despair) and then toward a resolve to understand, as David does, the sufferings of the present day as a paradoxical sign of God's support, a test of the soul's virtue: "We weren glad for þe daies in whiche þou madist us meke; for þe ʒeeris in whiche we siʒen yuelis. Lord, biholde þou into þin seruauntis, and into þi werkis; and dresse þou þe sones of hem" (Ps. 89:15–16 |**q**|). That this moment results at the end of |**q**| in new praises offered by the catenist to God (Ps. 91:2–5) suggests that the compiler may be dramatizing in the second half of his text a spiritual conflict within Lollardy, an emotional dialectic of despair and renewed trust in God that can be safely explored and perhaps resolved through the poetry of each soul's surrogate, David the Psalmist.

This penultimate section of the Huntington *catena* is the necessary prelude to its authoritative closing words. These are directed at those fools who refuse to learn the lesson that the catenist has internalized confidently enough to preach to others: that God will pronounce his judgment on the proud. He knows, as Augustine observes in commenting on Psalm 93:9, that God spares the wicked only in order to give them one last opportunity to reform. The catenist continues to ask in |**r**|, with the Psalmist, how long sinners will be permitted to prosper in this life ("Lord how longe schulen synners haue glorie?" Ps. 93:2), but his question is now rhetorical, like the final statement of his discourse: "Schal not he heere þat plauntide þe eere; eiþer biholdiþ not he þat made þe iʒe?" (Ps. 93:9). He has found a way, in constructing a homily entirely from the Psalter, to turn his misgivings into trust and interrogation of God's plan into an affirmation of faith.

Text

The Psalms *catena* edited below is one scriptural text of several in a Wycliffite biblical compendium, Huntington Library, San Marino, California MS HM 501, which begins imperfectly with selections from the Old Testament books of Deuteronomy, Baruch, and Tobit (WB Later Version, fols. 1r–19v), and thereafter consists largely of psalm-based materials: the four Psalter prologues discussed above (fols. 19v–24v); the Wycliffite Psalms in the Later Version, with the first three psalms given in full in Latin, before their English translations (fols. 25r–103v); the Canticles and a litany (fols. 103v–113r); and then the Lollard Psalms *catena*. The *catena* is followed immediately by *leroms Sautir*, as discussed above, and then by a series of other Wycliffite texts related to Scripture and elementary religion (e.g., on fols. 145r–146r, the twelve articles of faith).[77] The early leaves of the book have been damaged extensively by damp, in some cases half eaten away. The manuscript pages are now covered with crepeline, hence the lack of sharpness in Figures 1 and 3 accompanying this essay.

The text of the Huntington *catena* given below has been collated against the Wycliffite Bible, with which it agrees in most particulars. Underlined words are interpolated glosses that appear underlined both in the Wycliffite Bible and in HM 501. Punctuation and capitalization have been modernized.

All corrections, emendations, and other additions to the text are enclosed in square brackets. I have conjecturally restored psalm verses and parts of verses that I believe the scribe omitted due to eyeskip. In the case of the gap in the manuscript between folios 115v and 116r, however, I have restored only the missing portions of acaudate Psalm 13:2 and acephalous Psalm 88:43, indicating the bulk of the other missing material (one or more leaves) by an ellipsis.

I have provided boldface lowercase letters in square brackets to clarify the structure of the *catena* as I understand it (these letters appear as well as references throughout my discussion of the *catena*, above). The structure I propose is not entirely self-evident from the *catena* text, however, and should be understood as hypothetical.

I have also provided following my edited text an appendix that lists the Psalms and psalm verses compiled in the *catena*, according to my alphabetical designations of subsections.

***

|fol. 113v|

[a] God seiþ bi his profete, "My peple parseyue ȝe my lawe; bowe ȝoure eere into þe wordis of my mouþ. I schal opene my mouþ in parablis; I schal speke perfiȝt resouns fro þe bigynnynge. *Psalmus .lxxvij.* [Ps. 77:1–2]. Alle ȝe folkis heere þese þingis; alle ȝe þat dwellen in þe world parseyue wiþ eeris. Alle þe sones of erþe and þe sones of men; togidere þe riche man and þe pore into oon. *Psalmus .xlviij.* [Ps. 48:1–3]

[b] The lawe of þe Lord is wiþouten wem and conuertiþ soulis; þe witnessynge of þe Lord is feiþful and ȝeueþ wisdom to litil children. The riȝtfulnessis of þe Lord ben riȝtful, gladinge hertis; þe comaundement[78] of þe Lord is cleer, liȝtnynge iȝen. The holi drede of þe Lord dwelliþ into world of worlde; þe doomys of þe Lord ben trewe, iustified into hem silf. Desirable more þan gold, and a stoon myche precious; and swettere þan hony and hony comb. Forwhi þe seruaunt kepiþ þo; and myche ȝeldinge is in þo to be kept. *Psalmus .xviij.* [Ps. 18:8–12]

|**c**| Blessid is þe man þat ȝede not in þe counseil of wickid men; and stood not in þe wey of synners, and satt not in þe chaier of pestilence. But his wille is in þe lawe of þe Lord; and he schal biþenke in þe lawe of him day and nyȝt. And he schal be as a tree which is plauntid bisidis þe rennyngis of watris; þat schal ȝeue fruyt in his tyme. And his leef schal not falle doun; and alle þingis whiche euere he schal do, schulen haue prosperite. Not so wickid men not so; for þei ben as dust, þe which wynd castiþ awei fro þe face of þe erþe. Þerfore wickid men risen not aȝen in doom; neiþir synners in þe counseil of iust men. For þe Lord knowiþ þe wey of iust men; and þe wey of wickid men schal

|fol. 114r|
perische. *Psalmus .j.* |Ps. 1:1–6|
|**d**| And now ȝe kingis vndirstoonde; ȝe þat deemen þe erþe be lerned. Serue ȝe to þe Lord wiþ drede; and make ȝe ful ioie to him wiþ tremblyng. Take ȝe loore; lest þe Lord be wrooþ sumtyme, and lest ȝe perische fro iust wey. Whanne his ire brenneþ out in schort tyme; blessid ben alle þat tristen in him. *Psalmus .ij.* |Ps. 2:10–13| Deeme ȝe to þe nedi and to þe modirles child; iustifie ȝe þe meke man and pore. Rauysche ȝe out a pore man; and delyuere ȝe þe nedi fro þe hond of þe synner. *Psalmus .lxxxj.* |Ps. 81:3–4| Be ȝe wrooþ and nyle ȝe do synne; and for þo þingis whiche ȝe seien in ȝoure hertis and in ȝoure beddis, be ȝe conpunct. Sacrifise ȝe þe sacrifise of riȝtfulnes; and hope ȝe in þe Lord. *Psalmus .iiij.* |Ps. 4:5–6|
|**e**| The Lord is in his holy temple; he is Lord, his seete is in heuene. Hise iȝen biholden on a pore man; his iȝe liddis axen þe sones of men. The Lord axiþ a iust man |and vnfeiþful man|;[79] but he þat loueþ wickidnes hatiþ his soule. He schal reyne snaris on synful men; fier and brymstoon and þe spirit of tempestis ben þe part of þe cuppe of hem. For þe Lord is riȝtful, and |l|oueþ[80] riȝtfulnessis; his cheer siȝ equyte eiþir euennes. *Psalmus .x.* |Ps. 10:5–7| The Lord is maad refuyt[81] to a pore man; an helpere in couenable tymes in tribulacioun. Thei þat knowen þi name haue hope in þee; for þou Lord hast not forsaken hem þat seken þee.
|**f**| Synge ȝe to þe Lord þat dwelliþ in Sion; telle ȝe his studies, among heþene men. God forȝetiþ not þe cri of pore men; for he haþ mynde and sekiþ þe blood of hem. *Psalmus .ix.* |Ps. 9:10–13| 3e iust men, haue fulli ioie in þe Lord; preisynge togidere bicomeþ riȝtful men. Knowleche ȝe to þe Lord in an harpe; synge ȝe to him in

|fol. 114v|
a sautre of ten strengis. Synge ȝe to him a newe song; seie ȝe weel salm to him in criynge.
|**g**| For þe word of þe Lord is riȝtful; and alle hise werkis ben in feiþfulnes. He loueþ mercy and doom; þe erþe is ful of þe mercy of þe Lord. Heuenes ben

maad stidfast bi þe word of þe Lord; and al þe vertu of þo bi þe spirit of his mouþ. And he gaderiþ togidere þe watris of þe see as in a bowge; and settiþ depe watris in tresouris. Al erþe drede þe Lord; soþely alle men enhabitinge þe world ben moued of him. For he seide and |þe|⁸² þingis weren maad; he comaundide and þingis weren maad of nouȝt. *Psalmus* .32. |Ps. 32:1–9| Neiȝe ȝe to him and be ȝe liȝtned; and ȝoure facis schulen not be schent. This pore man criede, and þe Lord herde him; and sauede him fro alle hise tribulaciouns. The aungel of þe Lord sendiþ in þe cumpas of men dredynge him; and he schal delyuere hem.

|**h**| Taaste ȝe and se for þe Lord is swete; blessid is þe man þat hopiþ in him. Alle ȝe holy men of þe Lord drede him; for no nedynes is to men dredynge him. Men þat seken þe Lord; schulen not faile of al good. Come ȝe sones heere ȝe me; |and|⁸³ I schal teche ȝou þe drede of þe Lord. Who is a man þat wole lijf; looueþ to se Gode daies? Forbede þi tunge fro yuel; and þi lippis speke not gile. Turne þou awey fro yuel and do good; seke þou pees and perfiȝtly sue |þou|⁸⁴ it.

|**i**| The iȝen of þe Lord ben on iust men; and his |eer|en⁸⁵ ben to her preiers. |But þe cheer of þe Lord is on men doynge yuelis; þat he leese þe mynde of hem fro erþe.|⁸⁶ Iust men crieden and þe Lord herde hem; and delyueride hem fro alle her tribulaciouns. The Lord is nyȝ hem þat ben of troublid herte; and he schal saue meke men in spirit. Many tribulaciouns ben of iust men; and þe Lord schal delyuere hem fro |alle|⁸⁷ þese. The Lord kepiþ alle

|fol. 115r|

þe boonys of hem; oon of þo schal not be broken. |The deeþ of synneris is worst; and þei þat haten a iust man shulen trespasse.|⁸⁸ The Lord schal aȝenbie þe soulis of his seruauntis; and alle þat hopen in him schulen not trespase. *Psalmus* .xxxiij. |Ps. 33:6–23|

|**j**| The Lord haþ regnyd, he is cloþid wiþ fairsnes; þe Lord is cloþid wiþ strengþe, and haþ girt him silf. For he made stidfast þe world; þat schal not be moued. God þi seete was maad redy fro þat tyme; þou art fro þe world. |Lord, þe floodis han reisid; þe floodis han reisid her vois. Floodis reisiden her wawis; of þe vois of manye watris.|⁸⁹ The reisyngis of þe see ben wondirful; þe Lord is wondirful in hiȝe þingis. Thi witnessyngis ben maad able to be bileued greetly; Lord holynes bicomeþ þin hous, into þe lengþe of daies. *Psalmus* .lxxx|x|ij. |Ps. 92:1–5|⁹⁰ The iust man schal be glad in þe Lord and schal hope in him, and alle men of riȝtful herte schulen be preised. *Psalmus* .lxiij. |Ps. 63:11|

|**k**| Al þe erþe make ioie hertily to God, seie ȝe salm to his name; ȝeue ȝe glorie to his heriynge. *Psalmus* .lxv. |Ps. 65:2| Pore men se and be glad; seke ȝe God and ȝoure soule schal lyue. For þe Lord herde pore men; and dispiside not his bounden men. Heuenes and erþe herie him; þe see and alle crepinge beestis in þo <u>herie him</u>. For God schal make saaf Syon; and þe citees of Iuda

schulen be bildid. And þei schulen dwelle þere; and þei schulen gete it bi eritage. And þe seed of hise seruauntis schal haue it in possessioun; and þei þat louen his name schulen dwelle þerinne. *Psalmus .lxviij.* |Ps. 68:33–37| And alle kyngis schulen worschipe him; alle folkis schulen serue him.

|**l**| For he schal delyuere a pore man fro þe myȝty; and a pore man[91] to whom was noon helpere. He schal spare a pore man and nedy; and he schal make saaf þe soulis of pore men. He schal aȝenbie þe soulis of hem from vsuris and wickidnes; and þe name of hem is honourable bifore him. *Psalmus .lxxj.* |Ps. 71:11–14| A iust man schal floure; he schal be multiplied as a cedre of Liban men plauntid in þe hous

|fol. 115v|

of þe Lord; schulen floure in þe porchis of þe hous of oure God. Ȝit þei schulen be multiplied in plenteuous eelde; and þei schulen be suffrynge weel. That þei telle þat oure Lord God is riȝtful; and no wickidnes is in him. *Psalmus .lxxxxj.* |Ps. 91:13–15|

|**m**| Lord, who schal dwelle in þi tabernacle; eiþer who schal reste in þin holy hil? He þat entriþ wiþoute wem; and worchiþ riȝtfulnes. Which spekiþ truþe in his herte; which dide not gile in his tunge. Neiþer dide yuel to his neiȝbore; and took not schenschipe aȝens his neiȝboris. A wickid man is brouȝt to nouȝt in his siȝt; but he glorifieþ hem þat dreden þe Lord. Which sweriþ to his neiȝbore and disceyueþ not, which ȝaf not his money to vsure; and took not ȝiftis on þe innocent. He þat doiþ þese þingis; schal not be moued wiþouten eende. *Psalmus .xiiij.* |Ps. 14:1–5| The erþe and þe fulnes þerof is þe Lordis; þe world and alle þat dwellen in him is þe Lordis. For he foundide it on þe sees; and made it redi on þe floodis. Who schal stiȝe into þe hil of þe Lord; eiþir who schal stoonde in þe holy place of him? The innocent in hondis and cleene in herte;[92] which took not his soule in veyn, neiþir swoor in gile to his neiȝbore. This man schal take blessynge of þe Lord; and mercy of God his heelþe. This is þe generacioun of men sekynge him. Of men sekynge þe face of God of Iacob.

|**n**| Ȝe pryncis take vp ȝoure ȝatis, and ȝe euerlastynge ȝatis be reisid; and þe kyng of glorie schal entre. Who is þe king of glorie? þe Lord strong and myȝty, þe Lord myȝty in bateile. The Lord of vertues, he is kyng of glorie. *Psalmus .xxiij.* |Ps. 23:1–10| The Lord biheeld fro heuene on þe sones of men; þat he se if eny is vndirstondynge eiþir sekynge God. Alle bowiden awey, togidere þei ben maad vnprofitable; noon is þat doiþ good, noon is til to oon. The þrote of |hem is an open sepulcre, þei diden gilefuli wiþ her tungis; þe venym of snakis is vndur her lippis. Whos mouþ is ful of cursyng and bittirnesse; her feet ben swifte to shede out blood. Sorewe and cursidnesse is in þe weies of hem, and þei knewen not þe weie of pees; þe drede of God is not bifor her iȝen. *Psalmus .xiij.* | |Ps. 13:2–3|[93]

|. . .|[94]

|fol. 116r|

|o| |Thou hast enhaunside þe riȝt|[95] hond of men oppressynge him; þou hast gladid alle his enemyes. Thou hast turned awey þe help of his swerd; and þou helpidist not him in bateile. Thou distriedist him fro clensynge; and þou hast hurtlid doun his seete in erþe. Thou hast maad lesse þe daies of his tyme; þou hast bischeed him wiþ schenschip. Lord how longe turnest þou awey into þe eende? Schal þin ire brenne out as fier? Biþenke þo what is my substaunce, for wher þou hast ordeyn|i|d[96] veynly alle þe sones of men? Who is a man þat schal lyue and schal not se deeþ; schal delyuere his soule fro þe hond of helle? Lord where ben þin eelde mercyes; as þou hast swoor to Dauiþ in þi truþe? Lord be þou myndeful of þe schenschipe of þi seruauntis, of many heþene men; which I heeld togidir in my bosum. Whiche þin enemyes Lord diden schenschip fully; for þei dispisiden þe chaungynge of þi crist. Blessid be þe Lord wiþouten eende, be it doon, be it doon. *Psalmus .lxxxviij.* |Ps. 88:43–53|

|p| Lord þou art maad help to us; fro generacioun into generacioun. Bifore þat hillis weren maad eiþir þe erþe and world was foormed; fro þe world and into þe world þou art God. Turne þou not awey a man into lowȝnes; and þou seidist ȝe sones of men be conuertid. For a þousand ȝeer ben bifore þin iȝen; as ȝistirday which is passid and as kepinge in þe nyȝt. The ȝeeris of hem schulen be; þat ben had for nouȝt. Eerly passe he as an eerbe, eerly florische he and passe; in þe euentijd falle he doun, be he hard and wexe drie. For we han failed in þin ire, and we ben disturblid in þi strong veniaunce. Thou hast sett oure wickidnes in þi siȝt; oure world in þe liȝtnynge of þi cheer. For alle oure daies han failid; and we han failed

|fol. 116v|

in þin ire. Oure ȝeeris schulen biþenke, as an ireyne; þe daies of oure ȝeeris ben in þo seuenty ȝeeris. Forsoþe if eiȝte|ti|e[97] ȝeeris ben |in|[98] myȝty men; and þe more tyme of hem is traueile and sorewe. For myldenesse cam aboue; and we schulen be chastisid. Who knew þe power of þin ire; and durste noumbre þin ire for þi drede? Make þi riȝthond so knowun; and make[99] men lerned in herte bi wisdom.

|q| Lord, be þou conuertid sumdel; and be þou able to be preied on þi seruauntis. We weren fillid eerly wiþ þi mercy; we maden ful out ioie and we delitiden in alle oure daies. We weren glad for þe daies in whiche þou madist us meke; for þe ȝeeris in whiche we siȝen yuelis. Lord, biholde þou into þin seruauntis, and into þi werkis; and dresse þou þe sones of hem. And þe schynynge of oure Lord God be on us; and dresse þou þe werkis of oure hondis |o|n[100] us, and dresse þou þe werk[101] of oure hondis. *Psalmus .lxxxx.* |Ps. 89:1–17| It is good to knouleche to þe Lord; and to synge to þi name, þou hiȝeste. To

schewe eerly þi mercy; and þi truþe bi ny3t. In a sautree of ten coordis; wiþ song in harpe. For þou Lord hast delitid me in þi makyng; and I schal make ful out ioie in þe werkis of þin hondis. Lord þi werkis ben magnyfied greetly; þi þou3tis ben maad ful depe.

|r| An vnwijs man schal not knowe; and a fool schal not vndirstonde þese þingis. Whanne synners comen forþ as hey; and alle þei apperiden þat worchen wickidnes. That þei perische into þe world |of world|;[102] forsoþe þou Lord art þe hi3este wiþouten eende. For lo Lord þin enemyes, for lo þin enemyes schulen perische; and alle schulen be scaterid þat worchen wickidnes. *Psalmus .lxxxxj.* |Ps. 91:2–10| God is Lord of veniaunces; God of veniaunces

|fol. 117r|

dide freely. Be þou enhaunsid þat deemest þe erþe; 3elde þou 3eldynge to proude men. Lord how longe synners; |Lord|[103] how longe schulen synners haue glorie? Thei schulen telle out and schulen speke wickidnes; alle men schulen speke þat worchen vnri3tfulnes. Lord þei han maad low3 þi peple; and þei han dissesid þin eritage. Thei killiden a widowe and a comelyng; and þei han slayn fadirles children and modirles. And þei seiden þe Lord schal not se; and God of Iacob schal not vndirstonde. 3e vnwise men in þe peple vndirstonde; and 3e foolis lerne sumtyme. Schal not he heere þat plauntide þe eere; eiþir biholdiþ not he þat made þe i3e?" *Psalmus .lxxxxiij.* |Ps. 93:1–9|

Tulane University

APPENDIX

Psalm Extracts Assembled in the Huntington *Catena*

Section	Psalm	Verses	
a	77	1–2	
	48	2–3	
b	18	8–12	
c	1	1–6	(entire psalm)
d	2	10–13	
	81	3–4	
	4	5–6	
e	10	5–8	
	9	10–11	
f	9	12–13	
	32	1–3	
g	32	4–9	
	33	6–8	
h	33	9–15	
i	33	16–23	(verses 17 and 22 conjecturally emended)
j	92	1–5	(entire psalm)
	63	11	
k	65	1–2	
	68	33–37	
	71	11	
l	71	12–14	
	91	13–16	
m	14	1–5	(entire psalm)
	23	1–6	
n	23	7–10	(entire psalm, across m–n)
	13	2–3	(conclusion of verse 3 conjecturally emended)
	13	4–7?	(leaf missing; entire psalm?)
o	88	2–42?	(leaf missing; entire psalm?)
	88	43–53	(beginning of verse 43 conjecturally emended)
p	89	1–12	
q	89	13–17	(entire psalm, across p–q)
	91	2–6	
r	91	7–10	
	93	1–9	

NOTES

1. I wish to thank Edwin Craun, Ralph Hanna, Mary Robertson, and Elizabeth Schirmer for particular assistance. I am also pleased to thank the Bodleian Library, Oxford, the British Library, London, the Houghton Library, Harvard University, and the Huntington Library, San Marino, California, for permission to examine, quote from, and reproduce manuscript materials in their care.

2. *Doctor Evangelicus super omnes evangelistas*, as Wyclif was known in Bohemia. See Anne Hudson and Anthony Kenny, *Oxford Dictionary of National Biography*, online edition, http://www.oxforddnb.com.libproxy.tulane.edu:2048/view/article/30122.

3. See Anne Hudson, *The Premature Reformation: Wycliffite Texts and Lollard History* (Oxford: Clarendon Press, 1988), 249–259. Hudson notes that "Obscurity surrounds the use to which the *Glossed Gospels* were to be put" (256) but also suggests that they were assembled as "a library of materials" designed to foster Wycliffism (258).

4. General Prologue to the Wycliffite Bible (hereafter GP), chap. 5. See Josiah Forshall and Frederic Madden, eds., *The Holy Bible, Containing the Old and New Testaments, with the Apocryphal Books, in the Earliest English Versions, Made from the Latin Vulgate by John Wycliffe and His Followers* (Oxford: Oxford University Press, 1850), I:15 (hereafter WB).

5. For example, during his interrogation by Archbishop Arundel, William Thorpe cites three Old Testament texts together (Deut. 4:15–19, Ps. 96:7, and Ws. 14:12–15:19) in connection with the debate over images. See Anne Hudson, ed., *Two Wycliffite Texts: The Sermon of William Taylor 1406; The Testimony of William Thorpe 1407*, EETS 301 (Oxford: Oxford University Press, 1993), 57.

6. See "Types in Scripture," *The Catholic Encyclopedia* (New York: Robert Appleton, 1912), XV:107–108.

7. Indeed, Wyclif's followers insist that to confuse the literal and figurative senses is morally dangerous, for as Paul notes, "the lettre sleeth" (2 Cor. 3:6): "Whanne a thing which is seid figuratifly |in Scripture| is taken so as if it be seid properly |literally|, me vndirstondith fleschly: and noon is clepid more couenably |fittingly| the deth of the soule, than whanne vndirstonding |reason|, that passith beestis, is maad soget to the fleisch in suynge the lettre" (GP chap. 12 |WB I:44|). See also Kantik Ghosh, *The Wycliffite Heresy: Authority and the Interpretation of Texts* (Cambridge, UK: Cambridge University Press, 2002), 25–32.

8. John Wyclif, *Tractatus de Ecclesia, Now First Edited from the Manuscripts, with Critical and Historical Notes*, ed. Johann Loserth (London: Trübner and Co., 1886), 9.

9. For detailed descriptions of HM 501, see Consuelo W. Dutschke, *Guide to Medieval and Renaissance Manuscripts in the Huntington Library* (San Marino, CA:

126

Huntington Library, 1989), I:235–237; and Ralph Hanna, A *Handlist of Manuscripts Containing Middle English Prose in the Henry E. Huntington Library* (Cambridge, UK: D. S. Brewer, 1984), 25–30.

10. For a discussion of differences in construction between Scripture-based and scholastic sermons, see Woodburn O. Ross, ed., *Middle English Sermons, Edited from British Museum MS Royal 18 B.xxiii*, EETS o.s. 209 (London: Oxford University Press, 1940), xliii–lv. For Lollard concepts of preaching and the movement's disapproval of fraternal sermons, see Anne Hudson, *Premature Reformation*, 268–273.

11. <Here> *ben foure ful notable prologis <vpon þe sauter>. þe firste and þe secunde ben Ieromys <and þe þrid>de is Richard Hampollis wiþ þe fourþe* (in red, fol. 21v). All four prologues are printed in more expansive form at WB I:37–40 and II:736–738, although I quote from the manuscript's texts in this essay. Readings in angle brackets are lost due to extensive damp and are reconstructed from WB.

12. See Edwin Craun, *Ethics and Power in Medieval English Reformist Writing* (Cambridge, UK: Cambridge University Press, 2010).

13. Other vernacular translations of the Psalms predate the Wycliffite translation of the Bible. For a survey of these, with bibliography, see James H. Morey, *Book and Verse: A Guide to Middle English Biblical Literature* (Urbana: University of Illinois Press, 2000), 172–196. See also Margaret Deanesly, *The Lollard Bible and Other Medieval Biblical Versions* (Cambridge, UK: Cambridge University Press, 1920), 169–171 and 221–222.

14. Anne Hudson, ed., *English Wycliffite Sermons, Volume Three* (Oxford: Clarendon Press, 1990), 99.

15. On these revisions, many of which consist in extensive interpolations, see Dorothy Everett, "The Middle English Prose Psalter of Richard Rolle of Hampole. III. Manuscripts of Rolle's Psalter Containing Lollard Interpolations in the Commentary," *Modern Language Review* 18 (1923): 381–393; Michael P. Kuczynski, "Rolle among the Reformers: Orthodoxy and Heterodoxy in Wycliffite Copies of Richard Rolle's *English Psalter*," in *Mysticism and Spirituality in Medieval England*, ed. William F. Pollard and Robert Boenig (Woodbridge, UK: Boydell & Brewer, 1997), 177–202; and Kevin Gustafson, "Richard Rolle's *English Psalter* and the Making of a Lollard Text," *Viator* 33 (2002): 294–309.

16. For the primary Lombardian source, see *Commentarium in Psalmos, Patrologia Latina* 191: 61–1302 (hereafter PL).

17. Quoted from Harvard MS Richardson 36, fol. 5ra–b, a copy of the first of three Lollard revisions of Rolle. For a bibliographic map of the Lollard versions, which has in some respects been superseded, see Valerie M. Lagorio and Michael G. Sargent, "Richard Rolle," in *A Manual of the Writings in Middle English, 1050–1500* (New Haven: Connecticut Academy of the Arts and Sciences, 1993), IX:3055–3056 and 3415–3417.

18. Cf. H. R. Bramley, ed., *The Psalter or Psalms of David and Certain Canticles, with a*

Translation and Exposition in English by Richard Rolle of Hampole (Oxford: Clarendon Press, 1884), 11.

19. On the pronounced homiletic rather than theological character of the work, see Nicholas Watson, *Richard Rolle and the Invention of Authority* (Cambridge, UK: Cambridge University Press, 1991), 246–249.

20. Cf. Bramley, *Psalter*, 4; and PL 191:57.

21. On the history and medieval uses of these seven psalms (Pss. 6, 31, 37, 50, 101, 129, and 142 in the Vulgate numbering), see Michael S. Driscoll, "The Seven Penitential Psalms: Their Designation and Usage from the Middle Ages Onwards," *Ecclesia Orans* 17 (2000):153–201. Cassiodorus (*ca.* 485–580) was the first to name and list the subset, at the end of his commentary on Psalm 50 in *Expositio Psalmorum*, ed. M. Adraien, Corpus Christianorum Series Latina 97 (Turnhout, Belgium: Brepols, 1958), 469, although the special penitential character of certain psalms was already acknowledged by Origen (*ca.* 185–254) and Augustine (354–430).

22. On Davidic exemplarism in the Middle Ages, see Michael P. Kuczynski, *Prophetic Song: The Psalms as Moral Discourse in Late Medieval England* (Philadelphia: University of Pennsylvania Press, 1995).

23. See Anne Hudson, "A Lollard Sect Vocabulary?", in *Lollards and Their Books* (London: Hambledon Press, 1985), 165–180.

24. See "Psalms," *The Catholic Encyclopedia* (New York: Robert Appleton, 1911), XII:533–543.

25. GP, chap. 11 (WB 1:38–39).

26. I am currently completing an edition of this commentary, fragments of which survive in twenty-three other Wycliffite psalters.

27. On the history of Augustine's text, see "*Enarrationes in Psalmos,*" *Augustine through the Ages: An Encyclopedia*, ed. Allan D. Fitzgerald (Grand Rapids, MI: William B. Eerdmans, 1999), 290–296. Parts of the Augustinian material appear independently of the Lyran glosses in a single Wycliffite psalter manuscript, Trinity College, Dublin MS 70, fols. 29r–33v.

28. Lilian M. Swinburn, ed., *The Lanterne of Li3t*, EETS o.s. 151 (London: Kegan Paul, Trench, Trübner & Co., 1917), 62.

29. Deanesly, *Lollard Bible*, 446.

30. Ibid., 446.

31. PL 191:58.

32. See OED *catena*, a.; "*catenae,*" *The Catholic Encyclopedia* (New York: Robert Appleton, 1908), III:434–435; John O. Ward, "From Marginal Gloss to *Catena* Commentary: The Eleventh-Century Origins of a Rhetorical Teaching Tradition in the Medieval West," *Parergon* 13 (1996): 109–120; and N. G. Wilson, "A Chapter in the History of Scholia," *Classical Quarterly* 17 (1967): 244–256. The centrality of the scriptural text itself to the form and function of *catenae* is emphasized in Maurice Geerard and Jacques Noret, *Clavis patrum graecorum* (Turnhout, Belgium:

Brepols, 2003).

33. Merritt Y. Hughes, ed., *John Milton: Complete Poems and Major Prose* (New York: Odyssey Press, 1957), 740.

34. Nicephorus, *Catena in Octateuch. et libros Reg.* (Leipzig, 1772), which draws on and coordinates fifty-one distinct works of exegesis.

35. Hudson, *Premature Reformation*, 252–253. For a discussion of Aquinas's achievement in the *Catena aurea*, see James A. Weisheipl, *Friar Thomas D'Aquino : His Life, Thought, and Works, with Corrigenda and Addenda* (Washington, DC: Catholic University of America Press, 1983), 163–164 and 371. In the nineteenth century, the work was praised for its "masterly and architectonic skill," in contrast with other glosses, which were "partial and capricious"—that is, its form impressed as much as its content. See John Henry Newman, ed. and trans., *Commentary on the Four Gospels by S. Thomas Aquinas* (Oxford: Oxford University Press, 1864), I:iii–iv.

36. See Marcia L. Colish, *Peter Lombard* (Leiden, Holland: E. J. Brill, 1994), I:158–188, for a comprehensive discussion of the Lombard's sources and innovations.

37. Decimius Magnus Ausonius, *Ausonius*, ed. and trans. Hugh G. Evelyn White (New York: G. P. Putnam's Sons, 1921), I:370, 374.

38. "Proba, Faltonia Betitia," *Oxford Classical Dictionary*, 3rd ed., ed. Simon Hornblower and Antony Spawforth (Oxford: Oxford University Press, 1999), 1249; E. R. Curtius, *European Literature and the Latin Middle Ages*, trans. Willard R. Trask (Princeton, NJ: Princeton University Press, 1953), 459; and Filippo Ermini, *Il centone di Proba e la poesia centonaria latina* (Rome: Loescher, 1909).

39. J. R. H. Moorman, *Sources for the Life of S. Francis of Assisi* (Manchester, UK: Manchester University Press, 1940), 38.

40. Jean Leclercq, *The Love of Learning and the Desire for God: A Study of Monastic Culture*, trans. Catharine Misrahi (New York: Fordham University Press, 1961), 95–96.

41. Ibid., 91.

42. *Prophetae per excellentiam cum dicitur Propheta sine adjectione proprii nominis intelligitur David, ut cum dicitur Apostolus intelligitur Paulus, et Urbs Roma* (PL 191:59).

43. All biblical translations are from the Douay-Rheims version of the Latin Vulgate.

44. On the Romans *catena*, see Joseph A. Fitzmyer, *Romans: A New Translation with Introduction and Commentary* (New York: Doubleday, 1993), 333–334. Fitzmyer notes that the concatenating strategy itself is part of the text's meaning, since it implies "that all parts of a human being are involved in sin in God's sight and that the whole human being has participated in evil" (334). On the Hebrews *catena*, see Kenneth L. Schenck, "A Celebration of the Enthroned Son: The *Catena* of Hebrews 1," *Journal of Biblical Literature* 120 (2001): 469–485. The Psalms must have been an especially attractive biblical text for catenists due to their highly

repetitive verbal and rhetorical patterns. See Beth LaNeel Tanner, *The Book of Psalms through the Lens of Intertextuality* (New York: Peter Lang, 2001).

45. Hudson, *Two Wycliffite Texts*, 51.

46. Ibid., 72. Here the "scharpe auctoritees" include not only "holy writt" but also "þe sentence of doctours," that is, exegetical writings.

47. For summary descriptions of Laud Misc. 182, see WB I, no. 56 and Mary Dove, *The First English Bible: The Text and Context of the Wycliffite Versions* (Cambridge, UK: Cambridge University Press, 2007), 301, although Dove does not list the Old Testament extracts in the book.

48. In the manuscript, the glosses are keyed to their lemmata by a series of tie-marks like those that appear in MS Bodley 554, which seem to be derived from two of Grosseteste's concordantial signs. See S. H. Thomson, "Grosseteste's Concordantial Signs," *Medievalia et Humanistica* 9 (1955): 39–53.

49. *Psalmus .vj.* MS vj Psalmus (transposed).

50. See *"catena"* in Bayerischen Akademie der Wissenschaften, *Mittellateinisches Wörterbuch*, II. Band. Lieferung 3 (13. Lieferung des Gesamtwerkes), casalis-cereus (Munich: C. H. Beck, 1970), 369–370; and R. E. Latham, *Dictionary of Medieval Latin from British Sources*, Fascicule II C (London: Oxford University Press, 1981), 300. Latham does, interestingly, list under the verb *"catenare"* a passage from the anti-Lollard Thomas Netter (*ca.* 1375–1430) describing how Wyclif has "connected or linked together error to error" (*"sicut jam Witcleff facit, consequenter catenans errorem errori,"* Latham, *Dictionary of Medieval Latin*, 300).

51. Weisheipl, *Friar Thomas D'Aquino*, 171. The title *Catena aurea* is a Renaissance editor's invention.

52. See Hanna, *Handlist*, 28, item 12.

53. For the Latin text of pseudo-Jerome, see PL 115, 1449–1457; and Christopher Wordsworth, ed., *Horae Eboracenses, the Prymer or Hours of the Blessed Virgin Mary according to the Use of the Illustrious Church of York, with Other Devotions as They Were Used by the Lay-Folk in the Northern Province in the XVth and XVIth Centuries* (Durham, UK: Surtees Society, 1920), 116–122. (The author of pseudo-Jerome was actually Prudentius Trecensis, bishop of Troy, d. 861.) There is no complete edition of the Middle English version, although some brief extracts appear in Anna C. Paues, ed., *A Fourteenth Century English Biblical Version* (Cambridge, UK: Cambridge University Press, 1904), lxiii–lxiv. For pseudo-Bernard, see William H. Black, ed., *A Paraphrase of the Seven Penitential Psalms in English Verse, supposed to have been written by Thomas Brampton, S.T.P. in the year 1414, together with a Legendary Psalter of Saint Bernard, in Latin and in English Verse* (London: Percy Society, 1842). For Bede's Psalter, see Gerald M. Browne, ed., *Collectio psalterii Bedae Venerabili adscripta* (Leipzig, Germany: Saur, 2001); and Gerald M. Browne, trans., *The Abbreviated Psalter of the Venerable Bede* (Grand Rapids, MI: William B. Eerdmans, 2002).

54. See Morey, *Book and Verse*, 186–189.

55. Black, *Paraphrase of the Seven Penitential Psalms*, 51.

56. For advice on using certain psalms *contra inimicos* and *contra aduersarios et maliciosos* in an important fourteenth-century miscellany, see Michael P. Kuczynski, "An 'Electric Stream': The Religious Contents," in *Studies in the Harley Manuscript: The Scribes, Contents, and Social Contexts of British Library MS Harley 2253*, ed. Susanna Fein (Kalamazoo: Western Michigan University Press, 2000), 149.

57. PL 115:1449–1450.

58. Elizabeth Schirmer makes this suggestion in Schirmer, "Canon Wars and Outlier Manuscripts: Gospel Harmony in the Lollard Controversy," *Huntington Library Quarterly* 73 (2010):1-36.

59. The lowercase letters in square brackets refer to subsections of the *catena* in my edited text, above.

60. His full analogy is of the Psalter as a great house (*magna domus*) consisting of many small rooms, each with its own key. See Jerome, *Tractatus in Librum Psalmorum*, ed. Germanus Morin, Corpus Christianorum Series Latina 78 (Turnhout, Belgium: Brepols, 1958), 3.

61. Bramley, *Psalter*, 5. See also PL 191:61.

62. All of the Lyran glosses quoted in this paragraph appear in MS Bodley 554, fol. 1r. Text given in italics in these quotations is underlined in red in the manuscript.

63. MS Bodley 554, fol. 1r. Cf. Lyra's original: Quoniam nouit etc. *Id est, processum eorum per viam presentis vite nouit noticia approbationis, viam autem peruersorum nouit noticia reprobationis.* Nicholas of Lyra, *Postilla venerabilis fratris Nicolai de Lyra super Psalterium* (Strasbourg, 1492), 9, first column, section n.

64. The ultimate source for this type in patristic literature is Gregory the Great's (*ca.* 540–604) analysis of the figure of Job, whom at one point Gregory equates with Christ himself, "this very Poor Man of whom it is said by Paul, *Though He was rich, yet for our sakes He became poor* |2 Cor. 8:9|." See Gregory the Great, *Morals on the Book of Job, in Three Volumes*, trans. James Bliss (London: Walter Smith, 1883), 1:338.

65. See Hudson, "A Lollard Sect Vocabulary?" 169–171.

66. Hudson, "A Lollard Sect Vocabulary?" 171.

67. "Wherfore Poul seiþ þus, 'Þe Lord haþ ordeyned þat þei þat prechen þe gospel schullen lyue of þe gospel.' . . . for certis, in whateuere dignite or ordre þat ony preest is, if he conforme him not to sue Crist and hise apostlis in wilful pouerte and in oþer heuenli vertues, and specialli in trewe prechinge of Goddis word þou₃ suche oon be nempned a preest, he is no but a prest in name.'" Hudson, *Two Wycliffite Texts*, 69.

68. See ibid., 64. Also relevant here is the Lollard point that Christ chose "pore symple & ydiotis |uneducated people| to his prechyng," as opposed to the Antichrist, who chooses "sturdi & duble |deceitful| men & hauyng þe wisedom of þis world, for to preche his falshede." Swinburn, *Lanterne of Li₃t*, 6.

69. St. Augustine of Hippo, *Expositions of the Psalms, 1–32*, trans. Maria Boulding

and ed. John E. Rotelle (Hyde Park, NY: New City Press, 2000), 146 (on Ps. 9:10).
70. St. Augustine of Hippo, *Expositions of the Psalms*, 33-50, trans. Maria Boulding and ed. John E. Rotelle (Hyde Park, NY: New City Press, 2000), 32 (on Ps. 33:7).
71. Augustine, *Expositions of the Psalms*, 1-32, 167 (on Ps. 10:5).
72. Larry D. Benson, ed., *The Riverside Chaucer*, 3rd ed. (Boston: Houghton Mifflin, 1987), 88. See Derek Pearsall, "Poverty and Poor People in *Piers Plowman*," in *Medieval English Studies Presented to George Kane* (Woodbridge, UK: D. S. Brewer, 1988), 167–185. "The extensive medieval literature of poverty," Pearsall concludes, "is marked by its pursuit of philosophical and ideological issues: it rarely touches on the lives of poor people, except in a conventional way for purposes of demonstration" (168).
73. MS Bodley 554, fol. 1r–v.
74. Augustine, *Exposition of the Psalms*, 1–32, 179–180 (on Ps. 14:45).
75. On the importance of Lollard anxieties about God's wrath, in connection with a fragment of Rolle's *English Psalter*, see Michael P. Kuczynski, "An Extract from Richard Rolle's *English Psalter* in Beinecke Library Yale University MS 360," *Yale Library Gazette* 71 (1996):13–21.
76. Augustine, *Exposition of the Psalms*, 73–98, trans. Maria Boulding and ed. John E. Rotelle (Hyde Park, NY: New City Press, 2002), 294 (on Ps. 88:39–46).
77. Hanna, *Handlist*, 27, item 9, does not list the Latin texts of Psalms 2 and 3. Thirty-four folios from the head of HM 501, containing a fragment from GP and excerpts from WB Genesis and Exodus, are now at Keio University Library, Tokyo, Japan. I am grateful to Ralph Hanna for this information.
78. *comaundement*: MS comaundementis.
79. *and vnfeiþful man*: MS omitted.
80. *louede*: MS souede.
81. *refuyt*: WB refuyt, eþer help.
82. *þe*: MS omitted.
83. *and*: WB omitted.
84. *þou*: MS omitted.
85. *eeren*: MS iȝen.
86. *But þe cheer . . . hem from erþe|* MS entire verse omitted.
87. *alle*: MS omitted.
88. *The deeþ of synneris . . . men schulen trespasse*: MS entire verse omitted.
89. *Lord, þe floodis . . . of manye watris*: MS two verses omitted.
90. *lxxxxij*: MS lxxxij.
91. *a pore man*: MS a pore man fro þe myȝty.
92. *cleene in herte*: MS in cleene herte.
93. *hem is an open sepulcre . . . iȝen. Psalmus xiij.*: MS passage of indeterminate length omitted due to loss of at least one leaf.
94. *[. . .]*: MS missing at least one leaf at this point; Pss. 13:4–7 and 88:2–42 possibly lacking.

95. *Thou has enhaunside þe riȝt-*: MS passage of indeterminate length omitted due to loss of at least one leaf.
96. *ordeynid*: MS ordeynd.
97. *eiȝtetie*: MS ei3tene.
98. *in*: MS omitted.
99. *make*: WB <u>make</u> (underlined).
100. *on*: MS in.
101. *werk*: MS werkis.
102. *of world*: MS omitted.
103. *Lord*: MS omitted.

WORKS CITED

1. MANUSCRIPTS
Cambridge, Massachusetts
     Houghton Library, Harvard University, MS Richardson 36
Dublin, Ireland
     Trinity College, Dublin, MS 70
London, England
     British Library, MS Harley 2253
Oxford, England
     Bodleian Library, MS Bodley 554
     Bodleian Library, MS Laud Misc. 182
San Marino, California
     Huntington Library, MS 501

2. PRIMARY WORKS
Augustine. *Expositions of the Psalms*. Trans. by Maria Boulding and ed. by John E.
     Rotelle. 5 volumes. Hyde Park, NY: New City Press, 2000-2002.
Benson, Larry D., ed. *The Riverside Chaucer*. 3rd ed. Boston: Houghton Mifflin,
     1987.
Black, William H., ed. *A Paraphrase of the Seven Penitential Psalms in English Verse,
     supposed to have been written by Thomas Brampton, S.T.P. in the year 1414, together
     with a Legendary Psalter of Saint Bernard, in Latin and in English Verse*. London:
     Percy Society, 1842.
Bramley, H. R., ed. *The Psalter or Psalms of David and Certain Canticles, with a Translation
     and Exposition in English by Richard Rolle of Hampole*. Oxford: Clarendon Press,
     1884.
Browne, Gerald M., ed. *Collectio psalterii Bedae Venerabili adscripta*. Leipzig,
     Germany: Saur, 2001.
———, trans. *The Abbreviated Psalter of the Venerable Bede*. Grand Rapids, MI: William
     B. Eerdmans, 2002.

Fitzgerald, Allan D., ed. *Augustine through the Ages: An Encyclopedia*. Grand Rapids, MI: William B. Eerdmans, 1999.

Fitzmyer, Joseph A. *Romans: A New Translation with Introduction and Commentary*. New York: Doubleday, 1993.

Forshall, Josiah and Frederic Madden, eds. *The Holy Bible, Containing the Old and New Testaments, with the Apocryphal Books, in the Earliest English Versions, Made from the Latin Vulgate by John Wycliffe and His Followers*. Oxford: Oxford University Press, 1850.

Gregory the Great. *Morals on the Book of Job, in Three Volumes*. Trans. by James Bliss. London: Walter Smith, 1883. Hudson, Anne, ed. *English Wycliffite Sermons, Volume Three*. Oxford: Clarendon Press, 1990.

———, ed. *Two Wycliffite Texts: The Sermon of William Taylor 1406; The Testimony of William Thorpe 1407*. EETS o.s. 301. Oxford: Oxford University Press, 1993. Hughes, Merritt Y., ed. *John Milton: Complete Poems and Major Prose*. New York: Odyssey Press, 1957.

Jerome. *Tractatus in Librum Psalmorum*. Ed. by Germanus Morin. Corpus Christianorum Series Latina 78. Turnhout, Belgium: Brepols, 1958.

Newman, John Henry, ed. and trans. *Commentary on the Four Gospels by S. Thomas Aquinas*. Oxford: Oxford University Press, 1864.

Nicephorus. *Catena in Octateuch et libros Regnorum*. Two volumes. Leipzig, 1772-1773.

Nicholas of Lyra. *Postilla super Totam Bibliam, Liber Psalmorum-Liber Ecclesiastes*. Strassbourg, 1492.

Paues, Anna C., ed. *A Fourteenth Century English Biblical Version*. Cambridge, UK: Cambridge University Press, 1904.

Ross, Woodburn O., ed. *Middle English Sermons, Edited from British Museum MS Royal 18 B.xxiii*. EETS o.s. 209. London: Oxford University Press, 1940.

Swinburn, Lilian M., ed. *The Lanterne of Liʒt*. EETS o.s. 151. London: Kegan Paul, Trench, Trübner and Co., 1917.

White, Hugh G. Evelyn, ed. and trans. *Ausonius, with an English Translation*. New York: G. P. Putnam's Sons, 1921.

Wordsworth, Christopher, ed. *Horae Eboracenses, the Prymer or Hours of the Blessed Virgin Mary according to the Use of the Illustrious Church of York, with Other Devotions as They Were Used by the Lay-Folk in the Northern Province in the XVth and XVIth Centuries*. Durham, UK: Surtees Society, 1920.

Wyclif, John. *Tractatus de Ecclesia, Now First Edited from the Manuscripts, with Critical and Historical Notes*. Ed. by Johann Loserth. London: Trübner and Co., 1886.

3. SECONDARY WORKS

Colish, Marcia L. *Peter Lombard*. Two volumes. Leiden, Holland: E. J. Brill, 1994.

Craun, Edwin. *Ethics and Power in Medieval English Reformist Writing*. Cambridge,UK:

Cambridge University Press, 2010.

Curtius, E. R. *European Literature and the Latin Middle Ages*. Trans. by Willard R. Trask. Princeton, NJ: Princeton University Press, 1953.

Deanesly, Margaret. *The Lollard Bible and Other Medieval Biblical Versions*. Cambridge, UK: Cambridge University Press, 1920.

Dove, Mary. *The First English Bible: The Text and Context of the Wycliffite Versions*. Cambridge, UK: Cambridge University Press, 2007.

Driscoll, Michael S. "The Seven Penitential Psalms: Their Designation and Usage from the Middle Ages Onwards." *Ecclesia Orans* 17 (2000):153–201.

Dutschke, Consuelo W. *Guide to Medieval and Renaissance Manuscripts in the Huntington Library*. Two volumes. San Marino, CA: Huntington Library, 1989.

Ermini, Filippo. *Il centone di Proba e la poesia centonaria latina*. Rome: Loescher, 1909.

Everett, Dorothy. "The Middle English Prose Psalter of Richard Rolle of Hampole. III. Manuscripts of Rolle's Psalter Containing Lollard Interpolations in the Commentary." *Modern Language Review* 18 (1923):381–393.

Geerard, Maurice and Jacques Noret. *Clavis patrum graecorum*. Turnhout, Belgium: Brepols, 2003.

Ghosh, Kantik. *The Wycliffite Heresy: Authority and the Interpretation of Texts*. Cambridge, UK: Cambridge University Press, 2002.

Gustafson, Kevin. "Richard Rolle's *English Psalter* and the Making of a Lollard Text." *Viator* 33 (2002): 294–309.

Hanna, Ralph. *A Handlist of Manuscripts Containing Middle English Prose in the Henry E. Huntington Library*. Cambridge, UK: D. S. Brewer, 1984.

Herbermann, Charles G. et al. *The Catholic Encyclopedia: An International Work of Reference on the Constitution, Doctrine, Discipline, and History of the Catholic Church*. 18 volumes. New York: Appleton, 1907-1950.

Hornblower, Simon and Antony Spawforth, eds. *The Oxford Classical Dictionary*. 3rd ed. rev. New York: Oxford University Press, 2003.

Hudson, Anne. *Lollards and Their Books*. London: Hambledon Press, 1985.

——. *The Premature Reformation: Wycliffite Texts and Lollard History*. Oxford:Clarendon Press, 1988.

Kuczynski, Michael P. "An 'Electric Stream': The Religious Contents." In *Studies in the Harley Manuscript: The Scribes, Contents, and Social Contexts of BritishLibrary MS Harley 2253*. Ed. by Susanna Fein. Kalamazoo: Western Michigan University Press, 2000. 123-161.

——. "An Extract from Richard Rolle's *English Psalter* in Beinecke Library Yale University MS 360." *Yale Library Gazette* 71 (1996):13–21.

——. *Prophetic Song: The Psalms as Moral Discourse in Late Medieval England*. Philadelphia: University of Pennsylvania Press, 1995.

———. "Rolle among the Reformers: Orthodoxy and Heterodoxy in Wycliffite Copies of Richard Rolle's *English Psalter*." In *Mysticism and Spirituality in Medieval England*. Ed. by William F. Pollard and Robert Boenig. Woodbridge, UK: Boydell and Brewer, 1997. 177–202.

Latham, R. E. *Dictionary of Medieval Latin from British Sources, Fascicule* II C. London: Oxford University Press, 1981.

Leclercq, Jean. *The Love of Learning and the Desire for God: A Study of Monastic Culture*. Trans. by Catharine Misrahi. New York: Fordham University Press, 1961.

Matthew, H. C. G. and Brian Harrison, eds. *Oxford Dictionary of National Biography*. Online edition. Oxford: Oxford University Press, 2004-. http://www.oxforddnb.com.

Moorman, J. R. H. *Sources for the Life of S. Francis of Assisi*. Manchester, UK: Manchester University Press, 1940.

Morey, James H. *Book and Verse: A Guide to Middle English Biblical Literature*. Urbana: University of Illinois Press, 2000.

Pearsall, Derek. "Poverty and Poor People in *Piers Plowman*." In *Medieval English Studies Presented to George Kane*. Ed. by Edward Donald Kennedy, et al. Woodbridge, UK: D. S. Brewer, 1988. 167-85.

Schenck, Kenneth L. "A Celebration of the Enthroned Son: The *Catena* of Hebrews 1." *Journal of Biblical Literature* 120 (2001): 469–485.

Schirmer, Elizabeth. "Canon Wars and Outlier Manuscripts: Gospel Harmony in the Lollard Controversy." *Huntington Library Quarterly* 73 (2010):1-36.

Tanner, Beth LaNeel. *The Book of Psalms through the Lens of Intertextuality*. New York: Peter Lang, 2001.

Thomson, S. H. "Grosseteste's Concordantial Signs." *Medievalia et Humanistica* 9 (1955):39–53.

Ward, John O. "From Marginal Gloss to *Catena* Commentary: The Eleventh-Century Origins of a Rhetorical Teaching Tradition in the Medieval West." *Parergon* 13 (1996):109–120.

Watson, Nicholas. *Richard Rolle and the Invention of Authority*. Cambridge, UK: Cambridge University Press, 1991.

Weisheipl, James A. *Friar Thomas D'Aquino : His Life, Thought, and Works, with Corrigenda and Addenda*. Washington, DC: Catholic University of America Press, 1983.

Wilson, N. G. "A Chapter in the History of Scholia." *Classical Quarterly* 17 (1967):244-256.

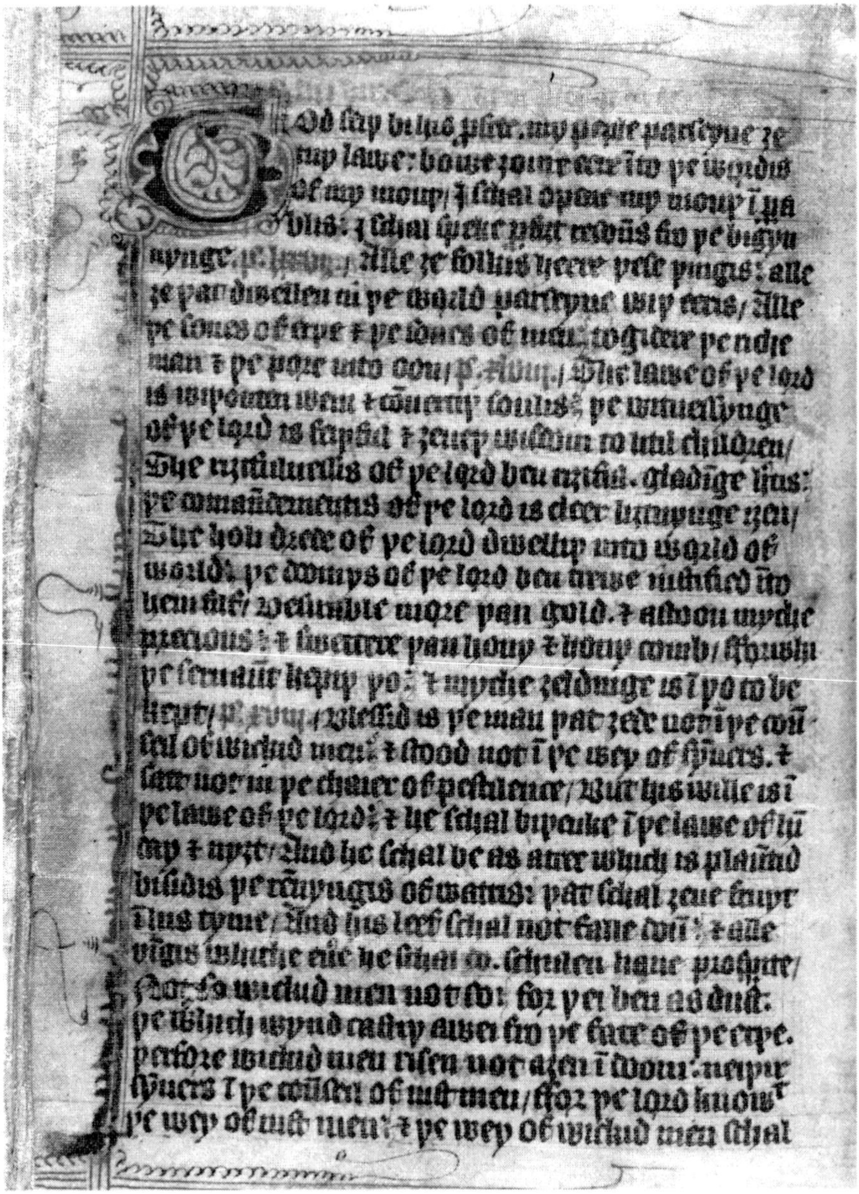

Figure 1: Beginning of the Lollard Psalms *catena*. Huntington Library MS HM 501, fol.

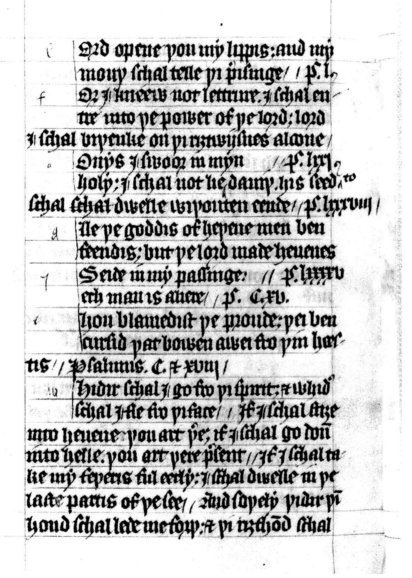

113v. By kind permission of the Huntington Library, San Marino, California.

Figure 2: Lollard Psalms excerpts. Bodleian Library MS Laud Misc. 182, fol. 311v. By kind permission of the Bodleian Library, Oxford.

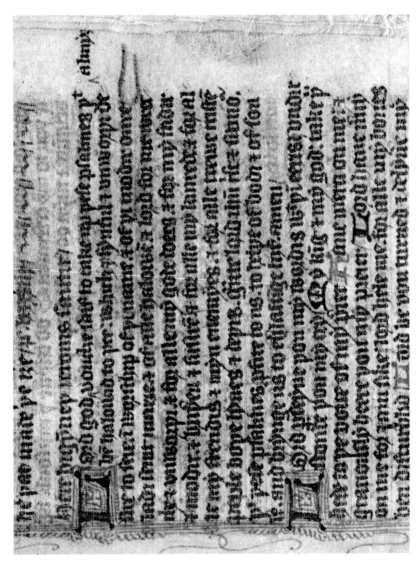

Figure 3: Ending of the Lollard Psalms *catena* and beginning of *Ieroms Sautir*. Huntington Library MS HM 501, fol. 117r. By kind permission of the Huntington Library, San Marino, California.

Fictions of Patronage:
The Romance Heroine as Sponsor in
John Metham's *Amoryus and Cleopes*

AMY N. VINES

Although several early studies of medieval patronage examine the system primarily from a financial standpoint,[1] many of the more recent scholars of medieval female sponsorship, such as June Hall McCash, Joan Ferrante, and Karen Jambeck, understand the patronage relationship as transcending economics.[2] These critics affirm a more varied concept of medieval women's intervention in the literary sphere—Joan Ferrante, for example, refers to their engagement as "urging" the productivity of male authors through "intellectual and emotional support"[3]—but confine their examples of such patronage to historical figures. This study furthers this understanding of extensive female patronage by considering evidence of this influence in literary texts such as John Metham's fifteenth-century romance *Amoryus and Cleopes*. In this article, I read the act of patronage not just as a system of financial exchange but more broadly as a system of social and intellectual support that may or may not include an element of financial remuneration.[4] Expanding the definition of patronage and considering multiple ways that women could learn the methods of cultural sponsorship expose women's dissemination of knowledge in the Middle Ages (such as medicinal recipes and chivalric and moral lessons) as culturally significant acts of largesse.

Medieval noblewomen learned how to commission textual compositions and translations, how to sponsor works of medieval art and architecture, and even learned about the social and spiritual benefits of establishing educational and religious foundations through examples set by family connections and the sociopolitical networks and textual communities in which they lived.[5] These networks of influence have been reconstructed to a certain extent through testamentary evidence and other extraliterary documents. However, I suggest that women might also have learned methods of patronage from the books they read, specifically medieval romances.

In these texts, the female reader encounters an explicit demonstration of how a woman's intellectual as well as financial resources can be used to influence cultural and literary productions. Even though these literary characters are sponsoring *knights* rather than *books*, the process of influence outlined in these romances marks a wide range of women's knowledge as socially significant and worthy of dissemination. By reassessing medieval patronage, broadening its scope and its potential as an avenue for women to express their intellectual expertise, this article examines Metham's *Amoryus and Cleopes* to consider how female characters functioned as models of cultural, intellectual, and social patronage in medieval romances read and patronized by women. Focusing on literary representations of women's sponsorship enables us to perceive the extent of women's influence on the medieval patronage system, an influence often unacknowledged in historical and extraliterary sources.

In *Amoryus and Cleopes* (1449),[6] we see how thorough specialized knowledge—in this case, the knowledge of natural science—can function as the primary means by which a romance heroine engages in sponsorship. In Metham's romance, Cleopes actively conveys her particular body of knowledge and implicitly offers specific instructions to female readers on how that knowledge could be used to promote the chivalric careers of the men they may seek to sponsor. This romance integrates the more immediately tangible benefits of women's patronage with the primarily intellectual and social influence (that is, not supplying riches or weaponry) enacted through Cleopes's scientific discourse. For example, Cleopes will give Amoryus several small but important gifts to ensure his success in battle. Although these items—gleaned from the medieval herbals and lapidaries on which her knowledge is based—do not compare to the lavish wealth and war gear the female patrons give their knights in other late-medieval romances such as *Partonope of Blois* and *Sir Launfal*, *Amoryus and Cleopes* demonstrates how female knowledge has practical applications in the life of a sponsored knight and in the lives of the readers of the romance as well.

Metham's text illustrates an aspect of female patronage not often explored in medieval romances where women are depicted as the arbiters of cultural influence. The success of the relationship between the lady and her knight, as well as his chivalric development, is predicated on Cleopes's proaction and the deployment of her scientific expertise; yet there is also a collaborative valence to their interactions, particularly toward the end of the romance, when the more traditional chivalric narrative transforms into a tale of religious conversion. At this point, Cleopes learns along with Amoryus about Christian truth from a hermit who performs a resurrection miracle. Despite this newfound religion, however, Cleopes's intellectual influence remains valid even after the conversion takes place; indeed, her new status as a Christian makes her patronage much more potent and persuasive for the audience of Metham's romance.

This element of collaborative as well as individual learning and influence is overtly mirrored by Metham's actual patrons, Miles and Katherine Stapleton. As I discuss at the end of this essay, Amoryus and Cleopes themselves are but thinly veiled characterizations of Miles and Katherine. Although we might read Katherine's influence over Metham and his romance as diminished because she acts in tandem with her husband,[7] the individual praise and attention Metham affords Katherine, both within the romance and in other texts, indicates that he considers her to be an influential patron in her own right.

Amoryus and Cleopes survives in a single manuscript located in the Princeton University Library: MS Garrett 141. At the conclusion to his text, Metham reveals to his audience the reason he began the business of "ryming": "To comforte them that schuld falle in hevynes / For tyme onocupyid, qwan folk have lytyl to do, / On haly dayis to rede, me thynk yt best so" (2210–2212). Metham's unorthodox suggestion, that the "tyme onocupyid" on holy days depresses people, could give many devout readers pause. Even more boldly, Metham suggests that the cure for this dismal lag time can be found in classically inspired romances such as *Amoryus and Cleopes* rather than a strictly devotional text or the Bible.[8] But for all the entertainment value contained in *Amoryus and Cleopes*, it is not a traditional romance either. The text draws heavily on scientific treatises and religious material in addition to the chivalric episodes.[9] Thus Metham's suggestion for holy day reading, placed strategically after the audience has read his unique romance, is not as inappropriate as it first appears; the romance is designed both to entertain and to provide spiritual inspiration for the reader.[10] Furthermore, this romance and the other texts owned by and dedicated to the Stapletons offer insight into fifteenth-century reading tastes, particularly those of a female patron.

This romance provides a steady trajectory of the status of scientific knowledge and chivalric activities that moves from their alliance with pagan religion and culture to a compatibility with Christianity. This article in part investigates this transformation of these activities from pagan to Christian—or their "conversion." I also consider the work's manuscript context, which situates the romance among other scientific texts written by Metham for his patrons.[11] These works suggest that the scientific portions of Metham's romance were not simply tedious digressions into scholarly learning, but that Katherine and Miles valued these parts of the romance, for this scientific material is reflected in the rest of the works in their manuscript.

In *Amoryus and Cleopes*, the audience witnesses not only a resurrection narrative and a moralized ending but also a Christian displacement of an older pagan belief system. In spite of this displacement, Metham maintains a continuity in his representation of two aspects of secularity in the romance: scientific treatises and feats of chivalry. These narratives are redefined or "converted" along with the characters in *Amoryus and Cleopes*. The pagans' conversion breaks the connection between classical paganism and science (an association often made in the Middle Ages) and forges a link between Christianity, scientific knowledge, and worldly pastimes. Whereas R. M. Lumiansky claims that "clearly, [the author's] chief interest is religious,"[12] Metham asserts the possibility of coexistence between science and salvation.

Most important, the character of Cleopes is the site at which natural science, the cultivation of knighthood, and newfound Christianity converge in Metham's romance. After the conversion, Cleopes's rehearsal of natural science, which enables Amoryus to succeed at worldly chivalric feats, is not condemned along with the pagans' idol worship. Rather, her secular knowledge and his chivalric victories are rendered as elements of a good Christian life; the actions and values of female patrons—both Cleopes and Katherine—remain consistent throughout Metham's romance. Thus the scientific information remains as valuable after the conversion as before, and valorous pursuits, those that bring the knight honor and respect, are not scorned by the newly baptized lovers and their fellow citizens. With *Amoryus and Cleopes*, Metham illustrates how Christians can enjoy the scientific and chivalric benefits of the world without jeopardizing their souls with pagan religion.

Cleopes's recitation of her natural scientific discourse, while at first glance a bit of a distraction or digression from the love narrative,[13] is part of a broader engagement with science both in the romance and in the manuscript in which it appears. It is clear from Metham's literary corpus that his patrons the Stapletons—and probably Metham himself—held a fervent interest in scientific texts.[14] Metham augments the more conventional elements often found in medieval romances, the chivalric episodes of jousting and dragon-slaying, with scientific treatises drawn almost entirely from classical sources.[15] This scientific information enhances Metham's scholarly image, provides narrative authority to his heroine, and functions as the foundation of her acts of patronage in the romance.

Unlike Metham's long and largely unprefaced digression into astronomical lecture (507–625), Cleopes's scientific monologue can be understood as the culmination of a comprehensive set of interventions in Amoryus's life. In her discussion of the relationship between Amoryus and his father, Jamie Fumo mentions Palamedon's "concern for his son's development, which mirrors the relationship between Chaucer's Knight and Squire in the *General Prologue*."[16] Indeed, there are significant parallels between these two sets of figures—Palamedon's knightly experience lies in stark contrast to Amoryus's frivolity and youthful rambunctiousness—but it is not clear that the father in Metham's romance is truly concerned with and supportive of his son's chivalric development. The question is, then: Who really teaches Amoryus?

Palamedon is doubtless an excellent source of knightly lessons; describing him as a true flower of chivalry, Metham notes that Palamedon's "prudent poyntys of were |skills of war| wer so dyvulgate |well known| / That in the chauncys of Mars he stode makeles |matchless| laureat" (90–91). Similarly, his son exhibits every bit of this chivalric potential. He is not only "manful and strong wythalle" (96) but "fulle of norture and curtesye; / And be hys wysdam, |he is| abyl an hole reme to gye" (97–98). Metham goes even further in his laudatory description of Amoryus, "of home |whom| this story in especyal / Makyth mencion" (94):

> And in hys governauns so demure and dyscrete was he,
> That iche creature he coude reverens be norturyd jentylnes
> Aftyr ther degré, that of pore and ryche yn the cyté.[17]
> The fame of hys manhod and of hys lovlynes
> Was in ryfe|.| (99–103)

Despite this chivalric promise—which extends beyond physical strength to include the subtle discernment and appropriate treatment of social rank—Metham is keen to remark that Amoryus was "makeles |matchless|, / Hys age consydyrryd" (103–105). Still a young man, Amoryus continues to act frivolously with his friends. As Palamedon, Amoryus, and their retinue ride to Albynest for the dedication of the newly constructed temple of Venus, one of Amoryus's young friends begins a discussion about love and fidelity. After elaborating on the perils of loving before one is certain of being requited, the friend shakes off the serious tone of their discussion and states, "lete yt pase, and syng now sum songe for this sesunne" (377). As these "fresch galauntys" (409) continue to sing their Maytime song, Palamedon notably "rode forth stylly, / Thynkyng alle but vanyté and foly" (407–408).

During the tournament, Palamedon reaches a similar conclusion when he sees the strange "kerchyf" that Amoryus wears, which is emblazoned with the same textual conceit Cleopes had pointed out to the young knight earlier: "'Qwat,' quod he, 'hath he yondyr? Yt ys sum nyseté.' / As he come nere—'Qwat have ye ther? qwat maner jape or foly?'" (871–872). When Amoryus explains that this badge will guarantee him victory, Palamedon dismissively and perhaps skeptically says "God yeve grace . . . yt be so" (877) and rides away. Finally, when Amoryus is faced with the challenge of fighting the dragon, Palamedon emphasizes the dangers inherent in the task but does not offer his son much encouragement:

> dare ye take this thyng?
> Be wele avysed, for yt ys no chyldys pleyng
> To fyght wyth sqwyche a devyl; for yf yowre wepyn brokyn
> Were in fyght, ye were but ded" (1193–1196).

Thus Palamedon displays concern not so much for his son's development as for his ability to maintain the seriousness and maturity necessary not only to succeed in but to survive knightly challenges such as jousting and dragon-slaying.[18]

Both of the young lovers in Metham's romance reflect their fathers' most notable attributes; while Amoryus demonstrates an undeveloped chivalric potential similar to Palamedon's, Cleopes mirrors the nurturing capacity of her father, Dydas. As co-ruler of Albynest, Dydas excels at negotiating the domestic and religious needs of the people, whereas Palamedon protects their interests in martial activities. Indeed, Metham describes Dydas as the people's patron; after a terrible earthquake strikes the region and destroys the temple of Venus,[19] "the cyteceynis for fere fled to Dydas palyse— / Bothe prest and seculerys, women and alle— / For socoure and comfort and to here hys avyse" (121–123). In response to their complaints about the loss of both the city's revenue and its main place of worship, Dydas reassures his people:

> Frendys, be noght abaschyd for this soden case.
> I schal a new tempyl reedyfye to owre goddes dere,
> And yt as rychely aray as the elde tempyl was.
> And eke as myche tresur as ye lest, more or las,
> I schal of my fre wyl restore that ye no los schal have. (135–139)

Channeling the people's fear and dismay into productive action, Dydas provides a rallying point for the citizens of Albynest after the devastating disaster. The people not only praise their benefactor and patron "on kneys . . . as thei aucte to do" (141–142), they begin the process of rebuilding the city, beginning with the construction of a "pyler [pillar] to Dydas Juno" (144).

Like her father, Cleopes stands as a beacon of inspiration to those around her. In addition to her beauty, she was "so benygne to yche creature, / That lusty yong knyghtys gret parte wold make / To breke huge sperys fersly for Cleopes sake" (152–153). Cleopes has the power to channel and instigate acts of chivalric prowess, an ability she readily applies to her relationship with Amoryus. Thus it is Cleopes and not Palamedon who takes control over Amoryus's knightly education; after meeting his lover, Amoryus rededicates himself to chivalry, setting aside his earlier childish songs and idle banter. The young man's successes in love, jousting, and dragon-slaying are based almost entirely on Cleopes's textual knowledge, patronage, and ability to communicate her knowledge, desires, and intentions even when she cannot speak to or influence her knight overtly.

The active role Cleopes plays in the romance is well illustrated in three scenes: the lovers' first meeting, Amoryus's tournament, and their meeting at the wall before the fight with the dragon. These acts of patronage are based almost exclusively on a woman's broad textual knowledge, which becomes a catalyst for male chivalric excellence; Cleopes recognizes the importance of texts as intellectual resources as well as physical objects that can function as a means of communication. At the dedication ritual for the magical sphere—the heart of the people's pagan religious practice—Amoryus and his coterie of "fresch yonge knytys" (732) are wandering through the temple of Venus when Amoryus's "eye began sodenly / To be set on one [i.e., Cleopes], abaschyd in maner of that soden chauns" (740–741). After this first glance, Amoryus feigns prayer in order to hide his love and circles the temple while forming a plan to approach Cleopes. His advance is hindered, however, because he is concerned about "the starerrys [those who stare]" (762) and his "fere of tungys [gossips]" (764).[20] When Cleopes notices his attention, she believes initially that he loves her only "in frendly maner" (771). Amoryus circles her several more times, and she begins to "consyder hys stature" and to "comend . . . hys semlynes" (782–783), until finally "lovys fyre had percyd here hert" (784). Although Amoryus and Cleopes feel the same for each other, Amoryus only comes close to look at her "in hope that he comfortyd schuld be yf he myght her behold" (787).

Rather than remaining satisfied with them merely gazing longingly at one another, however, Cleopes establishes a way "to make in love an entré" because "womannys wytt ys [ready] yn soden casys of necessyté" (796–797). She uses an illumination in her prayer book to convey her feelings, hoping only that "yf he wyse be, my menyng he schal perseyve in more and les" (811).[21] In this scene, the picture enables the lovers to pursue a relationship together rather than to love one another from afar. Indeed, without Cleopes's use of her book, the narrative could not continue.

Metham describes the textual illustration Cleopes uses to communicate with Amoryus in detail:

> an hynde lying as yt had bene on stonys,
> Holdyng an hert that bordyryd was wyth trw lovys,
> Beforn qwyche depeyntyd was a knyght knelyng,
> Holdyng in one hand an hart, in the odyr [a] ryng. (803–806)

While Stephen Page describes the subject of the illumination as a conventional medieval love allegory where the female deer is the object of a knight's hunt, the traditional dynamic of hunter and hunted is actually altered somewhat in Cleopes's picture. Here, the hind is reclining rather than fleeing from the hunter, and she holds the "hert," or her male counterpart, already in her grasp. Moreover, it is the hunter who kneels submissively before his prey and presents her with his h(e)art (a simultaneous symbol of his love and his masculinity) as well as a ring, to prove his faithfulness and devotion to the lady. Thus, in this configuration, the female holds the power, reserving the option either to accept or reject the knight's offer. It is to this picture that Cleopes gestures animatedly, "wyth her fynger demonstracion / Askauns |As if to say|, 'Construe now, for my menyng this ys the entencion'" (826–827). Cleopes creates a way for the lovers to communicate; it is very specifically through the medium of a text and the specific conceit it depicts (of which she has a thorough knowledge) that their relationship can progress.

While it is not uncommon to represent lovers using a book as a go-between to declare their feelings for one another in late-medieval literature,[22] it is significant that it is Cleopes who proactively solves the problem of their inability to convey their feelings. Cleopes's knowledge of her devotional text facilitates this communication and sets the tone for their future interactions. Indeed, her textual knowledge, whether devotional or scientific, enables Amoryus to succeed in his chivalric errands.

After Cleopes shows him the illustration in the temple, Amoryus adopts the mode of communication she has established and deploys it to his chivalric benefit. He commissions a painter to "steyn wyth colourys in a kerchyf of a qwarter brede |breadth| / The same conseyt that in Cleopes boke he sey" (858–859) and wears the kerchief openly at the tournament the following day. By replicating her textual sign, Amoryus may respond to Cleopes's expression of love and dedicate himself to her; in essence, Amoryus adopts Cleopes's ad hoc heraldic device, becoming her knight and accepting the patronage relationship she has begun to forge.

Not only does the badge serve to contact Cleopes, it proves to be the token that will ensure his success in the tournament, a talisman to protect the young knight from physical harm or social embarrassment. When Palamedon interrogates his son as to "qwat maner jape or foly" (872) he is wearing, Amoryus replies:

> this nyght for a specyal tokyn of vyctory,
> Venus apperyd, schewing this fygure to me,
> Byddyng me the symylytude to forme, wyth the qwyche wythowte fayl
> I schuld have vyctory in every tornyament and bateyl. (873–876)

Amoryus's explanation to his father, while cagey because of his reluctance to reveal the real reason for the badge, is not entirely untrue. By declaring that Venus motivated him to create the emblem, Amoryus appeals to his father's piety and gains his approval without denying the fact that Venus, the goddess of love, was the inspiration behind the drawing itself and Cleopes's choice of the picture as an intermediary for the lovers.[23]

The miniature Amoryus wears, inspired by Venus and chosen by Cleopes out of the many illustrations in her text, serves the knight well throughout the eight-day tournament. Because he fights only "for hys lady|'s| sake" (915), Amoryus is able to unseat over forty challengers and win the "laure of Marcyan vyctory" (1004). The subsequent fame and adulation Amoryus enjoys are due as much to Cleopes's industriousness as to his own physical prowess. The "lady sovereyn" (1008) for whose benefit Amoryus fights provides him with more than distant chivalric inspiration; Cleopes's assurance that his affection for her is requited (in the form of the textual symbol through which she establishes their patronage relationship) fosters a confidence in the knight that enables him to succeed in the tournament and to bolster his reputation.

After these initial interventions by the heroine in Amoryus's chivalric development, Metham indulges in a prolonged discussion of scientific information in *Amoryus and Cleopes*: the dragon lore that Cleopes offers her lover. As with the earlier astronomical information included to explain the workings of the magical sphere, the reader is taken through more than one hundred lines of little more than lists of dangerous serpents and the "remedyis of erbys and stonys" (1268) for their venom. In Book III, after Amoryus and Cleopes have fallen in love, word comes to Palamedon that a dragon is plaguing a neighboring city. When Amoryus tells Cleopes that he has accepted the challenge to fight the dragon, she immediately asks, "but qwat serpent ys yt? qwat do thei yt calle?" (1241). Before Amoryus can reply, however, Cleopes launches into almost ten stanzas of general information on the various venoms of serpents, such as "cokatrycys |basilisks|" (1251), the "draconia" (1253), and the "jaculus" (1259).

Cleopes even offers information on other poisonous animals that can counteract serpent venom: the "tode" and the "aramy |spider|" (1258). Her practical though obscure remedies are helpful to the reader as well as to Amoryus, for those who "fere thise chauncys to endure, / That in desertys must walke, thei purvey wysely |travel prepared|" (1266–1267). For example, if one should meet an "aspys |asp|" (1270), which can spit its venom forty feet (1279), they should drink "jacyntys and orygaun |hyacinth and wild marjoram|" (1284) to counteract it. For sea monsters, such as the "chyldrynys |water adder|," the "ydrys |hydra|," and the "ypotamys |a sea horse with teeth|" (1290), victims may be cured by applying the "egestyon of bolys |dung of bulls|" (1291).

At the conclusion to her long lecture on venomous creatures, Cleopes reaches the dragon that is "in specyal most foo / To alle lyvyng thing" (1292–1293), the serra cornuta. Finally, Amoryus interjects an answer to the question Cleopes posed fifty lines previously: "O! . . . lady, that same dragun yt ys / That I schuld fyght wyth" (1296–1297). Cleopes self-consciously reins in her lecturing and says apologetically, "I schal noght gab at alle, but telle yow the trwthys" (1299). At this point, Cleopes's intervention shifts from purely informational to practical, bestowing on the young knight the "charmys" (1300) he will need to defeat the dragon:

> In the begynnyng, loke that yowre harnes be sure for onythyng,
> And abovyn alle curyd wyth rede.
> And on sted of yowr helme, set a bugyl gapyng;[24]
> A bryght carbunkyl loke ther be set in the forhed.
> And in yowr hand, halde that ylke ryng
> Wyth the smaraged |emerald| that I here delyveryd yow this odyr day.
> Loke that the stone be toward hys eyn alwey. (1310–1316)

Furthermore, Amoryus must drink an elaborate concoction of wine, herbs, and ground stones or jewels because "alle venymmus thyng|s| fleyth fro her breth |their aroma|" (1329). Thus we witness in Cleopes's actions here not just a deployment of helpful knowledge but also the "Medea-like" giving of functional gifts.[25] Drawing on the extended natural-science lecture she has just given, Cleopes distills the encyclopedic information into a few key points that directly apply to the situation at hand. She further acts as Amoryus's patron when she presents him with the necessary tools to succeed in his chivalric endeavor.[26]

Hardin Craig suggests that Cleopes's knowledge of herbs and medicine "belonged to the education of a young lady in the Middle Ages and it is not surprising that it extended itself to all sorts of magic and sorcery."[27] However, Cleopes's text-based education, while probably gleaned from English translations of Latin, Greek, and Arabic sources rather than the originals, goes far beyond the practical, quotidian medical skills of the average young medieval woman.[28] Her knowledge of dragon taxonomy and the remedies for venomous bites is practical only because she is speaking with a knight who is about to enter combat with a hundred-foot serpent. Cleopes repeatedly refers to her sources as the more obscure encyclopedic texts of "clerkys" (1245 and 1295) rather than the household knowledge of the medicinal benefits of local herbs and minerals passed down from mother to daughter.

By the same token, Cleopes's expertise does not stray into the realm of sorcery any more than it remains in the domestic sphere. Metham is quite clear about his depiction of sorcery or "nygromancy" (471) in the character of Venus's secretary, the craftsman employed to create the sphere. Rather than the innocuous "erbys and stonys" (1268) that Cleopes uses, the secretary combines "gold, sylver and precyus stonys" (487) with a "multytyde of mennys bonys" (489). With this concoction, he conjures the "damnyd spyrytys" (491), seven hundred thousand to be exact, that will power the constantly moving sphere, performing an abomination to gain demonic power. Although Cleopes is a pagan throughout much of the romance, there is no indication that her scientific knowledge has its basis in the occult. As Metham does throughout the romance, Cleopes invokes authorities for her knowledge of dragons and natural remedies. At the beginning of her lecture, she notes that of this particular wisdom "clerkys wryte, of gret and smal, / |Their| namys and naturys, and qwerein they noy |do harm| be kend natural |according to their nature|" (1245–1246). Cleopes returns to these unnamed scholars when she discusses the most harmful dragon: "And serra cornuta yt ys namyd be clerkys" (1295).[29]

Although Cleopes's intervention is often rife with encyclopedic references to obscure scientific facts, the heroine plays a critical role as the patron and facilitator of Amoryus's chivalric career when she advises him on the correct way to slay the "serra cornuta." Amoryus accepts the challenge because if he succeeds, "of Amoryus men wryte schal / That he a dragon dyd sle be hys manhed in specyal" (1203–1204). While his father merely expresses the skeptical hope that the challenge will not result in the young knight's death, Cleopes offers a guarantee that Amoryus's specific desire for renown will be realized. If he follows her directions, she asserts:

> I dar sey savely |safely|
> That ye schal come hole and sound wyth victory;
> And aftyr qwyl ye lyve, be had the more in reputacion.
> Thys ys the fulle sentens of my counsel and conclusyon. (1335–1338)

After claiming victory over the dragon, Amoryus returns to Albynest, where Cleopes's predictions prove true:

> |The people| must nedys hym magnyfy wyth alle her myght,
> And hym excellent weryour and most hardy knyght
> Ever to name qwyl that her lyvys wold endure,
> To love hym beforn yche erthly creature. (1539–1542)

Thus it is not only by his manhood but also by Cleopes's expertise that Amoryus triumphs over the dragon. Indeed, she warns him, "but ye be reulyd be me, / Thow ye were as myghty as Sampson, ded ye schuld be" (1301–1302).

Ultimately, Amoryus's hopes for a distinctly masculine achievement and renown are somewhat compromised. When his story is written by Metham, the headnote to the romance in the Garrett manuscript gives credit where it is due: "Thys ys the story of a knyght, howe he dyd many wurthy dedys be the help of a lady, the qwyche taught hym to overcome a mervulus dragon" (Headnote, 1–2). Both Amoryus and the audience of Metham's romance witness the extent to which chivalric success depends upon the timely and thorough intervention of a female patron and lover.[30] Thus the scientific material in *Amoryus and Cleopes* provides more for Metham's narrative than a tinge of the exotic or erudite. The long treatises on astronomy and natural science, only loosely tied to the romance narrative, afford authorial credibility to both Metham and his heroine, allow Cleopes the opportunity to bring about genuine change in the life of her young knight, and function as a kind of reference book, a steady scientific background on which the religious conversion will take place.

Whatever *Amoryus and Cleopes* may lack in technical finesse, it makes up for in its wholly original Christian ending to a classical narrative: the story of Pyramus and Thisbe. This new ending emphasizes both religious conversion and the mitigation of paganism and is arguably the best example of Metham's considerable literary ambition in the romance. Throughout the Middle Ages the tale of Pyramus and Thisbe served as an Ovidian archetype of ill-fated love.[31] Metham appropriates the majority of the Ovidian version for *Amoryus and Cleopes*—including the lovers' communication through a fortuitous crack in the wall and the double suicide at the well—but ends his romance with the lovers' resurrection and conversion rather than their deaths.

Despite the inspiration Metham draws from his classical source, Book IV of *Amoryus and Cleopes* is wholly original, supplying a Christian ending to the tragic conclusion of Ovid's Pyramus and Thisbe tale. Ultimately, this new ending confirms that the scientific material which is so important to Metham's text and Cleopes's mode of patronage remains compatible with Christianity. Yet it also introduces a new aspect to Cleopes's participation in the romance; she not only sponsors Amoryus intellectually and tangibly, she also learns alongside her new love. They learn Christianity simultaneously rather than maintaining the strict model of patron and client, where the female sponsor teaches and directs the development of a young man. This collaborative learning, however, does not overshadow or replace the influence Cleopes has in Amoryus's life; rather, it mirrors the kind of equal and joint literary sponsorship of Katherine and Miles Stapleton, the actual patrons of Metham's romance.

As the lovers commit suicide because of a mistaken reading of the bloody handkerchief, a Christian hermit living nearby hears Cleopes's death cries. When the hermit continues praying, he has a divine revelation that he "was ment for the soulys savacion" (1826) of the people of the region. Upon seeing the dead lovers, the hermit prays to both Jesus and Mary that they "wold / Hem turne to lyfe yf thei krynsnyd wold be" (1837–1838). As he prays, the hermit lifts the lifeless bodies and declares, "yowre soulys into yowr bodyis / Entyr may ayen, fro the powere of the fend" (1864–1865). Amoryus and Cleopes return to life singing *"Salve . . . regina mater misericordye"* (1876), a famous medieval antiphon, for it was Mary who saved their souls from hell. They beg the hermit: "Make us Krystyn and teche us the wey ryght" (1892).

Following their baptism, the hermit leads Amoryus and Cleopes back to

Albynest and finds the people praying to the pagan sphere for the children's safe return. The hermit chastises the people for their idol worship and performs an exorcism on the temple, banishing the demons that were locked in the sphere. The people of Albynest witness the exorcism and, seeing the lovers' scars, which are "the tokynnys of ther woundys" (1969), they cry "Anone us krystyn make, wythowte delay, everychone" (2029). Before returning to his life in the wilderness, the hermit marries Amoryus and Cleopes in a Christian ceremony and establishes priests to remain in Albynest and teach the people the tenets of their new religion.[32]

Throughout the majority of the romance, the scientific information is introduced in conjunction with pagan ritual (with the temple sphere) or the chivalric acts, such as jousting and dragon-slaying, that Cleopes's patronage abets. Whereas the conversion narrative severs the connection between paganism and science by condemning one and leaving the other intact, it does not necessarily eradicate science altogether. Instead, Metham links science with Christianity, suggesting that the two categories can profitably coexist. Thus the focus of the heroine's sponsorship remains an important part of Amoryus's new identity as a fully matured Christian knight. Book IV of the romance illustrates Metham's "conversion" of science from the pagan to the Christian realm. Although the doctrine of Christianity officially supplants paganism, it does not undermine the validity of secular activities or the scientific information Metham has so conscientiously provided for his audience throughout the text. Both aspects of secularity in *Amoryus and Cleopes* are ultimately represented as part of a good Christian life.

The hermit's instruction of the two lovers just after their resurrection notably connects their previous religion with worldliness rather than the more egregious worship of false gods. Before the hermit agrees to baptize Amoryus and Cleopes, they must vow "to forsake alle the custum and governauns / Of paynymys secte" (1902–1903). Rather than imposing the Christian prohibition against idol worship—the first of the Ten Commandments and one of the primary elements of doctrinal instruction in the Middle Ages—the hermit begins an indictment of the transitory nature of the world.[33] During his lesson, the hermit reminds the lovers that "this world faryth as a feyre [fire], ever onstabyl" (1906) and if they "sofyr [i.e., endure] . . . thise transytory thingys" (1909), they will reap the "joys incomperabyl" (1908) of Heaven. "For Cryst seyth," the hermit continues, "that ful streyt [difficult] yt ys / A wordely wyse man to entyr hevyn blysse" (1910–1911).

Rather than insisting that Amoryus and Cleopes ask for forgiveness and perform penance for their suicides and idol worship, the hermit merely encourages them to turn their attention away from the impermanent world they now occupy and to concentrate instead on the everlasting world available to Christians after death. Too much of their attention, he suggests, has been turned toward worldly pursuits like tournaments, building temples, and slaying dragons.[34] These activities, conducted in large part to increase Amoryus's personal fame, seem to be the elements of pagan worldliness which must give way to Christianity. Their most extreme trespass, the one Metham counters explicitly with the hermit's teachings, is their total focus on the transitory world and personal advancement in it rather than the eternal one.

For the rest of the doctrinal information essential for newly converted Christians, Metham simply notes in passing that "of alle odyr thingys necessary, / Thys ermyght enformyd them fully in the feyth" (1912–1913). In this episode, the hermit appears to condemn all worldly activities as incompatible with Christianity. Soon after the hermit's lesson, however, Metham demonstrates that chivalric activities and worldly love—the very things Cleopes's patronage cultivates—are acceptable as long as they are part of a Christian culture.

In the final book of *Amoryus and Cleopes*, the misguided classical paganism the audience has pitied throughout the romance is demonized briefly and then eradicated and supplanted by Christianity. Once he has resurrected and converted Amoryus and Cleopes, the hermit does not expect that a love of a Christian God will supplant their love for one another. Rather, he expresses regret that two "so semly personys" should have committed suicide (1920) and inquires, "is [your] love . . . as gret now as yt was before" (1924)? Amoryus claims that his feelings for Cleopes have never been greater, and Cleopes answers that she is "wyth hert, wyll, and body, / Goddys *and* this knytys" (1930–1931; emphasis added). Although they have been converted to Christianity, they still share an earthly but virtuous affection for one another.

Prior to their deaths, the two lovers intended to spend the day in "lovely dalyauns . . . / Of that sqweete and plesaunt observauns" (1572–1574); their clandestine meeting is planned while they are fueled by the "flame of veneryan dysyre" (1549). Indeed, the sinful tryst is stopped just short of completion; Cleopes spills the "roseat blod of [her] pure maydynhede" (1764) when she stabs herself rather than when she consummates her relationship with Amoryus as she had intended. After their religious conversion, however, Cleopes still dedicates her soul and body to both Amoryus and Christ. In his Christian conclusion to the lovers' tribulations, Metham endeavors to reconcile *caritas*, or a love that transcends the secular world, with *cupiditas*, or passion.[35] Earthly love is not entirely supplanted by religious love; it is only placed within and legitimized by the structure of Christianity. Thus the pagan passion they almost indulged in the woods becomes a pious marriage sanctioned by God.

While the hermit strictly chastises the people of Albynest for their worship of demons, even ordaining "prestys and clerkys" (2074) to continue the Christian teachings after he is gone, the lessons he offers to the lovers—to avoid concentrating on earthly things—seem much more negotiable. Metham reports that Amoryus and Cleopes share a life of "long felycyté" (2087) in which

Amoryus rules Albynest while "ever encresyd in goode fame" (2080). Amoryus receives the personal renown he craved before his conversion not only through the acts of jousting and dragon-slaying—acts that were facilitated through his lover's patronage—but by governing his country "in joy, honour, and tranqwyllyté" (2081). The couple also have many "beuteus" children who "rychely / were beset" (2085–2086).

When their long lives are complete, Amoryus and Cleopes simultaneously "yeld . . . ther spyrytys to God" (2088) and are buried "in a tumbe of marbyl gray, / Platyd wyth ymagys of gold" (2089–2090). They are entombed with as much wealth and luxury as they enjoyed during their lives. Even if the hermit's lifestyle—living alone in the woods, "expendyng in prayere solytary" (2077)— is offered as a way to "eternal felycyté" (2079), Metham illustrates how good Christians may reap the benefits of both the worlds. Indeed, Metham's story never suggests that the hermit, a solitary, chaste, religious recluse, lives the better Christian life. Rather, the conclusion to the romance suggests that a Christian can enjoy both earthly pleasures and eternal ones and that a woman's patronage is fundamental to cultivating both. Thus Metham signals to his readers that natural science, chivalric pursuits, and Christianity are not mutually exclusive but are equally important to the lives of his patrons.

Amoryus and Cleopes is quite unique among late-medieval romances in that both the narrative and the manuscript in which it appears contain the unquestionable identification of the author's patrons: Lady Katherine and Sir Miles Stapleton. Since almost all Metham's works, both extant and lost, are dedicated to the Stapletons, we can assume that he spent a significant portion of his literary career under their patronage in Norfolk.[36] Although Metham's praise of each of his patrons is equally fulsome in *Amoryus and Cleopes*, the characteristics he emphasizes in each and the specificity with which he enumerates them vary significantly. Most critical treatments of *Amoryus and Cleopes*, including Craig's and Page's editions, consider Miles's and Katherine's patronage together. Indeed, both patrons are mentioned in the encomium section of the romance, and Metham's "Go now, lytyl boke" envoy asks the text to "Enterly me comende to my lord and mastyr eke, / And to hys ryght reverend lady" (2179–2180). As I discuss above, Amoryus's and Cleopes's simultaneous introduction to the tenets of Christianity corroborates the notion that women patrons may act and grow collaboratively while still maintaining their individual influence.

Despite the joint praise of the couple, Metham's praise of Sir Miles remains somewhat vague. Metham begins his tribute by "mervelyng gretly that noght nowe, as in eldtyme, / Men do noght wryte knyghtys dedys nowdyr in prose ner ryme" (2106–2107). He ascribes the dearth of knightly tales either to the "encresyng of vexacion" (2108) in late-medieval politics or to a lack of talent in medieval authors. Apparently, however, one modern English knight living in "este Ynglond" (2118) springs to Metham's mind. Like Amoryus, who lived his life as a "flowre of knyghthod" and as a "defensor of the cuntré, |and| keper of pes contynwalle" (2094–2096), Miles Stapleton lives a life of "gret prosperyté" (2117) with a "prudent porte of governans" (2118) and success in "Marcys chauns |battle|" (2119). Amoryus's father, Palamedon, is described in the romance as the most devout and powerful Roman warrior and a close confidante of emperor Nero; his mother was a descendent of Darius, the former Persian emperor. Similarly, Miles is:

> nobyl of lynage
> The qwyche decendyth of a gretyd aunsetré
> Of nobyl werrourrys that successyvely, be veray |true| maryage,
> The t|w|o and fyfty knyght ys computate to hys age. (2123–2126)[37]

Metham does not elaborate further on Miles's "gretyd aunsetré," choosing instead to refer the audience to his other works and insisting that "of hys |Stapleton's| dedys" he still has "many to wryte; / I purpose in odyr placys in specyall them endyghte" (2148–2149).[38]

Although both she and her husband were Metham's patrons, his praise of Katherine in *Amoryus and Cleopes* shows much more detail and specificity in honoring her admirable qualities. Throughout the several stanzas dedicated to praising Miles, Metham refers to him primarily as a modern-day "knyght" and a "wurthy werryur" (2134). Only after advertising his other texts does Metham give a name to his "champyon" (2137). When he turns to Katherine, however, she is named immediately, and all his comments are geared toward cultivating and cementing her patronage.

Metham begins his encomium to the Lady Katherine as he does her husband's, with a reference to her lineage. Whereas Miles's "gretyd aunsetré" (2124) is not named or traced specifically, Katherine has "decens be ryght lynage / Of wurthy and excellent stok lyneally / That Poolys men clepe" (2151–2153). Her legitimate family pedigree is as important as Miles's; after all, the Stapleton family maintained their position only by "veray maryage" (2125). Metham goes a step further in detailing Katherine's lineage by naming one of her powerfully connected relatives: her cousin, William de la Pole, duke of Suffolk (1396–1450).[39] The duke of Suffolk was a patron of John Lydgate, one of Metham's greatest influences,[40] and it is not by chance that Metham pauses to remark on a specific relative of Katherine's who is in particular a well-known literary patron. Perhaps by referring to Suffolk Metham is reminding Katherine that she comes from a family that supports literature; perhaps he is even attempting to secure the patronage of the de la Poles as well as the Stapletons. Whether the ultimate goal is to reaffirm Katherine's support or to procure the sponsorship of her family, Metham's concentration on Katherine in the final section of *Amoryus and Cleopes* indicates that he considers her goodwill to be key to his success.

When Metham indicates how he would like his book to be passed down to future readers, the lady Katherine is implicated in his wishes for the romance. For those readers, he writes, "the qwyche be nowe onborne," who "qwan this lady ys pasyd, schal rede this story, / . . . thei for her schal pray on evyn and morne" (2157–2159). Not only will *Amoryus and Cleopes* continue to be read after his patron's death, the story will place the future reader in immediate remembrance of Katherine. Even strangers who were not acquainted with the lady during her life will know enough about Katherine's character from the romance to pray for her after she is gone. This suggestion provides Katherine with an excellent reason to continue Metham's patronage; the more biographical encomia he writes for her, the more prayers she will receive. Although the patronage relationship between Katherine and Metham likely includes some aspect of financial compensation, the currency referred to in this passage goes beyond the monetary, outlining instead a connection predicated on esteem and poetic inspiration. Thus Katherine's comprehensive acts of intellectual and financial patronage during her lifetime extend well beyond her death, transcending any initial economic investment she or her family have made in Metham's work.

In addition to securing prayers for Katherine's soul, Metham grants her a certain amount of immortality in his dedication, which he calls "this memory" (2160).[41] His memorialization of Katherine reads like a blazon of womanly perfection:

> sche was namyd communly
> Modyr of norture, in her behavyng usyng alle gentylnes,
> Ever redy to help them that were in troubyl and hevynes.
> So beuteus eke and so benyngn, that yche creature
> Here |Her| gretly magnyfyid, commendyng her womanhede
> In alle her behavyngs, ireprehensybyl and demure
> And . . . sche toke gret heede
> To the necessyteys of the pore, relevyng them at every nede.
> (2161–2168)

Metham's extended praise of Katherine encompasses not only the standard womanly characteristics of beauty, virtue, and gentleness but also her more specific role as a common nurturer of all those she knew, her ability to help others in "hevynes" (2163),[42] and her generosity toward the poor. As with his depiction of her husband, Metham refers the audience to one of his other works for more about Katherine: "Of her beute and vertuys, here I sese; for yt ys so, / I hem declare in Crysaunt, and odyr placys mo" (2169–2170).[43] Having ceased in his direct praise of Katherine's attributes, however, Metham continues indirectly by comparing her to well-known literary figures. He regrets that he lacks the talent to represent his patron's qualities faithfully, wishing that he possessed "as gret a style . . . / As Chauncerys" (2172–2173). Metham lists the exemplary female characters about which Chaucer writes: "qwene Eleyne or Cresseyd," and "Polyxchene, Grysyld, or Penelopé" (2173–2174).[44] The lady Katherine, Metham claims, is "as beuteus, as womanly, [and] as pacyent as thei were wunt to be" (2175).

Just as Metham connects Miles with the character of Amoryus, highlighting his military accomplishments and noble ancestry, so the parallel Metham meticulously establishes between his lady patron and Chaucer's literary heroines begs the reader to consider the connections between Katherine and Cleopes. After all, *Amoryus and Cleopes* is a memorial text to her, one that will remind future readers of Katherine's virtues even after her death. However, aside from Cleopes's noble family and her surpassing beauty, what aspects of Cleopes's character might parallel most significantly with the lady Stapleton? Not only is Katherine beautiful, generous, and patient, she is the patron of a text that combines elements of the traditional chivalric romance, a genre often characterized as women's reading, with a practical knowledge of herbs, dragon taxonomy, and astronomical treatises.[45] Lee Ramsey asserts that "there are really only two kinds of heroines in romance: the vacuous and inactive object of the hero's desire and the lady in distress."[46] Metham's heroine, however, plays neither of these passive roles. Cleopes is the guardian of much textual knowledge; she is the problem-solver in her relationship with Amoryus; and she acts as the patron of his chivalric career.

Metham specifically makes his heroine's contribution to the narrative extend far beyond the vapid object of the hero's desire. It also exceeds both of Craig's categories of an educated female character: a purveyor of homespun remedies or a sorceress. Rather, Metham characterizes Cleopes as a savvy scholar, one who uses her knowledge of religious and secular scientific texts to facilitate a relationship with the man she loves and to keep him alive during his solitary masculine errands. Furthermore, she is converted to Christianity along with her lover and then embarks on a life of spiritual and earthly success secured in large part by her intellectual and practical sponsorship. With the listing of Chaucer's major literary heroines, future readers of Metham's text—perhaps even Katherine herself—could reflect upon the patroness's beauty, patience, and virtue. By reading about Cleopes, they could reflect on Katherine's intelligence and the value placed on the scientific texts that she and her husband commissioned.

It is telling that Metham wrote such a romance for a woman patron; the tale is entertaining, moral enough to read on holy days, and provides comprehensive information on astronomy and natural science. Considering that the other text Metham explicitly dedicates to Katherine is "Crysaunt," most likely a translation of a farming manual that treats of, among other subjects, animal husbandry and winemaking, *Amoryus and Cleopes* is not a metrical failure or an incongruous collection of scientific translation and fragments of romantic episodes. Rather it is a carefully selected and highly appropriate work for his female patron.

University of North Carolina-Greensboro

NOTES

1. See, e.g., Karl Julius Holzknecht, *Literary Patronage in the Middle Ages* (New York: Octagon Books, 1966); Joel T. Rosenthal, "Aristocratic Cultural Patronage and Book Bequests, 1350–1500," *John Rylands Library Bulletin* 64 (1981–1982): 522–548; and more recently Loveday Lewes Gee, *Women, Art and Patronage from Henry III to Edward III, 1216–1377* (Woodbridge, UK: Boydell Press, 2002). These influential studies of medieval patronage have been valuable but also restrictive because of their attention to material elements such as the exchange of money or prestigious political appointments; they privilege such materiality at the expense of a broader continuum that encompasses both tangible and intangible support. This narrow conception of patronage excludes most women from a vital aspect of medieval culture; only the most wealthy and to some extent independent aristocratic women could afford to sponsor literary, architectural, and cultural productions in the Middle Ages through strictly financial means.

2. June Hall McCash, "The Cultural Patronage of Medieval Women: An Overview," in *The Cultural Patronage of Medieval Women*, ed. June Hall McCash and Stephen G. Nichols (Athens, GA: University of Georgia Press, 1996), 1–49; Joan Ferrante, *To the Glory of Her Sex: Women's Roles in the Composition of Medieval Texts* (Bloomington: Indiana University Press, 1997); and Karen K. Jambeck, "Patterns of Women's Literary Patronage: England, 1200–ca. 1475," in *Cultural Patronage of Medieval Women*, ed. June Hall McCash and Stephen G. Nichols (Athens, GA: University of Georgia Press, 1996), 228–265. See also D. H. Green, "Chapter 4: Women's Engagement with Literature," in *Women Readers in the Middle Ages* (Cambridge, UK: Cambridge University Press, 2007), 179–255. Green specifically counters the narrow representation of patronage espoused in K. M. Broadhurst, "Henry II of England and Eleanor of Aquitaine: Patrons of Literature in French?" *Viator: Medieval and Renaissance Studies*, 27 (1996): 53–84. Broadhurst, Green asserts, confines herself to the "restrictive sense of 'the remuneration bestowed by the patron on the author,' to the exclusion of any other encouragement" (Green, *Women Readers*, 204). Mary Erler and Maryanne Kowaleski also set out to "broaden . . . the conventional understanding of power as public authority"; see Mary C. Erler and Maryanne Kowaleski, eds., "Introduction," in *Gendering*

the Master Narrative: Women and Power in the Middle Ages (Ithaca, NY: Cornell University Press, 2003), 1–17 |2|; I would suggest that part of that broadened understanding is a rejection of financially based discourses of power.

3. Joan Ferrante, "Whose Voice? The Influence of Women Patrons on Courtly Romances," in *Literary Aspects of Courtly Culture*, ed. Donald Maddox and Sara Sturm-Maddox (Rochester, NY: Boydell and Brewer, 1994), 3–18, 4.

4. While I seek to expand the concept of patronage in the Middle Ages to include acts of influence that are not monetarily based, I remain conscious of the risks of expanding the notion of patronage beyond critical usefulness. In this article, I follow Ferrante's policy of using the terms "patronage" and "sponsorship" interchangeably. Green notes that he differs from Ferrante in her use of the term "patronage" to refer to the act of supporting the writer or artist with "intellectual, emotional, and sometimes financial help" (Ferrante, "Whose Voice?" 4). Rather, Green prefers the "wider term 'sponsors'" (Green, *Women Readers*, 205). However, I adopt Ferrante's terminology because this article is invested in reevaluating the concept of medieval patronage as not necessarily financially based; to adopt the term "sponsorship" to refer to a "wider" category of influence would undermine that reassessment.

5. For a discussion of this mode of learning, see Rebecca Krug, *Reading Families: Women's Literate Practice in Late Medieval England* (Ithaca, NY: Cornell University Press, 2002); and Susan Groag Bell, "Medieval Women Book Owners: Arbiters of Lay Piety and Ambassadors of Culture," *Signs* 7.4 (Summer 1982): 742–768. One particularly rich example of these influential female networks is the women in the Neville and Beaufort families. See Jambeck, "Patterns," 228–265.

6. Metham informs his audience that he is writing his romance in "the sevyn and twenty yere of the sext Kyng Henry," or 1449 (2177). All line number citations from the romance and the other texts (cited by page number) in Princeton University Library, MS Garrett 141 are taken from Hardin Craig, ed., *The Works of John Metham*, EETS o.s. 132 (London: Kegan Paul, Trench, Trübner & Co., 1916). Page's TEAMS edition of the romance alone, Stephen F. Page, ed., *Amoryus and Cleopes* (Kalamazoo, MI: Medieval Institute Publications, 1999), updates Hardin Craig's textual apparatus and transcribes the final ten erased lines of *Amoryus and Cleopes*, parts of which are now visible under ultraviolet light (2213–2222). References to these recovered lines are taken from Page's edition.

7. Several scholars have discussed the increased patronage and literary activity of medieval women after becoming widows because of the greater financial and social freedom to pursue these activities. For example, Anne Neville Stafford (*ca.* 1414–1480) and her daughter-in-law Margaret Beaufort (1443–1509) both of whom became active literary sponsors after they were widowed.

8. We may also turn to an example found in William Caxton's Prologue to the chivalric romance *Blanchardyn and Eglantine* (1489). This English translation was undertaken at the behest of Margaret Beaufort (Caxton had previously produced

it for her in French); in his Prologue, Caxton suggests that reading a tale of the "noble fayttes and valiaunt actes of armes" is better than studying "ouer moche in bokes of contemplacioun"; W. J. B. Crotch, *The Prologues and Epilogues of William Caxton*, EETS o.s. 176 (London: Oxford University Press, 1928), 105. For more on Margaret Beaufort's patronage of Caxton's translation, see Jennifer Summit, "William Caxton, Margaret Beaufort and the Romance of Female Patronage," in *Women, The Book, and the Worldly: Selected Proceedings of the St. Hilda's Conference, 1993*, ed. Lesley Smith and Jane H. M. Taylor (Cambridge, UK: Brewer, 1995), 151–165; and Anne Clark Bartlett, "Translation, Self-Representation, and Statecraft: Lady Margaret Beaufort and Caxton's *Blanchardyn and Eglantine* (1489)," *Essays in Medieval Studies* 22 (2005): 53–66.

9. While this article considers primarily the nonromance sources used in *Amoryus and Cleopes*, Metham does draw significantly from the romance legends of Alexander the Great, which were popular in the late Middle Ages. Not only does Metham claim to have written a (no longer extant) story titled "Alexander Macedo" (Craig, *Works of John Metham*, 2143) for Miles Stapleton, but the narrative of *Amoryus and Cleopes* shows signs of this tradition's influence as well. For example, Craig suggests that Palamedon's and Dydas's marriages to Persian wives "off the lynage / Of Daryus" (ibid., 43–44) establishes a link between Metham's text and the Alexander legend (ibid., xiv). For further connections between *Amoryus and Cleopes* and other traditional materials, such as Lydgate's *Troy Book* and popular English romances, see ibid., xiii–xix; and Page, *Amoryus and Cleopes*, 8–15.

10. This combination of narrative elements serves Metham's purposes but has not recommended the romance to modern literary criticism. However, *Amoryus and Cleopes*'s low status in the eyes of modern scholarship is the result not of the many different kinds of material included in its narrative, a combination of which is often found in medieval romances, but rather of the long translations of scientific treatises and Metham's metrical ineptitude compared to other contemporary authors such as Lydgate. In several of his works on fifteenth-century English literature, Derek Pearsall remarks on *Amoryus and Cleopes*'s "metrical chaos" (Pearsall, "The English Chaucerians," in *Chaucer and Chaucerians: Critical Studies in Middle English Literature*, ed. D. S. Brewer [Huntsville: University of Alabama Press, 1967], 206), and the "technical . . .incompetence [which] make[s] it almost unreadable" (Pearsall, "The English Romance in the Fifteenth Century," *Essays and Studies* n.s. 29 [1976]: 69). Lee Ramsey chooses to indict the author for his "unskilled but serious-minded" attempt to write "a sentimental, pathetic love story" and "plunder . . . traditional romance for a jousting contest and a dragon fight to enliven the action" (Ramsey, *Chivalric Romances: Popular Literature in Medieval England* [Bloomington: Indiana University Press, 1983], 226). Technical inadequacies and generic looting aside, Metham's text is undoubtedly bookish, a fact that leads Ramsey to declare that he

was not "a romance writer, but rather a translator" (ibid., 225). Indeed, the long and seemingly unnecessary digressions into secular scientific material on astronomy and natural philosophy, which already appear incompatible with the more traditionally chivalric episodes, are particularly at odds with the resurrection and conversion narrative that concludes the tale. The text's objectionability for critics, however, lies not in its fusion of various secular and devotional genres but in the inelegant way they are combined.

11. The works of John Metham seem to have had a small readership in the late fifteenth century, perhaps limited to the Stapletons and their literary circle, which included the Pastons and Sir John Fastolf, and have seen little scholarly attention since then. For more on the literary circles in fifteenth-century Norfolk and Suffolk, see Samuel Moore, "Patrons of Letters in Norfolk and Suffolk, c.1450," PMLA 27 (1912): 188–207.

12. R. M. Lumiansky, "Legends of Alexander the Great," in A Manual of the Writings in Middle English; Fascicule I: Romances, ed. J. Burke Severs (New Haven: Connecticut Academy of Arts and Sciences, 1967), 112.

13. Jamie Fumo reads Cleopes's rehearsal of dragon lore as "extravagant . . . distracting and largely unintegrated"; Jamie Fumo, "John Metham's 'Straunge Style': Amoryus and Cleopes as Chaucerian Fragment," Chaucer Review 43.2 (2008): 215–237, 224. Furthermore, the jousting and dragon fighting scenes, she suggests, not only distract from the love story (they are "mood-killing") but also seem to be "indulged merely as romance necessity" (ibid., 224). However, judging from the centrality of the scientific material and chivalric pursuits within the romance and within the Garrett manuscript Metham prepared for his patrons, Cleopes's act of intellectual patronage at this point in the narrative is highly appropriate and timely.

14. In addition to Amoryus and Cleopes, the Garrett manuscript also includes treatises on physiognomy and palmistry and a set of prognostications based on the phases of the moon.

15. The term "science" in the Middle Ages often referred to a general body of knowledge or more specifically to book learning. Science was also part of the seven liberal arts (or sciences): grammar, rhetoric, and dialectic or logic (the trivium) and arithmetic, geometry, astronomy, and music (the quadrivium). See Edward Grant, "Medieval Science and Natural Philosophy," in Medieval Studies: An Introduction, ed. James M. Powell (Syracuse, NY: Syracuse University Press, 1992), 353–375, for a comprehensive outline of the development of all branches of medieval science and its place as a critical source for the scientific revolution of the seventeenth century.

16. Fumo, "John Metham's 'Straunge Style,'" 228.

17. Page provides a helpful explanatory note for this passage: "That he could treat each person with respect according to their rank because of [his] educated nobility" (Page, Amoryus and Cleopes, 34, n. 1).

18. Fumo, "John Metham's 'Straunge Style,'" 228–229, also discusses these three scenes, concluding that Palamedon's reactions to Amoryus's behavior constitute both an active interest in the young knight's chivalric progress and "the most substantial obstacle—albeit a symbolic and unintentional one—to the protagonist's otherwise seemingly unobstructed love" (ibid., 229). However, I read Palamedon's influence on his son as negligible.

19. This is the same earthquake that opens up the convenient crack in the wall between Amoryus's and Cleopes's gardens, allowing the lovers to communicate with one another.

20. The parallels between Amoryus's feelings of sudden love in this scene and the temple scene in *Troilus and Criseyde* are striking and suggest that Metham knew Chaucer's text well enough to imitate even the smallest of details in his account of the lovers' first meeting.

21. Metham's use of a textual device at this key point in the narrative is interesting. At the beginning of the romance, Metham pauses in his preface to the romance to describe why he is translating *Amoryus and Cleopes*: "noqwere in Latyne ner Englysch I coulde yt aspye, / But in Grwe Y had yt, wrytyn— lymynyd bryght " (58–59). Rather than simply dismiss a manuscript written in a language he cannot read, Metham asks "lettyryd clerkys" (62) about the content of the book and takes advantage of a Greek's arrival in Norwich to procure a Latin translation of the romance. His interest, he explains, is entirely piqued by the "lettyrys of gold that gay were wrowght to the ye" (60). The manuscript's beautiful illuminations, he continues, "causyd me to mervel that yt so gloryusly / Was adornyd, and oftyn I enqwyryd . . . / Qwat yt myght be that poyntyd was wyth so merwulus werkys" (61–63). Metham's detailed description of his own interest in manuscript illumination is recalled in the specificity he affords the depiction of Cleopes's picture. The character of Cleopes, like Metham and, hopefully, Amoryus, recognizes the impact and utility of illuminations as much as written text.

22. Page, *Amoryus and Cleopes*, 113.

23. It is apt that Amoryus credits Venus for his chivalric badge, as it is in the temple of Venus that he first sees Cleopes. During the ceremony, Amoryus uses the procession of the goddess's statue as an excuse to kneel in mock obeisance and examine the picture Cleopes shows him (818–821).

24. Page suggests that this could refer to heraldic helmet crests, which became popular in the late Middle Ages. Also, an oxlike animal is the crest of the Metham family in Yorkshire (Page, *Amoryus and Cleopes*, 120).

25. Fumo, "John Metham's 'Straunge Style,'" 224. Metham, Craig notes, draws considerably from the depiction of Medea in John Lydgate's *Troy Book* (Craig, *Works of John Metham*, 161–162). The women share comparable learning, and Medea offers a similar assurance that Jason will be killed in his endeavors without her help: "For noon but I may helpen . . . / In þis case" (John Lydgate, *Lydgate's*

Troy Book, Part I, ed. Henry Bergen, EETS e.s. 97 |London: Kegan Paul, Trench, Trübner & Co., 1906|, 2580–2581). Most significantly, however, Cleopes's gifts almost directly parallel Medea's. The "riche ymage of siluer" that works against "magyk and al enchauntemente" (2998–3002) is similar to Cleopes's "bugyl gapyng" (Craig, *Works of John Metham*, 1312), and the "oyntement, / To enoynte hym with, þat he be nat brent" (Lydgate, *Troy Book*, 3015–3016) is analogous to the potion Cleopes gives her love to protect him from venomous beasts. Finally, Medea gives Jason an agate ring (assuring him that "who-so-euer in his hond hit holde, / By vertu þat was infallible" |Lydgate, *Troy Book*, 3028–3029|), which closely parallels the emerald ring Cleopes instructs Amoryus to hold in his hand during the battle (Craig, *Works of John Metham*, 1314).

26. The giving of enchanted gifts such as rings and other accoutrements to knights before battle or chivalric errands is a commonplace in medieval romance. See, e.g., the Breton lay *Emaré*, where two separate women give the hero a magical ring and two magical hunting dogs. The difference between this instance (and others like it throughout the romance tradition) and the gift-giving and acts of sponsorship I outline in this article is that Cleopes's offerings are part of a larger program wherein the romance heroine deploys comprehensive knowledge and influence over the knight's chivalric identity and success.

27. Craig, *Works of John Metham*, 162.

28. Most medieval women did have some sort of training in the art of healing, such as basic first aid, setting broken bones, midwifery, and using herbs to combat illness. Two women in particular, Trotula of Salerno and Hildegard of Bingen, wrote medieval treatises about and for women. For more on the role of medieval women in medicine, see Monica H. Green, *The Trotula: A Medieval Compendium of Women's Medicine*, ed. and trans. Monica H. Green (Philadelphia: University of Pennsylvania Press, 2001); also Monica H. Green, "Documenting Medieval Women's Medical Practice," in *Practical Medicine from Salerno to the Black Death*, ed. Luis Garcia-Ballester (Cambridge, UK: Cambridge University Press, 1994), 322–353; and Monica H. Green, *Women's Healthcare in the Medieval West: Texts and Contexts* (Burlington, VT: Ashgate, 2000). Out of the three main Trotula texts, only one—the Trotula Minor—seems to have been actually written by a woman.

29. While Metham identifies no particular sources for Cleopes's encyclopedic knowledge, Page claims that Metham must have been familiar with texts such as medieval bestiaries and Trevisa's translation of *De proprietatibus rerum*, both of which discuss and describe poisonous animals at length. Metham could also have gathered his knowledge of stones and medicinal plants from comprehensive works like Trevisa's or from medieval lapidaries and herbals. For examples of medieval bestiaries, see Richard Barber, ed., *Bestiary: Being an English Version of the Bodleian Library, Oxford M.S. Bodley 764: with all the Original*

Miniatures Reproduced in Facsimile (Woodbridge, UK: Boydell, 1993); T. J. Elliott, ed. and trans., *A Medieval Bestiary* (Boston: Godine, 1971); and Debra Hassig, ed., *The Mark of the Beast: The Medieval Bestiary in Art, Life, and Literature* (New York: Garland, 1999). For medieval lapidaries and herbals, see Joan Evans and Mary S. Sergeantson, eds., *English Medieval Lapidaries*, EETS 190 (London: Oxford University Press, 1960); Pol Grymonprez, ed., *"Here Men May Se the Vertues off Herbes"*: A Middle English Herbal (MS. *Bodley* 483, *ff.* 57r–67v) (Brussels: Scripta, 1981); and Pol Grymonprez, ed., *A Medieval Herbal* (San Francisco: Chronicle Books, 1994).

30. In a testament to the importance this increased knightly status holds for Amoryus, when the young man commits suicide toward the end of the romance, he enumerates the loss of each part of the chivalric life Cleopes has helped him attain, seeming to mourn the individual trappings of knighthood—"aventurys new," "myry cumpany," "fame and vyctory" (1711–1713)—more than his lover.

31. Ovid's story of Pyramus and Thisbe was one of the most widely disseminated works from the *Metamorphoses* after becoming a popular subject of Latin rhetorical exercises in the twelfth and thirteenth centuries. See Robert Glendinning, "Pyramus and Thisbe in the Medieval Classroom," *Speculum* 61.1 (1986): 51–78, 54; and Stephen F. Page, "John Metham's *Amoryus and Cleopes*: Intertextuality and Innovation in a Chaucerian Poem," *Chaucer Review* 33 (1998): 201–208, 207. The most popular was the fourteenth-century French allegorical interpretation, the *Ovide Moralisé*.

32. Although the bulk of the Christian material added to the Pyramus and Thisbe legend is confined to the final book of *Amoryus and Cleopes*, Metham integrates the new narrative into the rest of the romance through an undercurrent of asides and personal commentary on the paganism in Albynest. Page suggests that Metham is not guilty of an "endless amplification or condemnation of the pagans" (Page, "Intertextuality and Innovation," 203), but that he refers to their religious beliefs constantly in either a matter-of-fact tone or an understated sadness at their misguided faith. See also Fumo, "John Metham's 'Straunge Style,'" 217. Indeed, Metham's discussion of the paganism in *Amoryus and Cleopes* seeks to engender a feeling of pity in the audience, or at least to neutralize any feelings of condemnation the Christian readers might have toward the Albynestian pagans.

33. For an example of how the Commandments were used to teach the laity in the Middle Ages, see Thomas Frederick Simmons and Henry Edward Nolloth, eds., *The Lay Folks' Catechism*, EETS o.s. 118 (London: K. Paul, Trench, Trübner and Co., 1901).

34. Shortly after the lovers' conversion, the reader will also witness the wholesale conversion of paganism in Albynest during the hermit's exorcism of the temple.

35. Roger Dalrymple, "*Amoryus and Cleopes*: John Metham's Metamorphosis of Chaucer and Ovid," in *The Matter of Identity in Medieval Romance*, ed. Phillipa

Hardman (Cambridge, UK: Brewer, 2002), 149–162, 155.

36. In addition to the glowing praise of the couple in *Amoryus and Cleopes*, the Garrett manuscript boasts two examples of the Stapleton–de la Pole coats of arms, one at the beginning of the romance (fol. 17r) and one on the first folio of the manuscript, which opens the treatise on palmistry. The arms are Stapleton impaling de la Pole: Stapleton, or, a lion rampant sable; de la Pole, azure, on a fess between three leopards' faces, or, a mullet sable (Craig, *Works of John Metham*, viii).

37. In other words, Miles Stapleton is the fifty-second in direct descent.

38. This statement not only confirms the Stapletons' past patronage of Metham but assumes their future sponsorship of his work. Page speculates that Metham was probably regularly compensated by the Stapletons either in the capacity of a "sometime-poet living in Norwich, or perhaps, more likely, [as] a member of the Stapleton retinue, perhaps the family secretary" (Page, *Amoryus and Cleopes*, 5). Given the long connection between Metham and the Stapletons and the likelihood of their consistent support of the author in whatever capacity he served them, we can begin to understand a patronage relationship not necessarily based on individual payments for texts either specifically commissioned or written speculatively in the hopes of remuneration. Rather, the broad definition of patronage with which this article begins—including intellectual and social as well as financial support—is a more accurate depiction of the relationship between Metham and the Stapletons.

39. William de la Pole became one of the most powerful men in England in the mid-fifteenth century. He engineered the marriage of Henry VI to Margaret of Anjou (1445). In 1430, he married Alice Chaucer (*ca.* 1404–1475), the granddaughter of Geoffrey Chaucer. Because Metham does not mention Suffolk's beheading in 1450, *Amoryus and Cleopes* must have been written before then. See George E. Cokayne, ed., *The Complete Peerage*, vol. 12: pt. 1 (London: St. Catherine Press, 1910–1959), 443–448.

40. At the end of *Amoryus and Cleopes*, Metham comments on Lydgate's "half chongyd Latyne" and "crafty imagynacionys of thingys fantastyk" (Craig, *Works of John Metham*, 2195–2196).

41. Metham's overt references to memorializing Katherine and to remembering her after death lead to some speculation about the state of Katherine's health during the romance's composition. Metham claims that "thys lady was, qwan I endytyd this story, / Floryschyng the sevyn and twenty yere of the sext Kyng Henry" (ibid., 2176–2177). While this statement establishes the date of the poem's composition, it also suggests that she was alive during the composition but not afterward. However, Katherine did not die until October 13–14, 1488, having remarried after Miles Stapleton's death in 1466.

42. This particular description recalls Metham's desire for *Amoryus and Cleopes* to comfort those who "falle in hevynes" (ibid., 2210) on holy days.

43. Page speculates that this text is a translation of *De omnibus agriculturae partibus et plantarium*, an encyclopedia of farming and animal husbandry written by Petrus de Crescentiis (1233–ca. 1320). See Will Richter and Reinhilt Richter-Bergmeier, eds., *Ruralia commoda* (Heidelberg: Universitätsverlag C. Winter, 1995). Page suggests that if the unknown *Crysaunt* text is indeed a translation of de Crescentiis's manual, then it is unlike the other texts Metham claims to have written. However, the practicality of a treatise on farming and livestock indeed dovetails with the other texts Metham wrote for the Stapletons. The scientific pieces, such as the treatise on physiognomy, and the sets of predictions (both for the year and for each day of the lunar cycle) provide practical, routine information to the reader. Furthermore, the kind of practical scientific discourse represented in a farming treatise is similar to those scientific discourses Cleopes marshals in her patronage of Amoryus; thus, praising Katherine's practicality and knowledge with *Crysaunt* easily recalls the praiseworthy practicality and knowledge of Cleopes.

44. "Qwene Eleyne" is Helen of Troy; Chaucer mentions her in several of his works, such as *The Book of the Duchess*, the *Parliament of Fouls*, *Troilus and Criseyde*, and the *Legend of Good Women*. Her great beauty is a commonplace in the Middle Ages. "Cresseyd" is Chaucer's heroine in *Troilus and Criseyde*; this is a dubious flattery considering how maligned Criseyde is in literature from the classical period through the Renaissance. She is, however, undoubtedly beautiful, and one hopes, for the sake of his future patronage, that this is the comparison Metham is drawing. "Polyxchene" is Polyxena, one of king Priam's daughters and the lover of Achilles. She is also mentioned in *The Book of the Duchess* and the *Legend of Good Women*. "Grysyld" is the heroine of *The Clerk's Tale*; she is a model of beauty and patience. "Penelope" is the wife of Odysseus and appears in several of Chaucer's works, such as *Anelide and Arcite*, *Troilus and Criseyde*, and the *Legend of Good Women*, as a model of fidelity.

45. For more on the notion that medieval romance audiences were at least partly comprised of noblewomen, see W. R. J. Barron, *English Medieval Romance* (New York: Longman, 1987), 231–235; Lee Ramsey, *Chivalric Romances*, 9 and 109–115; and Carol M. Meale, "'Gode Men / Wiues Maydnes and Alle Men': Romance and Its Audiences," in *Readings in Medieval English Romance*, ed. Carol M. Meale (Rochester, NY: D. S. Brewer, 1994), 209–226, 220.

46. Ramsey, *Chivalric Romances*, 177.

WORKS CITED

Barber, Richard, trans. and intro. *Bestiary: Being an English Version of the Bodleian Library, Oxford M.S. Bodley 764: with All the Original Miniatures Reproduced in Facsimile*. Woodbridge, UK: Boydell, 1993.

Barron, W. R. J. *English Medieval Romance.* New York: Longman, 1987.

Bartlett, Anne Clark. "Translation, Self-Representation, and Statecraft: Lady Margaret Beaufort and Caxton's *Blanchardyn and Eglantine* (1489)." *Essays in Medieval Studies* 22 (2005): 53–66.

Bell, Susan Groag. "Medieval Women Book Owners: Arbiters of Lay Piety and Ambassadors of Culture." *Signs* 7.4 (Summer 1982): 742–768.

Broadhurst, K. M. "Henry II of England and Eleanor of Aquitaine: Patrons of Literature in French?" *Viator: Medieval and Renaissance Studies* 27 (1996): 53–84.

Cokayne, George E., ed. *The Complete Peerage.* Vol. 12: pt. 1. London: St. Catherine Press, 1910–1959.

Craig, Hardin, ed. *The Works of John Metham.* EETS o.s. 132. London: Kegan Paul, Trench, Trübner & Co., 1916.

Crotch, W. J. B. *The Prologues and Epilogues of William Caxton.* EETS o.s. 176. London: Oxford University Press, 1928.

Dalrymple, Roger. "*Amoryus and Cleopes*: John Metham's Metamorphosis of Chaucer and Ovid." In *The Matter of Identity in Medieval Romance*, ed. Phillipa Hardman. Cambridge, UK: Brewer, 2002. 149–162.

Elliott, T. J., ed. and trans. *A Medieval Bestiary.* Boston: Godine, 1971.

Erler, Mary C., and Maryanne Kowaleski. "Introduction." In *Gendering the Master Narrative: Women and Power in the Middle Ages*, ed. Mary C. Erler and Maryanne Kowaleski. Ithaca, NY: Cornell University Press, 2003. 1–17.

Evans, Joan, and Mary S. Sergeantson, eds. *English Medieval Lapidaries.* EETS 190. London: Oxford University Press, 1960.

Ferrante, Joan. "Whose Voice? The Influence of Women Patrons on Courtly Romances." In *Literary Aspects of Courtly Culture*, ed. Donald Maddox and Sara Sturm-Maddox. Rochester, UK: Boydell and Brewer, 1994. 3–18.

———. *To the Glory of Her Sex: Women's Roles in the Composition of Medieval Texts.* Bloomington: Indiana University Press, 1997.

Fumo, Jamie. "John Metham's 'Straunge Style': *Amoryus and Cleopes* as Chaucerian Fragment." *Chaucer Review* 43.2 (2008): 215–237.

Gee, Loveday Lewes. *Women, Art and Patronage from Henry III to Edward III, 1216–1377.* Woodbridge, UK: Boydell Press, 2002.

Glendinning, Robert. "Pyramus and Thisbe in the Medieval Classroom." *Speculum* 61.1 (1986): 51–78.

Grant, Edward. "Medieval Science and Natural Philosophy." In *Medieval Studies: An Introduction*, ed. James M. Powell. Syracuse, NY: Syracuse University Press, 1992. 353–375.

Green, D. H. *Women Readers in the Middle Ages.* Cambridge, UK: Cambridge University Press, 2007.

Green, Monica. "Documenting Medieval Women's Medical Practice." In *Practical Medicine from Salerno to the Black Death*, ed. Luis Garcia-Ballester. Cambridge, UK: Cambridge University Press, 1994. 322–353.

. *Women's Healthcare in the Medieval West: Texts and Contexts*. Burlington, VT: Ashgate, 2000.

, ed. and trans. *The Trotula: A Medieval Compendium of Women's Medicine*. Philadelphia: University of Pennsylvania Press, 2001.

Grymonprez, Pol, ed. *"Here Men May Se the Vertues off Herbes"*: A Middle English Herbal (MS. *Bodley* 483, *ff*. 57r–67v). Brussels: Scripta, 1981.

. *A Medieval Herbal*. San Francisco: Chronicle Books, 1994.

Hassig, Debra, ed. *The Mark of the Beast: The Medieval Bestiary in Art, Life, and Literature*. New York: Garland, 1999.

Holzknecht, Karl Julius. *Literary Patronage in the Middle Ages*. New York: Octagon Books, 1966.

Jambeck, Karen K. "Patterns of Women's Literary Patronage: England, 1200–ca. 1475." In *The Cultural Patronage of Medieval Women*, ed. June Hall McCash and Stephen G. Nichols. Athens, GA: University of Georgia Press, 1996. 228–265.

Krug, Rebecca. *Reading Families: Women's Literate Practice in Late Medieval England*. Ithaca, NY: Cornell University Press, 2002.

Lumiansky, R. M. "Legends of Alexander the Great." In A *Manual of the Writings in Middle English; Fascicule* I: *Romances*, ed. J. Burke Severs. New Haven: Connecticut Academy of Arts and Sciences, 1967.

Lydgate, John. *Lydgate's Troy Book*, ed. Bergen, Henry. Part I. EETS e.s. 97. London: Kegan Paul, Trench, Trübner & Co., 1906,

McCash, June Hall. "The Cultural Patronage of Medieval Women: An Overview." In *The Cultural Patronage of Medieval Women*, ed. June Hall McCash and Stephen G. Nichols. Athens, GA: University of Georgia Press, 1996. 1–49.

Meale, Carol M. "'Gode Men / Wiues Maydnes and Alle Men': Romance and Its Audiences." In *Readings in Medieval English Romance*, ed. Carol M. Meale. Rochester, NY: D. S. Brewer, 1994. 209–226.

Moore, Samuel. "Patrons of Letters in Norfolk and Suffolk, c. 1450." PMLA 27 (1912): 188–207.

Page, Stephen F. "John Metham's *Amoryus and Cleopes*: Intertextuality and Innovation in a Chaucerian Poem." *Chaucer Review* 33 (1998): 201–208.

, ed. *Amoryus and Cleopes*. Kalamazoo, MI: Medieval Institute Publications, 1999.

Pearsall, Derek. "The English Chaucerians." In *Chaucer and Chaucerians: Critical Studies in Middle English Literature*, ed. D. S. Brewer. Huntsville: University of Alabama Press, 1967. 201-239.

. "The English Romance in the Fifteenth Century." *Essays and Studies* n.s. 29 (1976): 56–83.

Ramsey, Lee. *Chivalric Romances: Popular Literature in Medieval England*. Bloomington: Indiana University Press, 1983.

Richter, Will, and Reinhilt Richter-Bergmeier, eds. *Ruralia commoda*. Heidelberg, Germany: Universitätsverlag C. Winter, 1995.

Rosenthal, Joel T. "Aristocratic Cultural Patronage and Book Bequests, 1350–1500." *John Rylands Library Bulletin* 64 (1981–1982): 522–548.

Simmons, Thomas Frederick, and Henry Edward Nolloth, eds. *The Lay Folks' Catechism*. EETS o.s. 118. London: K. Paul, Trench, Trübner and Co., 1901.

Summit, Jennifer. "William Caxton, Margaret Beaufort and the Romance of Female Patronage." In *Women, The Book, and the Worldly: Selected Proceedings of the St. Hilda's Conference, 1993*, ed. Lesley Smith and Jane H. M. Taylor. Cambridge, UK: Brewer, 1995. 151–165.

The Manuscript Sources of
Divina auxiliante gratia

LINDA PAGE CUMMINS

Habent sua fata libelli.
—Maurus, *De litteris, syllabis et metris*

Traditional textual scholarship regarded manuscript witnesses as degenerate copies of the text the author intended; the critic's task was to eliminate the dross and recover the original. In his *Essai de poétique médiévale*, however, Paul Zumthor saw the variation among manuscript copies of the "same" text as an essential characteristic of medieval writing;[1] as Bernard Cerquiglini put it in his *Éloge de la variante*, the task of the medieval scribe was not to copy but to *rewrite*.[2] Present-day textual scholarship, accordingly, sees surviving witnesses not as deficient copies but as versions of a text valid in their own right, whose meaning is determined not only by the words that make them up but by the company in which they are placed and the manner in which they are presented; as Andrew Taylor notes in *Textual Situations*, the "meaning" of a text is not fixed but evolves diachronically.[3] Though a lost original may be said to have a destiny, in fact that destiny consists of multiple threads. Each copy of a text acquires a destiny bound to the physical document that contains it and subject to reinterpretation by later generations, based not only on its original creation but also on the conditions under which it has survived.

Traditional historiography of music theory placed such value on the lost original that it not only devalued variants, but also typically ignored those compendia that are dependent almost exclusively on sources recognized as significant, most particularly when these bear attribution to a named author. The fame of the parent work that originally assured their creation and preservation would today assure their virtual anonymity.

Divina auxiliante gratia (hereafter Divina) is a fifteenth-century music theory compendium whose content is drawn exclusively from the Lucidarium of Marchetto of Padua, a seminal work on plainchant theory by the leading music theorist of the Italian Trecento. Traditional views would dismiss Divina as a mere stepchild of its distinguished parent, likely undeserving of an edition of its own. Should it be deemed to merit one, the convention of tradition would certainly relegate its variant readings to the bottom of the page. Yet a study of its six surviving sources clearly shows that in the fifteenth century, Divina could literally stand in for its famous parent, was indeed considered a viable substitute, and was generally given a privileged position and enhanced decoration in its host manuscripts. Moreover, two redactors treated the text with exceptional liberty; their treatments (discussed below) are noteworthy, but cannot easily be accommodated in a conventional edition.

Divina's six manuscript sources confirm the distinction of Marchetto's reputation; in addition, they further corroborate the importance and necessity of the plainchant theory during the late Middle Ages and the Renaissance— importance and necessity that, though long recognized, have often been obscured by scholarly fascination with the concurrent development of polyphony. These sources also provide important evidence that compendia often have intentional design and purpose (though both may appear haphazard at first glance), as do the manuscripts that house them; and that a text's physical position in a manuscript and the size and decoration of its initials not only reflect the redactors' plans but also reveal a sense of the importance of particular works.

Biographical Excursus

Marchetto of Padua and his French contemporary Johannes de Muris were the preeminent music theorists of the fourteenth century. Both were influential for centuries, and the manuscript traditions of their works are entwined; the manuscripts considered here are typical in that respect. As I will make abundant reference to both in this essay, I will sketch their careers and influence at the outset,[4] beginning with Johannes, since the brief biography of Marchetto directly returns the discussion to Divina.

Johannes de Muris

Johannes de Muris was a mathematician and an astronomer as well as a music theorist. Known dates in his life extend from 1310, when he was implicated, along with his father, in the murder of a cleric; through the 1320s, when he was at the Sorbonne; to 1345, the year of his text on calendar reform, written in Avignon for the pope. His Notitia artis musice (1321) is the earliest treatise on the French theory of fourteenth-century rhythmic notation; he developed the theory further in the *Compendium musice practice*. The *Ars practica mensurabilis cantus* (formerly known as *Libellus cantus mensurabilis*), ascribed to him in more than fifty manuscripts, is the earliest complete statement of the theory, which became the foundation of the system of rhythmic notation that prevailed until around 1600. The *Ars contrapuncti secundum magistrum Johannem de Muris* (after 1340) is the most widely disseminated medieval treatise on counterpoint, with fourteen surviving sources.[5]

Marchetto of Padua

Marchetto of Padua was cantor at the cathedral of Padua during the first decade of the fourteenth century; recent research has placed him at the Naples court of Robert of Anjou and among the retinue of the royal couple when they departed for Avignon on May 18, 1318.[6] In the *Pomerium in arte musice mensurate* (between 1317 and 1319), dedicated to Robert, Marchetto set out the principles of an indigenous Italian system of rhythmic notation that differed in essential respects from Johannes's system and that flourished in Italy for a hundred years before its displacement by the more versatile French system. In the *Lucidarium in arte musice plane*, written shortly before the *Pomerium*, he proposed a division of the whole tone into fifths that contradicted the strictures of the prevailing "Pythagorean" tuning system of his time, removing an obstacle that could have blocked the eventual development of the present-day system of equal temperament. In this work he also developed a theory of chromatic progressions (those in which a melody proceeds directly from, say, C-natural to C-sharp), adapting earlier melodic theories to the musical realities of his day, and expounded a theory of modes in plainchant (predecessors of present-day major and minor keys) based on pentachord and tetrachord species (arrays respectively of five and of four consecutive pitches); his doctrine of modes became the basis of later such theories applicable to both plainchant and polyphony.[7]

In the *Lucidarium* and the *Pomerium* Marchetto spoke in a high scholastic mode, but he eventually fashioned a shorter treatment of rhythmic notation, the *Brevis compilatio*, which presents his theory of rhythmic notation without its scholastic vesture.[8] The anonymous *Divina* came to perform the same function for Marchetto's theory of mode.

Divina auxiliante gratia: Background and Extant Sources

Background

The destiny of Marchetto's *Lucidarium* has thus far not involved oblivion or anonymity. Only one of its eighteen surviving witnesses fails to name its author, and there are records of its having been read in every century since the fourteenth. But in the cut-and-paste world of the medieval text, that destiny did involve being broken into bits and pieces that were separated from the whole and scattered, with or without attribution, through countless other writings.[9] While traces of Marchetto's idiosyncratic doctrines are ubiquitous in Italian manuscripts of the fifteenth century, in two instances compendia drawn from the *Lucidarium*'s modal theory established their own manuscript traditions, became texts in their own right, and acquired their own destinies: the shorter *Sciendum est quod antiquitus* survives in three sources, the more expansive *Divina* in six, as mentioned above, one of which came to light only in the present decade.[10]

The Six Sources of Divina: *Similarities*

The six extant sources of *Divina auxiliante gratia* are:

Bergamo, Biblioteca Civica "Angelo Mai," MAB 21;
Florence, Biblioteca Medicea Laurenziana, Ashburnham 1119;
Florence, Biblioteca Medicea Laurenziana, Pluteus 29.48;
Pisa, Biblioteca Universitaria, 606;
Rome, Biblioteca Vallicelliana, B.83;
Venice, Biblioteca del Museo Correr, Correr 336, part 4.

Though in many respects the six versions of *Divina* are quite different, there are significant similarities.

1. Dating and origin: All are in fifteenth-century (or possibly very early sixteenth-century) Italian manuscripts (as witnessed by dates, watermarks, orthography, texts included). All now reside in libraries in Italy. As relatively few Italian fourteenth-century manuscripts of music theory are extant, the fact that all surviving copies of *Divina* are from the fifteenth or early sixteenth centuries does not preclude its having been compiled in the fourteenth century. In the sixteenth century, Marchetto's modal theory was absorbed into that of other major theorists whose works were propagated principally through prints rather than manuscripts.

2. Contents of the manuscripts containing *Divina*: All copies of *Divina* appear in manuscripts devoted either exclusively or primarily to music theory; and *Divina* keeps good company: four of the manuscripts include the Ars *practica mensurabilis cantus* ascribed to Johannes de Muris; five include the Ars *contrapuncti*, likewise ascribed to him; two include Book I of the Berkeley Compendium, notable as the earliest (1375) extensive treatment of accidentals (sharps and flats) outside the standard medieval array, which included only B-flats in addition to the "white" notes.[11]

3. Contents of the *Divina* text: In all versions, *Divina* includes the core of Marchetto's doctrine of mode along with its preliminary treatment of intervals.

The longer versions include as well an expanded treatment of modal theory, a discussion of musical punctuation, and material concerning elementary notation.

4. Attribution: With one exception (discussed below), the *Divina* text begins with a preface that reads:

> Diuina auxiliante gratia breuem tractatum compilare intendo de arte musicali plana, et hoc primo ad eruditionem mei, secundo ad proficuum adiscentium, tamen pro maiori parte ex libris boetij ac excellentissimi doctoris musice, videlicet Magistri marcheti paduani, extractum.

> With the aid of divine grace I intend to compile a short treatise on the art of plainchant, first for my own edification and second for the benefit of pupils. |It is| extracted for the most part from the books of Boethius and the most excellent teacher of music Master Marchetto the Paduan.[12]

The compiler thus intervenes between Marchetto and his text and forces Marchetto to share credit with—perhaps be validated by—Boethius; in fact, there is nothing from Boethius in *Divina*. Despite the admission that the text is a compilation and that credit must be shared, in all manuscripts but one (Venice 336) it is clear that *Divina* functions as a primary representative of Marchetto's work. His authority, in reality, goes uncontested.

5. Placement of the text in the manuscript and appearance of initials: In manuscripts from this time, the importance of a treatise is often indicated by its being placed at the beginning of a gathering or the top of a recto, and by the size and decoration of its initial. In all six sources, *Divina* is given a large decorated initial (often the largest in the manuscript) or has space left for one; in three, it is honored through placement at the beginning of a gathering, and in two others, at the top of a recto.

Individual Sources: Physical Condition, Contents Summary, *Divina's* Treatment

Turning now to the elements that distinguish one presentation of *Divina* from another in its sources, I will discuss the individual manuscripts and *Divina's* place in them, moving in progression from those which originally most respected the integrity of the text (or whose redactors intended to do so) to those which took the greatest liberties with it.

Pisa, Biblioteca Universitaria, 606, 189 pp. (Divina, part 1, pp. 111–125), paper, 263 x 180 mm, Northeast Italy, 1429

Pisa 606, copied in 1429, is one of only two *Divina* sources that bear a date. All published descriptions, beginning with Adrian de La Fage's,[13] treat the codex as two separate manuscripts bound together; recently Giuliano Di Bacco demonstrated that the two parts must have originally belonged to a single document that was later split in two and whose parts were then reassembled in the wrong order. The papers of both parts bear the same watermark; their writing blocks are identical in dimensions and lining, and (except for the item *Nota quod novem*) they were copied by the same hand. Moreover, if the present order of the sections were reversed to restore the manuscript's original layout, the largest (and most imposing) initial would come at the beginning of the manuscript, and what would become the last section would show the progressive decline in quality of execution often encountered toward the ends of manuscripts. Once the two parts are properly ordered, indeed, Pisa 606 emerges as a magnificent anthology representing, and distinguishing, French and Italian theoretical traditions: the first part is devoted to the French tradition—especially as represented by the work of Johannes de Muris—and the second to the Italian, represented by Marchetto of Padua.

Contents summary:[14]

> Original first part: Johannes de Muris and the French
> tradition
>> *Musica [speculativa] magistri Johannis de Muris;*
>> *Ars practica mensurabilis cantus [secundum Johannem de Muris];*
>> *Tractatus figurarum;*[15]
>> *Ars contrapuncti secundum Johannem de Muris;*
>> *Liber de proportionibus musice Johannis de Ciconiis;*[16]
>> *Contrapunctus secundum magistrum Johannem de Garlandia;*[17]
>> *Quoniam de canendi scientia;*[18]
>> "Jusquinus," *Nota quod novem sunt consonantie.*
>
> Original second part: Marchetto and the Italian tradition
>> *Lucidarium Marcheti de Padua in musica plana;*
>> *Pomerium musice mensurabili Marcheti de Padua;*
>> *Rubrice breves magistri Marcheti de Padua;*[19]
>> *Extractus Marcheti de Padua de tonis (= Divina auxiliante gratia);*
>> *Regule de tonis secundum illorum de Francia;*
>> *Exempla regularum Johannis de Muris.*[20]

The manuscript was beautifully prepared and executed in a neat, clear hand with few errors. Of all the manuscripts, this one most respects all its individual treatises as entities: each begins at the top of a fresh page; each begins with an initial or with space left for one (see fig. 1); most are clearly identified in a caption or a colophon (sometimes both). Evidently this document was intended not just to collect the texts it transmits, but to monumentalize them. As Di Bacco points out, the redactor seems to have made an effort to represent the main authors as broadly as possible; this is one of the few sources in which Johannes de Muris's unreservedly theoretical *Musica speculativa* rubs shoulders with the eminently practical *Ars practica mensurabilis cantus*, and the only source that contains *Divina* along with its parent *Lucidarium*. (Marchetto's *Brevis compilatio*, notably absent, had a very narrow dissemination; perhaps it was unavailable, or even unknown, to the redactor.)

The text of *Divina* is good but is truncated, closing near the bottom of a recto much earlier in the text than any other source and without a colophon; given the redactor's penchant for inclusion, it is likely that he was copying from a defective source. Aside from an excerpt on ligatures drawn from the *Brevis compilatio* in Rome B.83, only Pisa 606 contains works ascribed to Marchetto other than *Divina*.

Florence, Biblioteca Medicea Laurenziana, Ashburnham 1119, 80 fols. (Divina, 33r–46r), *paper, 194–198 x 139–140 mm, Italy, fifteenth century*

The redactor of Florence 1119 also seems to have had a clear design in mind, as a summary of the contents shows (here plotted against the manuscript's three constituent libelli).

Contents summary:[21]

Libellus 1
Opusculum de arte musica;
small treatises on music fundamentals.

Libellus 2
Divina auxiliante gratia;
treatise on ratios and intervals;
five small treatises on counterpoint.

Libellus 3
Ars practica mensurabilis cantus secundum Johannem de Muris;
six small treatises on counterpoint.

The manuscript was carefully prepared. The first treatise in each libellus is provided with an initial; both *Divina*, opening libellus 2, and the *Ars practica mensurabilis cantus*, opening libellus 3, have large initials within the writing block; *Divina's* is the most ornate (see fig. 2). No space was left for the first initial (on the first verso, not the first recto, of the manuscript), so that, unlike the other initials, it had to be placed in the margin. This makes the first libellus appear to be something of an afterthought; and, indeed, the writing block of the first libellus differs from that of the remainder of the manuscript in both dimensions and lining. So this redactor, like that of Pisa 606, appears to have intended, through the works that open the second and third libelli, to highlight plainchant theory and the notation of rhythm, Italian theory and French, Marchetto of Padua and Johannes de Muris, *Divina auxiliante gratia* and the *Ars practica mensurabilis cantus*. He then filled space remaining in the two libelli with smaller treatises addressing other aspects of music theory. The *Opusculum* covers fundamentals of music theory, as do the small treatises that follow it in the first libellus. If the addition of the first libellus was indeed an afterthought, it may have been prompted by a wish to provide elementary material to better prepare for the more advanced material covered in *Divina*.

Florence 1119 is one of three manuscripts that contain the full text of *Divina*. Comparison with the other manuscripts shows that the compiler intervened only minimally in the text, with occasional insertions that further explain or sum up a previous topic in language borrowed primarily from sections of the *Lucidarium* not found in other copies of *Divina*. Thus it appears that this version of *Divina* was compiled or copied by someone who wished to preserve Marchetto's ideas and who knew the *Lucidarium* well enough to turn to it when he felt the need for further clarity. The *Opusculum* supports that hypothesis, as it borrows frequently from the *Lucidarium*, often citing chapter and paragraph.

On the whole, Florence 1119 has one of the most accurate texts of *Divina*. Unfortunately, it has suffered because the ink, especially in the musical examples, has eaten the paper, making the notation nearly illegible and also obliterating words in the text on the reverse side (see fig. 2).

Rome, Biblioteca Vallicelliana, B.83, composite, music section 81 fols. (*Divina, 18r–29v*), *paper, 136–140 x 101–105 mm, Italy, fifteenth century*
The redactor of Rome B.83 evidently intended to collect a variety of texts on plainchant, counterpoint, ratios, and rhythmic notation, including some by major figures from the early fourteenth through the early fifteenth centuries. In addition to Johannes de Muris and Marchetto, he includes Philippe de Vitry, Johannes Ciconia (both composers as well as theorists), and Nicolaus of Capua, whose *Compendium musicale*, did it not break off on a verso after about the first tenth of its text as found in another manuscript, would have been its longest single item by far. But Rome B.83 was neither carefully prepared nor carefully written and—excepting the mere fact of its preservation—its destiny has not involved much better treatment. It now suffers not only from missing folios but also from a radical restoration, in the course of which leaves were arbitrarily

joined to make bifolios in such a way that it is now impossible to determine the original structure. From La Fage's description, it is clear that the leaves are not in the same order as they were when he saw it in the middle of the nineteenth century.[22] Almost every text in the manuscript is fragmentary, and a number of ascriptions, some evidently written by modern librarians, are incorrect.

Initials were never copied into the manuscript, but blocks of space, all of approximately the same size, were left for them at the beginnings of treatises—at least, of those treatises whose beginnings remain intact (see fig. 3). Thus it is impossible to know whether any treatises would have been given preference by more elaborately decorated initials. Of the eight treatise openings that survive, six begin at the top of rectos. Many are preceded by the doxology "Jhesus Maria" and close with phrases such as "Hec dicta sufficiant |Let what has been said suffice|." Thus we can see that the scribe respected the integrity of his texts, even though the gathering structure cannot be determined and we lack visual clues to establish a hierarchy of importance. Yet despite its present state, it is possible to discern vestiges of an organizational plan.

Contents summary:[23]

> Section 1: Counterpoint and ratios
> Ars contrapunctus Magistri Philippi de Vitriaco;
> notes referring to Franco of Cologne and Johannes de
>   Bulgundia (sic);
> Nova musica and De proportionibus of Johannes Ciconia
>   (fragments only);
> Ars contrapunctus secundum Johannem de Muris (fragments).
>
> Section 2: Plainchant theory and rhythmic notation
> (Marchetto and Muris)
> Divina auxiliante gratia;
> Brevis compilatio (fragment ascribed to Marchetto);
> Ars practica mensurabilis cantus secundum Johannem de Muris.
>
> Section 3: Plainchant theory, with material on counterpoint
> and ratios
> Anonymous text on fundamentals, plainchant theory,
>   counterpoint;
> Marchetto, Lucidarium, excerpts (here unascribed);
> Nicolaus de Capua, Compendium musicale (incomplete);
> miscellaneous verses on music theory;
> Sciendum est quod contrapunctus est fundamentum discanti
>   (counterpoint treatise elsewhere ascribed to
>   Philipoctus de Caserta);

texts on ratios here ascribed to Johannes de Muris;
fragments on plainchant and counterpoint.

Section 1 contains texts on counterpoint and ratios by major French theorists. Only the first bears an ascription, to Philippe de Vitry; the following two treatises, by Johannes Ciconia and Johannes de Muris, are incomplete at their beginnings and so lack the titles that appear in other sources.

Section 2 is devoted to Divina (with full credit to Marchetto) and to the Ars practica mensurabilis cantus, explicitly ascribed to Johannes de Muris. These two major works are separated by an excerpt from Marchetto's abbreviated treatment of rhythmic notation, the Brevis compilatio, also with an ascription. Thus, as in Florence 1119, Marchetto and Muris are juxtaposed through representative Italian and French texts on plainchant and rhythmic notation respectively, reflecting on a smaller scale the larger design of Pisa 606.

Section 3 offers texts on a variety of subjects and includes a set of unascribed excerpts from Marchetto's Lucidarium and the opening of the Compendium musicale of Nicolaus of Capua.

Marchetto is well represented here: of the eighty-one surviving folios, seventeen contain material by him, both ascribed and unascribed. The manuscript contains both the beginning and the end of Divina, and it is likely that it would contain the full text were it not missing a number of folios; aside from these, the text includes most of the material found in Florence 1119 and shares many variants with it—though not Florence 1119's few brief interpolations mentioned above. Clearly, Divina was chosen as the prime representative of Marchetto's plainchant theory, just as the Brevis compilatio was for his theory of rhythmic notation.

Florence, Biblioteca Medicea Laurenziana, Pluteus 29.48, 120 fols. (Divina, 93r–97v), paper, 225 x 165 mm, Tuscany, ca. 1475

Florence 29.48 still retains the chain that fastened it to the table in the old library. It is in excellent condition, and though not as extravagantly provided with initials as Pisa 606, it was carefully and exquisitely prepared in a clear hand, though with many mistakes. Padre Giovanni Battista Martini made a copy (now in the Civico Museo, Bologna) of parts of the manuscript that served as an exemplar for both Martin Gerbert and Edmond de Coussemaker.[24]

Even though the scribe left ample margins, he did not always take a new line to begin a treatise (sometimes leaving room only for some smaller initial in the middle of a line to mark a new work), much less leave blank space in order to begin a text at the top of a page. Only the three treatises that begin the libelli into which the material is organized are positioned at the top of a page: the treatise that currently opens the manuscript, De musica intervallosa, unascribed here but attributed to the fifteenth-century English theorist John

Hothby; the Ars contrapuncti secundum Johannem de Muris on folio 83r, considered by Di Bacco (on the basis of fascicle numbering and size of initial, among other factors) to be the original opening fascicle; and Divina on folio 93r.

The contents of Florence 29.48 are the most varied of any manuscript under consideration here. Like many medieval manuscripts, it groups treatises into categories that are clearly defined at the beginnings but sometimes fray toward the end, including works that do not always fit comfortably with their neighbors. Divina's importance (and that of other two that begin libelli) is indicated not simply by physical position but by being chosen to begin new topics, as the following outline of the manuscript shows. The material included covers a wide date range.

Contents summary:[25]

> Libellus 1
>> John Hothby, De musica intervallosa (here unascribed);
>> various musical topics;
>> Johannes Tinctoris, Proportionale musices;
>> treatises by and ascribed to Guido of Arezzo
>>> (early eleventh century);
>> notes on various theoretical topics;
>> Isidore of Seville, discussion of music from Etymologiae
>>> (ca. 600);
>> Aurelian of Réôme, Musica disciplina (late ninth century);
>> Regule de contrapuncto;
>> Ars cantus mensurabilis mensurata per modos iuris.
>
> Libellus 2: texts on counterpoint
>> Ars contrapuncti secundum Johannem de Muris;
>> Ars contrapuncti secundum Philippum de Vitriaco;
>> Post octavam quintam;
>> Ars contrapuncti secundum magistrum Zachariam;
>> notes on intervals and counterpoint.
>
> Libellus 3
>> Divina auxiliante gratia;
>> texts on various musical topics (some ascribed to
>>> Hothby).

The first libellus opens with Hothby's De musica intervallosa and the Proportionale musices of Johannes Tinctoris; the English Carmelite Hothby had a distinguished career as cantor and teacher in Lucca, and Tinctoris is generally considered the preeminent music theorist of the fifteenth century. These are followed by treatises of venerable age, among them the *Micrologus* and three shorter treatises by Guido of Arezzo (early eleventh century); the anonymous *Dialogus de musica* (*ca.* 1000) formerly attributed to Odo of Cluny but in this manuscript, as in many others, ascribed to Guido; Aurelian of Réôme's *Musica disciplina* (late ninth century); and the discussion of music from Isidore's *Etymologiae*.

Guido developed the *ut-re-mi-fa-sol-la* system of teaching singing and was the first to describe the staff; he is considered the most influential music theorist of the Middle Ages, and his works survive in more than eighty sources. The *Dialogus de musica* was the first treatise to use Latin letters for the notes of the scale in the manner still common today and was one of the sources from which Guido drew. Aurelian's *Musica disciplina* was a monument of the Carolingian revival, but by the fifteenth century its content would have been of only antiquarian interest. Isidore's so-called *Sententiae de musica* circulated separately from the rest of the *Etymologiae* in many music theory manuscripts. The first libellus closes with an anonymous counterpoint treatise and the extraordinarily interesting *Ars cantus mensurabilis mensurata per modos iuris*, a reworking of Muris's *Ars practica* argued through legal precepts.[26]

The second libellus includes five treatises on counterpoint, three of which are dignified with authors' names. The first, by Johannes de Muris, appears in five of the six *Divina* manuscripts; the second, by Philippe de Vitry, in Rome B.83 as well. *Post octavam quintam* is (after the *Ars contrapuncti secundum Johannem de Muris*) the second most widely disseminated medieval counterpoint treatise, appearing in eight manuscripts. The libellus closes with a collection of notes on contrapuntal practice.

In the third libellus, *Divina* introduces plainchant theory and is followed first by other material on that topic and then by a series of alternating treatises on counterpoint and rhythmic notation. In addition to its privileged location at the beginning of a libellus in Florence 29.48, *Divina* is further dignified through the acquisition of an exordium that not only serves as an introduction but treats letters and hexachords (arrangements of the syllables *ut-re-mi-fa-sol-la*) and thus gives information prerequisite to an understanding of *Divina*. Following the exordium, the *Divina* text proper merits space for an initial at the beginning of a line (see fig. 4). This is one of two versions that omit *Divina*'s musical examples, either through scribal intent or deficiency of the exemplar. Other treatises in the manuscript include examples; in *Divina* the scribe neither wrote them nor left room for them, though he copied the words *"ut hic patet* [as is evident here]" any number of times. Bergamo 21, whose text often varies with Florence 29.48, is missing the examples as well; the two may derive from a common source that also lacks examples. The discussions of clefs and registers of the voice that close *Divina* in most of its sources are lacking here.

Bergamo, Biblioteca Civica "Angelo Mai," MAB 21, 102 fols. (Divina, 67r–86v), paper, 210–215 x 155–160 mm, Bergamo, 1487

Unlike the other manuscripts considered in this essay, Bergamo 21 does tell us something of its origins:

> Hoc opusculum scriptum et notatum fuit per fratrem
> alexandrum de assolarijs de albino ordinis carmelitarum
> obseruancie in conuentu nostro bergomi . . . sub anno
> M.cccc.lxxxvij. die prima mensis decembris. [fol. 100r]

> This little work was written and notated by Brother
> Alexander de Assolariis of Albino, of the Carmelites of the
> Observance, in our convent at Bergamo in the year 1487, on
> the first day of the month of December.

Thus Alexander de Assolariis (whose given name honors a patron saint of Bergamo and whose family name is still common in the area) presents himself as a native of Albino (a nearby village) and a member of a Bergamasque order of Carmelite monks. The contents are primarily music theory treatises of the sort that would support the musical and liturgical activities of such a community, plus a few musical compositions that might have been part of their repertory. As we will see below, some of its contents have distinctly Lombard connections. The manuscript now resides in the Bergamo public library, only two blocks from the convent in which it was written (whose structure still stands, crumbling, its main portal now blocked by the extension of a neighboring building). Few music theory manuscripts are as redolent of the time and place of their origin as this one.

The handwriting of Bergamo 21 is neat if somewhat crude; the spelling is erratic, the grammar faulty. Though the manuscript is not lavishly made, it does include fanciful images—an initial depicting naked twins playing trumpets from the bells of which issue garlands; a colorful if uncharacteristically chubby "Guidonian" hand (a representation of the notes of the medieval scale and their syllables, ubiquitous in medieval and early modern music theory manuscripts); and on folio 19v, left blank at the end of the first treatise, sketches of what appear to be rooftops and human figures (perhaps in ecclesiastical robes); the head of one figure has been traced in ink that appears to be the same as the ink of the text.

Contents summary:[27]

Libellus 1
    Franchino Gafurio, *Practica musice*, Book I (early draft);
    treatise on division of the monochord (= Guido, *Micrologus*,
        chapter 3).

Libellus 2

> *Ad habendum noticiam artis musice* (= Berkeley Compendium, Book I);
>
> treatise on consonances and dissonances;
>
> *Circha contrapunctum* (similar to a treatment by Carmelite John Hothby);
>
> *De ratione contrapuncti* (a compendium of nine treatises on counterpoint and rhythmic notation organized into three chapters; the first is the Ars *contrapuncti secundum Johannem de Muris*);
>
> *De coniunctione moteti* (texts on counterpoint and rhythmic notation);
>
> Johannes de Muris, Ars *practica mensurabilis cantus* (a later hand has indicated, incorrectly, that Johannes was a member of the Carmelite order);
>
> treatise on ratios;
>
> treatise on rhythmic notation ascribed to *Magister Ricardus ordinis Carmelitarum*;
>
> *Cartula de cantu plano* ascribed to Stefanus de Laudosio (= Lodi).

Libellus 3

> *Sermo Sancti Bernardi abbatis de modo psalendi*;
>
> notes on ratios;
>
> tables of intervals and hexachords;
>
> treatise on music fundamentals;
>
> table of note values;
>
> table relating musical scale to planets, muses, etc.;
>
> diagram of monochord division.

Libellus 4

> *Divina auxiliante gratia* (with interpolations and additions; incomplete at end);
>
> texts on plainchant;
>
> musical compositions; exercises in singing, solmization, mutation;
>
> mnemonic verses pertaining to plainchant performance.

The treatise that opens the manuscript is an early draft of Book I of Franchino Gafurio's *Practica musice*, arguably the treatise of greatest influence on the musical thought of the sixteenth century;[28] its content is dependent in large part on Marchetto's *Lucidarium*, which Gafurio had copied in 1473. The draft of Gafurio's Book I was copied into Bergamo 21 nine years before the entire treatise was printed in 1496; Clement Miller recognized the importance of the Bergamo version as a key to the development of Gafurio's thought.[29] Gafurio was a native of Lodi, a Lombard village about forty kilometers south of Bergamo, and the treatise may owe its presence in this manuscript to his employment at the cathedral of Bergamo, though he was there for no more than eight months, beginning in May 1483.[30]

Divina is one of only three treatises that begin gatherings (Gafurio's Practica musice would almost certainly be a fourth if its opening were not missing). The scribe was fond of using large but plain initials to mark both the beginnings of treatises and subheadings within them, often making little distinction in size between the two, but as Di Bacco notes, he does use a combination of size and decoration to single out four (to which, again, Gafurio's Practica musice must be added): Ad habendum noticiam (a simply decorated initial, and beginning a libellus; on plainchant); De ratione contrapuncti (a larger initial, but without decoration; on simple counterpoint); Quedam cartula de cantu plano (featuring the most ornate initial, with the trumpet-playing twins mentioned above), ascribed to Stephanus de Laudosio, presumably, like Gafurio, a native of Lodi; and Divina (whose initial is almost twice as large as any other, but with one simple flower for decoration, and beginning a libellus; see fig. 5). These highlight the principal interests of the scribe, a practicing monastic musician for whom musica plana and counterpoint would be essential.

Bergamo 21's Divina is the most unusual version of its text. During the first twenty-three chapters of this version of Divina, the compiler coordinates Marchetto's modal doctrine point by point with another doctrine he says is that of Guido of Arezzo, labeling most of the chapters "secundum Marchettum" and "secundum Guidonem" in alternation. In fact, very little of the interpolated material can be found in treatises attributed to Guido, but much of it is identified by Jan Herlinger as excerpts from the Dialogus de musica, often ascribed to Guido in the Middle Ages, as in the version of Florence 29.48.[31]

The tag "secundum Guidonem" may have signaled for the Bergamo 21 redactor simply a theory of mode more conventional than Marchetto's, and he here sets up a dialogue between old and new: modal theory based on final and range on the one hand ("Guido"), or on species of pentachord and tetrachord on the other (Marchetto). After this dialogue he interpolates six chapters, four of which include material concordant with that of other Lombard theorists (Johannes Olomons, who maintained a singing school at Castiglione Olona, and Bonaventura da Brescia). Finally he tacks on additional chapters at the end of the Divina material, in one of which he represents Guido's pioneering description of the staff as a phenomenon characteristic of "our Lombard clerics." How long these additional chapters might have gone on we do not know, as the Bergamo 21 version's thirty-eighth chapter (Divina itself had sixteen) breaks off in the middle of a sentence at the end of a gathering.

Alexander introduces himself in the colophon only as the manuscript's textual and musical scribe. But he seems to have assumed a proprietarial role in the manuscript's contents: in Ad *habendum noticiam* (the Bergamo 21 redaction of what has come to be known as the First Book of the Berkeley Compendium), after dismissing other theorists' views on the number of *coniunctae* (accidentals other than the two B-flats that were the only ones in the traditional medieval scale), he replaces the other Berkeley sources' *"ego tamen* (or *sed ego*) *dico* |but I say|" with *"ego autem* Frater A. *dico* |but I, Brother A., say|." As the text of *Divina* is particularly idiosyncratic, it is tempting to see Alexander as its redactor and, indeed, as the redactor of the entire manuscript.

Venice, Biblioteca del Museo Correr, Correr 336, part 4, 32 fols. (Divina, 434r–444r),[32] *paper, 215–216 x 156–158 mm, Northwest Italy, late fifteenth–early sixteenth century*
       The bifolios of Venice 336, part 4, were originally numbered 1 to 8 and 9 to 16; thus we know that the pages that open this collection were intended as the opening of a work, but about the role of that work in a larger plan no more can be said. Venice 336, part 4, is currently the last of four manuscripts bound together in a composite volume. The first two do not concern music;[33] the third is a handwritten copy, dated 1502, of the 1496 print of Gafurio's *Practica musice.*[34] The table of contents of the composite volume does not mention the fourth and final component; overshadowed by its much larger neighbors, it was long overlooked.[35]
       The content of Venice 336, part 4, is concerned primarily with plainchant and music fundamentals.[36] It was copied in medium-brown ink in a not particularly refined cursive humanistic hand. The crudeness of the handwriting; the sometimes fanciful but rarely carefully drawn *paragraphi* in red ink; the notation of musical examples where what should be diamond-shaped notes are drawn as triangles with tails; a crowded writing block; initials that appear misplaced; a confusing array of captions in both brown and red ink, sometimes centered but more often placed in margins or at the ends of lines or squeezed between them, captions in red sometimes duplicating those in brown; and a repetitious sequence of topics that initially seem haphazard—all these give the first impression of a carelessly produced document, an impression far from correct. Identifying the sources from which the compiler borrowed and unraveling the visual clues, particularly initials and capitals, reveal a thoughtful and purposeful design.[37]
       Divina offers the most obvious clues to this unraveling. Just as in the other versions, it is singled out with a large initial—the largest in the manuscript and the only one written in red ink and within space left for it in the writing block. This copy includes *Divina's* chapter titles, which are present in four of the five other versions of the text (all but Florence 29.48); they are written in the brown ink, given adequate space and often centered, and appear to have been

part of the first layer of copying. (The only two red captions found in the Venice 336 *Divina* were inserted in space left below examples and do not appear in the other versions of that text.) Initials that mark subdivisions of the *Divina* text—much smaller than that at the opening of *Divina* but as large as or larger than any elsewhere in the manuscript—are also in brown, placed within the writing block, and often decorated with red; this also fits the pattern of other *Divina* copies. Thus it would appear that the Venice 336 scribe copied the *Divina* text from an exemplar not very different in layout from other known sources.

The two centered brown captions signal the two-part, large-scale structure of the compendium: *Ars cantandi* opens the manuscript (fol. 425); *Manus* follows (from fol. 444v). *Ars cantandi* is a comprehensive survey of the art of plainchant; the three enlarged initials mark the beginnings of its three main treatises from which material is borrowed: basic material on plainchant concordant with Vallicelliana C.105[38] (marked by the enlarged N of *Nota quod sunt tres modi cantandi*); more complex issues from Book I of the fourteenth-century Berkeley Compendium (marked by the enlarged S of *Sciendum quod mutatio*); and the fifteenth-century *Divina* (with its large red initial).

The caption of *Manus* refers to the "Guidonian" hand on which the notes of the scale and their syllables were often inscribed; here it serves as an emblem for elementary music theory. After an exhortation to students to learn terms, "since the beginning of all knowledge is to know terms, as the Philosopher (Aristotle) says in the first book of the *Posterior Analytics*,"[39] the compiler reviews the material from *Ars cantandi*, repeating some passages literally, directing the reader back to information "above,"[40] and once referring to examples "notated on folio 5,"[41] where such examples do in fact appear. He presents information in formats conducive to memorization, including mnemonic verses,[42] and urges students, "Let all these be committed to memory."[43]

Contents summary with concordances:[44]

> *Ars cantandi*
>> *Nota quod sunt tres modi cantandi* (~ Vallicelliana C.105, 119r–123v);
>> *De mutationibus, Mutatio sic diffinitur* (= *Ars musice plane optima et perfecta*, Lucca, Biblioteca Statale, MS 359, 107r–108r);
>> *Sciendum quod mutatio* (= Berkeley Compendium 1.2–8);
>> *De litteris musicalibus*, etc. (letters, hexachords, mutations, intervals);
>> *Divina auxiliante gratia*;
>> *Dico quidquid rite sonuerit* (= Martianus Cappela, *De nuptiis*, fragment).

Manus
> *Cupiens de rationibus cantus tractare* (letters, syllables, hexachords, mutations; intervals, modes).

Once the larger plan is obvious, it becomes clear that the compiler has made the material of music theory accessible by ordering topics so that each proceeds from the simple to the more complex, by omitting beginnings and endings and inserting short connectors to make smoother and more logical transitions from one topic or treatise to another, and by dividing his material into two units: knowledge (*Ars cantandi*), and the practical methods of absorbing that knowledge (*Manus*). As both Malcolm Parkes and A. J. Minnis have shown, much of the contribution of compilers in the later Middle Ages consisted of imposing order on the material they copied, often by dividing a large work into sections, providing new headings, making tables of contents, even reorganizing material, all to make the information more accessible to the reader.[45] The Venice 336 compiler, working with multiple sources, performed this same function.

Interestingly, the compiler maintained the integrity of his borrowed components except at their beginnings and endings, where he obscured primary identifiers such as opening sentences and attributions by abridgement or omission. The Venice 336 compiler seems to have felt little need of *auctoritas*, whether real or invented. In fact, the Venice 336 text lacks any appeal to authority other than God and Aristotle. Of the three major texts he chose, only *Divina* includes an authorial attribution in its other sources.[46] The Venice 336 compiler needed only the deliberate omission of the *Divina* attribution to create a text that lacks any attribution at all. He did this by truncating *Divina's* preface (see the original preface in the subsection "The Six Sources of *Divina*: Similarities" above) to read simply "*Divina auxiliante gratia, etc.*" Though he relocated to the opening of *Manus* the words that "etc." replaces (and it is this relocation that proves that his exemplar of *Divina* included the full preface), he never named Boethius or Marchetto, as the original preface does. Thus in this work *Divina*, along with all the other source texts, is literally swallowed, absorbed into the larger plan.

Here is the opening of *Manus*, the compiler's reworking of the remainder of *Divina's* preface (see the original preface in the subsection "The Six Sources of *Divina*: Similarities" above).

> Cupiens de rationibus cantus tractare, primo ad
> erudicionem mei, secundo ad profectum adissencium, non
> meis sed aliorum dictis quasi expleto flores decerpens,[47]
> domino inspirante hoc breue opusculum compilauj: |fol.
> 444v|

> Desiring to treat of the rules of song, first for my own
> edification, second for the profit of pupils, not in my own
> words, but almost completely in those of others—plucking
> flowers—with the Lord providing inspiration, I compiled this
> short little work.

The compiler relocated and refocused Divina's opening and in the process afforded us insights into his own view of his work. First, he revealed what is surely his primary purpose: "for the profit of pupils." Echoing St. Bonaventure's definition of a compiler, he claimed to have compiled "not in my own words but in those of others"; and he gave this definition quite literally in the words of another—the Divina compiler.[48] His "others" are not authorities; they are completely anonymous. Marchetto, originally forced to share credit with Boethius in the original preface, has now been reduced to the status of "other." And then the compiler issued one caveat: "not in my own words, but *almost* completely in those of others"—claiming a bit of credit for himself.

The Venice 336 compiler also described his working method; he chose his sources as though (using a common metaphor) "plucking flowers," but it is clear that he did not create this bouquet willy-nilly. It is a meticulously crafted document made of carefully chosen flowers that the compiler clipped, separated, and rearranged to create a bouquet whose design is logical, practical, and beautiful.

Conclusion

Traditional textual scholarship regarded manuscript witnesses as degenerate versions of a lost archetype; similarly, traditional historiography of music theory could dismiss Divina as a mere stepchild of its distinguished parent. Late-medieval readers, however, saw it differently—as a concise, more practical version. Stripped of the Lucidarium's scholastic apparatus, it was still capable of standing in for the longer treatise, as it does in five of its six sources. For that matter, the Lucidarium itself is complete, or nearly so, in only eighteen sources, so that the five additional Divina sources increase the array of manuscripts transmitting Marchetto's modal doctrine by almost one-third.[49]

Divina's practical approach to Marchetto's modal theory certainly lies behind its inclusion in Venice 336, whose purpose is indisputably didactic, and also in Bergamo 21, where the compiler could use both the concision of its content and its clearly marked chapters to set up his comparison of older modal theory with Marchetto's innovations. Divina's presence particularly in the five manuscripts oriented toward musical practice (excepting only Florence 29.48) further substantiates fifteenth-century musicians' concern for modal theory in particular and plainchant in general. The large initial that adorns (or was meant to adorn) Divina's opening in all six manuscripts may pay homage to Marchetto, but its positioning, marking major divisions in the organization of their topics, also speaks to the continued importance of the theories it presents.

Marchetto's pairing with Johannes de Muris shaped *Divina*'s destiny as surely as did its practicality, assuring its admission into the anthology Pisa 606 and also influencing its position in those manuscript collections (the two Florence manuscripts and Rome B.83) whose purposes—other than collecting—are less obvious. The distinction of the two theorists in the music theory of their respective countries almost certainly played a role in giving to *Divina*, as its almost constant traveling companions, Johannes's *Ars practica mensurabilis cantus* and the *Ars contrapuncti secundum Johannem de Muris*.

Historians succeed the musicians who copied and first read these texts, and scholars' interests ramify over time. In the eighteenth century, Martini had a copy made of Florence 29.48, the copy used by Gerbert (1784) and Coussemaker (1869); their publications and those of La Fage (1864) brought particular works to the attention of later scholars. One of the treatises Coussemaker published (*Ars contrapuncti secundum Johannes de Muris*) caught the attention, more than a century later, of Di Bacco (2001), who published a detailed study of its manuscript transmission. Without knowing *Divina* from five of his sources, Di Bacco would not have been able to identify Venice 336 as one further source. Thus the company in which *Divina* was placed reveals its past and continues to determine its fortunes.

Those fortunes, however, have not always been enhanced by that company: it was the presence of a copy of Gafurio's *Practica musice* in the composite Venice 336 that helped obscure the presence there of the relatively tiny compendium that includes *Divina*. Ironically, though, the presence of a preliminary draft of the *Practica musice* in Bergamo 21 led to publication of the entire manuscript on a commercial CD-ROM, which has made the text of *Divina* available to a wide audience.[50] And it may have been the famous array of theorists mentioned by name in Rome B.83 (Philippe de Vitry, Franco of Cologne, Marchetto, Boethius, Johannes de Muris, Nicolaus of Capua) that prompted the overzealous restoration that has obliterated all traces of its original structure.

From "extracted from the books of . . . the most excellent teacher of music Master Marchetto the Paduan" to "in the words of others"; from inclusion in a volume clearly meant to present the most important treatises of Italian and French fourteenth-century music theory to a bit of anonymous information; from the hand or direction of a collector to that of the practical musician; from pristine, intact, and filigreed to ragged and torn; from library shelf to microfilm to commercial CD-ROM, and more recently to my own digital photos—*Divina auxiliante gratia* has followed a rich, if patchwork, destiny. That destiny tells us much about the ways in which music theory was and continues to be transmitted, used, and regarded; and it reiterates for us both the reality of the ravages of time and the miracle of preservation. It also necessitates a rethinking of the edition—not only the edition of Divina, but editions of medieval texts in general.

Traditional textual scholarship, in its efforts to capture the text of an archetype, has sacrificed details of its witnesses, imprisoning them at the foot of the page, to paraphrase Cerquiglini.[51] But the grandeur of Pisa 606 is invisible there, the exordium of Florence 29.48 uncomfortable as a footnote. My own working collation in six parallel columns would also be condemned by Cerquiglini as an ineffective solution[52]—and it is—for my fragmentation by multiplication, with its subsequent blank spaces where other versions have interpolations, is every bit as misleading as the physical fragmentation of Rome B.83 or the compiler's fragmentation of Divina in Bergamo 21. And so the question hangs. How are we to construct a critical edition while respecting the individual identities and the richer views the Divina variants offer? This is a question that twenty-first-century editors have yet to address adequately, even as we move toward more online editions, and it haunts me—until I realize that ultimately, in whatever form my edition eventually takes, I become just another in this line of compilers, producing another version of Divina that suits my purposes and addresses my audience—yet another variant as I, in turn, rewrite.

University of Alabama

ACKNOWLEDGMENTS

I would like to thank a number of individuals and institutions for support in the preparation of this essay. Giuliano Di Bacco's book De Muris e gli altri: Sulla tradizione di un trattato trecentesco di contrappunnto (Lucca, Italy: Libreria Musicale Italiana, 2001) provides penetrating studies of the fourteen known sources of the Ars contrapuncti secundum Johannem de Muris, including five of the manuscripts of Divina auxiliante gratia; Giuliano also alerted me to the existence of the sixth source of Divina before it was announced in Christian Meyer et al., The Theory of Music: Manuscripts from the Carolingian Era up to c. 1500—Addenda, Corrigenda, Descriptive Catalogue, Répertoire international des sources musicales B III[6] (Munich: G. Henle Verlag, 2003). Jan Herlinger (with whom I am collaborating on an edition of Divina) and Matthew Balensuela offered many helpful suggestions. Research for the project was funded in part by a grant from the University of Alabama Research Advisory Committee. I received generous assistance and permission to publish figures from librarians at the Biblioteca Civica "Angelo Mai," Bergamo; the Biblioteca Medicea Laurenziana, Florence; the Biblioteca del Museo Correr, Venice; the Biblioteca Universitaria, Pisa; and the Biblioteca Vallicelliana, Rome.

NOTES

1. Paul Zumthor, *Toward a Medieval Poetics*, trans. Philip Bennet (Minneapolis and Oxford: University of Minnesota Press, 1992), 41–49, esp. 46. Originally published as *Essai de poétique médiévale* (Paris: Éditions du Seuil, 1972).

2. Bernard Cerquiglini, *In Praise of the Variant: A Critical History of Philology*, trans. Betsy Wing (Baltimore, MD, and London: Johns Hopkins University Press, 1999), 33–45. Originally published as *Éloge de la variante: Histoire critique de la philologie* (Paris: Éditions du Seuil, 1989).

3. Andrew Taylor, *Textual Situations: Three Medieval Manuscripts and Their Readers* (Philadelphia: University of Pennsylvania Press, 2002), 13.

4. For extensive discussions of writers and works, see Stanley Sadie, ed., *The New Grove Dictionary of Music and Musicians*, executive ed. John Tyrell, 2nd ed., 29 vols. (London: Macmillan, 2001); also Grove Music Online, at Oxford Music Online, http://www.oxfordmusiconline.com/subscriber/article/grove/music/17738 (accessed August 21, 2009). General introductions can be found in David Russell Williams and C. Matthew Balensuela, eds., *Music Theory from Boethius to Zarlino* (Hillsdale, NY: Pendragon Press, 2007).

5. Editions of the *Notitia* and the *Compendium musicale*: Johannis de Muris, *Notitia artis musicae, et Compendium musicae practicae*; *Petrus de Sancto Dionysio: Tractatus de musica*, ed. Ulrich Michels, Corpus Scriptorum de Musica 17 (n.p.: American Institute of Musicology, 1972); the *Notitia* appears in part in Martin Gerbert, *Scriptores ecclesiastici de musica sacra potissimum*, 3 vols. (St. Blaise, 1784), vol. 3, 312–315 (Book 1) and 292–301 (Book 2); the *Compendium musicale* appears in Gerbert, *Scriptores ecclesiastici*, vol. 3, 301–306. Editions of *Musica speculativa*: Gerbert, *Scriptores ecclesiastici*, vol. 3, 249–283; and Johannes de Muris, *Musica (speculativa)*, ed. Susan Fast, Musicological Studies 61 (Ottawa, Canada: Institute of Mediaeval Music, 1994). Editions of the *Ars practica*: Edmund de Coussemaker, ed., *Scriptorum de musica medii aevi nova series a gerbertina altera*, 4 vols. (Paris: Durand et Pedone-Lauriel, 1864–1876), vol. 3 (1869), 46–58; a critical edition is *Ars practica mensurabilis cantus secundum Iohannem de Muris: Die Recensio maior des sogenannten "Libellus practice cantus mensurabilis,"* ed. Christian Berktold, Bayerische Akademie der Wissenschaften, Veröffentlichungen der Musikhistorischen Kommission 14 (Munich, Germany: Verlag der Bayerischen Akademie der Wissenschaften, 1999). Editions of *Ars contrapuncti*: Coussemaker, *Scriptorum*, vol. 3, 59–68; and Giuliano Di Bacco, *De Muris e gli altri: Sulla tradizione di un trattato trecentesco di contrappunto* (Lucca, Italy: Libreria Musicale Italiana, 2001). On Johannes's musical treatises, see Ulrich Michels, *Die Musiktraktate des Johannes de Muris*, Beihefte zum Archiv für Musikwissenschaft 8 (Wiesbaden, Germany: Steiner, 1970).

6. F. Alberto Gallo, "Marchetus in Padua und die 'franco-venetische' Musik des frühen Trecento," *Archiv für Musikwissenschaft* 31 (1974): 42–56; Carla Vivarelli,

"'Di una pretesa scuola napoletana': Sowing the Seeds of the Ars nova at the Court of Robert of Anjou," *Journal of Musicology* 24 (2007): 272–296.

7. The best introduction to the theory of mode in medieval and early modern music is Harold S. Powers and Frans Wiering, "Mode," in *Grove Music Online* at *Oxford Music Online*, http://www.oxfordmusiconline.com/subscriber/article/grove/music/43718 (accessed August 21, 2009).

8. The *Lucidarium* and the *Pomerium* appear in Gerbert, *Scriptores ecclesiastici*, vol. 3, 65–121 and 121–188 respectively; The *Brevis compilatio* appears in Coussemaker, *Scriptorum*, vol. 3, 1–12. More recent critical editions are: Giuseppe Vecchi, "Su la composizione del *Pomerium* di Marchetto da Padova e la *Brevis compilatio*," *Quadrivium* 1 (1956): 153–205; *Marcheti de Padua Pomerium*, ed. Giuseppe Vecchi, Corpus Scriptorum de Musica 6 (Rome: American Institute of Musicology, 1961); Marchetto of Padua, *The "Lucidarium" of Marchetto of Padua: A Critical Edition, Translation, and Commentary*, ed. Jan W. Herlinger (Chicago and London: University of Chicago Press, 1985).

9. On the dissemination of the *Lucidarium*, complete and in excerpts and fragments, see Jan Herlinger, "Marchetto's Influence: The Manuscript Evidence," in *Music Theory and Its Sources: Antiquity and the Middle Ages*, ed. André Barbera (Notre Dame, IN: University of Notre Dame Press, 1990), 235-258.

10. For *Sciendum est quod antiquitus*, see Raffaello Monterosso, "Un compendio inedito del *Lucidarium* di Marchetto da Padova," *Studi medievali*, 3rd series, 7 (1966): 914–931, edited on the basis of Pavia, Biblioteca Universitaria, MS Aldini 361; the compendium is also transmitted in Pavia, Biblioteca Universitaria, MS Aldini 450 and in Seville, Biblioteca Capitular y Colombina, MS 5.2.25.

11. *The Berkeley Manuscript: University of California Music Library, MS. 744 (olim Phillipps 4450): A New Critical Text and Translation*, ed. and trans. Oliver B. Ellsworth, Greek and Latin Music Theory 2 (Lincoln: University of Nebraska Press, 1984).

12. All translations are the author's.

13. Adrian de La Fage, *Essais de diphthérographie musicale* (Paris: Legouix, 1864), 385–389.

14. Di Bacco, De Muris 162–173. Complete contents lists for Pisa 606 are available in id., 165–168; Pieter Fischer, ed., *The Theory of Music*, vol. 2, Italy, Répertoire international des sources musicales (RISM) B III² (Munich: Henle Verlag, 1968), 81–84; with additions and corrections in Christian Meyer et al., eds., *The Theory of Music: Manuscripts from the Carolingian Era up to c. 1500—Addenda, Corrigenda, Descriptive Catalogue*, RISM B III⁶ (Munich: G. Henle Verlag, 2003), 562–563.

15. The *Tractatus figurarum* is a treatise on French rhythmic notation ascribed alternately to Philippus de Caserta or Phillipotus Andrea, both late-fourteenth-century theorists.

16. The Paduan canon (and cantor, composer, and theorist) Johannes Ciconia was born in Liège; thus his *Liber de proportionibus* is placed here with other theorists in the French orbit.

17. Johannes de Garlandia was associated with the University of Paris in the late thirteenth century; the treatise is elsewhere ascribed to Philippe de Vitry, a French contemporary of Johannes de Muris.

18. *Quoniam de canendi scientia* is part of a treatise once associated with the twelfth-century "school" of St. Martial in Limoges.

19. Though the *Rubrice breves* is ascribed to Marchetto in its sources, it does not accord with his teaching in the *Pomerium*; the ascription is now considered spurious.

20. The captions of the last two items indicate that they are not from the Italian orbit. A redactor's design often breaks down near the end of a manuscript, which becomes a catchall for whatever items might fill available space.

21. Complete contents lists for Florence 1119 are available in Di Bacco, *De Muris*, 122–127; and RISM B III², 47–49; additions and corrections appear in RISM B III⁶, 481–483.

22. When La Fage saw the manuscript, the folio now numbered 64 followed that now numbered 70, so that the present 70v and 64r–v constitute the item he numbered IX and described as *"Vers latins sur des sujets dévots et musicaux, en trois pages"*; La Fage, *Essais*, 248.

23. Complete contents lists for Rome B.83 are available in Di Bacco, *De Muris*, 181–185; and RISM B III², 89–91; additions and corrections appear in RISM B III⁶, 602.

24. Giovanni Battista Martini (1706–1784) was an influential theorist, organist, and teacher (of Mozart, *inter alios*) who accumulated a large collection of music and writings on music. His own works include the unfinished *Storia della musica* (Bologna, 1761–1781).

25. Complete contents lists for Florence 29.48 are available in Di Bacco, *De Muris*, 104–111; and RISM B III², 36–43; with additions and corrections in RISM B III⁶, 483–484.

26. *Ars cantus mensurabilis mensurata per modos iuris*, ed. C. Matthew Balensuela, Greek and Latin Music Theory 10 (Lincoln: University of Nebraska Press, 1994); earlier edition in Coussemaker, *Scriptorum*, vol. 3, 379–398.

27. For detailed studies of the manuscript, including complete lists of the contents, see Di Bacco, *De Muris*, 41–58; RISM B III⁶, 434–448; and Angelo Rusconi, "Un manoscritto carmelitano di teoria musicale (Bergamo, Biblioteca civica 'Angelo Mai,' MAB 21)," *Rivista internazionale di musica sacra* 20 (1999): 255–300.

28. Cristle Collins Judd, *Reading Renaissance Music Theory: Hearing with the Eyes*, Cambridge Studies in Music Theory and Analysis 14 (Cambridge, UK: Cambridge University Press, 2000), 19–22.

29. Clement Miller, "Gaffurius's *Practica Musicae*: Origin and Contents," *Musica Disciplina* 22 (1968): 105–128; Clement Miller, "Early Gaffuriana: New Answers to Old Questions," *Musical Quarterly* 56 (1970): 367–388.

30. Bonnie J. Blackburn, "Gaffurius, Franchinus," in *Grove Music Online, Oxford Music Online,* http://www.oxfordmusiconline.com/subscriber/article/grove/music/10477 (accessed August 21, 2009).

31. Jan Herlinger, "Reflections of Guido d'Arezzo (?) in an Unpublished Treatise of the Fifteenth Century," paper delivered at the International Congress on Guido d'Arezzo on the Occasion of the Thousandth Anniversary of His Birth, Arezzo, December 2000.

32. Foliation runs continuously through the four manuscripts bound together as Venice 336, accounting for *Divina's* appearing on fols. 434r–444r of a 32-folio manuscript.

33. According to a table of contents on the second front flyleaf, the first manuscript contains the *Tractatus de admirandis et secretioribus philosophiæ arcanis* by Giovanni Mariano Buri, and the second, the *Opera spirituale* of Bartolomeo Mozzi da Saravalle, dedicated to Clement XI.

34. It is a witness to the dissemination of printed books through manuscript copies. On the *Practica musice* and its importance, see Judd, *Reading Renaissance Music Theory: Hearing with the Eyes,* Cambridge Studies in Music Theory and Analysis 14 (Cambridge, UK: Cambridge University Press, 2000).

35. The first description appeared in 2003 in RISM B III⁶, 627–630.

36. A collection of Psalm and Magnificat tones (fols. 448–456), copied in a more careful book hand using darker ink, seems to be the work of a different scribe and is not considered part of the compendium.

37. A detailed study of this source can be found in Linda Page Cummins, "Correr 336, Part 4: A New Source for Late Medieval Music Theory," *Philomusica Online* 5/1 (2005–2006), http://riviste.paviauniversitypress.it/index.php/phi/article/view/05-01-SG03/56 (accessed February 27, 2010).

38. Rome, Biblioteca Vallicelliana, MS C.105 is a tiny fifteenth-century manuscript containing short treatises on music (fols. 119-157) in a collection consisting mainly of religious writings.

39. "*Et quia principium alicuius scientie est scire terminos, ut ait philosophus in primo posteriorum*"; fol. 444v.

40. "*Responsum est antea in predicta carta*"; fol. 444v.

41. "*Exempla dictarum mutationum sunt antea scripta et notata: scilicet in carta quinta et sucessiue notata respice*"; fol. 446r.

42. On mnemonic verses in music theory treatises, see Anna Maria Busse Berger, *Medieval Music and the Art of Memory* (Berkeley: University of California Press, 2005).

43. "*Que omnia ista reducantur ad tui memoriam*"; fol. 446r.

44. Complete contents lists for Venice 336 are available in Cummins, "Correr 336," Appendix; and RISM B III⁶, 627-630.

45. Malcolm Parkes, "The Influence of the Concepts of *Ordinatio* and *Compilatio* on the Development of the Book," in *Medieval Learning and Literature,* ed. J. J.

G. Alexander and M. T. Gibson (Oxford: Clarendon Press, 1976), 115-141; A. J. Minnis, *Medieval Theory of Authorship: Scholastic Literary Attitudes in the Later Middle Ages* (London: Scolar Press, 1984).

46. The material concordant with Vallicelliana C.105 lacks attributions in that source, and the author (or compiler) of the Berkeley Compendium is not identified until long after the passage borrowed in Venice.

47. Cf., e.g., *"quasi quosdam ex prato flores carperes* |as if you were plucking flowers out of a meadow|," in Fabian Lochner, "Un Évêque musicien au Xme siècle: Radbod d'Utrecht (†917)," *Tijdschrift van de Vereniging voor Nederlandse Muziekgeschiedenis* (1988): 15; but for *ex prato* the Venice compiler has *expleto* very clearly.

48. Bonaventure on the ways of making books (St. Bonaventure, *In sententias Petri Lombardi* i.111): "Someone . . . writes the materials of others, adding, but nothing of his own, and this person is said to be the compiler." (Minnis, *Medieval Theory*, 94).

49. As stated above, only Pisa 606 contains both the *Lucidarium* and *Divina*. For a list of *Lucidarium* sources, see Herlinger, *Lucidarium*, 21–22; Herlinger, "Marchetto's Influence," 255.

50. Available from Glasor di Silvio Gallo e Tullia Valsecchi, v. Maglio del Rame, 13, 24127 Bergamo, Italy.

51. Cerquiglini, *In Praise of the Variant*, 47.

52. Ibid., 78.

WORKS CITED

Ars cantus mensurabilis mensurata per modos iuris. Edited and translated by C. Matthew Balensuela. Greek and Latin Music Theory 10. Lincoln: University of Nebraska Press, 1994.

Ars practica mensurabilis cantus secundum Iohannem de Muris: Die Recensio maior des sogenannten "Libellus practice cantus mensurabilis." Edited by Christian Berktold. Bayerische Akademie der Wissenschaften, Veröffentlichungen der Musikhistorischen Kommission 14. Munich: Verlag der Bayerischen Akademie der Wissenschaften, 1999.

Berger, Anna Maria Busse. *Medieval Music and the Art of Memory.* Berkeley: University of California Press, 2005.

The Berkeley Manuscript: University of California Music Library, MS. 744 (olim Phillipps 4450): A New Critical Text and Translation. Edited and translated by Oliver B. Ellsworth. Greek and Latin Music Theory 2. Lincoln: University of Nebraska Press, 1984.

Blackburn, Bonnie J. "Gaffurius, Franchinus." In *Grove Music Online* at *Oxford Music Online.* http://www.oxfordmusiconline.com/subscriber/article/grove/music/10477 (accessed August 21, 2009).

Cerquiglini, Bernard. In Praise of the Variant: A Critical History of Philology. Translated by Betsy Wing. Baltimore, MD, and London: Johns Hopkins University Press, 1999. Originally published as Éloge de la variante: Histoire critique de la philologie. Paris: Éditions du Seuil, 1989.

Coussemaker, Edmond de. Scriptorum de musica nova series a gerbertina altera. 4 vols., Paris: Durand et Pedone-Lauriel, 1864–1876.

Cummins, Linda Page. "Correr 336, Part 4: A New Source for Late Medieval Music Theory." Philomusica Online 5/1 (2005–2006). http://riviste. paviauniversitypress.it/index.php/phi/article/view/05-01-SG03/56.

Di Bacco, Giuliano. De Muris e gli altri: Sulla tradizione di un trattato trecentesco di contrappunto. Lucca, Italy: Libreria Musicale Italiana, 2001.

Fischer, Pieter, ed. The Theory of Music. Vol. 2, Italy. Répertoire international des sources musicales B III². Munich: Henle Verlag, 1968.

Gallo, F. Alberto. "Marchetus in Padua un die 'franco-venetische' Musik des frühen Trecento. Archiv für Musikwissenschaft 31 (1974): 42–56.

Gerbert, Martin. Scriptores ecclesiastici de musica sacra potissimum. 3 vols. St. Blaise, 1784.

Herlinger, Jan. "Marchetto's Influence: The Manuscript Evidence." In Music Theory and Its Sources: Antiquity and the Middle Ages, edited by André Barbera. Notre Dame, IN: University of Notre Dame Press, 1990. 235-258.

——. "Reflections of Guido d'Arezzo (?) in an Unpublished Treatise of the Fifteenth Century." Paper delivered at the International Congress on Guido d'Arezzo on the Occasion of the Thousandth Anniversary of his Birth, Arezzo, December 2000.

Johannes de Muris. Musica (speculativa). Edited by Susan Fast. Musicological Studies 61. Ottawa, Canada: Institute of Mediaeval Music, 1994.

——. Notitia artis musicae, et Compendium musicae practiae; Petrus de Sancto Dionysio: Tractatus de musica. Edited by Ulrich Michels. Corpus Scriptorum de Musica 17. N.p.: American Institute of Musicology, 1972.

Judd, Cristle Collins. Reading Renaissance Music Theory: Hearing with the Eyes. Cambridge Studies in Music Theory and Analysis 14. Cambridge, UK: Cambridge University Press, 2000.

La Fage, Adrian de. Essais de diphthérographie musicale. Paris: Legouix, 1864.

Lochner, Fabian. "Un Évêque musicien au Xᵐᵉ siècle: Radbod d'Utrecht (†917)." Tijdschrift van de Vereniging voor Nederlandse Muziekgeschiedenis 38 (1988): 3–35.

Marchetto of Padua. The "Lucidarium" of Marchetto of Padua: A Critical Edition, Translation, and Commentary. Edited by Jan W. Herlinger. Chicago and London: University of Chicago Press, 1985.

——. Marcheti de Padua Pomerium. Edited by Giuseppe Vecchi. Corpus Scriptorum de Musica 6. Rome: American Institute of Musicology, 1961.

Meyer, Christian, et al. The Theory of Music: Manuscripts from the Carolingian Era up to c. 1500—Addenda, Corrigenda, Descriptive Catalogue. Répertoire international des sources musicales B III⁶. Munich: G. Henle Verlag, 2003.

Michels, Ulrich. *Die Musiktraktate des Johannes de Muris*. Beihefte zum Archiv für Musikwissenschaft 8. Wiesbaden: Steiner, 1970.

Miller, Clement. "Early Gaffuriana: New Answers to Old Questions." *Musical Quarterly* 56 (1970): 367–388.

———. "Gaffurius's *Practica Musicae*: Origin and Contents." *Musica Disciplina* 22 (1968): 105–128.

Minnis, A. J. *Medieval Theory of Authorship: Scholastic Literary Attitudes in the Later Middle Ages*. London: Scolar Press, 1984.

Monterosso, Raffaello. "Un compendio inedito del *Lucidarium* di Marchetto da Padova." *Studi medievali*, 3rd series, 7 (1966): 914–931.

Parkes, Malcolm. "The Influence of the Concepts of *Ordinatio* and *Compilatio* on the Development of the Book." In *Medieval Learning and Literature*, edited by J. J. G. Alexander and M. T. Gibson. Oxford: Clarendon Press, 1976. 115–141.

Powers, Harold S., and Frans Wiering. "Mode." In *Grove Music Online* at *Oxford Music Online*. http://www.oxfordmusiconline.com/subscriber/article/grove/music/43718.

Rusconi, Angelo. "Un manoscritto carmelitano di teoria musicale (Bergamo, Biblioteca civica 'Angelo Mai,' MAB 21). *Rivista internazionale di musica sacra* 20 (1999): 255–300.

Sadie, Stanley, ed. *The New Grove Dictionary of Music and Musicians*. Executive editor John Tyrell. 2nd edition. 29 vols. London: Macmillan, 2001; also *Grove Music Online* at *Oxford Music Online*. http://www.oxfordmusiconline.com/subscriber/article/grove/music/17738.

Taylor, Andrew. *Textual Situations: Three Medieval Manuscripts and Their Readers*. Philadelphia: University of Pennsylvania Press, 2002.

Vecchi, Guiseppe. "Su la composizione del *Pomerium* di Marchetto da Padova e la *Brevis compilatio*." *Quadrivium* 1 (1956): 153–205.

Vivarelli, Carla. "'Di una pretesa scuola napoletana': Sowing the Seeds of the Ars nova at the Court of Robert of Anjou." *Journal of Musicology* 24 (2007): 272–296.

Williams, David Russell, and Balensuela, C. Matthew. *Music Theory from Boethius to Zarlino*. Hillsdale, NY: Pendragon Press, 2007.

Zumthor, Paul. *Toward a Medieval Poetics*. Translated by Philip Bennet. Minneapolis and Oxford: University of Minnesota Press, 1992. Originally published as *Essai de poétique médiévale*. Paris: Éditions du Seuil, 1972.

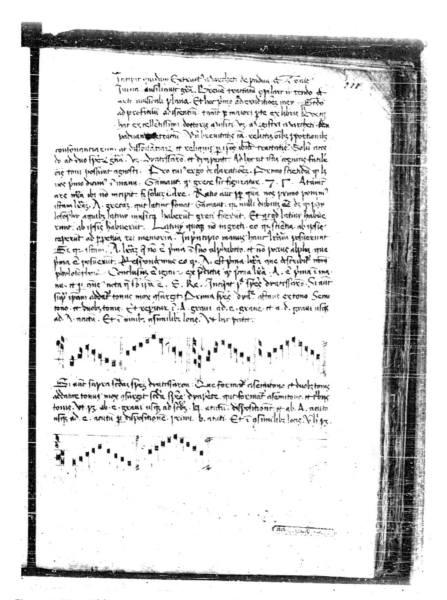

Figure I: Pisa, Biblioteca Universitaria, ms. 606, part I, p. 111 (=f. 58r). Pisa, Biblioteca Universitaria. By permission of the Ministero per i Beni e le Attività Culturali. The further reproduction by any means whatever is prohibited.

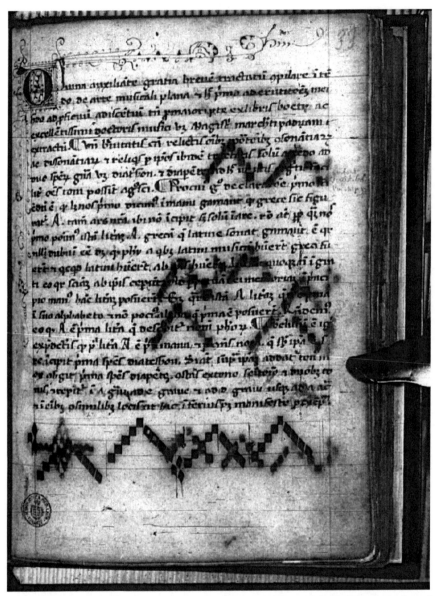

Figure 2: Florence, Biblioteca Medicea Laurenziana, Ashb. 1119, f. 33r. By permission of the Ministero per i Beni e le Attività Culturali. The further reproduction by any means whatever is prohibited.

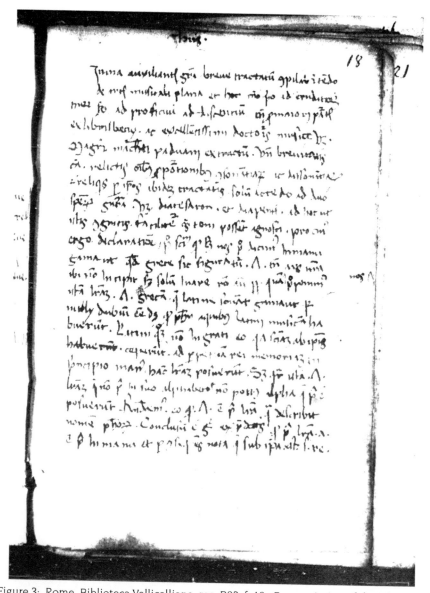

Figure 3: Rome, Biblioteca Vallicelliana, ms. B83, f. 18r. By permission of the Ministero per i Beni e le Attività Culturali. The further reproduction by any means whatever is prohibited.

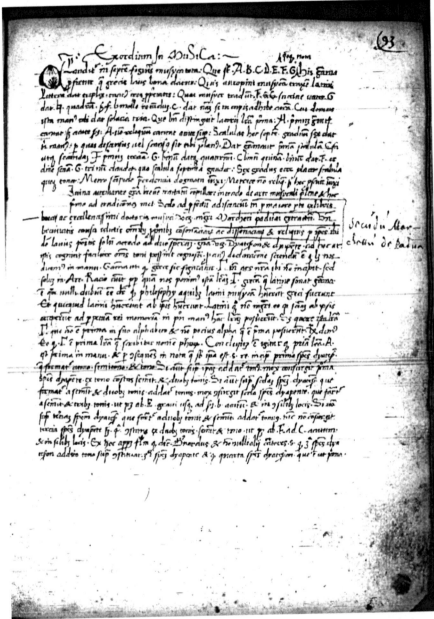

Figure 4: Florence, Biblioteca Medicea Laurenziana, Plut. 29.48, f. 93r. By permission of the Ministero per i Beni e le Attività Culturali. The further reproduction by any means whatever is prohibited.

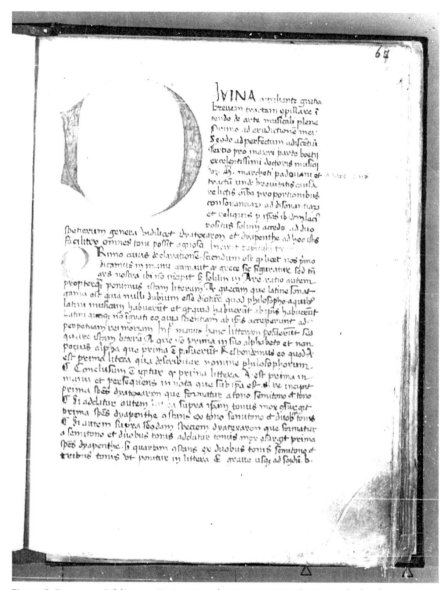

Figure 5: Bergamo, Biblioteca Civica "Angelo Mai," MAB 21, f. 67r. By the kind permission of the Library.

Nota Bene: Brief Notes on
Manuscripts and Early Printed Books
Highlighting Little-Known or Recently Uncovered Items or Related Issues

Two Recently Discovered Fragments of Nassington and Rolle

JORDAN ZWECK

In April 1677, the minister Nathaniel Heywood traveled from Lancashire to Yorkshire to visit his brother, Oliver Heywood, a prominent nonconformist minister, and to send his son, also named Nathaniel, to study at Richard Frankland's academy.[1] While at his brother's house, Nathaniel delivered two sermons, the notes for which have been preserved in a slim volume recently acquired by the Beinecke Library and now shelved as Osborn MSS File Folder 19558. While the sermon notes may prove useful for early modernists, historians of the early book will be more interested in the manuscript's binding material, two vellum leaves used as a wrapper and cover. Written on the leaves are fragments from two fourteenth-century texts, which I have identified as the minor Middle English religious poem *Tractatus de Unitate et Trinitate* by William of Nassington[2] and Richard Rolle's Latin prose work *De Emendatio Vitae*.[3] The discovery of these fragments is important for two reasons: first, it increases the number of known copies of the Nassington poem from two to three, and provides a better reading for one of the lines; second, evidence shows that the single medieval scribe who copied the fragments was working in the same geographical area as the authors and within about fifty years of their deaths.

Richard Rolle is one of the major figures of fourteenth-century English mysticism.[4] Probably born between 1305 and 1310 in Thornton, North Yorkshire, he left school early and became a hermit, establishing a wide following. He died at Hampole in 1349.[5] A large number of works by this prolific writer survive, and he seems to have been quite popular with medieval English audiences. Our perception of Rolle has been confused, however, by an early tendency to attribute authorship of anonymous texts to him.

While modern scholarship has now discredited many of the attributions to Rolle, including the *Pricke of Conscience*, the authorship of the work found in the Beinecke fragment, the *Emendatio Vitae*, is not in doubt. It survives in over one hundred manuscripts,[6] as well as in seven contemporary vernacular translations;[7] its most recent editor, Nicholas Watson, has called it "one of the most copied texts in late medieval England."[8] The twelve chapters of the work, which alternate between intense passion and sober Biblical scholarship, are designed to guide the reader on a progression from "conversion to contemplation."[9] The *Emendatio* has not received much critical attention, probably because scholars have tended to focus on Rolle's vernacular works and also because there was no good edition of the Latin text available until Watson's edition of 1995.

William of Nassington (or Nassyngton), the author of the other text of which a fragment is here preserved, was also a fourteenth-century poet of northern England. We have much less information about Nassington's life than we do about Rolle's, a problem which was exacerbated by the fact that until Ingrid Peterson's 1986 study, it was thought that Nassington was actually anywhere from two to six separate people. A member of a prominent Yorkshire family of ecclesiastics, William was a lawyer and held church offices in Exeter and York. He died in 1359, ten years after Rolle.[10] If he is known to literary critics at all, it is as part of the debate regarding the authorship of the *Speculum Vitae*. While the work was once attributed to Rolle, it is now generally accepted as the work of Nassington, on the grounds that he is named as the author in some manuscripts.[11] Whether or not Nassington is the author of the *Speculum Vitae*, his association with it provides a striking link between the two fragmentary links in the Beinecke manuscript. The *Speculum Vitae* is based, at least in part, on Richard Rolle's *Form of Perfect Living*,[12] of which Nassington may have written a versification.[13] Furthermore, Rolle's *Form of Perfect Living* has been said to "closely correspond" to his *Emendatio Vitae*.[14] In other words, then, there is a possibility that William Nassington, the author of our first fragment, wrote a versification of a late work by Rolle that has connections to Rolle's own *Emendatio Vitae*, which is our second fragment. I do not wish, here, to argue for or against Nassington's authorship of the *Speculum Vitae*, although the fact that Nassington and Rolle are linked both through the *Speculum Vitae* and the fragments in the Beinecke manuscript is suggestive.

Nassington's *Tractatus*, the poem found in the Beinecke manuscript, is a poem on the Trinity written in couplets. It is admittedly not a brilliant poetic composition, but it is at times moving, alternating between a narrative of the events of the life of Christ and direct appeals by the first person speaker of the poem for God's mercy. The section surviving in the Beinecke fragment, lines 223–237 and 260–274, describes the Passion. The *Tractatus* is one of several minor works attributed to Nassington. Attribution of the *Tractatus* to Nassington is based on incipits in the two other manuscripts in which it survives, the Thornton manuscript (Lincoln Cathedral 91, dated *c.* 1430–1450) and British Library MS Add. 33995 (late fourteenth century). Only the Thornton manuscript contains the entirety of the 432-line poem. BL Add. 33995, which titles the poem the "Band of Lovynge," has only lines 1–328. The other works in the British Library manuscript are the *Speculum Vitae*, a poem on "Hell, Purgatory, Heaven, the misery of human life, etc.," and the *Pricke of Conscience*.[15]

The celebrated Thornton manuscript, compiled and copied by Robert Thornton himself, is a larger and more disparate collection containing romances, religious works, and a medical treatise.[16] While it is true that medieval compilations sometimes had no guiding principles, with scribes copying texts as they came to hand, it is notable that the British Library manuscript contains both the *Speculum Vitae* and the *Pricke of Conscience*, and that the Thornton manuscript has many works attributed to Rolle. In addition, the poem on Heaven and Hell in BL Add. 33995 begins by addressing the Trinity, much as Nassington's *Tractatus* does, which suggests that the compiler might have been choosing his selections quite carefully.

To return to the seventeenth century, Osborn MSS File Folder 19558, the book in which our fragments are found, contains notes from two sermons that are indicated as having been delivered by Nathaniel Heywood at Northowram in 1677, written on paper in brown ink. The book measures roughly 9 cm x 15.5 cm, and the binding seems to be original. The manuscript identifies when the notes were copied, though not by whom or when the book was bound. A rubric indicates that the first sermon was delivered on April 22, 1677. At the end of this sermon is written "finis January 2 1677" (for January 2, 1678).[17] The second sermon was the "fore-noone sermon: April 29 1677." At the end of this section is written "finis Aprill 10 1678," a year after the sermon was delivered and some months after Heywood's death in December 1677.

It is clear that Nathaniel Heywood himself is not the scribe of our manuscript because, in addition to the fact that the notes were copied after his death, the colophon indicates that he is dead:

> Christian reader
> If there be any fault in this
> sermon blame not the disceased
> truely honourable & Able Auther
> but me the writer who could
> not take all pardon my faults
> inlarge it in thy meditations
> & practise it in thy conuersation

While we do not know anything about who was the scribe of our book, nor where it was produced, we do know something about the sermons, which might help us to further understand the production of the book. We know from Oliver Heywood's diaries that his brother Nathaniel came to visit him in Yorkshire on April 20, 1677. He stayed until about May 1, and, according to Oliver, "preacht two Lords days for [him]" at Northowram.[18] Nathaniel reportedly kept notes of all of his sermons, and Oliver posthumously published the two sermons recorded in the Beinecke manuscript as *Christ Displayed, as the Choicest Gift, and Best Master* because Nathaniel refused to publish anything while he was alive.[19] Comparison between these printed sermons and the sermon notes in the Beinecke manuscript reveal that they are based on the same sermons. Oliver Heywood's printed edition is much longer than the manuscript "notes," but it is clear that the notes would have produced the text as found in the printed book, and in any case, the colophon indicates that the notes are incomplete. Whoever copied the notes now found in the Beinecke must also have had access to Nathaniel's notes. I do not believe it was Oliver who made the Beinecke copy; Oliver tends to sign his work, and to inflate his own value as much as possible.[20] Rather I think that someone else, perhaps before Oliver had the work printed, made a copy for his own personal use. Oliver's records show that once the book was printed, he bought copies of it in bulk and distributed it to everyone he knew,[21] so it would make little sense for this other scribe to have had need to make his own copy after that. This would mean that the book was bound between 1678 and 1679, soon after the notes were copied and before Oliver's edition was published.

The Beinecke manuscript also includes three eighteenth-century owner identifications which provide us with a fixed date beyond which the book could not possibly have been bound. One, written on what is now the outside of the wrapper, and later crossed out, reads "Thomas Greenwoods Book 1786." The second, written upside down across the second column of the outside of the front cover, reads "Thomas Greenwoods Book," followed by a date that is difficult to read, but which is no earlier than 1785.[22] The third owner identification is not dated. I have not been able to identify this Thomas Greenwood, but Oliver Heywood knew several members of the prominent Greenwood family in Yorkshire, and it is tempting to believe that the book was produced at Northowram, where the sermons were given, and that it stayed in the area until at least the eighteenth century. If so, then it seems that the vellum used to bind it, which contains works by authors from Yorkshire written in a Northern dialect, must not have traveled far, if at all, in the time between its medieval copying and its use as binding material for the sermons. What can be said with some certainty is that our book was produced, probably in Yorkshire, sometime between 1678, when the sermon notes were copied, and 1786, the date given by Thomas Greenwood, but probably in or soon after 1678.

At this point, I must return to the medieval vellum and clarify what I have said about the binding. Though I have mentioned a wrapper, I have not heretofore noted that this wrapper is incomplete. It only protects the front of the book; there is no wrapper over the back. The cover proper is constructed from a single leaf, and the wrapper is made from a half leaf. This can be determined by reconstructing the original sheets of vellum from which the binding material was taken. The inside surface of the wrapper contains the Middle English poem by Nassington. Ultraviolet light shows that there was also writing on what is now the outside of the wrapper but cannot reveal enough to determine what that text was.

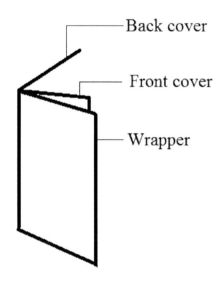

Figure 1: The Manuscript

The cover of the book is made from a single leaf of vellum containing Rolle's *Emendatio Vitae*. The leaf has been folded so that what was formerly the recto of the leaf is now the outside surface of the cover, with the top of the recto in front and the bottom of the recto in back. The top half of the verso is now the inside of the front cover. The bottom half of the verso is now the inside back cover. To have a wrapper on the front and not on the back is unusual. It is also unusual that the text on the front wrapper would be washed out when the text on the back cover was allowed to remain. There is no indication that the book has been rebound, or that there ever was a back wrapper.[23]

Since there are no real margins visible on the fragments, it would be foolish to try to reconstruct the full dimensions of the original vellum. We can, however, estimate how big the text block must have been (approximately 35.4 cm x 9 cm), and this reveals that there is very little text missing in our fragments from the edges of the text block due to trimming. Nassington's poem is written out line by line; couplets are linked by red brackets; and line initials are red-touched.[24]

A single scribe copied both the Latin and the Middle English texts. The only major difference in letter forms between the two is that in the Latin a two-compartment **a** is used throughout, whereas in the Middle English, a

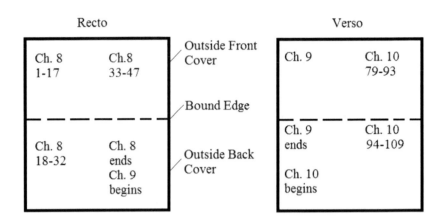

Figure 2: Reconstruction of Original Leaf

two-compartment **a** is used only for capital **a**. Elsewhere, a simplified single compartment **a** characteristic of Secretary hand is used.[25] It is my belief that the text of the Middle English was written somewhere in Yorkshire c. 1400.[26] The hand, which is cursive, primarily shows characteristics of less formal Anglicana, but has some features of Secretary hand, which, according to Parkes, began to be used in England c. 1375. Characteristics of Secretary hand in this manuscript include the simplified **a**, an **r** that looks like our modern printed **r**, and broken lobes.[27] Evidence of Anglicana includes the short **s** similar to Greek sigma, cursive **e**, long **r**, **g** with a closed bottom loop, and Anglicana **w**.

Comparison between our texts and the texts used by editors of the modern printed editions shows that our fragments are very accurate. The Nassington poem may have a better reading in the Beinecke fragment at line 236, but unfortunately, I have only been able to compare it to the Thornton manuscript and not to the British Library one, which is the earlier of the two. I also hesitate to claim that this proves that the scribe who copied the Middle English had access to a better exemplar than Thornton because Nassington's verse is at times uneven, and also because our fragment contains at least one, if not two mistakes, where we find a line ending with an unrhymed "yat."[28] However, the general accuracy of both the Nassington and Rolle texts makes sense, given they display characteristics of Northern dialect and that, since they were probably in Yorkshire in the eighteenth century, they may have been copied there as well. If the hand is indeed earlier than 1400, as Babcock claims, then it is possible that ours is the earliest surviving Nassington fragment. I hope one day to identify the Thomas Greenwood who owned the book in the eighteenth century, and I would like to believe that if I could trace its owners, I might be able to determine where the vellum came from—we do know Oliver Heywood kept an extensive library and that he kept at least one pocket book bound in vellum. Regardless of whether we ever learn the source of the medieval vellum, or whether our Nassington fragment is the earliest, or whether it has a more accurate line-reading, this book is still a significant discovery because it increases the number of known copies of Nassington's poem from two to three and provides what are at least alternate readings for several lines; it also suggests that there was a medieval compiler who saw fit to include two very similar works by Nassington and Rolle in a single collection. Finally, because Nathaniel Heywood's sermon notes represent an earlier stage of the sermons later published by Oliver Heywood, this early manuscript could also be of interest to early modern scholars.

      Yale University

Edition

A Note on Transcription:

    In transcribing the fragments, my goal has been to represent the text of the manuscript as accurately as possible without sacrificing readability. The scribe does not distinguish between **y** and *thorn*, so I have used only **y** in the transcription. Abbreviations have been silently expanded. The Tyronian nota is expanded as "and" or "et," as appropriate. Square brackets | | enclose letters which are visible on the vellum but of whose accuracy I am only relatively sure. Square brackets that enclose italicized letters indicate space where the letters are no longer visible at all. In order to ease reading and to give a sense of what was lost, and since our fragments are, in the main, very accurate, I have felt confident in filling in short illegible portions of words with the corresponding letters given in italics from the texts of the manuscripts printed by the editors. This has been necessary in a number of places because the binding material (and indeed the entire book) is dirty and worn from heavy use. In addition, it is impossible to read through the place where the later owner's name has been crossed out. Where only the ascenders or descenders of a line are visible, I have given a line of dots inside square brackets, thus |......................|. I have also indicated line numbers. For Nassington, I used the line numbering of the printed edition of the work by G. G. Perry (see note 2) for easier comparison. Since Rolle's text is prose, I have supplied numbering. Textual notes give substantive variants from Richard Rolle, *Emendatio vitae*; *Orationes ad honorem nominis Ihesu*, ed. Nicholas Watson (Toronto: Pontifical Institute, 1995). In the left column of Nassington's text, the left edge of the text block has been lost in trimming. I have provided what is missing, italicized and in square brackets ||, in order to facilitate reading. For the sake of legibility, I have decided to present the text of the EV in the order it would have originally been read, not as it is encountered in our fragments. That is to say, I present the full left column and then the full right column of the original page. In transcribing the Latin, I have decided to represent punctuation.

1. William of Nassington's *Tractatus de Trinitate et Unitate* (inside of wrapper)

Left Column

223　　　|...............||ya||............................||h|eued ya|t|
　　　　　|A *Crown*|e of thornys yat priked ye sar
225　　　|Of | whil|k| ye prikkis war |sa| scharp yan
　　　　　|*That the*||y| perched nere thurght ye herne pan
　　　　　|*They*| gaf ye a rede in yi hand
　　　　　|In-|sted of a scepture ye skornand
　　　　　|An|d kneled before ye in hethynge
230　　　|An|d said to ye haile Iewes kynge
　　　　　|Si||t|hen was yu demed at ye Iewes voce
　　　　　|*Thurg*||h| pilat to be hynged an ye croice
　　　　　|*The*| whil|k| yu bare toward ye sted
　　　　　|W||hare| yu was ordaynd to be done to ded
235　　　|S|ithen was yu strened on ye crosse sa fast
　　　　　|*Thurg*||ht| ye Iewes yat vaynes and synnes brast
　　　　　|An|d nayled yeron throght hand and fute

　　　　　..

Right Column

260　　　|*Þat mykil scha*|me ye did and velany
　　　　　At none of ye day yu cred, hely
　　　　　And |ȝ|heldid ye gast to yi fader all myghty
　　　　　yus yu died to make vs fre
　　　　　ffra ye gret thraldom yat in war we
265　　　Bot mykil payne and mykil reproue
　　　　　yu tholed befor ye ded for oure lufe
　　　　　And noght forto by vs agayne anely
　　　　　ffor whi yi ded mot suffice vs all forto by
　　　　　Bot for we suld yerby ensaumple take
270　　　to be pacient in angers for yi sake

---

223 For the sake of the rhyme, and based on Thornton, the final word should be yar, not yat. The manuscript is hard to read here, but an unrhymed yat is not unprecedented in this fragment. The scribe also mistakenly ends a line with an unrhyming yat in line 271. 236 Thornton: "Thurghe Þe Iewes Þat Þi vaynes & synows al to–braste." For metrical reasons, the number of syllables in our fragment is to be preferred.

And for ye thole all hard es yat
Als yu tholed for vs thurght yi gudnes
Elles thurt ye haf tholed nane oyer payn
Bot ye ded anely forto by vs agayn

275   ....

271 The word order here is wrong, so the line does not rhyme. This is the second time
in this fragment that an unrhymed "yat" has been mistakenly placed at the end of a line.
Thornton: "And for the to thole all Þat harde es."

2. Richard Rolle's *Emendatio Vitae*

Outside of front cover, column 1

1 |*affec=*|
|tuum|. ad illa|*m*| vel ad illam se|mitam|
diriguntur ¶Nullus op|*er*|ibus exterio=
ribus potest cognosci: quis sit ma=
5   ior vel minor cor|am| deo Stultum
est ergo de electis iudicare et dicere. Iste
excellit istum et illius merita ab istius
meritis longe distant. cum penitus
ignorent mentes illorum. quas si
10   scirent: licite possent iudicare
Ideo enim deus omni creature hoc
voluit esse secretum: ne hunc nimis
contempnerent: aut illum nimis
honorarent. quia sine dubio. si
15   possent videre corda hominum: multos
quos nunc velut electos honorant:
|. . . . .|

Continues on outside back cover, column 1 (very worn)

18 |*dei*| |d|ilectissimos |et| |*v*||e|lu|*t*| an|*ge*|los
sanctos ho|*nor*|arent ¶|Bo||ne| |*itaque*|
20   cogitaciones et me|d||*itaciones electo=*|
rum. a deo |sunt|. |*et tales per suam*|
gra|*ciam*| |sin|gulis |in|fundit: quales
illorum statui et condi|cioni| |*magis con=*|
gruere videt. Possem ergo medi=
25   taciones meas tibi dicere. |set| quales
|ti|bi amplius efficaces eru|*n*||t ne=|
|scio| aperire. quia interiorem affe|*c*=
cion|em tuam non vi|de|. |P|uto certe
|quod ille| meditaciones |*in te*| m|a|gis
30   de|*o*| placen|t| et tibi proficiunt quas
ipse deus per se |*in*| |a|nimam |tuam|
|infud|erit |*Verumptamen inicium*|

---

1 This line is not visible, but I have included it because it forms the first half of the word. This is Chapter 8, the end of line 56 (Watson's numbering system).
18 I have chosen not to arbitrarily skip line numbers to indicate lines of missing text. 17 words are obscured in the bound edge between the end of the previous section and the beginning of this one.

Continues on outside front cover, column 2

| . . . . ||*scrip=*|
tis suis. scito quod amorem Christi non
35   gustabis Insipientis enim est dicere
deus illos docuit quare ergo eciam me non
docebit: |*Respond*|eo t|*ibi quia*| non es
talis qual|*es*| ipsi f|*uerunt*| Superbus
enim es et a|*u*|ster|*us illi*| vero humiles
40   et mites e|*xti*|terun|*t et*| presumen=
do nichil de |*d*|eo a|*dq*|uisierunt. set
se sub omnib|*us h*|umilia|*n*|do scienci|*a*|m
sanctorum acceperunt Docuit ergo illos.
vt nos in eorum libris doceremur.
45   Si vero meditaciones tue amorem
Christi nunc desiderant. aut nunc eius
laudem sonant: vt michi videtur

. . . .

Continues on outside back cover, column 2, which is too worn to transcribe.
The only things visible are a line of red where the title of the new chapter (9)
was written and a large red s, the first letter of Chapter 9. Under Ultraviolet
light one can see that the column once held the end of Chapter 8 and the
beginning of Chapter 9.

This ends what was formerly the recto of the page.

Chapter 9 continues on the inside of the front cover, column 1. This begins
the verso.

vitare |*d*|ebem|us| |*et*| que |*a*|ge|*re*| Sub=
50   tilissime machine inimicorum nobis
aperiuntur. accendunt ad amandum. et

---

34 As a result of trimming, 28.5 words are missing between the end of the last section
and the beginning of this one.
36 *deus* Inserted in the space between the left and right column, but occurring in its
proper place in the text.
37 Here, the crossed-out owner identification begins to obscure the text.
49 From our knowledge of the text block, we can presume that roughly 5 lines of text
were lost between the end of the recto and the beginning of the verso, but this cannot
be proven because the end of the recto is too worn to read.
vitare |Watson: *visitare*| It is possible that there is an abbreviation mark above the word,
but it is too obscured to read.

ad lacrimas compungunt. preparant
nobis mensam delicatam. Si in il=
lis sicut in omnibus diuiciis delecta=
55   ti fuerimus Si nulla cupiditas
honoris vel fauoris vel laudis homi=
|num| succendat nos ad scienciam scrip=
|tur|arum. set sola intencio placen=
|di d|eo. vt sciamus quomodo ipsum di=
60 |ligamus| et idem proximum docea=
mus Non vt reputemur scientes
|apud| populum. immo magis debemus
| . . . . |

Continues on the first column of the inside of the back cover, which is
difficult to read due to wear.

scilicet a |v|ana orentacione. vt no|n|
65   p|eccem| tibi Causa ergo locucionis nostre
sola sit laus dei et edificacio prox=
imi vt illud de nobis impleatur
S|em|per laus eius in ore meo. quod
F|it| q|uando| la|u|dem nostram non querimus
70 |et contra| |eius| laudem non loquimur.
De puritate mentis. Capitulum. ix.
P|er hos| nouem gradus pretac=
|tos ad purita||tem| mentis ascen=
|ditur qua uidetur Deus| . Puritatem
75 |dico que in via haberi po|test Nam
|quomodo perfecta carita|s adquiritur hic.
|ubi tociens homo u||eni||ali||b||us| |sa|ltem
|peccatis sordidat|ur Lauandi sunt

---

53 *delicatam* |Watson: *delicatem*|
55 Si |Watson: *sed*|
64 Sixteen words are obscured in the bound edge between the end of the previous
section and the beginning of this one.
70 *loquimur.* This period is red and indicates the end of Chapter 9.
71 This whole line is written in red and is the same size as the main text. It should read
"Capitulum 10," not "9."
72 Per The **P** is red and 3 lines tall.

Chapter 10 is continued on the back side of the front cover, column 2

|Si l|otus fuero aquis niuis |id est ve=|
80   ra penitencia et effulserint velut |m||un=|
dissime manus mee propter innocen=
cie opera: tamen sordibus intinges me
propter peccata venialia: que vitari
non possunt Et abhominabuntur
85   me vestimenta mea id est me ab=
hominabilem reddit caro mea |et|
sensualitas que tam fragilis est
et labilis. et prona ad amandum de=
lectabilem mundi speciem quod me
90   sepe peccare cogit, Ideo dicit. A=
postolus ¶Non regnet peccatum in
nostro mortali corpore. quasi diceret pec=
catum in nobis potest non regn|are|

The verso concludes on the inside of the back cover, column 2

si se iuste exercuerit in studio
95   leccionis. oracionis et meditacionis v|t|
prenotatum est. Quamuis enim peccet
aliquando venialiter: cito tamen propter inte=
gram intencionem suam ad deum di=
rectam. deletur fferuor namque
100   caritatis in ipso existens: omnem ru=
biginem peccatorum consumit: quasi si
gutta aque in camino ardenti
mitteretur ¶Virtus ergo purg|a=|
ti animi est: mentem ad deum habere inten=
105   tam quia in hoc statu tota cogi=
tacio in christum dirigitur. tota memo=
ria in ipsum extenditur. eciam quando
|a|l|iis| loqui vide|t|ur |In| munda enim
| . . . . |

---

79 Between the end of the last section and the beginning of this section, 26 words are
missing due to trimming.
85 *me* |Watson: *me michi*|
89 *quod me* |Watson: not present|
94 Between the end of the last section and the beginning of this section, eighteen
words are obscured by the binding.
98 *suam* |Watson: *suam integram intencionem*|
108 Chapter 10, line 28.

APPENDIX

Letter Forms and Abbreviations[29]

a is found in the simplified single compartment form.[30]
b has an ascender that loops to the right.
c is flat-topped.
d has an ascender that loops to the left.
e is found as cursive **e**.
f is always found as a tall **f**.
g is closed.
h has a limb that descends below the line and curves to the left.
k is easily confused with **l**.
l has an ascender that loops to the right.
ll is often written with a cross-stroke, as a ligature.
n - I have chosen not to indicate what is either an otiose line or an
abbreviation at the ends of lines ending in **n**. Instead of finishing the minim,
the scribe brings the line back up and then crosses it. In the Latin text, this
represents a missing nasal, but in the Middle English, it is only found in
words at line-ends that end in vowel+**n**. It is possible that it represents a
final **e**, but there is an equal chance that it means nothing. The same mark is
found in the Thornton manuscript.
r is found in three forms: The Anglicana long-tailed **r** occurs initially and after
c, a, g, and **th**. The 2-form is found only after **o**. The Secretary **r** (r) is found
finally after **a** and medially after **f** and **a**.
s occurs in two forms: The Greek or Anglicana short **s** is found finally and
initially. The tall **s**, which hooks to the right, generally occurs medially. It is
found initially only in *strened* (line 235) and *synnes* (line 236).
t has a shaft that always extends above the cross-bar.
u/v has an otiose stroke forming a loop above the left side when it is used
initially.[31]
w - Anglicana **w** is found medially and initially.
y is indistinguishable from *thorn*.
The *yogh* might occur once, in ʒheldid (line 262).

There are no unusual abbreviations.
The Tyronian nota is cursive and 2-shaped.

NOTES

1. These events were recorded in Oliver Heywood's diary, J. Horsfall Turner, ed., *The Rev. Oliver Heywood, B.A., 1630–1702; his autobiography, diaries, anecdote and event books; illustrating the general and family history of Yorkshire and Lancashire.* 4 vols. (Brighouse: A. B. Bayes, 1881–85), III:178.

2. Nassington's poem was edited, without knowledge of this manuscript, by G.G. Perry, *Religious Pieces in Prose and Verse* (1913; New York: Greenwood Press, 1996), 60–72.

3. For an edition of the *Emendatio Vitae*, see Richard Rolle, *Emendatio vitae; Orationes ad honorem nominis Ihesu*, ed. Nicholas Watson (Toronto: Pontifical Institute, 1995), cited as "Watson."

4. For a consideration of whether Rolle should be labeled a mystic, see Denis Renevey, "Richard Rolle," in *Approaching Medieval English Anchoritic and Mystical Texts*, ed. Dee Dyas, Valerie Edden, and Roger Ellis (Cambridge: D.S. Brewer, 2005), 63–74.

5. For a brief account of Rolle's life, see Watson, 6–8.

6. Rüdiger Spahl, "Richard and William or To Whom was Richard Rolle's *Emendatio Vitae* Dedicated?" *Revue d'Histoire des Textes* 32 (2002): 301.

7. According to John Alford, the *Emendatio Vitae* was Rolle's "most frequently translated" piece. "Richard Rolle and Related Works," in A.S.G Edwards, ed. *Middle English Prose: A Critical Guide to Major Authors and Genres.* (New Brunswick: Rutgers University Press, 1984), 35–60, at 45.

8. Watson, 5.

9. Watson, 20.

10. Ingrid J. Peterson, who has done the only major study of Nassington, provides a chronology of his life and gives 1359 as the year of his death. *William of Nassington: Canon, Mystic and Poet of the Speculum Vitae* (New York: Peter Lang, 1986), 18–20. The DNB gives his year of death as 1354. Matthew Sullivan, "Nassington, William (d. 1354)," *Oxford Dictionary of National Biography* (Oxford: Oxford University Press, 2004). Valerie Lagorio and Michael Sergent accept Peterson's account. "English Mystical Writings," in A *Manual of the Writings in Middle English 1050–1500*, ed. Albert E. Hartung (New Haven: Connecticut Academy of Arts and Sciences, 1993), 3049–3137, at 3087.

11. Peterson's study was written with the primary goal of convincing scholars that no one except Nassington could be the author of the *Speculum Vitae*. Others, however, have been less sure. When Hope Emily Allen studied manuscripts of the *Speculum Vitae* in the early twentieth century, she found Nassington's name associated with only two of the thirty-one copies she examined, and concluded that "he may or may not be the author of the *Speculum*." "The *Speculum Vitae*: Addendum," *PMLA* 32.2 (1917): 133–162, at 136.

12. Robert R. Raymo, "Works of Religious and Philosophical Instruction," in A *Manual of the Writings in Middle English* 1050–1500, ed. Albert E. Hartung (Hamden: Archon Books, 1986), 2255–2378, at 2261.

13. Peterson disputes Nassington's authorship on the grounds that it lacks the "section on contemplation, which is central to his own thought" (163).

14. Alford, 43.

15. British Library Manuscripts Catalogue Online, http://www.bl.uk/catalogues/manuscripts/HITS0001.ASP?VPath=html/26565.htm&Search=33995&Highlight=F (accessed 16 April 2007).

16. *The Thornton Manuscript* (*Lincoln Cathedral* MS 91), ed. D. S Brewer and A. E. B. Owen (London: Scolar Press, 1975).

17. The civil year began in March, not January.

18. Turner, III:178.

19. Henry Ashhurst, *Some Remarks upon the life of that painful servant of God, Mr. Nathanael Heywood* (London: Tho. Cockerill, 1695), 18.

20. This claim might be proven by comparison to Oliver Heywood's handwriting in other manuscripts; unfortunately, I have not had an opportunity to do so.

21. Turner, II:213.

22. The third number is obscured, and could be either 8 or 9.

23. If one were to conjecture, one might be tempted to say that the vellum was being used as the flyleaf for some other book and was cut out to provide the cover for this collection of sermons. This would be based on the fact that there is very little text missing from the vellum, while what *is* missing would have been from the top and bottom of the text block (see below). It still would not adequately explain why Greenwood's name is written upside down on the front cover. There is no proof for this claim, and it is just as likely that trimming the vellum sheet to fit the dimensions required by the sermon collection explains the loss of lines.

24. By contrast, Thornton has one full couplet per line. There are brackets, but they do not seem to indicate rhyme.

25. Analysis of the hand is based on M. B. Parkes, *English Cursive Book Hands* (Oxford: Oxford University Press, 1969). For a detailed list of the letter forms of our manuscript, see appendix.

26. Robert Babcock, in a recent conversation (April 2005), agreed that there was a single scribe, but asserted that the manuscript is earlier than 1400 based on his knowledge of Latin paleography. While it is possible that the two fragments were copied at different times by the same scribe, their overall similarity, as well as the fact that they survived in places near enough to each other to have been selected for use as binding material together, suggests that they at least came from a single original manuscript. I make the claim that the fragments were written in Yorkshire because the Middle English has characteristics of Northern dialect, such as *mykil*.

27. The **a**, at least, confirms my proposed date of *c.* 1400, as it is the primary letter form assigned by A. I. Doyle to this time period: "The gradual introduction of Secretary **a**, and the associated letter-forms of **g**, **r**, and **s**, singly or together, into otherwise traditionally Anglicana hands, is a common phenomenon in the period of about 1375–1420." A. I. Doyle, "The Copyist of the Ellesmere *Canterbury Tales*," in *The Ellesmere Chaucer: Essays in Interpretation*, ed. Martin Stevens and Daniel Woodward (San Marino: Huntington Library, 1995), 49–67, at 54.

28. See below.

29. Letter forms are based on the ME. Abbreviations are based primarily on the Latin. There is no substantial difference between the two, unless indicated. I do not address capital letters.

30. In the Latin, as noted above, it is found only in the two-compartment form.

31. In the Latin, there is an alternative form in which the approach stroke sometimes comes from far below the line.

St. Birgitta of Sweden's *Revelationes* (1492) in York Minster Library

BRIDGET MORRIS

The seven hundred revelations of St. Birgitta of Sweden were first printed in Lübeck in 1492 at the press of Bartholomaeus Ghotan in an edition that was commissioned by the mother-house of the Birgittine order at Vadstena in Sweden. According to the colophon, two men, a brother named Petrus Ingemari (later confessor general at Vadstena, d. 1526), and a lay brother named Gerhardus (a German by birth, d. 1515, who was described in the *Diarium Vadstenense* as a "bonus pictor"), went to Lübeck on September 27, 1491, to oversee the printing. Both brethren returned to Vadstena on November 25, 1492, taking with them several unbound copies.[1] The edition opens with the *Epistola domini Johannis Cardinalis de Turrecremata*, an abbreviated version of the defense by the Spanish Dominican Cardinal Juan de Torquemada (1388–1468) in response to the controversy surrounding the *Revelationes* at the Council of Basel in the 1430s.[2] Then follows the defense by Birgitta's Swedish confessor, Master Matthias of Linköping, which is widely known from its incipit as the *Stupor et mirabilia*, and constitutes a prologue to the seven Books of *Revelationes*. The main part of the volume is taken up with Books I–VII which are followed by certain additional materials: the *Epistola solitarii ad reges* (an endorsement of the saint by her later confessor and general editor, Alphonso of Jaén), Book VIII (a collection of political revelations), the *Regula s. Salvatoris* (the Birgittine Rule), *Sermo Angelicus* (the liturgy for the Birgittine nuns), *Quattuor orationes* (four prayers in praise of Christ and the Virgin), and *Revelationes Extravagantes* (various additional materials that were not incorporated into the canonization edition). At the end is the *Vita abbreviata sanctae Birgittae*, an extensive alphabetical index, and a prayer addressed to St. Birgitta.[3]

The Ghotan printing marks the end of a long and complex process of textual transmission that began in the 1340s with Birgitta writing down her visions in her native tongue.[4] Her Swedish text was then translated into Latin, and after her death in 1373 a revision was carried out by Alphonso of Jaén to meet the requirements of the canonization committees appointed by the papacy. None of the earliest drafts in Swedish or Latin survives, except for two fragments in Birgitta's own hand that are now housed in the National Library in Stockholm.[5] From the late fourteenth century until the early sixteenth century, hundreds of copies in Latin were made. The estimated 180 manuscripts that survive today fall into four main groupings that are broadly associated with centers or regions of Birgittine influence, in particular, Naples, Prague, Vadstena, England and Germany. During this period the text was augmented with supplementary and explanatory materials, and the ordering of the Books of Revelations was subject to rearrangement. In fact, it was not until Ghotan's first printed edition that the Birgittine corpus became properly defined for the first time.[6] This printing had a run of eight hundred copies on paper and sixteen deluxe copies on parchment. Today, about fifty copies of the 800 volumes printed on paper survive in libraries throughout the world, and just four copies of those printed on parchment are extant.[7]

York Minster Library possesses a paper copy of Ghotan's edition (Library Class mark XII. J.9). The volume is first mentioned in the catalogue of the Minster Library, which was compiled in 1638, and entered as *"Turra Cremata de Revelacionibus S. Birgittae,"* referring to the opening text, Torquemada's *Epistola.*[8] This catalogue was compiled as a consequence of the substantial donation of more than three thousand books to the library in 1628 by the widow of Archbishop Tobie Matthew, who was born in Bristol in 1546 and spent the years from 1559 to 1583 in Oxford before becoming bishop of Durham 1583 and archbishop of York in 1606.[9] Although it is quite likely that the Birgittine volume was part of Matthew's library, there is no evidence that it was, for it bears none of his hallmark signatures, initials or motto as bishop of Durham or archbishop of York. However, he was a learned bibliophile with a broad interest in theology and was a collector of books from foreign printing presses, so this is the sort of book in which he might well have been interested.[10] It is unlikely that it was already in the Minster library at the date of the Matthew donation, for books before this time were chained, as suggested by an inventory record from 1624 for the purchase of eight dozen chains, and there are no chain marks on the Ghotan edition.[11]

Equally possible is that the volume found its way into York Minster Library from another library, perhaps from a local monastic community or a recusant group in Yorkshire that had been closed at the Reformation. There is a record, for instance, from an inventory made in 1558 of the library of the Cluniac Priory of St Mary Magdalene at Monk Bretton —a house that had a particular interest in printed books — which lists a volume of the Revelations of "Birgitte virginis," together with thirty other volumes that the Cluniac monks were attempting to keep intact after the dissolution; this record expresses a wish to return the collection to the priory if it were ever restored.[12]

St. Birgitta had a strong following in Yorkshire even within a few years of her canonization in 1391. Henry Fitzhugh, lord of Ravensworth and nephew of the martyred Archbishop Richard Scrope, went to Sweden in 1406 with Henry IV's daughter, Philippa, for her marriage to the Scandinavian ruler, Erik of Pomerania. Fitzhugh later donated his estate at Cherry Hinton, near Cambridge, as the economic foundation for a Birgittine establishment. Even before he went to Sweden, he appears to have had an interest in mystical writings, and his family was connected with Richard Rolle's immediate circle. Between 1408 and 1415 he maintained two Vadstena brethren in England at his own expense. Henry IV petitioned the pope for permission to found a Birgittine abbey in York, possibly at St. Nicholas's or St. Leonard's hospital.[13] In the event, none of these plans ever came to fruition, and instead it was Henry V who established the new royal foundation of Syon at Isleworth on the Thames, within easy reach of London.

Many of the Syon brethren were scholars who had taken their degrees at Oxford or Cambridge before entering Syon, where they became authors and translators of spiritual works. One such person was Clement Maydestone (d. 1456), originally a Trinitarian of Hounslow, who wrote a history of the death in 1405 of Archbishop Scrope.[14] Thomas Gascoigne, the chancellor of Oxford University, was a staunch defender of Birgitta and translator of her *Vita* into English; as a young chaplain he had taken part in the visit to Vadstena with Henry Fitzhugh to arrange for the royal marriage between the houses of England and Sweden, mentioned above. He annotated several manuscripts to do with Birgittine texts, and his *Liber veritatum*, written between 1433 and 1457, makes mention of the preeminent Syon manuscript, London, British Library MS Harley 612. Thomas also fostered the cult of Richard Scrope, after giving a speech on the five wounds of Christ and using typically Birgittine iconography (seen most notably in the nuns' black headdress that has a white crown and cross and a red spot at each intersection of the cross).[15]

Copies of the Revelations were clearly in circulation in Yorkshire at an early date. A priest named Peter donated a collection of twelve books to the Cistercian house of Swine in the late fourteenth or early fifteenth century, including a volume of the revelations, wrongly attributed to Birgitta as "regine."[16] Lord Henry Scrope (d. 1415) is alleged to have bought a copy of the Revelations from a bookseller in Beverley.[17] Archbishop Richard Scrope and St Birgitta occur together as devotional figures in the Bolton hours manuscript in York Minster Library (MS add. 2 fol.). The pretty miniature of St Birgitta in this book of hours contrasts with the harsh-faced woman of the Neapolitan manuscripts of the 1390s and the heavy-featured representations of her in Sweden by northern German artists.[18] The Bolton hours, which may even predate the foundation of Syon, illustrates how quickly the Birgittine cult had spread after the canonization and seemingly penetrated into the English mercantile class, an indication of the growing popularity of a saint who otherwise appears so closely associated with royalty and the aristocratic class.[19]

Description of the York volume

The York volume of Ghotan's printed edition is complete, with no leaves at all missing.[20] It is in its original calfskin binding, with original boards, although the fore-edge is in nineteenth- century leather. The total binding measurement is 35 cm by 25 cm. The very fine-quality binding is from the workshop that had the monogram WG-IG, a large commercial stationers operating in Cambridge and perhaps later in London between 1478 and 1533.[21] It has a lattice-shaped design set diagonally on both the upper and the lower boards, and inside the lozenges are a fleur-de-lys, a rose in a circle, a griffin in a flat-topped lozenge, and shield with the double WG-IG monogram. A floral stamp in a rectangular frame forms the border. Traces of five round metal bosses can be seen on the upper and lower boards. On the lower board there is also the mark of a plate for a shelfmark label measuring 6 cm by 3 cm, with four nail holes along the top and four along the bottom. The label itself is lost but the mark is clearly apparent. On the fore-edge are indexing tabs at each subsection of the book, made of parchment strips measuring approximately 6 cm by 2 cm and pasted down to either side of the leaf where they sit. They are well-worn, and most of them are still in situ. Books II and III still have legible tab titles ("secundus liber," "tercius liber") written in a fine Gothic hand.[22]

Inside the volume, the initials and rubrics are colored in red and yellow with both colors used in particular at the beginning of the book. The colored capital letters finish at chapter 42 of Book I. Titles and paragraph signs are decoratively underlined in red with many capitals in yellow. In Book IV, chapters 8 and 9, there is a page using silver coloring in two revelations spoken by the Angel.

The full-page woodcut of the crucifixion at Book IV, chapter 70, contains several colors: green for the plants and the crown of thorns, brown for the skull, pink for faces, and red for Christ's body, which is also sprinkled with drops of blood. The style and character of this coloring suggest that it was done locally and not in a professional workshop. At this page opening the book is slightly worn in appearance, indicating perhaps that it was left open for the contemplation of the image. Some of the other full-page illustrations, which total fourteen in all, also have some light shading in color.[23]

The front endpaper contains an epigram in a cartouche in a contemporary English hand. It contains the name of "Frye" in the right margin. The text appears to be an extract from a sermon and contains a criticism of those who wish to take vengeance for injuries inflicted upon them, quoting Deuteronomy and Proverbs, and afterwards referring to a sermon by St Augustine:

> Duo sunt que Christus sibi retinuit et quasi desponsauit sibi scilicet vindictam et gloriam. Vindictam sibi retinuit, vnde ipse dicit deuteronomij tricesimo secundo. Michi vindicta et ego retribuam. Certe stultissimus est qui vindictam vult accipere de iniuriis sibi illatis, quando ipse vult suum vulnum de alio vulnere sanare. Ipse querit sanitatem in aliena infirmitate et in alieno malo bonum suum. Ipse est similis illi qui querit ignem in aqua, in felle dulcedinem, in spinis et tribulis ficus. Vnde Augustinus: Qui de aliena querit medicamentum, ipse adquerit sibi grande tormentum. Ideo nullus debet vindictam sibi querere, sed illa disposicioni diuine dimittere. Et ideo dicit Salomon Prouerbiorum vicesimo secundo. Ne dicat Malum reddam sed expecta Dominum cui est vindictam reddere. [24]

After a space, halfway down the page, is an unidentified two-line epithet:

> Quando bonum faris et in corde malum meditataris,
> Oscula que Iudas Domino dedit hec tu michi das.[25]

The volume also contains some contemporary bookmarks in situ.[26] One is a pentrial of minims on parchment, and a second, which points to a possible provenance within a monastic environment, refers to "reverentissime pater" in the vocative case. It looks like part of a letter containing just two lines on each side of the paper. Another bookmark, written on both sides, contains only a smattering of words and may be a piece of text rather than a letter.

Marginalia

The most distinctive feature of this volume is that it is annotated throughout with markings of some kind on almost every page. There are also signs that the book was closed quickly before the ink was allowed to dry. The hands of between one and five scribes are present in every Book of Revelations, with some overlap between scribes in the different Books. Books II and III, on the knights and clergy of Sweden, have fewer marginalia than elsewhere, while Book V, the Liber Quaestionum, has several different hands. Most notably, the Vita has no marginalia. All the hands are contemporary, from the late fifteenth or early sixteenth century, with the exception of a gloss from the later sixteenth century that gives a definition of the Latin verb "refollicare" in the Regula, chapter 3:

"refuseth to refresh, to strengthen and make lustie again." The presence of this later gloss is an indication that the volume (or at least the Birgittine Rule) was being carefully read well into the sixteenth century. Another sixteenth-century hand occurs on the final page, giving the name of one John Johnson.

Some of the marginal marks are written in red ink in the same hand, and these appear to relate primarily to the passages that concern the Virgin Mary. At least one of them is written in brown plummet first and overwritten in red ink. Throughout the volume there are frequent marginal indexes in the shape of a pointing finger in a clawlike hand. There are also many fine undulating vertical lines in ink down the margins against specific sections of text, and a distinctive circular lozenge nota sign recurs. Occasionally, there is a correction to a mistake in the Latin text (for example, Book VI chapter 52, "bonis et bonis" is changed to "bonis et malis"), and grammatical or orthographical errors are adjusted. The phrase "optima lectio" occurs quite commonly (e.g., in Regula, chapter 5, on the duties of monks). Another comment is "aureum capitulum" (for example, in Book VI, 66, which concerns the qualities of a good soul, using the metaphor of a house). In the Quattuor orationes, a numbering sequence is used for the paragraph divisions in the first prayer section, but in the subsequent prayers there are simply division marks without numbers. The index at the end of the volume has a modest number of highlighting pointers, most notably to the devil, death, and purgatory, to baptism before the age of discretion is reached, and to the well-known revelation about the three generations of women in judgment in Book VI chapter 52, which is also depicted in one of the woodcuts at the opening of the book.

The marginal comments seem for the most part to be mnemonics that summarize the main theme or subject for attention, rather than commentaries on the content. They often repeat the key words of a passage or summarize in short phrases the main point being made. St. Birgitta as a person was not of particular interest to the readership, nor, understandably, was Swedish history; nor indeed did her well-known criticism of the fourteenth-century Church receive much attention. The political interest is reflected in the passages that relate to English history, such as the French-English war in Book IV, chapters 103 to 105, in which the saint proposes a marriage alliance as a solution to the hostilities.

In the main, the commentaries reflect a devotional readership, most likely within a monastic environment. The most commonly highlighted passages concern the spiritual life of the ordinary clergy as well as the sacraments. All manner of very ordinary passages are highlighted that draw attention to the spiritual life, such as the private concerns of a priestly cleric and reader in his everyday devotions, and on almsgiving at a monastery (for example, Book VI 99). The good moral life, the dangers of vanity and the ways of the world, the imitation of the lives of the saints, purgatory, the devil, and the terrors of hell are also noted; and revelations in praise of Christ and the Virgin are frequently highlighted. The marginalia are suggestive of a high level of education among the readers, but in the main they do not cite authorities from the traditional teachings within the Church and they may even be intended as an expression and affirmation of the orthodoxy of the Revelations.

Provenance of the York copy

At first sight some of the bibliographical features of this volume suggest an affinity with the English Birgittine foundation of Syon. The Syon Birgittines were a richly endowed, centrally placed, and well-favored community, and intellectually at the very heart of late- medieval and early Reformation England. The Birgittine monks assiduously promoted and retained orthodox texts to defend the old faith, but at the same time they were at the forefront of new changes, such as the introduction of printing. Within the order, the Revelations formed part of the practice of regular communal reading, although the exact details are unclear and rules seem to have varied from house to house. The *Syon Additions*, which are the additional monastic regulations used at Syon, do not refer specifically to the reading of the Revelations in the house, although they do list as a "greuous defaute" the describing of the Revelations as dreams and their being held in contempt in any way.[27] On the other hand, the *Liber usuum*, which was produced in the Birgittine monastery of Gnadenberg in southern Germany in the mid-fifteenth century for the entire Birgittine order, states that members of the order were supposed to read the Revelations at meal times in four-yearly cycles, getting through three or four books each year.[28] Two other works that figure prominently as reflections of Birgittine spirituality in practice are the *Sermo Angelicus*, the specially composed weekly reading by the nuns at Matins, and the *Rule*, both of which were read aloud weekly in the community.

The York Minster volume contains several features that are similar to those of Syon books, in particular the presence of a book label and fore-edge tabs, and the absence of chain marks, foliation numbers, class marks, ex libris and other curatorial marks.[29] Furthermore, the *secundo folio* cataloguing system at Syon appears to be reflected in the subsequent cataloguing of the book in York.[30] It seems unimaginable that the house at Syon did not own a copy of the first printed edition of the Revelations; but there is no unequivocal evidence that it did. The register of the brethren's library, compiled by Thomas Betson, contains an entry, *Septem libri reuelacionum beate Birgitte cum tabula* (item M 115), that might refer to Ghotan's printed edition.[31] Although Betson's description and wording are not consistent with his method elsewhere, especially in respect of the *secundo folio* reference, Vincent Gillespie concludes that "the apparent absence of this famous edition of Bridget's works, seen through the press by brethren from the mother house of Vadstena, from elsewhere in the collection makes it likely that that edition is the one indicated here."[32]

Elsewhere, Gillespie comments that the printed edition could have been held in one of the other collections of books known to have been in the abbey; in other words, it was not held in the library itself.[33]

However, two features of the York volume point away from a Syon provenance. First, the size of the book label is different from those on Syon books, being slightly larger than the Syon labels, and therefore not immediately recognizable as a Syon label.[34] Second, there is no evidence that the liturgical texts in the volume were the subject of particular study or use, as might be expected of an edition that had belonged to Syon.

The other great foundation of the later medieval period was the Carthusian order, whose history often interweaves with that of the Birgittines in England, especially the Charterhouse of Sheen, which, like Syon, was founded by Henry V on the banks of the river Thames —the two houses stood opposite and were, as Shakespeare puts it, "two chantries where the sad and solemn priests / Sing still for Richard's soul" (*Henry* V. 4.1).

Birgitta must have known the Carthusians from her pilgrimage to Santiago de Compostela in 1341, although they were not established in Sweden until some 150 years later. They are one of the few orders that she does not openly criticize in her revelations. Indeed, in the *Extravagantes*, chapter 4, she exhorts the Birgittine nuns to follow the model of the Carthusians in their song:

> Imitentur illorum cantum, qui Cartusienses vocantur, quorum psalmodia plus redolet suauitatem mentis humilitatemque et deuocionem quam aliquam ostentacionem. Nam non vacat a culpa animus, quando cantantem plus delectat nota quam res, que canitur, omninoque abhominabile est Deo, quando vocis eleuacio plus fit propter audientes quam propter Deum.[35]

The Carthusians had an interest in mystical writers in particular, and the surviving lists of their books include the name of St Birgitta alongside those of Richard Rolle, Walter Hilton, and Catherine of Siena.[36] They were known for their "spiritual reading" and for making marginal notes in printed books, and, together with the Birgittines, they contributed greatly to the spiritual following of the devotion to the heart of Christ, and of Christ's passion in the late Middle Ages. Some of the features in the York volume are suggestive of a possible Carthusian provenance, most notably the religious epigram on the front endpaper of the type that often occurs in Carthusian volumes and the abundant use of marginalia.[37] The frequent references to the Virgin Mary and the contemplative image that is created in the carefully colored image of the crucifix in Book IV are also in keeping with Carthusian observance.[38] Further, the lack of class marks makes it possible that the book was used in a cell rather than in a library. The most explicit suggestion of a Carthusian connection is the passage quoted above relating to Carthusian singing, which is highlighted with a pointing index, with a marginal gloss that summarizes the text itself.

In keeping with the pattern of the frequent loan and exchange of books between monastic houses, including Syon and Sheen, it is possible that the York copy of Ghotan's edition was loaned from one monastic community to another. The Carthusian house in London, for instance, is said to have lent a copy of the *Revelationes* to a house in Coventry in 1500 and one to Beauvale in 1510.[39] Donations of books from one monastic community to another also happened frequently. For instance, a copy of the second edition of the *Revelationes* (printed by Koberger in Nuremberg 1500) was donated by David Curson, a brother of Syon, to John Doo, fellow of Fotheringham College, and after him "to the comune use for euermore of the company." This copy is now in Lambeth Palace Library.[40]

The York Minster Library copy of the *Revelationes* was clearly a valued volume that existed within a stable monastic environment, and the evidence on balance points to the likelihood that it was in Carthusian hands in the early sixteenth century. This conjecture now seems the most fruitful line for a more detailed expert study of the different hands and scribes within the general context of marginal references and commentaries in early English printed devotional books. The book can also take its place among considerations of Birgittine compilations that were so extensively produced throughout Europe in the century after St. Birgitta's death; for although it is not a compilation itself, the highlighted revelations and passages, if drawn together, would comprise a compilation of their own and a unique reading of the Birgittine corpus in its entirety.[41]

Whatever the provenance and readership of this book, whether for preaching, teaching, or for silent reading in a cell, or as part of a communal and shared activity of monastic reading, this volume in York Minster Library retains its bibliographical integrity possibly to a greater degree than any other existing printed copy of the Revelations, and with the exceptional richness of its marginalia, it provides an important insight into the very private world of the contemporary English reader who was reading St. Birgitta's Revelations at the end of the Middle Ages.

ACKNOWLEDGMENTS

Earlier versions of this paper were read at the Manchester Medieval Society, the Leeds Medieval Seminar, and the International Conference for the 600th Jubilee of St Birgitta, Vadstena, August 2002, and the Archbishop Scrope Conference, York, 2006. I am grateful for the conversations and correspondence I have had with the following: Stephan Borgehammar (University of Lund),

Ian Doyle (University of Durham Library), Mirjam Foot (University College, London), Monica Hedlund (University of Uppsala); Veronica O'Mara (University of Hull), Christopher de Hamel (Corpus Christi College, Cambridge), Sue Powell (University of Salford), Vincent Gillespie (Lady Margaret Hall, Oxford), Elizabeth Westin-Bergh (Skokloster Library, Sweden). In particular, I wish to thank Deirdre Mortimer, formerly Librarian of York Minster Library, for her enormous generosity and encouragement while I was pursuing my research.

NOTES

1. See Claes Gejrot, *Diarium Vadstenense. The Memorial Book of Vadstena Abbey*. Acta Universitatis Stockholmiensis. Studia Latina Stockholmiensia 33 (Stockholm, Sweden: Almqvist & Wiksell International, 1988), 390. According to the same source, seven copies of the *Revelationes* were destroyed in a fire in Vadstena in 1495, together with a newly-installed printing press:

> Consumpsitque et in favillam redegit singula, que in illa domo servabantur, cum tecto et intersticiis etc. Tunc combusta fuit ibi inter alia una tunna plena cum septem voluminibus Revelationum celestium sancte matris nostre beate Birgitte, quam deponi hic fecerat quidam civis Lubecensis pro librorum huiusmodi venditione. Item, conflagraverunt etiam ibidem diversa instrumenta pro impressura librorum realiter aptata et iam per medium annum in usu habita, videlicet torcular cum litteris stanneis in brevitura et in textura in magnis expensis et laboribus comportata.

> [Everything that was preserved in this building [i.e., the infirmary], together with the roof and dividing walls, was consumed and transformed into ash by the fire. Among the destroyed items was a barrel containing seven volumes of the *Revelationes* of St Birgitta, our mother; this barrel had been deposited here by a citizen of Lübeck for the sale of its contents. In addition, various printing machinery was burnt that had only been fully installed and used for six months. This was a printing press with metal letters for large and small type, and it had been procured for a great sum of money and with enormous effort.]

2. On this controversy see further Claire Sahlin, *Birgitta of Sweden and the Voice of Prophecy* (Woodbridge, UK: Boydell, 2001), 221–223; Carl-Gustaf Undhagen, "Une source du prologue (chap. 1) aux Révélations de Sainte Brigitte par le

cardinal Jean de Turrecremata," Eranos 58 (1960): 214–226; Heymericus de Campo: Anna Fredrikson Adman, ed., Dyalogus super Reuelacionibus beate Birgitte." A Critical Edition with an Introduction, Acta Universitatis Upsaliensis, Studia Latina Upsaliensia 27 (Uppsala, Sweden: Uppsala Universitet, 2003). Torquemada's Epistola also includes the Bulla canonizationis beatae Birgittae issued by Pope Boniface IX on October 7, 1391, and Martin V's Confirmatio canonizationis beatae Birgittae, dated July 1, 1419, in Florence.

3. For further bibliographical information, see Isak Collijn, Sveriges bibliografi intill år 1600, Svenska Litteratursällskapet, 10: 15 (Uppsala, Sweden: Almqvist & Wiksell, 1935), 117–128; Gesamtkatalog der Wiegendrucke. Herausgegeben von der Kommission für den Gesamtkatalog der Wiegendrucke, Band IV (Leipzig, Germany: Karl W. Hiersemann, 1930).

4. On St. Birgitta in general, see Bridget Morris, St Birgitta of Sweden (Woodbridge, UK: Boydell, 1999), and for an account of the process of the recording of the revelations, see Denis Searby and Bridget Morris, The Revelations of St. Birgitta of Sweden, Volume 1. Liber Caelestis, Books I–III (New York: Oxford University Press, 2006), 11–25.

5. See Bertil Högman, Heliga Birgittas originaltexter (Uppsala, Sweden: Almqvist & Wiksell, 1951).

6. The Ghotan text is most closely related to the Swedish "Vadstena" branch of manuscripts, although it also introduces several errors and independent readings of its own. See further Birger Bergh, "Tillförlitligheten i olika versioner av Birgittas Uppenbarelser," in Birgitta, hendes værk og hendes klostre i Norden, ed. Tore Nyberg, Odense University Studies in History and Social Sciences 150 (Odense, Denmark: Odense University Press, 1991), 397–405.

7. Two of the parchment copies are in private hands; the others are in Skokloster Castle, Uppland, and the Bodleian Library, Oxford; and there are forty-three leaves in the National Library in Stockholm). See further on the location of the paper copies in the British Library's electronic Incunabula Short-title Catalogue (ISTC), available at http://www.bl.uk/catalogues,istc/.

8. This catalogue was compiled as a penance for the offence of simony by a cleric named Timothy Thurscross; see G. E. Aylmer and Reginald Cant, A History of York Minster (Oxford, UK: Clarendon Press, 1977), 502–507.

9. See further James Raine, A Catalogue of the Printed Books in the Library of the Dean and Chapter of York (York, UK: Sampson, 1896), vi.

10. His books reflect some of the religious controversies in the early years of English Protestantism; the Jesuit Edmund Campion threw some doubt on his loyalty to the Church of England, and two of his sons later joined the Catholic Church. See Raine, Catalogue, vii.

11. Before the Matthew donation, the holding of the Minster Library was extremely modest, especially compared with the fine collection held by the nearby Abbey of St Mary's in York, as was noted at a visitation during the reign of Henry VIII; see Raine, Catalogue, v.

12. See Richard Sharpe, James P. Carley, R. M. Thomson, and A. G. Watson, *English Benedictine Libraries: The Shorter Catalogues*, Corpus of British Medieval Library Catalogues 4 (London, UK: British Library in Association with The British Academy, 1996), 266. See also Claire Cross, "Monastic Learning and Libraries," in *Humanism and Reform: The Church in Europe, England, and Scotland, 1400-1643. Essays in Honour of James K. Cameron*, ed. James Kirk (Oxford, UK: Blackwell Publishers, 1991), 263; and James P. Carley, "The Dispersal of the Monastic Libraries and the Salvaging of the Spirits" in *The Cambridge History of Libraries in Britain and Ireland, Vol. 1, to 1640*, ed. Elisabeth Leedham Green and Teresa Weber (Cambridge, UK: Cambridge University Press, 2006), 285–287. "Virginis" is a misleading —but not uncommon— description of Birgitta, a mother of eight children; and she is sometimes confused with St. Brigid of Kildare, as, for example, in the catalogue of Gloucester Cathedral Library, which also houses a copy of the Ghotan edition of 1492; see Suzanne Mary Eward, ed., *A Catalogue of Gloucester Cathedral Library* (Gloucester, UK: Dean and Chapter, 1972), 39.

13. See further Neil Beckett, "St Bridget, Henry V, and Syon Abbey," in *Studies in St Birgitta and the Brigittine Order*, ed. James Hogg, 2 vols, *Analecta Cartusiana*, Salzburg, 35:19 (New York: Edwin Mellen Press, 1993), 2. 127.

14. See also Vincent Gillespie, ed., *Syon Abbey, with the Library of the Carthusians*, ed. A. I. Doyle, Corpus of British Medieval Library Catalogues 9 (London, UK: British Library in Association with The British Academy, 2001), 228.

15. See Julia Bolton Holloway, *The Life of Saint Birgitta by Birger Gregersson and Thomas Gascoigne* (Toronto, CA: Peregrina, 1991), 7–9.

16. David N. Bell, *The Libraries of the Cistercians, Gilbertines and Premonstatensians*, Corpus of British Library Catalogues 3 (London, UK: British Library in Association with The British Academy, 1992), 146.

17. K. J. Allison, ed. *The Victoria County History of York, East Riding, vol VI: Beverley* (London, UK: Institute for Historical Research, 1989), 62.

18. For examples, see Hans Aili and Jan Svanberg, *Imagines Sanctae Birgittae: The Earliest Illuminated Manuscripts and Panel Paintings Related to the Revelations of St Birgitta of Sweden*, 2 vols (Stockholm, Sweden: Royal Swedish Academy of Letters, History and Antiquities, 2003); Mereth Lindgren, 2nd ed., *Bilden av Birgitta* (Stockholm, Sweden: Proprius, 2002).

19. See Jeremy Goldberg and Patricia Callum, "How Margaret Blackburn taught her Daughters: Reading Devotional Instruction in a Book of Hours" in *Medieval Women: Texts and Contexts in Late Medieval Britain: Essays for Felicity Riddy*, ed. Jocelyn Wogan-Browne, *et al.* (Turnhout, Belgium: Brepols, 2000), 217–236; Sarah Rees Jones and Felicity Riddy, "The Bolton Hours of York: Female Domestic Piety and the Public Sphere" in *Household, Women and Christianities in Late Antiquity and the Middle Ages*, ed. Anneke B. Mulder-Bakker and Jocelyn Wogan-Browne (Turnhout, Belgium: Brepols, 2005), 215–254. Although there are several

studies of the Birgittine influence in the axis of London, Oxford, and Syon and in East Anglia (the home of her defender at the canonization, Adam Easton), less work appears to have been done on the Birgittine influence in northern England.

20. According to the information given in existing catalogues and judging by those copies I have had the opportunity to see in libraries in Sweden, Denmark and Britain, most other copies are defective in some way. For example, the preeminent copy in Sweden, which is in the library of Skokloster Castle (one of the four surviving parchment copies), is wanting the woodcut of the crucifixion in the middle of Book IV. The Skokloster parchment was bought in London in 1897 by Count Per Hierta på Främmestad, and had earlier been owned by Lord Ashburnham.

21. I am grateful for this information to Professor Mirjam Foot, who in a private communication writes:

> A bindery that was at work in Cambridge and links through one or two tools with work produced by the Unicorn binder, used a signed tool with the monogram WG, as well as a roll signed with two monograms: WG and IG; the shop also used two panels signed IG. J. B. Oldham suggested that this shop belonged to two generations of binders, WG, the father and two sons, the elder: WG and the younger: IG, and indeed the (large) output from this bindery that covers books printed between 1478 and 1537, can be divided into three periods, linked either by the WG tool or by the WG/IG roll. The first period covers books printed between 1478 and 1507. It is possible that IG and WG were booksellers who employed this bindery rather than being binders themselves.

See further J. Basil Oldham, *English Blind-stamped Bindings* (Cambridge, UK: Cambridge University Press, 1952), 17–19, pl. XI; G. D. Hobson, *Bindings in Cambridge Libraries* (Cambridge, UK: Cambridge University Press, 1929), pls. XIV, XV; G.D. Hobson, *English Binding before* 1500 (Cambridge, UK: Cambridge University Press, 1929), 21–22, pls. 47–51. G. Pollard, "The Names of some English 15th-century Binders" *The Library*, 5th ser. 25 (1970): 208, 212–213; M. M. Foot, "English Decorated Bookbinding," in *Book Production and Publishing in Britain* 1375–1475, ed. Jeremy Griffith and Derek Pearsall (Cambridge, UK: Cambridge University Press, 1989), 65–86.

22. The missing tabs are in Book VII (but the mark, measuring about 5 cm by 4.5 cm, is still visible), *Quattuor Oraciones* (5 cm by 2.5 cm), and *Extravagantes* (5 cm by 2.75 cm). For each letter of the index there is a tab, with the exception of "r" (where the tab mark shows), and "s" to "z" have no tab marks at all. The fore-

edge tabs appear to be more a feature of continental than of English books. For a comparative example of the functional purpose of the Syon tab marks, in a manuscript copy of the Bible where each book is indicated with a small gothic hand, see Christopher de Hamel, *Syon Abbey: The Library of the Bridgettine Nuns and their Peregrinations after the Reformation* (Otley, UK: The Roxburghe Club, 1991), 106–107.

23. Of these fourteen, four (including this one of the crucifixion) are whole woodcuts, while the other ten are formed from three or more blocks. This crucifixion block, which shows the Ghotan coat-of-arms at Mary's feet, is also found in a missal produced by an anonymous printer for the diocese of Lebus in Brandenburg. See K. Haebler, "Das Missale für die Diözese Lebus (Missale Lubucense)," *Nordisk tidskrift för bok- och bibliotekshistoria*, årgång 2 (1915): 53–76.

24. "There are two things that Christ kept for himself and as it were betrothed to himself, viz. vengeance and glory. He kept vengeance for himself, as he himself in the 32nd chapter of Deuteronomy said: 'Vengeance is mine and I shall repay.' [Deut. 32:35] Certainly that man is foolish who wishes to take vengeance for the injuries that have been inflicted upon him; when he wishes to cure his own wound from the wound of another. He seeks health in the sickness of someone else and he his own good in someone else's misfortune. He is like a man who seeks fire in water, sweetness in bile and figs on thistles and thorns. About this Augustine says: 'he who seeks a remedy from what is not his own is heaping up for himself a great torment.' And so no one ought to seek for vengeance for himself, but leave that to divine will. And so Solomon says in Proverbs 22: Let no-one say 'I shall return the evil' but wait for the Lord to whom it belongs to exact vengeance." The quotation from St Augustine may be found at Sermo 132 (*Patrologia Latina*, xxxviii. 684).

25. "When you speak good and meditate evil in your heart, You give me the kisses that Judas gave the Lord."

26. They were found at Books IV, ch. 111, Book VI, ch. 34, and Book VI, ch. 40.

27. See further G. J. Aungier, *History and Antiquities of Syon Monastery, the Parish of Isleworth, and the Chapelry of Hounslow* (London, UK: J. B. Nichols and Son, 1840), 258.

28. See Sara Risberg, ed., *Liber usuum fratrum monasterii Vadstenensis: The Customary of the Vadstena Brothers. A Critical Edition with an Introduction*, Acta Universitatis Stockholmiensis. Studia Latina Stockholmiensia 50 (Stockholm, Sweden: Almqvist & Wiksell International, 2003), 182–183. However, as Risberg observes (*ibid.*, 14–18), the monks of Syon did not participate in the general chapter at Gnadenberg, where the *Liber usuum* was ratified in 1487, and the *Liber usuum* was not very widely circulated, so it is possible that it was not observed at Syon.

29. The Syon Abbey collection (containing some 1,500 entries) has now been reconstructed and updated in Gillespie, *Syon Abbey*.

30. The fore-edge classification and cataloguing of the book under "Turrecremata" in the York Minster Library catalogue of 1638 may also explain

why it appears to have been overlooked; when I first discovered this book in York Minster Library the catalogue entry gave the impression that it contained simply Torquemada's defense rather than the complete text of the *Revelationes*.

31. The donor of this volume was a man named Copynger, who probably entered Syon in the 1520s and was elected confessor general in 1536; *Ibid.*, 573.

32. *Ibid.*, 257.

33. "The absence from this collection of the great Ghotan 1492 Lübeck edition of the works of Bridget raises serious doubts about the extent of their later commitment to studying her writings. If there was one printed book I had assumed would be in the collection it was this edition: its absence is eloquent, although it could have been held in one of the other collections of books known to have been in the house." Vincent Gillespie, "Dial M for mystic: mystical texts in the library of Syon Abbey and the spirituality of the Syon brethren," in *The Medieval Mystical Tradition, England, Ireland, and Wales: Exeter Symposium VI: Papers Read at Charney Manor, July 1999*, ed. Marion Glasscoe (Woodbridge, UK, and Rochester, NY: D.S. Brewer, 1999), 265.

34. I am grateful to Vincent Gillespie who drew my attention to this point. On the Syon labels see Gillespie, *Syon Abbey*, xlvii, and pls. 5a and 5b.

35. "They should imitate the song of those who are known as Carthusians, whose singing is more redolent of the sweetness of the mind, and of humility and devotion, rather than any ostentation. For the soul is not blameless when the singer finds more joy in the music than in what is being sung; and it is altogether abhorrent to God when the voice is raised more towards the listener than towards God." On the Birgittines and Carthusians in Scandinavia, see Alf Härdelin, "In the Sign of the Rosary" in *Medieval Spirituality in Scandinavia and Europe*, ed. L. Bisgaars, S. S. Jensen, Kurt Villands Jensen, and John Lind (Odense, Denmark: Odense University Press, 2001), 285–93. See also Bridget Morris, "Birgittines and Beguines in Medieval Sweden," in *The Holy Women of Liège* ed. Juliette Dor, Lesley Johnson and Jocelyn Wogan-Browne (Turnhout, Belgium: Brepols, 1999), 159–176.

36. E. Margaret Thompson, *The Carthusian Order in England* (London: SPCK, 1930), 313–334.

37. It is to Dr. Ian Doyle that I owe this line of argument. Dr. Doyle kindly spent time looking through this volume in York Minster Library and sharing his observations with me in 2003.

38. On the relationship between image and text, see further Jessica Brantley, *Reading in the Wilderness. Private Devotion and Public Performance in Late Medieval England* (London and Chicago: University of Chicago Press, 2007), 27–77.

39. See Gillespie, *Syon Abbey*, 626–627. The Ghotan edition was followed by eight further editions. The second was produced in Nuremberg in 1500 by Anton Koberger, with the patronage of the Austrian nobility and the emperor Maximilian. It contains seventeen woodcuts that have been associated with

the atelier of Albrecht Dürer. The third edition, based on Koberger's, was also published in Nuremberg in 1517 by F. Peypus. The fourth was produced in Rome in 1557 by the Swedish historiographer and exiled Catholic Olaus Magnus, who had charge of St Birgitta's house in the Piazza Farnese in Rome, where he installed a small printing press. The fifth edition was published in 1606 by the bishop and theologian Consalvo Durante, who made an attempt to emend some of the errors in Ghotan's edition and introduce commentaries of his own. Then followed three editions that were all based on Durante's, and printed respectively in Antwerp in 1611, Cologne in 1628, and Rome in 1628. The last edition was based on the 1628 edition and was produced in Munich in 1680 by Simon Hörmann, the confessor general at the Birgittine abbey of Altomünster. See Isak Collijn, *Sveriges bibliografi*, 117–128; Isak Collijn and A. Lindblom, *Birgitta-utställningen* 1918: *Beskrifvande förtechning öfver utställda föremål* (Uppsala, Sweden: Almqvist & Wiksell, 1918), 131. Over the past fifty years a critical edition of the entire corpus has been published by the Fornsvenska Fornskrift-sällskapet [Medieval Swedish Texts Society], and there is an online version of the Latin text produced by Svenska Riksarkivet (The National Archives of Sweden), *Corpus reuelacionum samcte Birgitte*, available at: http://62.20.57.210/ra/diplomatariet/CRB/index.htm.

40. Gillespie, *Syon Abbey*, lxxii; Michael Sargent, "The transmission by the English Carthusians of some Late Medieval Spiritual Writings," *Journal of Ecclesiastical History* 27, no. 3 (1976): 225–240.

41. On the uses of the Revelations in England, see Roger Ellis, "'Flores ad fabricandam ... coronam': an Investigation into the Uses of the Revelations of St Bridget of Sweden in Fifteenth-century England," *Medium Ævum* (1982): 163–186. On some of the major vernacular compilations, see Bridget Morris and Veronica O'Mara, eds., *The Translation of the Works of St Birgitta of Sweden into the European Vernaculars*, The Medieval Translator 7 (Turnhout, Belgium: Brepols, 2000).

Cambridge University Library, Additional MS 2604: Repackaging Female Saints' Lives for the Fifteenth-Century English Nun

VERONICA O'MARA and VIRGINIA BLANTON

Of late, scholars interested in East Anglia have focused their attention on devotional practices, and these contributions have enriched our understanding of book production, manuscript circulation, and issues of literacy.[1] Especially useful is the increased understanding of women, both religious and lay, as readers of hagiographical texts. Our work-in-progress, an edition of Cambridge University Library, Additional MS 2604, promises to enhance current discussions of devotional reading by making readily available a manuscript containing twenty-two (mainly female) saints' lives in Middle English. The brief description of this edition offered here includes an examination of the contents and physical composition of this manuscript, which has not hitherto received any serious scholarly attention, and a discussion of the Latin sources, which present a complicated tangle of manuscript and print in the late-medieval period.[2] Alongside the discussion of these complications will be an investigation of the identity of the possible convent for which the lives were intended. By focusing on issues of content, manuscript decoration, and postmedieval provenance, we hope to unravel the complicated history of Add. 2604 and provide some indication of how Latin lives were being repackaged for reading by English nuns. The present brief article serves as an introduction to the larger project.[3]

As may be seen in the appendix, this manuscript consists almost entirely of female saints, all of whom are virgins, martyrs, or nuns. At first glance it may seem odd that the collection opens with two male saints, John the Baptist and John the Evangelist, and closes with another male saint, Leonard. Yet in medieval tradition the chastity of the Evangelist was emphasized, just as the Baptist's link to the virgin martyrs was evident in many roodscreen paintings.[4] Moreover, the two St. Johns share an iconographic tradition from the fifth century onward, and they, together with Leonard, are often found as the dedicatees of medieval nunneries.[5] The lives of these three male saints frame a rather eclectic mixture of female saints, beginning with the Roman virgin martyrs Columba, Agatha, Cecilia, and Barbara, followed by ten English saints, whose lives have familial ties and geographical associations with East Anglia and Kent. We then return to the Bible with Martha, then back again to Rome with Domitilla, Justina, and Benedicta before going to Ireland with Modwenna and France with Leonard.

The manuscript, which is in a single hand of the second half of the fifteenth century and consistent linguistically, has definitely been copied from another manuscript, as is evident from the frequent examples of dittography, and it is missing many pages (sometimes entire quires).[6] The saints' lives cross quire boundaries, and so any argument about the individual groupings being found in separate booklets is not tenable. The only saints that are each separately contained within the same quire boundaries are Modwenna and Leonard at the end of the manuscript, so they could have conceivably circulated independently.

This manuscript seems to comprise three little cycles broadly following the order of the liturgical calendar, although they look to be anything but a coherent whole.[7] The manuscript opens with the universal saints, starting with the two biblical Johns and ending with the virgin martyr Barbara, whose feasts run from June 24 to December 4. Put physically in the center are ten English saints, whose feasts run from June 23 to November 17, starting with Æthelthryth and finishing with Hild. Then the manuscript ends with another universal group, starting with the biblical Martha and ending with Leonard, whose feasts run from July 29 to November 6 (with Modwenna in a decidedly odd placement). For complicated textual and codicological reasons, it is clear that the collection must also have originally included two other lives.[8]

The manuscript contains chapter summaries as well as decoration throughout, and on the decoration between lives or on the headings, occasional cadel heads can be found. Spray work indicative of East Anglian artistry adorns champ letters at the opening of each legend except Modwenna's, the penultimate life, which has only the standard large initial used for new sections of a life.[9] This detail may provide more evidence for the suggestion that Modwenna was not intended for the present volume, a conjecture somewhat negated by the fact that Leonard, which follows, has the typical opening decoration.

Moving to the content of the manuscript, the obvious question is: What sources underlie this very diverse though codicologically intentional collection? Not surprisingly, the sources fall into two groups: those for the universal saints and those for the English saints. As will be obvious to anyone familiar with that medieval best seller the *Legenda aurea*, a number of the universal saints figure in that collection, namely, Agatha, Cecilia, John the Baptist, John the Evangelist, Justina, Leonard, and Martha. Of these, only the legends for Cecilia, John the Baptist, John the Evangelist, and Martha are actually translated from the *Legenda aurea* proper. The lives for Agatha, Justina, and Leonard come from other sources. In addition, Barbara, Benedicta, Columba, and Domitilla also have sources or analogues outside the *Legenda aurea*.

Just one example will suffice to show how the *Legenda aurea* is used.[10] In the life of John the Baptist, Add. 2604 combines the Nativity with the Decollation—starting with the Nativity (fols. 1r–3v), then moving to the Decollation (fols. 3v–10v) interrupted by a short passage from the Nativity (fols. 5v–6r), and then finishing with reordered exempla from the Nativity (fols. 10v–11v). The translator's general method is to provide a very close rendering with only a few minor stylistic changes, such as the omission of the names of patristic authors and sources and the addition of questions to clarify matters. Long explanatory material is excluded completely. From this example, it is very obvious that the hagiographer is interested in narrative, and this focus becomes especially clear with the number of miracles packed in at the end. Moreover, the Add. 2604 writer cleverly rearranges the order of these so that his life finishes with the story of how two devotees argue about the merits of the respective St. Johns, only to be told by the saints themselves that they are in accordance in heaven, so there is no need for dispute about them on earth. Ending this way, the story neatly connects the Baptist with the Evangelist, who comes next in the volume.

In trying to locate the sources of the other legends that are not straightforward translations from the *Legenda aurea*, it is necessary to investigate not only various manuscripts but also early printed sources. The most important of the latter for current purposes is Bonino Mombrizio's *Sanctuarium*, printed in Milan by 1480 and commonly referred to as Mombritius, followed by the anonymous *Historiae plurimorum sanctorum*, which was published as an addition to the *Legenda aurea* in Cologne in 1483 and in Louvain in 1485 by a certain Johannes of Westfalia.[11] There is a degree of overlap in content among all three works. Indeed preliminary work has shown that just because one so-called source for a text has been isolated, this does not mean that another so-called source for the same text cannot be found; for instance, Add. 2604 Barbara shares elements with the *Historiae* and Mombritius; Justina seems to follow Mombritius very closely but with a section in the middle not found in Mombritius or the *Legenda*; while the Leonard in the *Legenda* is identical with Mombritius but neither of these two is the source of the Add. 2604 text. Moreover, the identification of sources is further complicated by the intractable interaction of potential manuscript and printed sources at this period.

It is obvious, then, that much work remains to be done in disaggregating all these different potential sources, something that is not a problem with the English saints, which are closely translated from John of Tynemouth's *Sanctilogium Anglie, Walliae, Scotiae et Hiberniae*. John was a monk of the Benedictine house at St. Albans and finished his legendary in the late fourteenth century.[12] The collection features some 156 Latin legends designed for daily reading that were later reordered alphabetically before being printed in English and in Latin in 1516.[13] The translation of these eleven lives here indicates some desire to make this collection available to a non-Latinate audience earlier than previously thought.

If we return to a consideration of the three cycles of devotional readings, leaving aside Modwenna and Leonard, we see that the English cycle in the middle begins with the Ely saints: Æthelthryth; her sisters Seaxburh and Wihtburh; Seaxburh's daughters Eormenhild and Eorcengota; and Eormenhild's daughter Wærburh of Chester. There is also a brief account of Æthelburh, another of Æthelthryth's sisters, appended to the end of the life of Eorcengota. The Ely saints are presented in calendar order (their original feasts having been collapsed and celebrated together in July alongside Seaxburh's feast and Wihtburh's translation feast). All of the Ely women were nuns and all but Eormenhild were abbesses. Together they comprise more than a quarter of the saints represented in the codex. This grouping suggests, therefore, that the manuscript was produced near the cult center at Ely, Cambs., where four of the women were buried, or in some other locale in East Anglia, where devotion to Æthelthryth and her family is most densely attested.

Particular attention to the Ely saints is made manifest in the incipits for each of the Ely lives. In these are added genealogical details designed to inform and remind a reader of the relationship between the women even as they serve to connect the lives into a larger narrative. For example, the incipit for Æthelthryth reads as one would expect: "The life of Seynt Audry of Hely" (fol. 52v).[14] The incipit for Seaxburh is augmented to stress her relationship to her sister featured in the previous life: "Here begynnyth the life of Seynt Sexburge, sister to Seynt Awdre, which was the next abbess of Hely aftir hir" (fol. 59v). Eormenhild and Wærburh's introductions follow this pattern, but at the life of Eorcengota we have: "Here begynnyth a shorte lyfe of Seynt Erkengoode, the secunde doughter of Seynt Sexburgh and the awnte of Seynt Wereburgh, and of Seynt Alburgh þat was sistir to Seynt Awdre of Hely" (fol. 65r). The incipit not only shows how Eorcengota is related to Seaxburh, it also indicates how she is related to Wærburh, who is featured in the previous life. The final incipit for Wihtburh returns to the common phrasing, which suggests that she was as well known as Æthelthryth and needed no other introduction. That said, all the lives open with details connecting the women.

The incipits of the other native lives featured in Add. 2604 do not show such a pattern. Eadburh's, however, does indicate a connection to her institution and to the abbess who preceded her there: she is the "abbess of Tenett aftir Seynt Mildrede" (fol. 76r), linking her to the most famous saint of Kent, whose life does not appear in this manuscript. As noted earlier, there is at least one missing life between Eanswith and Hild, where quire 11 is missing. It would be tempting to think that Mildred, who is named in Eadburh's incipit, was included here, but her feast day of July 13 does not fall between Eanswith's, on August 31, and Hild's, on November 17. Moreover, Mildred's life would need to come before Eadburh's for the referencing in the incipit to work properly.[15]

One might fully expect Æthelburh from Barking, one of the most important Benedictine nunneries in southern England, to be featured in Add. 2604— and clearly she was known to the translator, who made sure to mention that Æthelthryth's sister was not *that* Æthelburh. The omission of the Barking abbess, perhaps because she was not royal, indicates that at the very least, this is not a manuscript intended for reading in her community.

Unfortunately, the other native women featured in Add. 2604 do not solve the puzzle of the missing life in any way. Like the Ely women, they are all Anglo-Saxon or Irish royal abbesses of Benedictine houses. Hild is the Northumbrian abbess of Whitby who lived for one year in East Anglia, where her sister had married the King of East Anglia, but there seems to be little veneration of her outside the north. Modwenna is an Irish saint whose missions to England led her to choose Burton-on-Trent for her burial rather than her home in Ireland. The inclusion of her life at the end, with Leonard, suggests that we might not read her in quite the same way as the others. Eadburh and Eanswith are Kentish saints; Edith's mother was Kentish, even though her father was Edgar of Wessex. This may well indicate that there was some intention to highlight both East Anglian saints and those with links to Kent. Yet in comparing the translations of these legends to the source text in John of Tynemouth, it is obvious that the elaborate genealogies of the Kentish saints in the Latin text are excised. Thus a saint's Kentish royalty is highlighted, but not people in her extended family. One consequence of this change is that the connections between the Kentish saints and the Ely saints are not emphasized. Eadburh, for example, is Seaxburh's sister-in-law and aunt to Eorcengota, Eormenhild, and Wærburh. These relationships are not made manifest nor are they highlighted in the incipits. Given the importance of genealogical details regarding the Ely saints, these omissions are striking and suggest a desire to set the East Anglian sororal family apart from the other saints in this collection.

Although the manuscript provides no indication of author, audience, or patron, it is not difficult to narrow it down to a particular region. There are a number of clues, with the most striking one being art-historical. As noted at the outset, the spray work is clearly East Anglian, and this provenance tends to be supported by the language in which these legends are written. Moreover, not only is the cult of the Ely saints firmly established in this region, but some of the universal saints, for example, Barbara, Cecilia, and Martha, were particularly popular in the area.[16]

There are a number of competing claimants for the nunnery in question, however. The focus on abbesses and royal service to monastic communities would indicate a convent of high status and undoubtedly one that is Benedictine or Augustinian, based on the inclusion of Benedictine saints. As noted earlier, it is unlikely to be Barking, but this leaves the whole of East Anglia and somewhat beyond as possibilities.[17] There is a range of intertwined evidence, which we offer here.

With regard to the saints, much depends on the weight given to individual aspects. For example, if one comes fresh from reading the Syon lives of John the Baptist and John the Evangelist in Cambridge, St. John's College MS N.16 and N.17, one might be inclined to see the present volume as part of the same sort of production. Yet it has to be said that the presence of the two Johns, linked as they may be to Syon in some respects, are hardly unusual in any manuscript.[18] Much more important in this respect is Leonard. His presence could easily indicate a convent such as Denney in Cambridgeshire, which not only was dedicated to Leonard but also had firm connections with the monastery at Ely and thus to the Ely saints.[19] The Augustinian friar Osbern Bokenham, moreover, wrote individual lives of female saints at the request of several laywomen, and these were gathered together as a legendary, possibly for the Franciscan nuns at Aldgate or Denney.[20]

Even more support from book ownership may highlight the claims of Campsey Ash in Suffolk. Add. 2604 seems very like the Anglo-Norman collection known as the Campsey Ash manuscript in its compilation and scope as well as in its presentation as a vernacular, devotional text.[21] This unusual manuscript of lives, both universal and native saints, written in Anglo-Norman, was produced for the reading of the Augustinian nuns at Campsey Ash and so begs the question of whether a similar vernacular compilation was produced for them in the fifteenth century.

Yet another possible home for this manuscript is Minster in Sheppey, which is not only dedicated to Seaxburh, one of the Ely saints, but being in Kent provides an interesting base for this novel combination of East Anglian and Kentish royal saints; most tantalizingly, we know that at the Dissolution, Minster had "a boke of Saynts lyfes," a description that suggests a legendary written in English.[22]

Finally, there is the manuscript itself. It was owned in the eighteenth century by George Tasburgh, a Roman Catholic from Bodney Hall in Norfolk, who died in 1783. There is strong evidence that certain of the Tasburghs, with family homes in South Elmham in Suffolk and Bodney in Norfolk, remained Catholic throughout the Reformation and beyond, and it may well be that the manuscript had been in the family at least since that period.[23] If one wants to argue that the manuscript derived from a convent in East Anglia and ended up with the Tasburgh family, it is interesting to note that the nearest convent to Bodney Hall is Thetford in Norfolk and the nearest to South Elmham are Bungay and Flixton in Suffolk.

Whatever its ultimate provenance, this legendary, currently comprised of eleven native and eleven universal saints, is a welcome addition to other collections that feature only universal saints (such as Bokenham's *Legendys of Hooly Wummen*) or native saints (such as British Library, Lansdowne MS. 436, a Latin collection that was owned by Romsey Abbey, a Benedictine nunnery).[24] Indeed, Add. 2604 provides the earliest known example of its type to show a concerted interest in native female saints (the *South English Legendary*, for example, has very few such legends). This translation from a mixture of Latin sources into Middle English prose, clearly made available for a readership of women religious in the environs of East Anglia, offers a new and particularly significant avenue of research for those engaged in studies of female reading and piety and the transmission of religious texts.

University of Hull
University of Missouri–Kansas City

APPENDIX

Contents of Cambridge University Library, Additional MS 2604

fols. 1r–11v	John the Baptist	June 24	
fols. 11v–21v	John the Evangelist	December 27	fol. 14 cut out
fols. 22r–25v	Columba of Sens	December 31	
fols. 25v–32v	Agatha	February 5	ending incomplete
(fols. 33r–40v)	quire 5 missing		
fols. 41r–47v	Cecilia	November 22	opening incomplete + fol. 44 cut out
fols. 47v–52v	Barbara	December 16	
fols. 52v–59r	Æthelthryth	June 23	fol. 58 cut out
fols. 59v–61r	Seaxburh	July 6	
fols. 61r–62v	Eormenhild	July 6 for February 13	
fols. 62v–65r	Wærburh	July 6 for February 3	
fols. 65r–66v	Eorcengota	July 7 for February 26 & Æthelburh July 7	
fols. 66v–69r	Wihtburh	July 8, translation feast	
fols. 69v–75v	Edith of Wilton	September 16	
fols. 76r–79r	Eadburh	December 13	
fols. 79r–80v	Eanswith	August 31 or September 12	ending incomplete
(fols. 81r–88v)	quire 11 missing		
fols. 89r–93r	Hild	November 17	opening incomplete
fols. 93r–97v	Martha	July 29	
fols. 97v–98r	Domitilla	May 12?	
fols. 98r–105v	Justina	October 7	ending incomplete + fols. 106–107 cut out
fols. 108r–112v	Benedicta	March 16?	opening incomplete + fols. 106–107 cut out
fols. 113r–136v	Modwenna	July 5 or 6	fol. 126 cut out
fols. 137r–152v	Leonard	November 6	fols. 138, 140, 143, 146–151 cut out

NOTES

1. Some important contributions to the discussion of English devotional reading that inform this study include Gail McMurray Gibson, *The Theater of Devotion: East Anglian Drama and Society in the Late Middle Ages* (Chicago: University of Chicago Press, 1989); Karen A. Winstead, *Virgin Martyrs: Legends of Sainthood in Late Medieval England* (Ithaca, NY, and London: Cornell University Press, 1997); Mary C. Erler, *Women, Reading, and Piety in Late Medieval England* (Cambridge, UK: Cambridge University Press, 2002); Virginia Blanton, *Signs of Devotion: The Cult of St. Æthelthryth in Medieval England, 695–1615* (University Park: Pennsylvania State University Press, 2007); Simon Horobin, "Politics, Patronage, and Piety in the Work of Osbern Bokenham," *Speculum* 82 (2007): 932–949; as well as two articles by A. S. G. Edwards, "The Transmission and Audience of Osbern Bokenham's *Legendys of Hooly Wummen*," in *Late-Medieval Religious Texts and Their Transmission: Essays in Honour of A. I. Doyle*, ed. A. J. Minnis (Woodbridge, UK, and Rochester, NY: Brewer, 1994), 157–167; and "Fifteenth-Century English Collections of Female Saints' Lives," *The Yearbook of English Studies* 33 (2003): 131–141.

2. We are working on a study and edition of these saints' lives. Jayne Ringrose has just published a description of Add. 2604 in: *Summary Catalogue of the Additional Medieval Manuscripts in Cambridge University Library Aquired before 1940* (Woodbridge, Suffolk: Boydell, 2009), 16-17. Before this catalogue, the only notice in print was by Oliver Pickering in his survey of "Saints' Lives," chapter 15 in *A Companion to Middle English Prose*, ed. A. S. G. Edwards (Cambridge, UK: Brewer, 2004), 249-270, 258.

3. A draft of this article was presented at the Early Book Society conference held at the University of Exeter in July 2009.

4. See, e.g., John Mirk's reference to John the Evangelist's "grace of vyrgynyte, þat ys, of maydenhode" in Theodor Erbe, ed., *Mirk's Festial: A Collection of Homilies, by Johannes Mirkus (John Mirk)*, EETS e.s., 96 (1905), 30–34, 31, l. 4. For the Baptist's links with virgin martyrs, see Katherine J. Lewis, "Becoming a Virgin King: Richard II and Edward the Confessor," in *Gender and Holiness: Men, Women and Saints in Late Medieval Europe*, ed. Samantha J. E. Riches and Sarah Salih (New York: Routledge, 2002), 86–100. See also Blanton, *Signs of Devotion*, 277–285.

5. See Jeffrey F. Hamburger, *St. John the Divine: The Deified Evangelist in Medieval Art and Theology* (Berkeley and Los Angeles: University of California Press, 2002), 65; cited in Claire M. Waters, ed., *Virgins and Scholars: A Fifteenth-Century Compilation of the Lives of John the Baptist, John the Evangelist, Jerome, and Katharine of Alexandria*, Medieval Women: Texts and Contexts 10 (Turnhout, Belgium: Brepols, 2008), 20, n. 63. In the country as a whole there were more than fifteen dedications of nunneries to either of the two Johns or to Leonard, including Buckland (John the Baptist); Canonsleigh (Mary, John the Baptist, and Etheldreda); Carrow (Mary and John [the sources do not make clear which John]); Denney (James and

Leonard); Esholt (Mary and Leonard); Godstow (Mary and John the Baptist); Kilburn (Mary and John the Baptist); London, Holywell (John the Baptist); and Nun Appleton (Mary and John the Evangelist). For these dedications, see David N. Bell, *What Nuns Read: Books and Libraries in Medieval English Nunneries* (Kalamazoo, MI, and Spencer, MA: Cistercian Publications, 1995).

6. Besides the saints' lives, the manuscript also contains varied items that include pages from a medieval antiphoner, pasted-in pages from a late-sixteenth-century writing master's book, and some eighteenth-century notes.

7. The monks at Ely moved a number of the Ely feasts, which were originally in February and March, to July, when they celebrated them along with the feast of Seaxburh: Seaxburh's daughter Eormenhild (February 13) and granddaughter Wærburh (February 3) were moved to July 6 and her daughter Eorcengota to July 7, the feast of Seaxburh's sister Æthelburh; Wihtburh, whose feast of March 17 is added to Add. MS 2604 on her translation feast of July 8. It is unclear when this practice began of celebrating Seaxburh's daughters' feasts in July. See Rosalind C. Love, ed. and trans., *Goscelin of Saint-Bertin: The Hagiography of the Female Saints of Ely* (Oxford: Clarendon Press, 2004), xxiii–xxvi.

8. Quire 5, which would have contained the end of Agatha and the beginning of Cecilia, and quire 11, which would have contained the end of Eanswith and the beginning of Hild, are missing. A comparison of the remaining texts with their sources demonstrates that in each case there would have been enough space for another life to have followed Agatha and Eanswith (discussed further below).

9. In a private communication, Kathleen Scott kindly dates this East Anglian spray work to the third or fourth quarter of the fifteenth century.

10. The edition used for comparative purposes is Jacobus de Voragine, *Legenda Aurea*, ed. T. Graesse, 2 vols. (Leipzig: Arnold, 1846); translated in Jacobus de Voragine, *The Golden Legend: Readings on the Saints*, trans. William Granger Ryan, 2 vols. (Princeton, NJ: Princeton University Press, 1993).

11. Mombritius is most accessible in *Sanctuarium, seu Vitae Sanctorum* (Paris: Albert Fontemoing, repr. 1910); see also *Hystorie plurimorum sanctorum noviter et laboriose ex diversis libris in unum collecte* (Cologne, Germany: Johannes de Westfalia, 1483; Louvain: Johannes de Westfalia, 1485). In addition to the current study, we are also working on a description of the *Historiae plurimorum* for future publication. For a superlative investigation into some of the complexities surrounding the *Legenda aurea* and related material, see Sherry L. Reames, *The Legenda Aurea: A Reexamination of Its Paradoxical History* (Madison and London: University of Wisconsin Press, 1985).

12. Manfred Görlach, *Studies in Middle English Saints' Legends* (Heidelberg, Germany: Universitätsverlag C. Winter, 1998), 148; and Carl Horstmann, ed., *Nova legenda Anglie*, 2 vols. (Oxford: Clarendon, 1901), ix–xxi.

13. For a discussion of the relationship between the different versions, see the edition of the 1516 English version, *The Kalendre of the Newe Legende of*

Englande, ed. Manfred Görlach, Middle English Texts 27 (Heidelberg, Germany: Universitätsverlag C. Winter, 1994), 7–12; the printed Latin 1516 edition is available in Horstmann, *Nova legenda Anglie*.

14. In all quotations from the manuscript, we quote from our own edition, which is in progress

15. Various other possibilities will be explored in our forthcoming study and edition of the texts.

16. Eamon Duffy, "Holy Maydens, Holy Wyfes: The Cult of Women Saints in Fifteenth- and Sixteenth-Century England," in *Women in the Church: Papers Read at the 1989 Summer Meeting and the 1990 Winter Meeting of the Ecclesiastical History Society*, ed. W. J. Shiels and Diana Wood, Studies in Church History 27 (Oxford: Basil Blackwell, 1990), 175–196. For discussions of devotional art in East Anglia, see D. P. Mortlock, *The Popular Guide to Suffolk Churches*, 3 vols. (Cambridge, UK: Acorn, 1988–1992); Ann Eljenholm Nichols, *The Early Art of Norfolk: A Subject List of Extant and Lost Art* (Kalamazoo, MI: Medieval Institute Publications, 2002); H. M. Cautley, *Suffolk Churches and Their Treasures*, 4th ed. (Ipswich, UK: Boydell, 1975); H. M. Cautley, *Norfolk Churches* (1949; repr. Woodbridge, UK: Boydell, 1979); and M. R. James, *Suffolk and Norfolk* (London: Dent, 1930).

17. For a list of nunneries in East Anglia known to have owned books, see Bell, *What Nuns Read*.

18. Waters, *Virgins and Scholars*.

19. There are some unusual choices in the saints represented, for example, Domitilla (who is also out of sequence in the third little cycle) and Columba of Sens; there is at present no obvious reason why these should be found in a collection of saints native to or popular in East Anglia.

20. This attribution was made by A. I. Doyle in 1958 and is noted in Edwards, "Transmission and Audience," 157 and n. 4.

21. For an extensive discussion and description of this manuscript, British Library, Additional MS 70513, see Emma Campbell, *Medieval Saints' Lives: The Gift, Kinship and Community in Old French Hagiography*, Gallica 12 (Cambridge, UK: Brewer, 2008), 181–204, 231–232, and 235.

22. Bell, *What Nuns Read*, 155. For details on Minster, see "Houses of Benedictine Nuns: The Priory of Minster in Sheppey," in *A History of the County of Kent*, vol. 2 (London: Archibald Constable and Co., Ltd., and St. Catherine Press, 1926), 149–150; see also E. C. Walcott, "The Priory of Minster in Sheppey," *Archaeologia Cantiana* 7 (1868): 287–306.

23. References in local records to the Tasburghs as recusants are fairly extensive, although the early religious history of the family is particularly complicated.

24. For the most recent discussion of Bokenham, see Horobin, "Politics, Patronage, and Piety"; for information on the Lansdowne manuscript, see Bell, *What Nuns Read*, 161.

Richard James and the Seventeenth-Century Provenance of British Library MS Cotton Caligula A.XI

SIMON HOROBIN

In a recent article published in this journal Lawrence Warner drew attention to four manuscripts of *Piers Plowman* which appear to have connections with Matthew Parker and his circle.[1] One of these manuscripts, now British Library MS Cotton Caligula A.XI, was first associated with Parker by N.R. Ker, whose opinion that the table of contents on folio 2r was in a sixteenth-century hand belonging to Parker's secretary was cited by Kane and Donaldson in their description of the manuscript.[2] The association with Matthew Parker was also quoted by C.D. Benson and Lynne Blanchfield in their description of the manuscript.[3] In addition to the table of contents, Benson and Blanchfield also attributed the heading "Pierce Ploughman" at the head of the first folio of the poem to the same hand. It is not clear to which of the many Parkerian scribes Ker was referring here, although the title of "secretary" is most clearly associated with John Joscelin.[4] However, the hand that added the table of contents is quite different to that of Joscelin and I can find no similarities with that of any other member of the Parker circle.[5] The solution to this problem is apparent, however, if we compare the hand responsible for the table of contents in Caligula A.XI with other manuscripts in the Cotton collection. For the scribe responsible for adding the contents list to this manuscript, as well as many other manuscripts owned by Sir Robert Cotton, is Richard James, the first person to be employed by Cotton as librarian of his impressive collection.

Richard James was born in 1591 on the Isle of Wight, eldest son of Richard James and nephew of Thomas James (1572/3–1629), the first librarian of the Bodleian Library in Oxford. Richard James took a scholarship at Corpus Christi College Oxford in 1608, and was admitted BA in 1611 and MA in 1615. Later that same year he was made a probationary fellow of Corpus. He subsequently took holy orders and graduated BD in 1624. His formal association with the Cotton library began c.1625 and among his duties were contributing to the cataloguing of the library, identifying manuscripts and their contents, and supplying them with tables of contents. As T.B. James writes: "If Cotton the collector of manuscripts was the father of the British Library collection, then James's scholarly and administrative work of collecting and identifying manuscripts and supplying contents' lists, which largely stand today, make him the godfather of that collection."[6] While Cotton himself added tables of contents to a small number of manuscripts in his collection, and another anonymous scribe using a distinctively florid hand added others, the majority of such lists were the work of Richard James. In his discussion of James's contribution to the organisation of Cotton's library, Colin Tite notes the impressive accuracy of James's identifications of the texts found in these manuscripts, especially given the lack of reference resources that would have been available to him.[7] Tite also provides a facsimile of contents lists supplied by James and the anonymous stylized hand in Cotton Claudius E.IV, containing the *Gesta Abbatum Albani*. In James's list we can see the same combination of palaeographical features found in Caligula A.XI: especially characteristic are the two forms of **g**: one a straightforward secretary form, the other a distinctive humanistic form in which the lower bowl forms a figure 8. Also distinctive are the upright ascenders on **l**, **h**, **d** with wedge-shaped serifs at the top.

Richard James's interest in *Piers Plowman* was not limited to his cataloguing responsibilities; he also transcribed extracts from the poem into one of his notebooks, now Bodleian Library James MS 2. The extracts begin on page 149 with the title "Peter Plowman. MS. Eius vita et visio explicit" and finish on page 159. These extracts were discussed briefly by Charlotte Brewer in her discussion of the poem's seventeenth-century readership and the manuscript was included by Ralph Hanna in his list of copies of the B Version.[8] Brewer suggests that the extracts are textually related to Robert Crowley's printed edition of 1550 and that this was the source used by James, while Hanna noted textual similarities with a manuscript related to the three closely affiliated manuscripts: Bodleian Library MS Bodley 814 |Bo|, British Library MS Additional 10574 |Bm| and Caligula A.XI |Co|. Hanna also notes the fact that, as Cotton's librarian, James would have have had access to the Caligula manuscript. The identification of James's hand in the Caligula manuscript above strengthens the association of the extracts with that manuscript, while collation of James's text with the variants listed in the Athlone editions of the poem makes it clear that this was the source of James's extracts. The extracts comprise the following lines: C Pro 47-65, 76-77, 85-94 (omitting l.88), A Pro 90-5, 206-207, 1.177-80, B 2.218-235, 3.35-3.63 (omitting lines 39 and 58), 4.147-153, 3.165-6, 3.201-8, 5.30-31, 8.14-16, 10.311-332, 11.75-77, 17.254-259, 18.423-431, 20.216-226, 20.285-290, 20.325-350, 20.364-372, 12.186-191, 13.40-92, 13.269-270, 15.70-72, 15.101-127, 15.213-215, 15.228-231, 15.286-288, 15.348-351, 15.412-415, 15.441-444, 15.490-495, 15.542-567, 15.502-507, 15.527-8. The mixture of lines taken from all three versions of the poem immediately suggests a connection with the BmBoCot group as these manuscripts show a similar textual configuration. Kane and Donaldson described the contents of this group as follows: C Pro 1-2.131, A 2.90-212 and B 3-20. Two of the three lines omitted within the extracts (3.39 and 3.58) are paralleled in the BmBoCot group, while an additional line found after 2.231, "To ben of her counsail whan thei carieden abouȝte" is only found in these three manuscripts and in one closely related A manuscript: British Library MS Harley 6041 |H2|.[9] There are numerous smaller substantive variants that indicate an affiliation with BmBoCot, as the following selection of examples from passus 3 indicates. The first citation is from the Kane and Donaldson edition of the B Version, the second is taken from James's transcription:

3.37   And seide |wel| softely, in shrift as it were,
        And seid ful softly shrifte as it were
in shrifte| shrifte BmBoCot
3.53   While ye loue lordes þat lecherie haunten
        While ye loue of lordis, leccherie haunteth
loue| loue of BmBoCot; þat| om. BmBoCot
3.55   It is a freletee of flessh-ye fynden it in bokes-
        Hit is a freelte of fleisch. Þei finde hit in bokis
ye| Þei BmBoCot
3.62   Do peynten and portraye |who| paie|d| for þe makynge
        And peynte and pourtraie: and paie for þat making
Do|And BmBoCot

There are a number of unique variants, but the nature of these suggests that they were probably introduced unconsciously by James himself during the process of transcription.

    If we consider the various passages James extracted from the poem it becomes clear that his interest in the poem was particularly focused on Langland's satire of the friars and his treatment of Catholic doctrine. The lines from the prologue chosen by James show a particular interest in Langland's satire of pilgrimage and professional pilgrims. His transcription begins with C P.47-65, with its satire of pilgrimage and the hypocrisy associated with pilgrims, while his addition of the marginal subheading "pilgrimages" makes clear his view of the passage's central theme. The remaining extracts that James chose to include from the prologue centre on Langland's satirical portrayal of the church, holders of ecclesiastical office and the friars. By contrast he shows little interest in the satirical presentation of other secular groups, while he dismisses the political allegory of the fable of the belling of the cat with a mere summary of its content:

> The rats and the mice haue a conspiracie and counteth to hange a bell abought the courte cats coller. what this meneth the author sais |h|e dare not tellen ye men that be merrie Divine ye for I dare not by deare God of heaven but the little mouse tells them though they kill this kat, yet shuld there come another. To catch vs and all our kinde, though we crepe vnder benches and he sais that if the rats had their will they could not rule themselfs and þat the mees did destroie manni mens mault he wishes them not to mischeef þe cat. (p. 150)

An enjoyment of Langland's satire of the friars is apparent elsewhere in his selection of 2.218-2.235, an account of Liar's protection by the friars, introduced by James with the following subheading: "He saith that falsenesse being pursued by the kings commaund fled to the Freris. Gyle to the marchauntis who apparrelled him like an apprentis." James's copy of the poem skips from 2.235 to 3.35, introducing the exchange between Mede and her friar confessor in which he offers her absolution in exchange for financial gifts. Once again we see James glossing over the political dimension to the Mede episode; he dismisses the discussion of Mede's marriage to Conscience with the briefest of summaries: "Conscience will not be entreatid by the king to marrie Mede because she corrupteth all things." The remainder of his extracts from passus 3 focus on Mede's involvement in clerical corruption, while a further historical and political reference is again summarily discarded: "Mede reprehends Conscience for auerting the king from his victorie in Normandie." His selection of just three lines from passus 8 (8.14-16) further highlights his focus on Langland's treatment of the friars, as shown by his marginal heading "Frier Minours." Predictably James included 10.322-332, with its prophecy of the dissolution of the monasteries, although interestingly James omitted the second half of 10.332: "Have a knocke of a king. |and incurable the wounde|," perhaps an attempt to stress the more positive impact of the reformation. He also included the lines which call for the disendowment of the monasteries, under the subheading: "Dos Constantin destruenda" (15.555-567). Lines 11.75-77 question the practice of convents with regard to confession and burial, lines 17.254-9 deal with the efficacy of pardons and indulgences, while his extracts from passus 20 concern the figure of Sir Penetrans Domos, though significantly break off before Conscience's call for friars to have a "fyndyng," which would remove their need to beg for money (20.384).

James also selected passages that question the efficacy of Catholic practices and doctrine, such as 1.177-80 with its emphasis on Christian charity over Catholic sacraments:

> But if ȝe loue leelich, and lene þe pore
> Of such good as God you sente goudliche parteth
> ȝee ne haveþ no more merite in masse ne in hours
> Þan malkyn of her maydenhed. whan no man her coveiteth,
> (1.177-80)

The majority of James's extracted passages may therefore be categorised as concerned with fraternal practices, Catholic doctrine or ecclesiastical satire. There are, however, a few short selections that are harder to explain. The inclusion of the following two lines, the only lines selected from passus 5, is hard to explain, but may suggest an antifeminist interest:

> And he warnid Wat, his wife was to blame
> That her hed was worth half a mark and his hod not worth a grot
> (B 5.30-31)

James's antiquarian concerns seem to lie behind his inclusion of the following two lines, with their reference to the mayoralty of John Chichester which was used to date the poem:

> A thousand and thre hundred, twies thritty and ten,
> My wafres there were gesene, whan Chichestre was maire.
> (13.269-270)

His selection of these lines for their chronological reference is apparent from James's adding of the following marginal note alongside them: "Piers P. quando vixit."

The passages extracted from *Piers Plowman* by James demonstrate how he saw in the poem support for his efforts to summon antiquarian learning as support for his anti-papist campaign. Since his uncle's resignation of his post as Bodley's librarian in 1620, Richard and Thomas James had plundered the library's resources in search of ammunition in the war against Catholic doctrine. A major focus of this campaign was a projected study of the 'decanonization' of Thomas Becket: *Decanonizatio Thomae Cantuariensis et suorum.* James's exploitation of the copy of *Piers Plowman* in Caligula A.XI in support of his anti-papist agenda shows how he drew upon the manuscripts of the Cotton

Library for a similar end. James evidently saw in Langland's poem support for his Protestant project and it was this that motivated him to extract this selection of passages and to copy them into a notebook, alongside extracts from Becket's letters clearly destined for the same purpose.[10]

Magdalen College, Oxford

NOTES

1. Lawrence Warner, "New Light on *Piers Plowman*'s Ownership, *ca.* 1450-1600," *Journal of the Early Book Society* 12 (2009): 183-95.

2. *Piers Plowman: The B Version*, eds George Kane and E. Talbot Donaldson, rev. edn (London: Athlone; Berkeley and Los Angeles: Univ. of California Press, 1988), 5, n. 33.

3. C. David Benson and Lynne Blanchfield, *The Manuscripts of Piers Plowman: The B-Version* (Cambridge: D.S. Brewer, 1997), 69.

4. See the account of Joscelin's life, including his appointment as Parker's Latin secretary, in G. H. Martin, "Joscelin , John (1529–1603)," in *Oxford Dictionary of National Biography*, ed. H. C. G. Matthew and Brian Harrison (Oxford: OUP, 2004), http://www.oxforddnb.com/view/article/15130 (accessed February 3, 2010).

5. For a facsimile of Joscelin's hand and those of other Parkerian scribes see C. E. Wright, "The Dispersal of the Monastic Libraries and the Beginnings of Anglo-Saxon Studies. Matthew Parker and his Circle: A Preliminary Study," *Transactions of the Cambridge Bibliographical Society* 3 (1951): 208-37.

6. Tom Beaumont James, "James, Richard (*bap.* 1591, *d.* 1638)," in *Oxford Dictionary of National Biography*, ed. H. C. G. Matthew and Brian Harrison (Oxford: OUP, 2004); online ed., ed. Lawrence Goldman, January 2008, http://www.oxforddnb.com/view/article/14617 (accessed February 3, 2010).

7. Colin G.C. Tite, *The Manuscript Library of Sir Robert Cotton*, The Panizzi Lectures 1993 (London British Library, 1994), 57-63.

8. Charlotte Brewer, *Editing Piers Plowman: The evolution of the text* (Cambridge: Cambridge University Press, 1996), 20 and n. 5; Ralph Hanna, *William Langland* (Aldershot: Variorum 1994), 40.

9. *Piers Plowman: The A Version*, ed. George Kane, rev. edn (London: Athlone; Berkeley and Los Angeles: Univ. of California Press, 1988), 48. For the line's appearance in BmBoCot, see *Piers Plowman: The B Version*, 1 n.3.

10. For a description of the contents of this manuscript see Falconer Madan, H.H.E Craster, and N. Denholm-Young, eds., *A Summary Catalogue of the Western Manuscripts in the Bodleian Library* (Oxford: Clarendon Press, 1953), no. 3839.

The Transmission of "The Book of Shrift"

RALPH HANNA and KATHERINE ZIEMAN

"The Book of Shrift," a 4000-line penitential handbook in verse (*Index of Middle English Verse* 694), forms one of the typical additions to the original text of *Cursor Mundi*.[1] In the early (s. xiv[1]) circulation of this massive biblical history, "The Book" usually appears at the very end of the work. As a result, it has been subject to those vicissitudes that typically afflict the ends of manuscripts, and although all early copies of the *Cursor Mundi* seem originally to have included it, "The Book" now only survives in full in a single one of them, British Library, Cotton Vespasian MS A.iii.[2]

Nevertheless, "The Book of Shrift" does not exist simply as a pendant to the enormous *Cursor*. Much later in the fourteenth century, perhaps in the 1390s, a pair of scribes copied what would appear to be excerpts from the text. These are found in BL, MS Cotton Galba E.ix, which Morris printed (scribe hereafter designated **G**) and in Bodleian Library, Rawlinson poet. 175 (hereafter **R**).[3] On the basis of considerable overlap of contents, as well as remarkably close textual relations (most pronounced in their versions of *The Prick of Conscience*), the two books appear to have emanated from the same copying center, probably somewhere in northern Yorkshire. Indeed, the two scribes contributed independent portions to a third book, British Library, Harley MS 4196, where scribe **G** copied quires 18–21 and scribe **R** quires 27–34.[4] The two versions of "The Book" copied by these scribes will provide some further evidence for their connection and typical behavior.

One's initial response to the renditions of "The Book of Shrift" in **G** and **R** is one of difference. Neither book offers quite the same text nor in the same order. In **G**, one finds the following presentation: folios 67ra–73va: two large chunks, comprising Morris's lines 27548–28063+ and 28614–29547+ (edn. pp. 1527–51, 1560–86).[5] The break between the two selections is marked by a large, centered "Amen" on folio 69rb, and a similar colophon appears at the end of the selection. In addition, immediately following, at fols 73vb–75ra, **G** presents a versified Pater Noster, with exposition (*Index* 788). This, excepting the same three *Cursor* manuscripts which have "The Book of Shrift," is a unique text.[6]

In contrast to this presentation, **R** provides, *in some respect or another*: folios 80va–93rb, 101va–103vb, lines 25864–27523, 27548–28063+, 28614–29547+ In other words, **R** presents the text from its opening, as it appears in Vespasian, while **G** appears as probably engaged in editorial behavior, tailoring a full text by selection. Neither of the two books contains lines 28064–28613, for which Vespasian remains the only witness.[7] Finally, although **R** takes up, after this hiatus, at the same point as **G**, it then lacks altogether lines 27523–547.

However, **R**'s presentation of "The Book of Shrift" is considerably more erratic than this summary would suggest: folios 80va/1–87ra/23 provide the rubric "Here bigyns a schort tretyce of schryft" and lines 25684–27161 (edn. 1470–1514). At this point, seven couplets past the rubric "Of þe poyntes þat falles to þe preste," the manuscript unexpectedly provides: folios 87ra/24–91ra/24, lines 28660–29547+ (edn. 1561–86). The selection ends with the couplet "And tyll his kyngdom he vs ken l Thurgh prayer of his moder Amen." It is succeeded by the rubric "Of þe seuen dedly synnes and of þair braunches," and there follows: folios 91ra/27–93rb/40: lines 27548–28063+ (edn. 1527–51), concluding with the same centered "Amen" as appears after both segments presented in **G** and with a further pair of blank lines at the column foot.

In addition, more of the poem appears later in **R**, and in a most unexpected place. These materials are buried in the center of another text that has been copied later in the book. This is a verse translation from Latin called "The Gast of Gy" (*Index* 3028). It begins at the head of folio 96ra and is separated from **R**'s consecutive copying from "The Book of Shrift" by a passion lyric also in **G** (*Index* 2080) and two extraneous verse texts of wide circulation (*Index* 1781 and 1718). Here **R** presents: folios 101va/41–103va/26: "The Book of Shrift" lines 27162–27523+ (edn. 1514–24; a short bridging passage occurs), followed by folios 103va/27–103vb/28 lines 28614–59 (edn. 1560–61). The lines appear as a single block, inserted between the couplets ending with line 1012 and beginning with line 1013 of Schleich's edition of "The Gast."[8] Even in the absence of evidence provided by the other copy of "The Gast of Gy," which lacks them, these selections would stand out as thoroughly extraneous here. At this point in "The Gast," the ghost is being asked whether he knows whether he will eventually end up in the same part of heaven as the saints; in the subsequent lines of the consecutive text, he is being informed that his time in Purgatory will end at Easter. Between these discussions, one finds more than four hundred lines explaining the gambits priests can use to extract efficacious confessions from their parishioners.

The text of **R** has plainly been subjected to some form of dislocation. Moreover, this dislocation interfaces intriguingly with the text, as presented consecutively (allowing for omissions) in **G**. The longer displaced portion of **R** includes those materials of "The Book of Shrift" that occur just before **G** begins his representation of the text, but the succeeding twenty-five lines presented in Vespasian appear in neither **G** nor **R**. The briefer, concluding displaced lines correspond to the head of the second selection in **G**. Plainly, some feature associated with the boundaries of what the scribes present is at issue here.

To get further with this problem, one needs to convert this textual or editorial perception into a codicological one. It is fairly plain, simply from local readings, that, so far as we can now know, both **G** and **R** were engaged in copying from the same exemplar; their texts simply include too many unique crotchets to be independent of one another.[9] As a consequence, one needs to try to imagine the shape of the exemplar shared by the two scribes but so differently deployed.

Here a few salient hints offer some guidance for proceeding. There is a certain implied consonance among one set of textual features that is not the property of either **G** or **R** and thus, inferentially, might represent features of their common source.[10] The last bit of "The Book of Shrift" copied by **R** on folio 103[vab] comprises lines 28614–59, i.e., 46 lines. Rather unexpectedly perhaps, the Vespasian manuscript, in which "The Book of Shrift" appears in its original *Cursor Mundi* context, offers evidence for this as an important number in production, for the text there appears in double columns of 46 lines to the page.[11] Finally, when **R** copied the exemplar, he included some sort of break after line 27161, at which point the scribe resumed copying about 1500 lines further on in the consecutive text (only to return to eventually copy nearly all the materials here omitted). Line 27161 would fall 1478 lines into this copying stint. This is a sum suspiciously close to an even product of 46: 46 multiplied by 32 produces 1472.[12] Moreover, the multiplier revealed by this product is also significant, for it implies, given a double-column format (four columns to the leaf), that one might expect such an exemplar to have been composed of eight-leaf quires.

If one attempts to follow through on such a hypothesis, one might imagine that the exemplar underlying "The Book of Shrift" in **G** and **R** had the form:

quire 1 = lines 25684–27161 (1478 lines)
quire 2 = lines 27162–28613 (1452 lines) + (either here or at the start of the next) an odd 46-line column, with lines 28614–59[13]
quire 3 = lines 28660–29547+ (888 lines).

In the final quire of this reconstruction, materials from "The Book of Shrift" should have filled about 19 columns (46 x 19 = 874), thus at least five leaves. This final unit, if it were restricted to presenting "The Book of Shrift" in isolation, would thus have been minimally a quire of six leaves. But it could conceivably have contained other items and have been a full eight leaves like the preceding examples. If so, it could have accommodated 584 additional lines of some text or another.

Imagining the exemplar common to **G** and **R** in this way casts a somewhat different light on this textual situation. At least to begin, we assume, although it will emerge that it is not the only possible explanation, that **G**'s behavior with "The Book" was simply selective. This scribe began his text at a major textual division, the treatment of the Seven Deadly Sins, within quire 2. He failed to copy through to the end of quire 2, and his second textual block, shared with **R**, simply reproduced the contents of quire 3.

The **R** presentation of "The Book" reveals, however, that **G**'s consciousness that he was looking at two separate textual chunks may indicate something about the nature of quire 2 in the exemplar. One can clarify the situation by unpacking the quire, deploying what should have been its contents, leaf by leaf. In the postulated format, 46-line columns, each leaf should have contained 184 lines (46 x 4), and thus:

> leaf 1 = lines 27162–345
> leaf 2 = lines 27346–529
> leaf 3 = lines 27530–713
> leaf 4 = lines 27714–897
> leaf 5 = lines 27898–28081
> leaf 6 = lines 28082–265
> leaf 7 = lines 28266–449
> leaf 8 = lines 28450–633[14]

This breakdown by the leaf immediately shows that, when **R** copied "The Book of Shrift," apparently planning to represent the text fully (and in sequence), he did not find quire 2 in place at all. His sequential text (the second report of **R**'s contents displayed above) simply passed silently from the end of materials in quire 1 (ending with line 27161) to those that probably stood at the head of quire 3 (taking up with line 28660).

Eventually, of course, **R** did acquire the immediately following materials. That is, later in his work, he copied the lines that should have appeared on leaves 1 and 2 of the second quire. But he copied them in an alien place, in the middle of "The Gast of Gy." Moreover, he also had there materials, which he copied immediately following the contents of quire 2, leaves 1–2, that could have come either from leaf 8 or, thanks to the bit of finagle we have introduced in our initial formulation, from an odd column on an added slip (lines 28614–59). However, when **G** copied the text, that column's worth of text was almost certainly *in situ* and copied in its appropriate position.

Equally, **G** may not have been selectively grouping large chunks of text. Had leaves 1 and 2 of this quire (and perhaps quire 1) been absent at the time he copied, he might well have begun with text on the first leaf that he saw. That would have been leaf 3 of quire 2 (in our symmetry-driven argument, it would have begun with line 27530). Looking at this leaf, the scribe would have spotted the rubric introducing a major textual division, the discussion of the Seven Deadly Sins, which marks the onset of his copying, at line 27548 of the edited text.[15] From that point, he copied straight on through three leaves of the exemplar, concluding at the foot of leaf 5^v of the original quire 2, at line 28063 (in the symmetrical form displayed above, this side would have ended with line 28081).

The scribe **R** also had access to these same leaves 3 to 5. But these were apparently displaced at the time he copied them, and their materials (executed as lines 27548–28063+) now followed quire 3. Apparently, neither scribe could lay hands on (or may not have recognized the absence of) the remainder of quire 2, the sixth, seventh, and eighth leaves. They had simply been misplaced, and it is possible that **G**'s presentation of "The Book of Shrift" as large fragments reflects this state of affairs.

In short, part of the exemplar available to both scribes, its second quire, had disintegrated. **R** reflects a point in the history of this exemplar when pieces of the quire were available, apparently the loose leaves preserved by being tucked inside another quire with another text (and not a text that **G** seems ever to have thought of copying). It may be worth noting that, if the exemplar of "The Gast of Gy" were in the same format as that the two scribes apparently were accessing for "The Book of Shrift," double-column pages with 46-line columns, the 1012 lines of Schleich's edition would have exactly filled 22 columns (46 x 22 = 1012), i.e., five full leaves and the recto of a sixth. On turning this leaf, **R** may have found an extra two leaves (plus a slip bearing a single column of text?) stuffed in, and he may have decided (if not been directed by a note left by some earlier hand exposed to the same mishap) that their materials should precede the verso of the quire's sixth leaf.

To conclude this portion of the argument, we offer two further schematic diagrams of the transmission of "The Book of Shrift." When **G** received these materials, he appears to have found them in the form:

> |quire 1 —not certainly present|
> quire 2, leaves 3–5 (approximately lines 27530–28081)
>   an odd 46-line column, with lines 28614–59
> quire 3 (lines 28660 onwards)

On the other hand, when **R** began copying, the exemplar was apparently in the form:

quire 1 (lines 25684–27161)
quire 3 (lines 28660 onwards)
quire 2, leaves 3–5 (approximately lines 27530–28081), and then,
detached from the rest, incorporated into "The Gast of Gy":
quire 2, leaves 1–2 (approximately lines 27162–529)
an odd 46-line column, with lines 28614–59

The two scribes copy the same materials, but in differently arranged and
fragmentary orders, apparently dependent on the state of the archetype, when
each worked with it at different times.

Of course, neither **G** nor **R**'s scribal labor was limited to presenting "The
Book of Shrift." Leaving aside their other work (on Harley 4196, for example),
each, at the moment of copying, was engaged in contributing to a large
continuous anthology of substantial texts. For both of them, "The Book of
Shrift" was not entirely self-substantial but always conceived as "situated,"
part of an ongoing complex of diverse materials.

In **G**, such a contextualization is signalled by the text that immediately
follows "The Book," mentioned above. The metrical Pater Noster (*Index* 788)
is a staple of early *Cursor Mundi* manuscripts, but, outside that siting, appears
only here. One might well suggest that were the third quire of "The Book of
Shrift" exemplar a full one of eight leaves, that **G** could have found the text
there, immediately following "The Book." (The three hundred lines of *Index*
788 would comfortably fit within the remaining space.) Just as **G** never chose
(was never instructed or commissioned?) to copy "The Gast of Gy," where **R**
inadvertently discovered bits of "The Book of Shrift" exemplar, **R** will similarly
have chosen (or been instructed) to ignore this material.

The compilation procedures underlying **R** reveal what could be a more
deliberate adjustment of materials from exemplars also available to **G**. In
R, "The Book of Shrift" is sandwiched between two passion lyrics, *Index* 110
at folio 80rb and *Index* 2080 at folio 93va. **G** also copied these two poems, but
consecutively, at folio 51^{vab}. Presumably, **G** here is faithful to the received
exemplar, for his presentation of the poems as immediate companion-pieces
in this order is echoed in the only other manuscript with parallel contents,
Bodleian Library, MS Don. c.13, fols. 165vb–66ra.[16] **R** has deliberately split the
poems apart, while retaining their exemplar-order, and he has inserted "The
Book of Shrift" between them.

R's choice here represents a combination of fidelity to received exemplars
and what one may call compilatory aesthetics. That is, **R** shows a strong
predilection for beginning texts, so far as possible, at the head of a leaf (column
a, line 1). His presentation of the small exemplar with these two lyrics has
been misrepresented in order to respond to this aesthetic. Hence, the first
poem (*Index* 110) is clearly disposed as page-filler; it appears in the middle of

the mostly blank column, with a following centered explicit and sixteen blank lines, which are spaced out around the colophon of this text and at the column foot. The second lyric (*Index* 2080) begins at folio 93va/1 and occupies most of the column; again, **R** leaves blank lines at the foot, here six of them, so that his subsequent text may begin at an appropriately emphatic point, folio 93vb/1.

Finally, the behavior of the two scribes offers concrete evidence about the extended book-community of which the two are a part, evidence elsewhere only implicit or inferential. This well-organized community includes at least ten scribes – four (one very briefly) in **G**, one of these overlapping with Harley and one with Tiberius E.vii; five in Harley, the two discussed here overlapping with **G** and with **R**; two in **R**; and two in Tiberius – as well as at least six decorating hands (one, perhaps the first scribe of **G**, shared between **G** and Tiberius, and one between a bit of Harley and **R**). This community, elsewhere argued to be centered at Ripon Minster (see note 4), strikingly displays the imposition of a "house spelling-system" and quite substantial signs of learned intervention and revision of texts, most evident in the "expanded" *Northern Homily Cycle*, partly copied by **G** in Harley 4196. To this evidence, **G** and **R**'s handling of "The Book of Shrift" fills in further details about working practices. First, all scribes' reliance on a similar format of book-production, double columns of 44–48 lines, most normally quired in twelves, may be directly linked with the prevalence of this format in early full copies of *Cursor Mundi*, from which **G** and **R** derived "The Book of Shrift." Their reliance upon presentations of this full text is so pervasive that, even when receiving a portion of *Cursor* in a different format ("The Book of Shrift" must have been in eights), they converted it into their normal house form.

Second, while all these scribes were driven by piecemeal presentation of texts, probably in response to the demands of a patron or patrons, the various states of "The Book of Shrift" imply a quite considerable underlying organisation. **R**'s unique fragments from quire 2 of this exemplar cannot have ended up within "The Gast of Gy" unless the team had both exemplars at hand simultaneously. While the confusion of the two texts may not instil great confidence in the efficiency of proceedings, the loose leaves of "The Book" can only have appeared in the exemplar for "The Gast" if these two separate runs of quires were retained proximately. As is further clear from various texts repeatedly copied across this community's run of manuscripts, the group clearly had and preserved through some period a library of exemplars. Quite in contrast to the usual hand-to-mouth procedures followed in most fourteenth-century collections, even in books as grand as the London Auchinleck manuscript or British Library, Harley MS 2253, this was a carefully controlled book community—and one with some degree of continuity and permanence.

Oxford University and University of Notre Dame

NOTES

1. Carleton Brown and Rossell Hope Robbins, eds., *The Index of Middle English Verse* (New York: Columbia University Press, 1943), and *Supplement to the Index of Middle English Verse*, ed. Carleton Brown and Rossell Hope Robbins (Lexington, KY: University of Kentucky Press, 1965); hereafter collectively "Index"): *Cursor Mundi* is number 2453.

2. See the edition, Richard Morris, ed., *Cursor Mundi, Part V*, EETS o.s. 68 (1878), lines 25684–29546+, at pp. 1470–1586: all further references to this edition will cite it as "edn.," giving pages. For the remainder of the early circulation, in the Fairfax and Göttingen MSS, see Morris's summary note at p. a n.3 and the extensive and illuminating discussion by John J. Thompson, *The Cursor Mundi: Poem, Texts and Contexts*, Medium Ævum Monographs, n.s. 19 (Oxford: Society for the Study of Medieval Languages and Literature, 1998), particularly 23–28, 58–60, 174–76, 182.

3. For descriptions, see, respectively, *Ywain and Gawain*, ed. Albert B. Friedman and Norman T. Harrington, EETS o.s. 254 (1964), ix–xi; and Falconer Madan et al., *A Summary Catalogue of Western Manuscripts in the Bodleian Library at Oxford*, 7 vols in 8 (Oxford: Oxford University Press, 1895–1953), 3:321–22 (no. 14667). A portion of the text also appears at Wellesley College, MS 8, pp. 5–12, but is irrelevant here. This book of s. xv^{in} may have been produced proximately to **GR** but presents only the excerpt lines 29238–547+ (part on a now-lost leaf, edn. 1577–86).

4. On these scribal connections and the ambience of copying, see Ralph Hanna, "Yorkshire Writers," *Proceedings of the British Academy* 121 (2003): 91–109, esp. 92–100; and Hanna, "Some North Yorkshire Scribes and their Context," *Medieval Texts in Context*, ed. Denis Renevey and Graham D. Caie (New York, USA and Abingdon, Oxon, UK: Routledge, 2008), 167–91.

5. Here and elsewhere, + indicates that **G** and **R** contain have additional lines after the final line cited from Morris's edition.

6. See Morris, *Cursor Mundi*, lines 25103–402, at 1437–55 (again printing **G**). In the original context, *Cursor Mundi*, this exposition precedes "The Book of Shrift" and is separated from it only by two prayers, unique in the lengthy *Cursor* as being composed in stanzaic verse, rather than short couplets.

7. See Morris, *Cursor Mundi*, 1552–59.

8. See Gustav Schleich, ed., *The Gast of Gy: Eine englische Dichtung des 14. Jahrhunderts nebst ihrer lateinischen Quelle De spiritu Guidonis*, Palaestra 1 (Berlin: Mayer and Müller, 1898). This corresponds to line 1074 in the more readily available edition, C. Horstman, ed., *Yorkshire Writers: Richard Rolle of Hampole, an English Father of the Church, and his Followers*, Library of Early English Writers, 2 vols (London: S. Sonnenschein and Co., 1895–96), 2.313. Horstmann prints the poem from the only other copy, in British Library, MS Cotton Tiberius E.vii, another volume produced by the team of which **G** and **R** are part. The fragment was first identified

by Max Kaluza in his review of Schleich's edition (*Literaturblatt für germanische und romanische Philologie* 10 |1900|: 334), who identified it as part of *Cursor Mundi*. Edward Foster more accurately identified the lines as belonging to 'The Book of Penance' in his recent edition for TEAMS (*Three Purgatory Poems: The Gast of Gy, Sir Owain, The Vision of Tundale* |Kalamazoo: Medieval Insititute, 2004|, 140), although he apparently did not realise that the manuscript contained other parts of the text. See Katherine Zieman's re-edition of "The Gast," to appear as "Les traductions en moyen anglais du De Spiritu Guidonis," in a forthcoming volume of the Corpus Christianorum, continuatio mediaevalis, Marie Anne Polo de Beaulieu, gen. ed., *Le De Spiritu Guidonis et ses traductions...* (Turnhout: Brepols, forthcoming 2011?).

9. For merely a few examples, cf. Morris's parallel presentation of the source in Vespasian with readings of **G** (which we have verified are also the readings of **R**), *Cursor Mundi*, at 28816, 28888, 28898, 28922, 28926, 28937, 28949, 28953, 28960, 29117.

10. In contrast to the module introduced in the next sentence, **G** is pretty universally in double columns of 48 lines to the page (sometimes 47), **R** universally in those with 44 lines to the page.

11. See Thompson, *Cursor Mundi*, 32–33. Indeed, for a space near the end of the materials intruded into "The Gast of Gy," **R** and Vespasian have nearly synchronous column breaks, viz., **R** folio 103ra begins with line 27410, as does Vespasian folio 152rb; **R** 103rb with 27456, as Vespasian 152va; **R** 103va with 27500, Vespasian 152vb with 27502.

12. We have simply, for convenience, followed the lineation of Morris's edition, which, since it is keyed to the full Vespasian text, will introduce small anomalies. There are a number of brief passages omitted in both **G** and **R** and several others added in both; Morris's lineation takes no account of rubrics, although these diminish the number of verse lines that can appear in any column or folio.

13. One textual detail would support the hypothesis of such a loose slip bearing a textual correction. Line 28614 is the opening of a new discussion, headed by a large capital A, and a second large capital A appears at the opening of line 28658 (cf. edn. 1560–61). The archetypal scribe may have resumed copying at the seond of these, rather than the first, and his omission supplied by a corrector.

14. Recall that accompanying this leaf, either here or at the start of the next quire, there was perhaps an odd 46-line column, with lines 28614–59.

15. It is also germane here to recall that **R** never found lines that should appear at just this juncture and lacks 27523–48 altogether.

16. For a description of this book, see Ralph Hanna, *Richard Rolle: Uncollected Verse and Prose, with Related Northern Texts*, EETS o.s. 329 (2007), xxiii–iv. One should note that **G**'s copy of the lyrics appears in a portion of the manuscript bibliographically separate from that in which the scribe copied "The Book."

"Documentum Roberti Grosehede": An Unpublished Early Lollard Text

RALPH HANNA

Cambridge, Trinity College, MS O.1.29, but for one of its texts, might be described as an almost boilerplate mid-fifteenth-century religious miscellany. More or less pocket-sized (about 195 mm x 140 mm overall), it provides a succession of standard prose tracts of instruction, with a strong Northern and Rollean emphasis. The volume begins and concludes with Rolle's epistles: at the head a relatively unusual isolated copy of "The Commandment" (fols. 1–8), at the end, the ubiquitous "Form of Living" (fols. 99v–117v). About forty percent of the book is devoted to the explicitly yet inauthentically ascribed "Pater noster of Richard Ermyte" (fols. 18–66v). The collection also includes the companion pieces "The Abbey of the Holy Ghost" and its "Charter" (fols. 77–99).[1] Given the placement of the scribal language in east central Lincolnshire by the *Linguistic Atlas of Late Mediaeval English*, the book would appear in most respects to represent the familiar southward spread of Northern texts into Humberside and thence into the East Midlands more generally.[2]

There is, however, one exception, a single textual item, one of the volume's three unpublished texts, an omission this note will seek to rectify.[3] At fols. 73–74v, the compiler presents a text he identifies as "Documentum Roberti Grosehede episcopi Lincolniensis." This brief work, enjoining priests not to harass poor parishioners for their tithes, would appear to be of origins quite distinct from the remainder of the book. In its argument, it relies upon what is relatively easily identifiable as Wycliffite "cant," e.g., associations of post-apostolic "innovative" behaviors with Satan and Antichrist (lines 6–7, and following), use of the phrase "pore mennes godes" as a more relevant term than "tithes" (lines 15–16, etc.), and a passing reference to worldliness as a form of "mamentrie" (i.e., idolatry, the worship of a false god, line 99).[4]

Moreover, like a good many similar polemics, the text is presented as a series of excerpts from materials deemed authoritative. This is perhaps nowhere more evident than in the opening move that provides the slightly misleading title for the piece. Robert Grosseteste here stands for a local English tradition of clerical concern. The great bishop of Lincoln replaces the orthodox and conventional model, Thomas Becket, who is anathema in these contexts because of his steadfast vindication of clerical rights.

At the same time, one should probably insist that, within a range of Lollard invective at abuses perpetuated by the established church, the brief tract strikes a relatively conciliatory note. It is not addressed simply, or indeed primarily, to sectarians, as a muckraking revelation of abuse. Rather, the author directs his comments to the "villains," grasping priests themselves, and he imagines that he offers, through his citations, a case that his audience should recognize as compelling—and that should lead to self-reform. In the context of Trinity O.1.29, one might imagine this to be a priest's book that includes not just basic catechetical information, but an admonition about how its owner should behave.

Any doubts one might have about the sectarian origins of the "Documentum" will be vitiated by a second, and partial, record of the text. This occurs added at the end of a booklet, on a blank leaf (and on part of a supplied extra leaf), in Bodleian Library, Bodley MS 647.[5] This manuscript represents the collaborative work of four scribes, all of whom write English in comparable Derbyshire languages.[6] The Bodley manuscript has been recognized, ever since John Bale handled it in about 1550, as a central exhibit of early vernacular Wycliffism. Virtually all its contents (once again, the exception is this unpublished text) are well-known, for Bodley 647 provided materials for the two early anthologies, edited by Thomas Arnold and F. D. Matthew, through which vernacular Wycliffite interests have always been known.[7]

The Bodley manuscript shows many signs of having been derived from materials close to the origins of the vernacular Lollard movement, for example, its inclusion of the eucharistic confessions printed by Aston. The scribe who added his version of the "Documentum" to the ensemble (and who appears nowhere else in the volume) clearly responded to the thematic emphases of the whole. In the most general terms, the book provides a protracted discussion of proper priesthood (and the many perverse modern representations of that order). Among its other original texts, it includes a brief diatribe derived from and ascribed to Grosseteste. The topic of unnecessarily coerced tithes emerges elsewhere, in one of the book's Latin portions. There a different scribe gives an approving reference to a passage in Gratian, a discussion of unneedy priests taking tithes.[8] This citation, ascribed to Jerome, is probably alluded to in line 13 of the text appended here.

I present below the text, as it appears in Trinity O.1.29. The copy in Bodley 647 is only a fragment; it breaks off at midpage, with "to" (line 69). The scribe who offered this portion may have lost interest, once it became clear that the text actually did not reproduce an extensive Grosseteste commentary, but as with the other texts in Bodley 647, the scribe was transmitting an extremely good copy of the tract. In a number of local readings, the Trinity scribe clearly is misrepresenting materials satisfactorily communicated by his early fifteenth-century predecessor, perhaps most notably the eyeskip error I repair at lines 58 through 60 of the text below. A number of other examples litter the Trinity text and require correction, for example "fitrid" in line 37 (a rare word, but one also appearing in another early Lollard text).

However, in addition to providing only a fragment of the whole, the "Documentum" in Bodley 647 appears truncated in a second respect. This manuscript offers a considerably less lengthy account than does the Trinity copy, even of those portions where they run in parallel. Phrase by phrase and line by line, Trinity provides a fuller text, of great grammatical specificity, and often, local detail.

This situation does not, however, exemplify the editors' paradox *recentiores, non deteriores*. Rather, in every other text of the manuscript where comparison is possible, the scribe of Trinity O.1.29 reveals himself as a compulsive (and often irritating) rewriter of received materials.[9] This scribe seems unable to leave anything as he received it, and from the collations of texts he produced, one can assemble a rich array of evidence for his customary "prosaics." Certainly, his case might provide a salutary caution to editors. Typically concerned with the transmission of a single work, editors might well broaden their scope to consider the customary practices, displayed across a range of writings (and potentially, diverse manuscripts), that can be associated with those individuals providing evidence for their editions.

In this situation, where the Trinity scribe is most usually a unique witness to the text, one has to admit that an edition, as opposed to a transcription, of the "Documentum" is impossible. After Bodley 647 breaks off in line 69, one has no real check on the Trinity scribe's activities, other than his customary practices elsewhere. One must acknowledge this constraint, and I present below the text in its only full extant form. Where the two copies of the "Documentum" run in parallel, I make no effort to bring their readings into conformity, although I do correct what seem to me manifest errors in Trinity. For the first 42 lines of the version below, I provide a separate second set of collations, limited to presenting what I imagine to be the Trinity scribe's intrusions, generally readings of the type that have been noted by past editors of the manuscript's texts. This list follows a more conventional one, a full collation of other deviations between the two witnesses, including those dozen or more occasions where Trinity seems to me, for one reason or another, to have misrepresented a reading recorded in Bodley (and inferentially, in Trinity's exemplar as well). There are a number of further examples that, although I remain dubious about them, I have let stand.

|fol. 73ʳ|

Hic incipit documentum Roberti Grosehede episcopi Lincolniensis.

Þe worthi clerke Roberte Grosehede, beschope of Lincoln,
says in a sermone þat he made vnto þo pope þat kepers or
curatoures of mannez saulez, nought prechynge Cristes gospelle
by worde and lyfynge like vnto þe werkez of Ihesu Criste and
5   fore loofe of Cristenne saulez, wille for to be dedd in þemeseluen
and |sleers of| saules taken vnto þeire cure. Þei Antecriste and
Sathanas transfigure into an aungell of lyght. And also Saynt
Bernard says in his epistille vnto þe curatez of Holykirke, "Whatso
10   þinge þat þou holdes of þe auterage ouer a strayte and bare
lyf|lode| and simple clethyng, it es nouȝt þin þat, bot it es othere
mennes and it es thefte and it es sacrilege."

And also Saynt Bernarde and Seynt Ierome in þaire Epistelle
sayes on þis manere: "Whatsoeuer þinge þat þies clerkes of
15   Holykirke haue in þeire possessione, it es nouȝt þeirs, bot it es pore
mennes godes of þeire subditez. |fol. 73v| For to resayue pore
mennez |godes| and þan nought to gyffe þeme vnto pore menne
bot for to withdraugh þeme fro þeme, it passes alle maner of cruelte
of thefte or of robrye."

20   And also Saynt Bernarde þusgates saies in his epistele vnto
þo prelatez of Holykirke, "A ȝe prelatez and mased folez in þo
gouernale of Holykyrke, what doose golde or syluere in ȝoure
sadellez, in ȝoure bridelles? And also ȝoure horsez are chargedd
with gemmes and with iewells, and pore men hungire and thirste
25   and haue nakyde syddes."

"We are Cristez heritage, bought with his preciouse blode,"
sayes þies ilke pore men. "And it es cruelly withdraughen fro vs,
þat þinge þe wilke ȝe so outragely wastez." And þerfore sais þis
pore men þus, þat two wikkidnes comez þereof. "ȝe prelatez
30   p|eres|chez in ȝoure doynge vanite, and wee hungire and thirste
and also suffere mekille kare and mekille woo."

"Thynke, ȝe prelatez," sai|s| Saynt Bernarde, "How orribull
sall þe crye of pore menne be at þe daye of dome agayns all ȝow.
Thynke also, ȝe curatourez of Holykirke, what it profites now to
35   waste tythyngez and offeryngez of Holykirke in gaye peloure or in
grisse and in festes of ricche men and iaggedd sqwyers and
|fitred| clothez, as it were þe feende tormentourez. And ȝoure
+ pore paryschenez suffers mekile disease, in hungure, thriste,
and colde. And fore schame and sclaundere of þe warlde, þai
40   borough oftetyme þe penees þe wilke þat þei offere vnto ȝou
into encresynge of ȝoure lyuynge, gretely hynnderand þeire
awne astate."

And ȝee fynde written in ȝoure laughe þat all þinge þat
euer ȝee haue in ȝoure possessione is pore mennez gode, and
45   not ȝourez. And also ȝee are not lordes þerof, bot ȝe be þeire
procuratores. Thynke, if þat ȝe be procuratores, to lyue so
lustely þat þe pore men, þat are lordez of ȝoure temperellez
godez, farez oftetyme so harde þat vnneese þei may sustene
þeme in þer lyfynge?
50   Thynke also weel and haue it sadely in mynde þat Criste
Ihesu and alle his holy aposteles for all þeire holy lyfe and trew
prechynge hade no more bot a poore and naked lyflode for to
do þeire office þerby. And Gode ordende no more vnto a|ny|
preste |in þe laughe| of grace bot foode and hylynge and for
55   to |lyue of| þe gosspell to þame þat it preches. Who has graunted
vnto ȝou so many markes and poundes by noumbre of hundrethe,
when ȝee preche nouȝt þe gosspell in worde and in dede, but
gyues sclaundere to Cristen, bothe be pride and couetyse |and
lecchorie sumtyme and glotonye and ydelnesse?
60   And to stoppe couetyse|, of prestez say|s| God in his laughe
þus, þat prestez and dekounes |fol. 74r| sulde nought take of þe
possessione of þeire brothire, bot be fully weel appayede with
offerynge of tythes comand vnto þe chirche. Bot ȝe now vpon
deyes brynge vp amonge ȝou many and diuersez new |custom|es,
65   of þe wilke God noþinge spekes in Holy Write. And ȝit ȝe do full
eueil ȝoure office, bothe in techyng and in example of gode lyfe
geuynge.
Thynke also, ȝee prelates þat curses men þat offers nouȝt at
ȝoure liste and likynge, bot spendes mekile bettere þaire almus to
70   pore nedy men and counsels othere men to do þe same. Þere ȝe
may by noo laughe ne resoune compelle þeme to offire as þat þei
weere woont at do bot allonely be eueile techynge of couetous
prestez.
And thenkes þus in ȝoureseluen þat ȝe are be a thousand
75   partie for to gyfe trewe techynge of þe gosspelle and ensaumple
of holy lyfe vnto ȝoure subiettez, ȝa, þan þei are bounden to paye
to ȝow tithynge or offerynge. And þerfore ȝe be a thousande
partie more acursed þan are þei, for þe withdraughynge of gostely
dette, þan þat þei be for withdraughynge of any maner of tythez or
80   offerynge.
If it so be þat ȝe couetis to do weel and treuly ȝoure office,
thynkez it well in ȝoure þoughtez þat Criste Ihesu in his epistele
cursed neuer man ne woman for tithes? And þusgatez þei didd
weel þer office when wikked men wild nethire gyue þeme mete ne
85   drynke. How and what manere made Sathanas ȝou so herdy and
stoute and outrage for to curse trew men in Holykirke, for þat þei

spend þeire almusdede on þaire brethire, beand in gret pouerte,
and þerto also þai counseile Cristene men to do þe same, as Criste
hymseluen comaunded in his gosspell? A, ȝe masede folez,

90 wantande fully alle þe lyght of grace þat in ȝow suld be passandly,
ȝe oftetymes cursez þeme expressely fore þat þei do willfully þe
precepte of God.

Bot were is now on þies dayes more schame, velany,
heresy, and open tyrantrye of Antecriste þa|n| es regnand among

95 ȝou day be daye and ȝhere be ȝhere? And þerfore I counseill ȝou
to þinke how þat þe holy Tobie departed all his tithes vnto poore
nedy men at þe thride ȝhere. Fore prestez worchipped þan fals
goddes, as þe Bibille vs openly |telles|. |fol. 74v| Þan sethyne
couetys and gloteny is mamentrie, as Saynte Paule, þe holy apostole

100 of Criste, sais. Fore men maye not withdraughe laughfully and
waste þe offerynge, nowt to ȝou dewed of longe tyme fore ȝoure
couetouse, pride, and wastynge, and also pore men þeire godes.

A, thynke þus in ȝoure hertez, I counseill, if it so be with
ȝou þat ȝee seeke mekile more þe temporell godez of ȝoure

105 subiettez, ȝa, þan ȝe do in any tyme þe heel of þeire saule. Sothely,
alle ȝe þat sogatez do are acursedd of God almyghty. Forewhi ȝe
are fully oute of his preciouse vertu, þat es calledde Charite.
And þerfore all ȝe do, standande in þat case, es not bot dyme
and darke and withouten þe lyght of grace.

110 Also thenkez in ȝoure myndes, if þat ȝe haue ought comon
to ȝoure kirkes or to ȝoure orders or to any maner benefice of
Holykirke þorough þis wharied synne, Symonye. Forewhi if so
be þat ȝee so haue done, ȝe are acursedd be ȝoure aune laughe.
ȝa, ryght as cursede heretikes vnto þe tyme þat ȝe be fully

115 amended of þat ilke fals symonye and recounseild of ȝoure
prelate. Whethire þat ȝe may be saaue in þis maner of doynge
withouten resynynge or naye? And þerfore it es þe moste
|h|este for ȝou all fore dred of vengeaunce of God þat ȝe ceese
now forward of ȝoure sclaundre and cursynge. Fore in

120 sothfastnes to saye, temporell godes are not dette to ȝow.

And þerefore preches treuly and frely Cristes gosspell
vnto ȝoure subdites and schewes vnto þeme in all þinge mekenes,
deuocioun, and resonable lyfe in mete and drynke, withouten
any outrage. And lokes also þat ȝe haue competent howsynge

125 and honeste seruandes. And sellez nouȝt Cristez bodie in messys
fore offerynge or fore any othere vntrew wynnynge.

Forwhi if ȝe sogatez do, þan do ȝee mekile more
cursedlyere þen Iudas didd. Fore he sulde Criste Ihesu when þat
he was dedely and nouȝt knawen fore verray God. Bot if þat ȝee

130 sell his body sacried in þe messe, þan ȝee sell hym glorifyede and

knawen for God almyghty in trinite. And þerfore be ȝe wyese
and waare in ȝoure wyrkynge, and ȝe sall haue to ȝoure mede þe
blis þat nere sall haue endynge.

***

Emendations and other variants from Bodley 647 (B)

3 curatoures| curatis B   mannez| mennus B   4 lyfynge| lyf B   like vnto|
licly to B *6 sleers of| B, sorye es for MS   vnto| to B   6 Þei| And B   Antecriste|
Antecristes B   7 transfigure | transfigurid B   8 epistille| pistels B   -so| -euere B
10 þe auterage| outrage B   *11 lyflode| B, lyfynge MS   13 Bernarde...lerome|
trs. names B   Epistelle| pistils B   16 For| And for B   *17 godes| B; þinge MS
vnto| to B   18–19 alle...robrye| þo cruelte of alle robbers (thus an extra doublet in
MS) B   20 saies| after epistele B   epistele| pistils B   vnto| to B   21 þo prelatez|
prelates þus B   A| Say B   23 in[1]...bridelles| in þo bridel and þo sadel B   24
with[2]| precious stones and B   25 and haue| with B   26 his| Cristis B   28 þe
wilke| þat B   wastez| adds þus B   28–29 And... þat| seyn pore men after þereof B
*30 pereschez| B, prechez MS   *32 sais| B, said MS   33 þe| þis B   at...ȝow| trs.
phrs. B   daye of dome| domusday B   34 Thynke| And now thynke B   curatourez|
curatis B   35 in| adds gret B   *37 fitred| B, taterynge of MS (cf. MED fit(e)red
pp.)   *38 pore| B, propure MS   hungure| adds and B   39 fore... þai| om., but for
wordly schame appears after borough (thus another added doublet in MS) B   40 þei|
for to B   vnto| to B   43 And...written| Sith ȝe write B   ȝoure| adds owne B   44
gode| godis B   45 ȝe be þeire| om., but of pore men appears after procuratores[1]
B   46 if| wheþer B   procuratores[2]| trew p. of pore men B   þat| and B   *53 vnto
any| B, vnto a MS   *54 in þe laughe| B, om. MS   *55 lyue of| B, trowe on MS
(having confused the form with leve 'believe')   56 vnto| to B   43 Cristen| adds men B
*58–60 couetyse...couetyse| B, om. MS (an eyeskip)   *60 says| B, sayde MS   61
nought| noþing B   62 brothire| breþer B   appayede| payed B   *64 customes|
B, laughes MS   65 noþinge spekes| spekes not B   68 also| wil B   prelates|
prestes B   69 liste and likynge| wille B   to| B ends   *94 þan| þat MS   *98 telles|
om. MS (along, probably, with more, at the page-boundary)   *118 heste| beste MS

Words and phrases unique to Trinity, lines 1–42 only

5 wille for to   7 an, And   9 vnto...Holykirke, þat   10 and bare   11 þat bot,
and[1,2]   13 And[1]   14 on þis manere   -so-, þinge þat þies, of Holykirke   15 in
þeire...bot   16 of þeire subditz   17 þan, to[1], for to   18 fro þeme it (and cf. the
variant cited above)   20 And, þusgates   21 of Holykirke   21–22 and...Holykyrke   22
or syluere, And also   27 þies ilke   And, with-, so outragely   30 ȝoure, also   31
and mekille woo   32 Saynt   33–34 all, also, of Holykirke   34 now, of Holykirke
35–36 or in grisse, in   37 it...feende   38 cf. the variant cited above   40 oftetyme...
þei   41–42 into...astate

NOTES

1. For descriptions, see Montague R. James, *The Western Manuscripts in the Library of Trinity College, Cambridge: A Descriptive Catalogue*, 4 vols. (Cambridge: University Press, 1900–1904), 3:33–34; Linne R. Mooney, *Manuscripts in the Library of Trinity College, Cambridge*, Index of Middle English Prose, Handlist 11 (Cambridge: D. S. Brewer, 1995), 74–75; Florent G. A. M. Aarts, ed., *The Pater Noster of Richard Ermyte: A Late Middle English Exposition of the Lord's Prayer* (Nijmegen: University Press, 1967), xiv–xv.

2. The book appears in Angus McIntosh, M. L. Samuels, and Michael Benskin, *A Linguistic Atlas of Late Mediaeval English*, 4 vols. (Aberdeen: University Press, 1986), as LP 180 (coordinates 514/344); see 3.261–62.

3. The unique texts include an Annunciation sermon (fols. 66v–73) and a discussion of prayer, identified in its colophon as being derived from a "liber qui vocatur pupilla oculi interioris hominis" (fols. 8–17v). For this item, not related to the lengthy discussion in the Rollean *Holy Boke Gratia Dei*, see P. S. Jolliffe, *A Check-List of Middle English Prose Writings of Spiritual Guidance* (Toronto: Pontifical Institute of Mediaeval Studies, 1974), item M.13.

4. The phrase, "pore men's goods," is the English shorthand answering two of Wycliffe's "errors" condemned at Blackfriars in May 1382, the fifth ("Quod decimae sunt purae eleemosynae...") and ninth ("est contra sacram scripturam, quod viri ecclesiastici habent possessiones temporales"). See further G. H. Martin, ed., *Knighton's Chronicle 1337–1396* (Oxford: University Press, 1995), 254–57 passim. For "maumetry," see the first three texts edited Edward P. Wilson, "A Critical Text, with Commentary, of MS. English Theology f.39...," 2 vols. (unpub. Oxford B.Litt. thesis, 1968 [Bodleian, MS B.Litt. c.177–78]); and the comments and description at Ralph Hanna III, *Smaller Bodleian Collections*, Index of Middle English Prose, Handlist 12 (Cambridge: D. S. Brewer, 1997), xxii–iii, 14–15.

5. Anne Hudson mentioned the two copies, *The Premature Reformation: Wycliffite Texts and Lollard History* (Oxford: University Press, 1988), 342, note 142, amid a customarily concise summary of Lollard views on tithing, pp. 341–45.

6. See *Linguistic Atlas* LP 61, described 3:68–69.

7. For Bale, see *Index Britanniae Scriptorum...*, ed. Reginald L. Poole and Mary Bateson, 2nd ed., with a new introduction by Caroline Brett and James P. Carley (1902; Cambridge: D. S. Brewer, 1990), 270–71. For the seminal editions, see Thomas Arnold, ed., *Select English Works of John Wyclif*, 3 vols. (Oxford: University Press, 1869–71), esp. volume 3 passim; Frederic David Matthew, ed., *The English Works of Wyclif Hitherto Unprinted*, EETS o.s. 74 (London: Trübner, 1880, 1902; repr. 1998), 40–51. For further materials overlooked in these volumes, see Margaret Aston, "Wyclif and the Vernacular," *Studies in Church History*, Subsidia 5 (1987), 281–330, at 328–30 (cf. the discussion at 297–300). A protracted discussion of MS Bodley 647 and its reception will appear in *Essays and Studies* for 2010.

8. For the first of these, "Lincolniensis" (fols. 62v–63v), see Arnold, 3.230–32. The Jerome citation appears at fol. 83, and refers to *Decretum* C.1, q.2, c.6 ("Qui sumptibus propriis sustentari possunt, ab ecclesia stipendia non accipiant"), ed. Emil Friedberg, from the original edition of Aemilius Luduvicus Richter, *Corpus Juris Canonici*, 2 vols. (Leipzig: Tauchnitz, 1879–1881; repr. 1959), 1.409.

9. See Aarts, *Pater Noster*, xx–xxii (mentioning a similar report on the "Abbey" texts of this manuscript); and, for Rolle's epistles, S. J. Ogilvie-Thomson, ed., *Richard Rolle Prose and Verse*, EETS o.s. 293 (1988), xxxix and xlvi.

Descriptive Reviews

ANTHONY BALE and A.S.G. EDWARDS, EDS.
John Lydgate's Lives of Ss Edmund & Fremund and the Extra Miracles of St Edmund.
Heidelberg: Universitätsverlag Winter, 2009.197 pp.

This volume contains an edition of John Lydgate's *Life of St. Edmund*, including its Prologue, his *Life of St. Fremund*, and three posthumous miracles of St. Edmund, known as the *Extra Miracles*. The two *Lives* are edited from British Library MS Harley 2278, described by A. S. G. Edwards in his introduction to the facsimile of this manuscript as "probably the most important illustrated manuscript of Middle English verse to be produced in the fifteenth century" (*The Life of St Edmund King and Martyr: John Lydgate's Illustrated Verse Life Presented to Henry VI: A Facsimile of British Library MS Harley 2278* [London: British Library, 2004]; reviewed *JEBS* 9 [2006], 178–9). It was presented to King Henry VI to commemorate his extended stay at the Benedictine Abbey at Bury St. Edmunds in 1433/34. The abbot, William Curteys, had charged Lydgate with the task of translating the work from Latin. Surviving in thirteen manuscripts, Lydgate's *Ss Edmund and Fremund* was popular and influential in the fifteenth century. As the editors of this volume note, it was key in establishing the freestanding saint's life as a popular literary form in fifteenth-century East Anglia. Despite its historical and literary importance and the popularity of Lydgate studies in the last two decades, this is the first critical edition of all the materials which arguably constitute Lydgate's work in its fullest form. Its appearance is a welcome addition to Middle English studies.

The introduction to this edition begins with a summary of the text of the works and brief descriptions of the thirteen manuscripts in which the *Lives* survive completely or in fragments, including the four manuscripts in which the *Extra Miracles* were added. Further sections discuss the circulation of the manuscripts, as well as the occasion, authorship, and composition of both the *Lives* and the *Extra Miracles*. In discussing whether the *Extra Miracles* were written by Lydgate, the editors provide a helpful summary of previous debate and, in support of Lydgate's probable authorship, add details regarding the likely dates of the occurrence and recording of each miracle. The concise and informative section on Lydgate's use of sources will be a great aid to scholars working on these texts in the future. The introduction ends with short entries on the editors' reasons for choosing the base manuscripts, their transcription and editorial procedures, and the illustrations. Sensibly, the editors have not attempted to provide a full analysis of the illustrations in Harley 2278 or the other two illustrated manuscripts but instead provide brief descriptions of each illustration within the textual commentary and direct the reader to A. S. G. Edwards's facsimile edition.

The editors selected Bodleian Library MS Ashmole 46 as the base-text for their edition of the *Extra Miracles* because it is more metrically and orthographically regular than the other manuscripts. Substantive variants are included in the end notes. For the edited text of the *Lives*, Harley 2278 was selected due to its claim to authority as a presentation copy made at Bury St. Edmunds, possibly under Lydgate's supervision. On the basis of this textual authority, the editors have chosen not to include variants in this edition except where there is a manifest error in the base manuscript or where readings seem otherwise problematic. For those readers interested in subsequent scribal variations or the rewriting of religious and political texts, it is regrettable that substantive variant readings from the base manuscript are not included in this edition, which is likely to be the standard reference for quite some time. Helpfully, however, the editors direct the interested reader to the University of Harvard PhD thesis of Dr. James I. Miller, who records the variants in all but one of the manuscripts, the exception being His Grace the Duke of Norfolk, Arundel Castle MS (*Biblioteca Norfolciana*), *sine numero* which was not rediscovered until after Dr. Miller completed his thesis.

The edited text is accompanied by a detailed commentary supplemented by a comprehensive glossary of proper names, a selective glossary of difficult words or constructions, and a bibliography. The second glossary is slightly frustrating to use, as not all instances of glossed words are recorded. This is, however, a minor quibble about a well-presented edition that will provide a sound basis for future work on these texts.

Joni Henry, University of Cambridge

JANETTA REBOLD BENTON
Materials, Methods, and Masterpieces of Medieval Art.
Santa Barbara, CA: Praeger, 2009.
xxiv + 303 pp. 26 color and 45 B&W plates.

Janetta Rebold Benton's *Materials, Methods, and Masterpieces of Medieval Art* is a book that is destined to find its way onto a great many shelves. Written in a no-nonsense, straightforward, and approachable style, its twelve chapters outline the basics of the most common types of medieval artistic production. Individual chapters function as basic guides to manuscript illuminations, wall and ceiling paintings, mosaics, ivory carving, metal, stone and woodwork, enamel, stained glass, textiles, secular and ecclesiastical clothing, and armor. Along with easy-to-understand descriptions of materials and processes, each chapter provides a few key examples, usually drawn from those works that are best known in the field—the illuminations in *Les très riches heures du Duc de Berry*, the frescos of Giotto, the mosaics of Ravenna's San Vitale, the stained glass of Chartres Cathedral, the Bayeux Tapestry, and so on.

Benton's structure is based on the output of select medieval artisans' guilds, and the book understandably focuses on what would today be considered the high arts. Likewise, most of the examples are drawn from Western Europe—France, Italy, Britain, Germany, and the Low Countries—with a slight bias towards the late rather than early Middle Ages. Indeed, Benton seems most at home when discussing artworks from the years immediately preceding the great calamities that ended the Middle Ages, in that liminal space between anonymous and named artists. Most of the book's chapters open with a brief introduction outlining the basic social function of a given type of artistic production, then move into a highly detailed but generally lay-oriented description of materials and methods, before outlining approximately a half dozen of the more famous examples of a given type of art. Interpretations of individual works of art are mainstream but nevertheless acknowledge minority opinion where appropriate or immediately accessible. There is a short contextualizing introduction in which the basics of guild production are documented and some key terms defined, as well as a short conclusion discussing medieval working conditions and the problems we face today in properly contextualizing medieval works in terms of their original appearance and presentation.

Although the selection of the representative art works, the lucidity of description, and the wealth of factual information presented make this book an ideal reference work for serious medievalists momentarily working outside of their immediate specialty, *Materials, Methods, and Masterpieces of Medieval Art* would be especially useful to an undergraduate or graduate audience. Indeed, although it is certainly not a textbook, it would be easy to imagine structuring an upper-level course on medieval art along its outlines. In this regard, the bibliography, rather than serving as a compendium of information relating to specific issues in the interpretation of the examples Benton provides, instead offers a way for the interested reader to begin to encounter each type of artistic production. Each section of the bibliography contains precisely those works that best exemplify current scholarly thought on the generalities of a given field.

The volume might have been improved through the inclusion of more black and white illustrations—not necessarily more images of works of art, but helpful diagrams illustrating unfamiliar procedures or the components of objects. For example, the descriptions of ecclesiastical vestments could have been much improved with a few simple illustrations. Although Benton's description of the nine types of vestment worn by a bishop is lucid, an illustration to show how the individual items interacted might have been beneficial. Nevertheless, most of the examples chosen are so well-known that countless images of them are readily available online.

Materials, Methods, and Masterpieces of Medieval Art will be an invaluable reference tool to those art historians whose scholarly focus is narrow rather than broad, and Benton's book will be of particular interest to literary, political, and historical scholars or musicologists and the like who lack a significant training in art history.

Carl James Grindley, The City University of New York

MARGARET CONNOLLY AND LINNE R. MOONEY, EDS.
Design and Distribution of Late Medieval Manuscripts in England.
York: York Medieval Press, 2008. 352 pp. 15 B&W illustrations.

Most of the essays in this volume were first delivered as papers at the York Manuscripts Conference in 2005. The title of the conference was "Making the Medieval Book," a focus reflected in the "Design" part of the title, which is addressed in the first two sections, "Designing the Canterbury Tales: Chaucer's Early Copyists" and "Designing Devotion: Individual and Institutional." The titles are self-explanatory: Daniel W. Mosser, Jacob Thaisen, and Takako Kato write respectively on "'Chaucer's Scribe': Adam and the Hengwrt Project," "The Trinity Gower D Scribe's Two *Canterbury Tales* Manuscripts Revisited," and "Corrected Mistakes in Cambridge University Library MS Gg.4.27." The three essays offer evidence of the difficult process (in terms of organizing the material and establishing the text) by which Chaucer's unfinished papers were prepared for consumption. Linne Mooney's identification of Adam Pinkhurst as the Hengwrt scribe and thus Scribe B of the Trinity Gower (Cambridge, Trinity College MS R.3.2) lies behind the essays of Mosser (who considers, if Adam was the scribe, how far Chaucer might have been involved in Hengwrt) and Thaisen (who investigates Scribe D of the Trinity manuscript). Kato details the types of mistakes made by the "careless" scribe of another *Canterbury Tales* manuscript, Cambridge University Library MS Gg.4.27.

In the second section, the focus is similarly on the preparation of texts for readers, specifically the evidence for design dictated by different demands. The target audience might be an individual (such as the one who owned the York Pavement Hours and had eight images sewn into it, or the Tudor gentlewoman Anne Bulkeley, discussed by Amelia Grounds and Alexandra Barratt, respectively), an institution (the Bridgettines, also discussed by Barratt, or the clergy revising the Sarum lections, discussed by Sherry Reames), or a regional or social network group (arguably the focus of Julian M. Luxford in his essay on the Founders' Book of Tewkesbury Abbey). The four essays in this section are "Late Medieval Efforts at Standardization and Reform in the Sarum Lessons for Saints' Days" (Reames), "Evolution of a Manuscript: The Pavement Hours" (Grounds), "Singing from the Same Hymn-Sheet: Two Bridgettine Manuscripts" (Barratt), and "'Secundum originale examinatum': The Refashioning of a Benedictine Historical Manuscript" (Luxford).

In the final section we move to "Distribution" with "Development and Distribution: Mapping Manuscripts and Texts." Although the section starts with Linne R. Mooney's study of vernacular literary manuscripts from 1375 to 1475, "Locating Scribal Activity in Late Medieval London," the issue of distribution is really introduced by Michael G. Sargent in "What do the Numbers Mean? Observations on Some Patterns of Middle English Manuscript Transmission," a thought-provoking and original essay. (The numbers mean that very few texts survive in large numbers of manuscripts; distribution often shows a rising rate for up to fifty years, followed by a plateau—but this bald summary does not do the essay justice.) The other essays, appropriately, take up the theme of numbers. *Brut* scores high (over 180 manuscripts), whereas a text like *Contemplations of the Love and Dread of God* survives in thirty-six manuscripts and two printed editions (still quite respectable). John J. Thompson and Margaret Connolly, respectively, look at their distribution in "The Middle English Prose *Brut* and the Possibilities of Cultural Mapping" and "Mapping Manuscripts and Readers of *Contemplations of the Love and Dread of God*." Ralph Hanna studies the twenty-one "Yorkshire Manuscripts of the *Speculum Vite*" (out of a total of forty-five), and George R. Keiser looks at the distribution of one particular herbal and then English herbals in general in "Vernacular Herbals: A Growth Industry in Late Medieval England."

In the introduction by Connolly and Mooney (which provides a clear synopsis of the essays), the editors argue for the primacy of manuscript study: "Linguistics, dialectology, stemmatics, palaeography, and codicology all make important contributions to the study of the literature, over and above—or, more rightly, before—the critical studies that one undertakes for literary works of all periods." The veracity of this statement is fully proved by the essays in this volume. JEBS readers need not be told, but literary critics, take heed!

Sue Powell, University of Salford

CYNTHIA J. CYRUS
The Scribes for Women's Convents in Late Medieval Germany.
University of Toronto Press: Toronto, Buffalo, and London, 2009.
xix + 387 pp.

For anyone already enthralled by the subject of manuscript production in nunneries, this volume makes a riveting read; for anyone not yet interested in the subject, this volume provides an ideal scholarly welcome. Based on a wealth of detailed information, the book is divided into five main chapters ("Of Monasteries and Their Scribes," "Structuring Scribal Relationships," "The Content of Convent Manuscripts," "Scribe as Individual," and "Why Scribes Serve"), preceded by an introduction and a conclusion that makes up chapter six. There are two very informative appendices ("Distribution of Known Scribes and of Surviving Manuscripts by Monastic Order" and "Forty-eight Women's Convents with Active Scriptoria in Late Medieval Germany"), and the notes fill over eighty pages. There are also various helpful tables and three specific indices (of people, convents, and manuscripts) as well as a general one. Not only is there an extensive bibliography, but in the list of abbreviations, Cyrus provides a most useful list of finding-aids.

There is so much of interest in this book that it is difficult to decide where to begin, so the easiest thing to do is to let readers know about Cyrus's working methods and her statistics. Rather than restricting herself to a "'top ten' or 'top fifty' sort of investigation" (10), Cyrus assiduously assessed all surviving monastic materials from women's convents from the beginning of the thirteenth century to the start of the Reformation, that is, some 4,000 manuscripts from approximately 450 convents. Besides perusing documentary material and library catalogues, she also worked her way through the 23,774 colophons found in *Colophons de manuscrits occidentaux des origines au XVIe siècle*, alongside the various other aids both published (such as the *Germania Benedictina*) and online (such as the *Matrix Monasticon*), to locate her material. These thorough investigations have revealed 361 named and fifty-five unnamed female scribes who between them were responsible for 561 manuscripts. A total of 133 convents used women scribes, with roughly equal distribution among the Dominicans, Cistercians, Clares/Tertiaries, and Benedictines (34–35).

The material is set out in a systematic fashion so that each chapter is divided into various headings and subheadings. In Chapter 3, which deals with the content of convent manuscripts, the liturgical manuscripts are all scrupulously divided into books for the choir, for soloists, for male clerics, for readings within the services, for reference, for planning, and for private reading. This means that readers not only get the specific information, such as that "[t]he single sequentiary manuscript in a woman's hand that stems from this period was copied in part by the Freiburg Clarissan scribe Elsbeth Töpplin" (100) but also telling comments that can help them in the interpretation of the evidence. For example, Cyrus suspects "that soloists' manuscripts were more ephemeral than their choral counterparts ... and did not necessarily have lasting value for the community once the manuscript's creator had passed away" (101). This tiny example is indicative of the procedure throughout, so that in the course of the study a reader learns about the influence exerted by changes of a monastic rule and the consequent demands for new books (25), that more women's convents were linked to internal than external scribes (50), that the books copied by women for themselves were most often the Psalter and the *Gebetbuch* (61), and that (unsurprisingly) Observant women's houses produced more books that the non-Observant (177), and so forth, besides the precise detail, for example, that there are thirty-nine named scribes and 124 surviving manuscripts written by women associated with St Katarina in Nuremberg (69), or that of the sixty-six missals from convent libraries, only two are associated with men (102).

One may follow the fortunes of the better-known female scribes who recur through the volume, such as Loppa von Spiegel of Cologne (actually an illuminator), Kunigund Niclasin of Nuremberg (both scribe and librarian), or Clara Hätzlerin of Augsburg (most strikingly of all, an independent scribe producing works by commission). Or one may also discover gems for oneself, such as the colophon of Margaretha von Schonbergk, who tells us that she wrote "mit yrer lyncken hant," or Alheydem Kalves, who wrote "in anno meo 73 cum magno labore." It is a measure of the author's scholarship that when she paraphrases or semi-quotes such material in the body of the text, the full quotation is always given in the original language, as here on page 148 in notes 54 and 55.

Having read this volume with great enthusiasm from cover to cover and having benefited at every turn from information on my areas of interest both new (for example, antiphonals and table books) and old (for example, book circulation and colophons), the only criticisms are that the publisher did not see fit to ensure the inclusion of a map of the somewhat dizzying succession of convents and, more seriously in my view, any reproductions of the scribal hands represented here. Although such a map might have been difficult to prepare, the second omission is less easy to understand. Admittedly, this is not a subject to which Cyrus devotes space. On page 6, she simply alludes to the palaeographical work of Karin Schneider on the most famous example of female scribal activity in Germany, St Katharina in Nuremberg, and to Albert Bruckner's well-known study focusing on the case of Dorothea Schermann of Gnadental in Basel, as well as to the recent study by Alison Beach on female scribes in twelfth-century Bavaria. Thereafter Cyrus only makes incidental mention of what she terms "handwriting style" (for instance, on pages 43, 45 and 96). Nevertheless, particularly for the benefit of those who work in areas where the survivals of authenticated female hands (either lay or religious) are so rare, it is a shame that the publishers did not urge the author to provide such material, especially given the fact that she is familiar with so many manuscripts (all listed on pages 303–15). These two criticisms aside, Cynthia Cyrus should be warmly congratulated for producing such a scholarly volume that will both amply satisfy the hardened manuscript specialist and do much to encourage the neophyte.

Veronica O'Mara, University of Hull

A. S. G. EDWARDS, ED.
Regional Manuscripts 1200–1700.
English Manuscript Studies 1100–1700, 14.
London: The British Library, 2008.
268 pp. 24 B&W illustrations.

This is a rich volume, beginning with a study of how Anglo-Saxon texts were supplemented from the thirteenth to sixteenth centuries as *inspeximus* charters and ending with a sixteenth-century ballad manuscript. Listing titles is essential to convey the range and interest of the volume: "The Exchequer, the Chancery and the Abbey of Bury St Edmunds: Inspeximus Charters and their Enrolments" (Kathryn A. Lowe), "Anglo-Norman Prose Chronicles and their Audiences" (John Spence), "The *Tabula medicine*: An Evolving Encyclopaedia" (Peter Murray Jones), "Chapter and Worse: An Episode in the Regional Transmission of the *Speculum Christiani*" (Vincent Gillespie), "Newly Discovered Booklets from a Reconstructed Middle English Manuscript" (Kathleen L. Scott), "A Manuscript Found in the Library of Abbotsford House and the Lost Legendary of Osbern Bokenham" (Simon Horobin), "Three Marian Texts Including a Prayer for a Lay-Brother in London, British Library, Additional MS 37049" (Marlene Villalobos Hennessy), "Robert Bale, Scrivener and Chronicler of London" (Anne F. Sutton), "'A breif collection of matters of Cronicles': Notes by John Stow in Lambeth Palace Library MS 306" (Christopher Lay), and "Bodleian MS Ashmole 48 and the Ballad Press" (Andrew Taylor). The final pages before the customary "Manuscripts at Auction" (A. S. G. Edwards) provide the text of six typescript notes on significant features of medieval manuscripts, particularly ruling and quiring, made by Neil Ker when, as a conscientious objector, he was working as an Oxford hospital orderly. This (valuable) curiosity is introduced by A. I. Doyle; it is perhaps not intended as part of these *Regional Manuscripts*.

Indeed, the title is the only strange thing about this volume. No allusion is made to the title at all, and it will be clear that the volume is arranged chronologically, not by region (place-names occur in several, but by no means all, the titles above). Quite apart from the fact that regionality (although fashionable) is hardly unusual in Middle English manuscripts, at any rate, there seems no reason to label the volume in this way, and several contributors barely, or never, mention the word "region" (Gillespie is an exception in having "regional transmission" in his title and actually dealing with it in his essay). While his title is not explanatory of region, Spence discusses the provenance of his chronicles; Scott has two sentences on dialect; Horobin associates his very interesting manuscript with Clare in Suffolk (although the title would suggest a far more northerly region); and Hennessy's manuscript comes from Axholme or Beauvale (but we are not told that these are in Lincolnshire). The closest connections of the last three essays are, perforce, with London.

This is not to denigrate the authors of these very valuable essays on a wide range of topics of interest to codicologists. One does question, however, whether they should have been directed more closely to discuss the over-arching focus of the book's title, or, much more simply, the title could have avoided the word "regional" altogether.

Sue Powell, University of Salford

SUSANNA FEIN, ED.
My Wyl and My Wrytyng: Essays on John the Blind Audelay
Kalamazoo, MI: Medieval Institute, 2009. xix + 355 pp. + 2 plates.

This collection of essays edited by Susanna Fein is in some ways a natural sequel to the collection she previously edited for the Medieval Institute, *Studies in the Harley Manuscript: The Scribes, Contents, and Social Contexts of British Library* MS *Harley* 2253. Like the previous collection, *My Wyl and My Wrytyng* investigates the scribes, contents, and social contexts of a single manuscript (Oxford, Bodleian Library MS Douce 302), reevaluating its significance to the histories of literature and of the book in the process. Unlike *Studies in the Harley Manuscript*, however, this collection operates as a companion to *John the Blind Audelay: Poems and Carols: (Oxford, Bodleian Library MS Douce 302)*, the TEAMS volume also edited by Fein. Fein's intention is to renew attention to John the Blind Audelay's book and writing, and to redefine his place in Lancastrian literary culture.

Fein's influence over the collection is palpable—she contributes essays that introduce and conclude the volume—although her influence is perhaps less discernable than Audelay's on Douce 302. Fein's introductory essay, "John Audelay and his Book: Critical Overview and Major Issues," revises our understanding of how Audelay's book is structured and of his place in literary history, while introducing the range of issues that are addressed by the collection's other authors. Fein places Audelay in the company of Thomas Hoccleve, Margery Kempe, and John Lydgate, "writers who sought and wrote themselves into traditional forms (orthodox, hagiographic, Chaucerian)" during the "profound contradiction and uncertainty" of the Lancastrian age. She argues that "Audelay truly fits" because his "oeuvre . . . displays idiosyncratic autobiography, orthodox yet troubled allegiances, authorial proclivities and preoccupations, earnest refashioning of traditions, and dependency on scribal fidelity" (3). She suggests that the "issues to be faced in assessing the significance of the Audelay manuscript are perpetually two-pronged: on the one hand, there is the book itself, and on the other, there is the man it names and gives voice to: John the Blind Audelay" (15).

Some essays in the collection take a comprehensive view of Audelay and his book, while others focus on sections and even individual texts within Audelay's book. Notably, two essays, one by Derek Pearsall and another by Richard Firth Green, consider the influence of William Langland on Audelay and his book, and come to differing conclusions. The essays by Michael J. Bennett, Robert J. Meyer-Lee, and Susan Powell shed light upon Audelay's biography and also on his book as well. Bennett's "John Audelay: Life Records and *Heaven's Ladder*" might be considered a slight misnomer, since the records of Audelay's life are scant and just barely plural, but the essay opens an issue that will claim varying degrees of attention throughout this collection of essays: how can we reconcile the John Audelay who participated "in a bloody affray in a London church on Easter Sunday 1417" (30) with the John Audelay who was chantry priest at Haughmond Abbey in Shropshire, while compiling and perhaps composing the majority of the texts in MS Douce 302? Bennett concludes that "the [life] record of 1417 and the codex of 1426 [Douce 302] obviously inform each other in a biographical sense: they give the participant in the affray in the London church a future, and the poet at Haughmond a past" (38). In "The Vatic Penitent: John Audelay's Self-Representation," Meyer-Lee draws out the details of Audelay's scant biography further and argues that "Audelay's book, therefore, in aim, literary form, and material realization may be understood as the codicological equivalent of a perpetual chantry chapel, although with two crucial changes: in the codex he takes the place of Lord Lestrange, and the reader takes his place" (67). Susan Powell takes a more circumscribed approach to Audelay's writing in "John Audelay and John Mirk: Comparisons and Contrasts," where she does as advertised. She says that Audelay and Mirk were priests who lived close to one another in time and place, and shared an association with the Austin canons. She concludes that whatever the difference between them, the works of both Audelay and Mirk arise within a common medieval culture where true penitence and dying well were important values.

Some of the essays in the collection engage directly with individual texts within the collection or with sections of Audelay's book, and address two other issues relating to Audelay's "wrytyng": how much of his book did Audelay compose, and what were the influences on his composition and compilation practices? The first few of these more narrowly focused essays also concentrate upon the first section of the manuscript, known as the *Counsel of Conscience* or the *Ladder of Heaven*. Oliver Pickering's "The Make-Up of *Counsel of Conscience*" considers the first eighteen works in Douce 302, which Audelay conceived of as a complete work or book, and perhaps originally standalone. Pickering argues not only that this section of the codex was compiled chronologically and that Audelay's poetic ability seems to have declined with age, but also that given the lost opening to the codex, "John Audelay may have been a much more considerable poet than he now appears" (132). Both Derek Pearsall's "Audelay's *Marcolf and Solomon* and the Langlandian Tradition" and Richard Firth Green's "Langland and Audelay" examine the possible influence of *Piers Plowman* on Audelay's alliterative poem *Marcolf and Solomon*. Pearsall, who first wrote about Audelay thirty years ago and argued that *Marcolf and Solomon* was profoundly influenced by Langland and the alliterative traditions that he adapted, has become less sure of direct influence in the interim. He offers "an alternative explanation of the resemblances between *Piers Plowman* and *Marcolf and Solomon*, other than that of direct influence," an alternative influenced partially by a deeper appreciation of the problems of asserting the influence of one medieval text on another where the evidence is "fragmentary at best" (148-149). Green ends where Pearsall began, seeing influence among the fragments of evidence, and reckons that "if we accept this view of Audelay's quest as both a spiritual as well as a literary one, there is one obvious earlier model for him to have drawn on—Will's lifelong search for Saint Truth in *Piers Plowman*" (162). Robert Easterling's essay, "'Choose Yourselves Wither to Go': John Audelay's *Vision of Saint Paul*," examines Audelay's activities as a translator and reveals "the inventiveness with which Audelay Englished and versified this well-known visionary homily" (172).

The rest of the collection focuses on the other three sections of the manuscript identified by Fein. In "John Audelay and the Bridgettines," Martha W. Driver provides some context for a single text in the second section of Douce 302, the so-called "Salutation to Saint Bridget." Driver demonstrates that "as history Audelay's *Salutation to Saint Bridget* . . . refers to topical events in the author's own lifetime, and the stanzas reveal much about the Bridgettine rule and associated ideas, most specifically the promotion and circulation of indulgences" (208). Moreover, Driver concludes that Audelay's poem also functions as an indulgence "and readers are encouraged to pray through its text for Audelay's salvation" (208). In her essay, "Audley's Carol Collection," Julia Boffey tackles the sequence of twenty-five Middle English carols occupying folios 27v–32r of Oxford, Bodleian Library MS Douce 302, which Fein identifies as the third section of the manuscript. Boffey concludes that while the carols collected in this section of the manuscript function "as a semi-autobiographical part of the oeuvre that the manuscript attributes to Audelay," they also "constitute a small anthology of useful pieces" that may very well have been useful to later owners of the manuscript, as well as its original audience (225). By contrast, John C. Hirsch's "'Wo and Werres . . . Rest and Pese': John Audelay's Politics of Peace" focuses on only one of the carols collected in Douce 302, the *Henry VI Carol*. Hirsch asserts not only that the Audelay carol favors Henry VI over his more renowned father, but that it espouses a politics of peace that resembles the work of George Herbert. Hirsch argues that the two poets "shared not only a secular past and a sacred poetic present, but also the Anglican poet's sense of human contingency and divine love, finally liberating categories that applied as equally to king as to commoner" (245). In the collection's penultimate essay, Eric Gerald Stanley writes about "The Alliterative *Three Dead Kings* in John Audelay's MS Douce 302." Stanley surveys Audelay's alliterative practice in *Three Dead Kings* from Douce 302's fourth section in order to re-examine Audelay's disputed authorship. He concludes that "there are no grounds for doubting" Audelay's authorship, in part because "Audelay showed his mastery of the craft of versifying in the poems in MS Douce 302, responding with linguistic and poetic skill to the varied demands made by each verse form and literary kind" (278). Fein ends the collection with "Death and the Colophon in the Audelay Manuscript," which discusses "how the life story and penitential consciousness of a shamed chaplain conjoin with the make-up—especially the drawn-out endings—of Audelay's book"(295).

My Wyl and My Wrytyng succeeds admirably as a companion to the TEAMS volume of Audelay's poems because its essays open up areas and methods of inquiry in MS Douce 302, although they do not provide many definitive answers. In addition, the collection demonstrates why the time has come to reevaluate Audelay and his book: Audelay's self-aware persona makes him interesting to postmodern sensibilities, as well as susceptible to theoretical approaches, and his book makes him interesting to bibliographers and historians of the book.

Bryan P. Davis, Georgia Southwestern State University

PAUL GEHL

Humanism for Sale: Making and Marketing Schoolbooks in Italy, 1450-1650.
http://www.humanismforsale.org/ (accessed 15 Feb. 2010).

Paul F. Gehl, the curator of the John M. Wing Foundation on the History of Printing at the Newberry Library in Chicago, published his first book, *A Moral Art: Grammar, Society, and Culture in Trecento Florence*, in 1993 at Cornell University Press. His second monograph, *Humanism for Sale: Making and Marketing Schoolbooks in Italy*, 1450-1650, serves as a continuation of *A Moral Art*, covering the centuries after the Trecento. However, *Humanism for Sale* is a radically different kind of publishing venture: it is available for free online, will ultimately include some 250 digital photos of the books it discusses, and is open to readers' comments and questions. Therefore, even though the book does not have the imprimatur of a university press, it merits review here not only because it is by an renowned expert in its field but also because its unique form may well provide a model for online publishing by scholars of book history in the future.

Humanism for Sale charts how humanists in the first two centuries of printing marketed and sold their program of educational publishing to the public through what Gehl has called "the long sixteenth century." Although his basic subject is schoolbooks, his study engages with not only specific textbooks that enjoyed great popularity, such as the plays of Terence and the grammar book known as the Donat, but also textbook writers such as the humanist Latin grammarian Antonio Mancinelli and the Jesuit Manuel Alvares. Terence's works receive a good deal of attention early in the book; Gehl discusses not only the manuscript history of the plays but also their early printings in folio, quarto, and smaller formats intended for specialized audiences. Donatus's grammar, commonly called the Donat, was a popular hold-over from the Middle Ages, and pedagogical techniques associated with it were adapted to texts with humanist content. By 1550 numerous pedagogical alternatives had appeared, so the Donat underwent revisions to reflect some of these developments in its sixteenth- and seventeenth-century printings. Even so, it lost its place as the leading grammar textbook to the immensely successful *Syntaxis* by the sixteenth-century Jesuit Manuel Alvares, which remained in print until the late nineteenth century.

According to Gehl, early humanism had to be specially modified and packaged in order to appeal to northern European markets, and among its greatest advertisers was Erasmus, who lent prefatory matter to publishing projects from which he apparently profited. Among these were printed editions of the *Disticha Catonis*, the collection of Latin proverbs that had already been a staple of the grammar school curriculum for centuries. Erasmus's attempt to put his stamp upon this work was consistent with his interest in elaborating upon proverbs, which were considered the building blocks of philosophical discourse.

Gehl discusses the changing contents and pedagogical techniques of textbooks in terms of the politics of the Reformation, and especially the Counter-Reformation, since his focus is on Italy; those politics include, of course, added interest in the intersection of Latin learning and vernacular literacy. Gehl moves well beyond language textbooks to discuss not only extra-curricular books that teach bookkeeping, handwriting, and music, but also emblem books and the so-called *ricettari*, a term initially based on the word for "recipe" in the culinary sense but which broadened to include "how-to" advice, such as home remedies, cleaning agents, and cosmetics. Such books were of special interest to lower-class readers attempting to imitate higher classes, but Gehl also shows that such books had an upper-class readership.

Interspersed in his discussion of general trends in these areas of publishing is a good deal of attention to packaging, presentation, and consumption of this printed material. Gehl masterfully analyzes innovations in typography, page layout, and other physical aspects of the page. He also provides insights into the complex, ever-changing intersection between prefatory or dedicatory material and advertizing, which generally follows the age-old strategy of praising one's own product while insulting one's competitors. Often this prefatory material also suggested likely readers of the texts, and during these two centuries, the readership in most of Italy was growing rapidly because of the rise of vernacular literacy. All of this valuable information is conveyed in a lucid and often witty prose style that makes the book a pleasure to read.

The kind of on-line publishing represented by *Humanism for Sale* offers to scholars of the early book a number of advantages that standard book publishing does not. First, there is the possibility of interactivity. In a recent lecture Gehl described the desirability of interactivity in this way:

My thought was that a monograph on line should be a dynamic object, at least as interactive as a blog. It would be open to comment and addition by readers, and revision by the author. In such a model, moreover, a book written for one purpose and with one audience in mind might also become useful for other audiences. After all, that is one value and pleasure of online files, that they grow and change. And it is typical of the online documentary archives we so admire.

So by using the Word Press blog format augmented by an add-on called Comment Press, he created the format that he thought would work best, and it is fairly user-friendly. Readers who would like to comment must register with their e-mail address, a user name, and a password, and this allows them to comment on any part of the monograph: the text as a whole, a chapter, a section of a chapter, or even a single paragraph. Gehl has responded to a number of these comments, expressing his gratitude for emendations of translations and other corrections. So the monograph is a scholarly dialogue of sorts, directed by Gehl.

The social networking aspect of *Humanism for Sale* pales in comparison to its chief advantage: the monograph at this point has over 200 digital photos of books from the Newberry's holdings that Gehl discusses, and he intends to include up to 250. The illustrations, roughly the same width as the column of text, appear in the text exactly where they are needed, and two clicks on any illustration will enlarge it to full-screen size for viewing details. Needless to say, the prodigious number of illustrations that this format allows and the opportunity to see the digital images enlarged represent enormous advantages over similar material in printed books. (Gehl's position at the Newberry means that he has not had to pay fees for photographs or reproduction rights, so other online books might not provide the wealth of images that this one does.) Yet another advantage of the digital format is the search function, which allows readers to search for any term in the book and thus efficiently eliminates the need for an index.

Even so, there are disadvantages to this online format. For ease of citation and on-screen reading, the chapters are divided into relatively short sections; three chapters have 20 or more sections, each with a different heading. As one reader wrote in a comment, this format tends to fragment Gehl's argument rather than emphasizing its continuities, so the discomfort that some people experience in reading on screen may be augmented by this feature of the work. The other great disadvantage at this point affects the reader less than it does Gehl: tech support. Gehl wanted to use a program with some likelihood of a decent shelf life, and the reason he chose the combination of Word Press and Comment Press was that it was developed and supported by the Institute for the History of the Book, a New York- and London-based group that had an institutional meltdown in December 2008, just as Gehl's book was posted online, and no longer supports the Comment Press program. What that will mean for the long-term availability of Gehl's work remains to be seen.

Gehl's decision to publish digitally anticipates the move from printed books to digital ones at university presses. In March 2009, the University of Michigan Press announced that within two years, 50 of the more than 60 monographs that it publishes each year will be released only in digital editions. Other university presses, including Duke, are making some of their books available through online purchase. These university presses will have print-on-demand services, so readers who do not want to spend hours before a computer screen or a personal reading device such as a Kindle will be able to have a hard copy if they choose to. When university presses begin digital publication in earnest, they will have to take on the responsibility of supporting whatever software they deem to be best suited to their monographs, so that they will not face the kind of problem that Gehl currently confronts. One of the great advantages of digital publication is that more can be published. Thus a university press can pay more attention to a book's contribution to scholarship, rather than simply its potential profit or loss, a concern that has become too common as the economics of print publishing have deteriorated. Interestingly, Gehl's *Humanism for Sale* has appeared in its current form because of worries about its profitability: in spite of the enthusiastic reception of his earlier book *A Moral Art*, he was unable to interest university presses in this book because it was too specialized to sell the 500 copies that now represent a standard press run of a scholarly book.

Paul Gehl's *Humanism for Sale* is worth reading on the basis of its own merits, but also because it behooves scholars to begin to understand the options that are available in online publishing, including the decision of whether or not to make online books interactive. If work on the history of the book is to derive maximum benefit from the inevitable shift to digital publication, then scholars in the field need to make their preferences known to university presses. Otherwise, they will make the same mistakes that Gutenberg made in the last great technological shift from manuscript to print: Gutenberg was too concerned with making his books look like manuscripts to explore unique possibilities presented by the new technology. If we do not take a hand in the online publishing revolution, we may be condemned to an analogous conservatism in which online books are reproduced as dead PDFs and exploit none of the exciting possibilities of digital publications that Gehl's *Humanism for Sale* does.

Edward Wheatley, Loyola University, Chicago

RALPH HANNA, ED.
The Knightly Tale of Golagros and Gawane.
Scottish Text Society, Fifth Series, Volume 7.
Woodbridge: Scottish Text Society, 2008. xlv + 145 pp.

Ralph Hanna's edition of the alliterative romance, *The Knightly Tale of Golagros and Gawane*, made a timely appearance in 2008: this text is known only from a single source, a pamphlet (STC 11984) printed in Edinburgh in 1508, which is now bound with ten other small printed books in National Library of Scotland, Advocates MS 19.1.16. Hanna's introduction begins with a discussion of the 1508 print and its producers, Walter Chepman and Androw Myllar, who are the first printers known to have operated in Scotland. A royal patent from King James IV gave these men an astonishingly wide remit: they were licensed to print law books, acts of parliament, chronicles, liturgical books, "and al utheris bukes that sal be sene necessar, and to sel the sammyn for competent pricis" (p. xiii). As well as printing books "efter the use of our realme" (p. xiii), they were privileged to import foreign books without incurring duty, giving them an advantage in the market. Hanna stresses Myllar's connections with Rouen and suggests that some of the errors in the 1508 print of *Golagros* may be attributed to his French laborers' lack of familiarity with both Scots secretary script and the artificial poetic language of Middle Scots. The introduction also covers matters of language and date: while acknowledging that the poem could have been composed at any time between the 1420s and 1508, on linguistic grounds Hanna favors a date in the final quarter of the fifteenth century. The text's sources are also discussed. The poem is believed to be derived from a later prose redaction of the *Conte de Graal*, the first continuation to Chrétien de Troyes's *Perceval*, but Hanna argues for the much greater influence of another source, the early fifteenth-century romance *The Awntyrs off Arthure*. He also claims that the latter may have had a Scots provenance even though the four surviving manuscripts demonstrate evidence of circulation only within England.

This edition is not all Hanna's own work. As the title-page acknowledges, the edition is based upon materials collected by the late W. R. J. Barron, and the preface very clearly demarcates which sections are to be attributed to which editor. At the time of his death in 2005, Barron had produced a punctuated transcription of the text which incorporated many provisional emendations; Hanna's version of the text has retained almost all of these. As Hanna notes (p. xxxviii), producing a critical edition of a text which survives only in a single witness is a "completely hypothetical endeavour," though he is able to rely upon his considerable knowledge of the diction and conventions of alliterative poetry to tackle transmissional errors. All emended readings are clearly signalled in a separate list. The glossary, initiated by Barron, has been completed and extended by Hanna who has also single-handedly compiled the extensive textual commentary. I noticed one typo, on p. xxxi: "for what generally been" should read "for what have generally been."

Margaret Connolly, University of St Andrews

LOTTE HELLINGA, ED.

Printing in England in the Fifteenth Century: E. Gordon Duff's Bibliography with Supplementary Descriptions, Chronologies and a Census of Copies. London: The Bibliographical Society and The British Library, 2009. xvii + 278 pp. 53 B&W illustrations.

Under the slightly misleading title of *Printing in England in the Fifteenth Century*, Lotte Hellinga has given us a handsome revised edition of E. Gordon Duff's *Fifteenth Century English Books*, a landmark catalogue and study of the incunabula that were printed either in England or on the continent for the English market. Hellinga's *rifacimento*—in many ways, a poor man's *Catalogue of Books Printed in the XVth Century Now in the British Library, XI: England* [= BMC XI], published in 2007 and currently available for €1325—is divided into five main sections: (1) a facsimile reprint of Duff's 1917 edition, selectively revised with strike-outs and insertions on pages 8 (no. 28), 22 (no. 79), 24 (no. 88), 78 (no. 278), 94 (no. 339), and 100 (no. 361); (2) a 46-item supplement listing fifteen complete or substantially complete books (nos. 1, 7, 11, 26, 27, 31, 32, 35–37, 40–42, 45, 46), twelve indulgences, many of which are fragmentary or damaged (nos. 13–24), twelve fragments of devotional, grammatical, legal, literary, liturgical, and other works (nos. 3–6, 12, 28, 29, 33, 38, 39, 43, 44), three items known only from offsets or a faint double impression (nos. 2, 8, 9), and four replacements for original Duff entries (nos. 10, 25, 30, 34); (3) fifty-three pages of plates reprinted from Duff's edition but updated with new captions reflecting the typographical discoveries reported in BMC XI; (4) an index of all of the more than 470 items by printing house, including those on the continent; and (5) a revised concordance and census of copies. The relatively small number of additions, most of which have been familiar to experts for decades, shows just how little was left for Hellinga's rake after Duff's broom.

Most people who consult this catalogue will probably be interested in the revised dates assigned to a large number of items, a consequence of the painstaking research undertaken for BMC XI. In fact, a copy of the latter is essential for making sense of Hellinga's shorthand references to types, initial alphabets, and devices, and serious users of Duff can look forward to routine trips to their local research library, at least until BMC XI becomes available in a handier format. From my own notes, I can already offer one revision of consequence: STC 1987 (Duff 44), the celebrated fragment of *Bevis of Hampton* in the Bodleian Library (Douce Fragm. e.13), was not printed by Wynkyn de Worde around 1500—as has also been suggested by Alan Coates, et al., A *Catalogue of Books Printed in the Fifteenth Century now in the Bodleian Library*, Oxford (2005), II, 700–01 (B-591)—but rather by Hugh Goes around 1506. The entry for Duff 44 should therefore be revised on the model of Duff 361 (STC 13689.3—mistakenly referred to as STC 13687 on page 265), where another reattribution to Goes is duly noted.

As far as the other information in this catalogue is concerned, a few general comments are warranted. Since connecting catalogue entries to actual STC items is a perennial problem for rare book researchers, the inclusion of shelfmarks in the revised census, which appears to have been compiled partly from unverified sources, would have been welcome. Despite diligent searching and repeated enquiries, I have never been able to locate the following three listed copies of extremely rare editions: STC 15882 (Duff 188) at Gonville and Caius College, Cambridge (probably misplaced), STC 16254 (Duff 355) at Corpus Christi College, Cambridge (probably misplaced), and STC 17962 (Duff 307) at King's College, Cambridge (most likely a phantom). The absence of such unique identifiers also complicates Hellinga's proposal to distinguish copies of the same edition by Duff and census number. Which of the three British Library copies of STC 1536 (Duff 40), for instance, would be intended by 40.12, 40.13, and 40.14, assuming that 40.15 is reserved for the fragment at C.18.d.9(292)? The situation is not clarified by ISTC or the BL integrated catalogue, which list only two copies of this book in the library (IB.55241, IB.55242) in addition to the fragment.

The heavy burden of tradition makes itself felt in Hellinga's work, and one might say that this catalogue takes a remarkably old-fashioned approach to the study of England's earliest books. Mentioned only in passing—if mentioned at all—are the major digital resources that twenty-first century bibliographers have come to rely on, most notably EEBO (Early English Books Online), ESTC (English Short Title Catalogue), and ISTC (Incunabula Short Title Catalogue), all of which convey a great deal of relevant or duplicated information, and often for free. My alternative vision for "Duff redux" would have been an open-access and fully searchable website with individual bibliographical records containing the relevant information from Duff plus, at minimum, a complete high-resolution digital scan of every item (the best copy where multiple copies exist), a list of locations with verified shelfmarks, and a comment box where other experts could add their own emendations, notices, queries, etc., for possible incorporation into the permanent record. This online cataloguing model would go a long way towards melting the ice block of print publication and harnessing the widely dispersed energies and expertise of bibliographers, literary scholars, rare book cataloguers, and other historians of the book. It would also facilitate the mammoth task of verifying the conclusions reached in BMC XI.

Known for his uncompromising standards and irascible character, Duff left his position as librarian of the John Rylands Library in 1900, eventually earning a living from his own publications as well as from dabbling in the rare book trade. (In 1924, he died a wealthy man, leaving an estate valued at £16,242, approximately equivalent to £487,000, according to <http://www.nationalarchives.gov.uk/currency/>, or £690,000, according to <http://www.measuringworth.com>.) I am confident that Duff would have been flattered by Hellinga's bibliographical *homage*, which serves as an effective portal to more up-to-date scholarship on English incunabula, but I am equally confident that his own revision of *Fifteenth Century English Books* would have looked very different.

Joseph J. Gwara, US Naval Academy

DANIEL HOBBINS
*Authorship and Publicity Before Print: Jean Gerson
and the Transformation of Late Medieval Learning.*
Philadelphia: University of Pennsylvania Press, 2009. 335 pp.

The corpus of work devoted to Jean Gerson (1363–1429), the famed chancellor of the University of Paris and leading light of the Council of Constance, has expanded in recent decades as the desire to provide a unitary outlook on his career has grown more pressing. The multiplicity of roles that he performed and the amount of his writing that is preserved complicate the task, as indeed does the growth of scholarship, focusing on aspects of his achievement as diverse as his re-evaluation of Ockhamist covenant theology and his promotion of the cult of St Joseph. Brian Patrick McGuire and Gilbert Ouy have both made attempts to place a more singular definition on Gerson: the recent biography written by the former, *Jean Gerson and the Last Medieval Reformation* (2005), besides providing a detailed chronological summary, attempted to piece together certain aspects of Gerson's character, while Ouy has drawn on certain literary traits within his writing to define him as a "humanist." Daniel Hobbins also wishes to bridge the divisions that have "left Gerson unintelligible as a single, coherent historical actor" (7). His approach, embodied in *Authorship and Publicity*, certainly draws much impetus from the manuscript-led methodology pioneered by Ouy, but it also emerges as unique and arguably more intuitive than the paths forged by his contemporaries. He draws our attention to the Gerson who is most readily apparent through the sea of manuscripts and texts, Gerson the prolific writer. He aims, moreover, to place the Chancellor and his works within a distinctive later medieval culture of writing, notably avoiding the "humanist" label applied by Ouy or alternatively that of "scholastic." "Writing," Hobbins states, "unifies his life and thought, just as it links Gerson to the cultural landscape that produced him" (7). The literary and textual culture in which Gerson existed indeed proves to be as important a focus for the work as the man himself.

The introduction presents a promising argument, that the intellectual culture surrounding Gerson produced a greater interest in viewing writings in relation to their writers and in the form and manner of their distribution than is apparent with schoolmen of preceding generations. Here, Hobbins also pre-empts the more controversial, but nevertheless stimulating, arguments contained in his work, that we can speak of Gerson as an "author" and moreover as a "public intellectual" "publishing" his works. Chapter 1 unveils Gerson "the bookman." Having far greater access to books than a thirteenth-century schoolman, the Chancellor and his contemporaries became more concerned to identify works in their original form, to treat them in their entirety, and to associate them with the qualities of their writers. Gerson promoted books that were approved by age, that upheld a consistent and accepted terminology throughout, that did not divorce speculation from applied ethical questions, and that were written by men who blended learning with upright life and piety. Chapter 2 frames the place Gerson saw for himself as an "author," or at least as the writer of those short works that Hobbins defines as "tracts." Despite his strong desire to delineate a "common school of theological truth" founded on a long existing canon, Gerson was nevertheless anxious to find a place for the writer of his own day, focusing on the application of moral theology to contemporary affairs in these shorter texts. Gerson also wrote longer, more unifying, and more esoteric works, as well as a swath of poetry, especially in his later career, and chapter 3 handles a cluster of such writings, those he wrote in exile and at Lyon (between 1418 and 1429). Such writings he could only justify more thinly, as a concession to those bored of reading the same, old material, nevertheless he drew strength at this point in his career from the "ideal of permanence, the prospect of lasting writing" (73) that he saw in the older writings he so admired. The analyses offered here are noteworthy because they undoubtedly open windows for further study of such little known works as the Monotessaron, the Treatise on songs, and the Compilation on the Magnificat.

The fourth chapter forms the hinge of the book, drawing our attention to how Gerson tailored the style of his writing. The Chancellor saw rhetoric as "another logic," an alternative and independent corollary to the "pure logic" he thought recent schoolmen to be too reliant upon. Gerson certainly saw a place for the latter, but he especially disapproved of its use before untrained audiences, who would only be confused by it. Rhetoric, on the other hand, could serve a "deep moral purpose" of the sort that speculative logic could not, "to stir the passions through preaching and writing" (116). Here, Hobbins is able to offer a well-argued critique of Ouy's definition of Gerson as a humanist, arguing that such an approach to literary style reflected "not a story of declining scholasticism or of nascent humanism, but of challenge and adaptation" (125), as schoolmen like Gerson were able to find wider audiences than ever before.

The final three chapters evoke both the manner in which Gerson's work was distributed to this audience and his interest in this process. Chapter 5 details how Gerson and some of his contemporaries broke free from the established forms favored by the writers of the university, in writing "tracts," short treatises often designed to be contained within a single quire, which could be disseminated readily. Chapter 6 describes how Gerson's concern to write for prompt distribution distinguished him from those vernacular and humanist authors who wrote for patrons and moreover reveals his concern for the integrity of his works, both in form and in interpretation, throughout the process of their distribution. His *De laude scriptorum* encourages devoted and careful scribal practice, but Gerson sought moreover to "authorize" texts in circulation. Hobbins draws our attentions again beyond the printed editions, where rubrics and other apparatus such as indices, tables, and even diagrams are treated "like so much scribal rubble accumulated over the centuries and hindering our encounter with the naked text" (169), and back to the manuscripts. Our attention is drawn to the rubrics of the *Monotessaron*, which are organized in a table of contents with corresponding Gospel references, and to the mnemonic verse to aid the memorization of its contents; Gerson himself most likely created these himself since he accurately described them in a letter to a Celestine monk. Such devices did more than just aid memory or enable the work to serve as a reference tool: they also attempted to place constraints on how the work was read and understood. Through a careful comparison of manuscripts, it is also asserted that Gerson himself promoted his colophon to the head of the text in at least four works, an act which served to further associate the writing with the identity of the author and the historical context of its composition. His occasional attempts to correct and edit texts are also brought to life in the same manner. Chapter 7 deals with the means by which Gerson's works found such a wide contemporary readership in most quarters of the West within the lifetime of the writer. Hobbins shows a considerable grasp of the manuscript tradition behind the surviving texts in outlining how they were given an audience throughout most quarters of the West through exchange at the church councils of Constance and Basel and also via the labors of the Carthusian and French Celestine orders and the Benedictine congregation of Melk. Throughout these chapters, the reader's impression of this distinctive world of later medieval writing and manuscript exchange is strengthened by a number of evocative illustrations, such as the startling reproductions of the textual and diagrammatic apparatus employed in certain manuscripts, and maps charting the early spread of Gerson texts. The volume concludes with a useful appendix listing the manuscripts derived from Carthusian and Celestine collections that contain his works.

Authorship and Publicity certainly has much to commend it, and should be considered a fine volume. Hobbins's analysis of Gerson "the writer" emerges as the most convincing overview to date of the Chancellor of Paris and his career, as it is the one that sits most naturally with the textual evidence. But perhaps the greatest strength of this approach is its ability to securely contextualize a nevertheless vibrant and unique character within his times. Whereas the psychoanalytical tendencies of McGuire and the "humanist" label applied by Ouy have arguably made it more difficult to place Gerson in his own times, he is here described within a distinctive later medieval literary and textual culture, largely avoiding such difficulties. Hobbins's effort to understand "the late fourteenth and early fifteenth centuries as a distinct cultural period" (12) is laudable, and it is nowhere more effective than in his exposition of the growing and vibrant world of manuscript production and distribution in this era. The textual culture described here, that which allowed Gerson to reach audiences that earlier schoolman could not have imagined, would of course be radically transformed by print, but might also be said to have given birth to it: above all, as Hobbins emphasizes, it was no mere last gasp of a medieval manuscript culture, nor a simple prototype for the world of the printing press, but possessed a character of its own. It is a character that the influence of Elizabeth Eisenstein has often obscured; in *Authorship and Publicity*, however, it emerges vividly. Given the successes of the book in this area, eyebrows might be raised at the use of terms such as "publishing," "author," and "public intellectual," which, in spite of strong efforts to contextualize them, ultimately draw the mind to later times, but even terms like these will provide worthy fuel for future debate and are not stressed so far as to seriously distort the analysis. Rather, the emphasis throughout remains simple but expressive – focused on Gerson, the writer of his times. The result is a book that will not only please Gerson specialists but also scholars across a broad field of study. Those with interests in textual culture will certainly be enlightened by this fine work, which resists presupposed models of transition in the later Middle Ages.

Robert Shaw, Oriel College, Oxford

EMMA LIPTON
*Affections of the Mind: The Politics of Sacramental Marriage
in Late Medieval English Literature.*
Notre Dame, IN: University of Notre Dame Press, 2007. 246 pp.

In what sense is marriage a Christian sacrament? *The Catholic Encyclopedia* quotes Calvin and Luther's denials that it was any such thing. They concede that it was "instituted by God," "good and holy" (Calvin), and that it may be a "figure of Christ and the Church" (Luther), but they cannot find any Scriptural foundation for considering it a sacrament. In the later Middle Ages, it was generally accepted that marriage *was* a sacrament, but there was no clear agreement as to how and why. Did it consist in the words of the marriage vow, the inner consent of bride and groom, the love between them, their life together, or the priest's blessing? Did it involve sexual union? There was no consensus among theologians and jurists, as Christopher Brooke and James Brundage have shown, and even greater confusion at the pastoral level.

In this original and thought-provoking book, Emma Lipton nods towards this chaotic state of affairs but asserts that the sacrament had a clear "orthodox definition," expressed by Hugh of Saint Victor: it did not involve the priest or sexual union, but instead free consent, love, and mutuality. This assertion underpins her central claim, that the sacramental status of marriage was used by the lay middle strata of late medieval England to create a new vision of their place in the world. Since marriage was a sacrament, lay married people could assert their claim to virtue and piety alongside the clergy. Since marriage could involve a horizontal, mutual view of social relations, it provided an embryonic social vision, and, Lipton argues, marriage itself was the middle-strata alternative to the aristocratic adultery of courtly love. Moreover, the texts exploring these ideas introduced new, generically hybrid forms that threw off the conventions of aristocratic and clerical tradition.

Some of these claims are pushed too far here. Given the real controversies surrounding marriage as a sacrament, it would seem to offer unstable ground on which to build a coherent social model, and the argument of the book tends to falter whenever it comes to pinning down the social implications of particular presentations of marriage. The "middle strata" also fail to convince, in this formulation, as a clear social class in need of a distinctive ideology, which is unsurprising, given that the four writers considered are John Gower (described in what records we have as squire and "armiger"), the sometime courtly poet Geoffrey Chaucer, and the probably clerical compiler of the N-Town manuscript, alongside the more straightforwardly bourgeois Margery Kempe. However, taken individually, the four chapters offer compelling investigations of the ideologies of marriage in Chaucer's "Franklin's Tale," Gower's *Traitié pour essampler les amantz marietz*, the N-Town Mary plays, and *The Book of Margery Kempe*.

The surprising shift from Arveragus and Dorigen's marriage to the relations between the three men at the end of the "Franklin's Tale" provides a good starting point for the argument that marriage is being used to discuss social relations in medieval literature. "Married Friendship: An Ideology for the Franklin" is most valuable in its presentation of new evidence that the marriage at the center of the "Franklin's Tale" is based on traditions of friendship; it is less persuasive in its claim that friendship governs the happy ending of the tale or that this amounts to "an egalitarian social vision." I was ultimately unconvinced, moreover, that Arveragus and Dorigen's marriage is either a rejection of aristocratic values or a sacrament.

"Public Voice, Private Life: Marriage and Masculinity in John Gower's *Traitié*" discusses Gower's little-read French ballade sequence. Lipton shows that Gower offers, to an audience that he clearly constructs as male, an ideology of sexual self-regulation within marriage that he presents as spiritually superior to military conquest. At the same time, he rejects the courtly love of romance as sinful and inconstant. This in itself is striking, but it is hard to agree that this French poem with Latin glosses, which deals for the most part with the acts of kings and the nobility, is really about and for the middle strata. In fact, given that most of the poem is dedicated to harping on the evils of adultery, it is remarkably difficult to read from it any marital ideology beyond sexual continence. Lipton's claim that the poem's focus on adultery and rape "shifts power to the lay realm" because these crimes happened to be the province of both civil and ecclesiastical courts reads as a rather farfetched basis for a new vision of society, particularly since divine justice is far more prominent than civil justice in the poem.

The next chapter, "Performing Reform: Marriage, Lay Piety, and Sacramental Theater in the N-Town Mary Plays," turns away from civic virtue to present some fascinating material on the positive valuation of marriage in these plays. In "The Marriage of Mary and Joseph," the merits of marriage versus virginity are overtly discussed and marriage is commended, and Lipton shows that marital love is presented in "Joachim and Anna" as a locus for piety that functions as an alternative to the corruption of the temple. Lollard claims that marriage was superior to celibacy are interestingly connected to the plays' East Anglian origin, though Lipton does not claim that the plays are Lollard. Again, the argument is perhaps taken too far when Lipton contends that the play invokes the idea of lay people performing the sacraments because Mary's parents bless the marriage and because, in performance, lay actors performed clerical roles.

Finally, "The Marriage of Love and Sex: Margery Kempe and Bourgeois Lay Identity" discusses how Margery uses her experience of earthly marriage to develop her sense of mystical marriage to God, and how the traditions about marriage and sex inherited by Margery create complications both in her life and in her *Book*. On the religious side, Margery's experience of the affection and intimacy of marriage allows her to create a distinctive account of her mystical marriage to God. On the earthly side, Margery seems to start off with a typically bourgeois affectionate and supportive marriage, and Lipton examines why she comes to portray it as sexually coercive. She identifies conflicts between the marriage sacrament and the doctrine of marital debt and suggests that sexual coercion brings Margery's story into conformity with the rhetoric of the lives of other holy women.

Affections of the Mind makes some large claims that will not persuade all readers. But by showing how the complexities of late medieval marriage ideology provided new ways of thinking about lay religion and the individual's place in society, Lipton has opened up each of her chosen texts in new and stimulating ways; her exemplary bibliography will help interested readers to think more about these subjects.

Cathy Hume, University of Leeds

R. M. THOMSON
A *Descriptive Catalogue of the Medieval Manuscripts*
of Merton College, Oxford, with a description
of the Greek Manuscripts by N. G. Wilson.
Cambridge: for Merton College, Oxford, by D. S. Brewer, 2009.
488 pp. 18 color plates. 92 B&W illustrations.

This splendid volume is the latest in the series of Rodney Thomson's catalogues of medieval manuscripts in British libraries. He has already covered the cathedrals of St Alban's, Lincoln, Worcester, and Hereford, but this production is the most splendid of them all, partly through two generous bequests. There are 18 color plates of manuscript illuminations and a further 92 in black and white, which, apart from manuscript text, include photographs of Merton College Library itself, interior and exterior, and a variety of interesting phenomena, such as the fourteenth-century book-chest (where pledges were deposited), the bindings and clasps of some of the volumes, inscriptions, explicits, pledge notes (*cautiones*), and other fascinating material. The preface by the librarian of Merton notes that during his visits to the College, "Professor Thomson's lively accounts of discoveries, and even of vexing textual and codicological tangles, inspired in widely diverse members of the College an enthusiastic interest in the manuscripts and in the progress of the catalogue." That enthusiasm is conveyed in the clever choice of these illustrations to the catalogue.

In introducing the book, one need only paraphrase the first paragraph of Thomson's introduction, which is admirably lucid and pertinent. Merton College Library contains 328 medieval, mainly Latin, manuscripts, dating from the ninth to the late fifteenth centuries, plus many fragments dating from about 1550 to 1625. This is more than other Oxford college libraries, except Balliol, but less than the great Cambridge collections—Trinity, for example, has nearly 1,500 items. It is important, however, because most of the manuscripts are survivals of the medieval library, because many of them have *ex dono* inscriptions, because excellent archival records survive (23 booklists), and because the "New Library" (now the Old Library) is the oldest (late fourteenth-century) functioning library in Western Europe.

The introduction is organized chronologically: "From the Beginnings until the Late Fourteenth Century," "William Reed and the 'New Library'," "The Fifteenth Century," "Reviewing the Medieval Library," "Religious Upheaval and the Coming of Print," "From the Seventeenth Century until Modern Times," "Former Catalogues," and "This One," the last title suggesting the general informality and readability of the catalogue as a whole. One risks reproducing the whole introduction in an attempt to describe its interest and range. Suffice it to say that the history of the library is a microcosm of the history of college libraries in general and that Thomson comes up with many interesting and even exciting facts on book chests, *ex libris* and *ex dono* inscriptions, book distribution, wardens and fellows, booklists, authors, furniture, Marian visitations, vandalism, catalogues, and much more.

The catalogue itself provides comprehensive descriptions of the 328 manuscripts (structure, contents, hands, decoration, history, bibliography), followed by brief descriptions of the fragments, including (separately catalogued) those "still in printed books, not mentioned above." Appendix A covers the three Greek manuscripts, Appendix B the 151 extracts relating to the books and library from the Merton account rolls, Appendix C Bale's account of the books he found in the Merton College Library, and Appendix D the section on 289 Merton manuscripts in Thomas James' *Ecloga* (as annotated by Neil Ker). There is a page index of manuscripts, early printed books, and records, followed by a general index. The latter might be fuller and would be much improved if it included all the names for which Thomson gives details in the "History" section of each manuscript entry. It is also a pity that it does not include the plates. For this, perhaps one must await the online version that the Merton College librarian promises in his preface.

However, my wish is not to cavil with this impressive work. Intended to appeal to alumni, as well as academics, it must satisfy both, a difficult and unusual task to accomplish successfully. Thomson is to be congratulated!

Sue Powell, University of Salford

R. M. THOMSON
From Manuscript to Print.
Hobart: University of Tasmania Press, 2008.
125 pp. 200 color plates.

This publication is the catalogue of an exhibition of pre-1600 books that was held at the Morris Miller Library, University of Tasmania, Hobart, from December 2008 to January 2009. Unlike Thomson's other catalogue reviewed here, this one describes a tiny library of medieval manuscripts and incunables. However, the catalogue is very well produced, with at least one (and generally more) color illustrations of every one of the exhibits, eight of which are from the State Library of Tasmania, which has twenty-eight pre-1600 books or fragments, and one from St David's Cathedral. Illustrations are of all sizes, often crammed onto sometimes margin-less pages, though not to disadvantage—the book is beautifully designed and photographed, and ample room is given for the text. Where of interest, the binding is showcased; indeed, "showcase" is a perfect description of this catalogue. One can appreciate the books much better and see more of them than in many an exhibition vitrine.

Part of the collection, and most of the pre-1600 material, came to the university very recently, when it gained the early library of Christ College, which disbanded in 1856, only ten years after its founding, but which has undergone various reincarnations since. A remarkable collection of early printed books had been acquired by the college from the Rev. Robert Rowland Davies, Archdeacon of Hobart. Despite making it clear that "I cannot afford to give them to the college," he appears never to have been paid for his 222 titles, and only seventeen of the fifty-three pre-1600 books survive. Later in the century, the college suffered bad losses through fire, and in 1971 through theft. All but one of the early books which were at the college then are now safely stored in the university library once more. The other main source of the university collection came through donations of printed classical texts (but no incunables) by Robert Dunbabin, Professor of Classics in the first half of the twentieth century, who donated twenty pre-1600 books, and his contemporary, Frank Woodward, who, after a strange career, retired to Tasmania and left the University 337 books (fourteen from the period 1553–1601).

The collection may therefore seem parochial and the product of happenstance: the books themselves were largely picked up in bookshops, and elsewhere, by their owners. However, it has examples (sometimes only a page) of most of the main European presses (barring Spain), notable early copies of classical texts, and several original or early bindings. The catalogue entries are arranged chronologically, from a manuscript fragment of a Passional of about 1150 (acquired by Thomson himself), through five other manuscripts, twelve incunables (one a single leaf from Caxton's edition of the *Polychronicon*, STC 13438), with the remaining entries (pages 39–116) covering books from 1505 to 1590, ending with Ortelius' *Theatri Orbis Terrarum* printed by Plantin at Antwerp (over a dozen illustrations). A chronological handlist of the pre-1600 books owned by the university and the State Library of Tasmania ends the volume.

Sue Powell, University of Salford

About the Authors

Virginia Blanton is Associate Professor of English at the University of Missouri-Kansas City, where she serves as doctoral faculty in English and Religious Studies. Her research focuses on medieval hagiography and religious ritual. She is the author of *Signs of Devotion: The Cult of St. Æthelthryth in Medieval England*, 695-1615 (2007), which was awarded the Society of Medieval Feminist Scholarship First Book Prize in 2008. She is also co-editor of *Intertexts: Studies in Anglo-Saxon Culture Presented to Paul E. Szarmach* (2008).

Emily Butler is a doctoral candidate at the Centre for Medieval Studies in the University of Toronto. She will defend her dissertation, "Textual Community and Linguistic Distance in Early England," in April 2010. Her most recent publication is "Alfred and the Children of Israel in the Prose Psalms," *Notes and Queries* 57.1 (2010): 10-17. She is currently at work on a study of a series of short texts from Cambridge, Corpus Christi College, MS 201, as well as an edition of Matthew Parker's editorial prefaces. She is serving for the first time as Associate Editor for the *Journal of the Early Book Society*.

Margaret Connolly teaches at the University of St Andrews and is a general editor of the Middle English Texts series. Her most recent publication is *Index of Middle English Prose, Handlist XIX: Manuscripts in the University Library, Cambridge (Dd-Oo)* (2009). She has also published editions of Middle English religious prose texts; the monograph *John Shirley: Book Production and the Noble Household in Fifteenth-Century England* (1998); and, jointly with Linne Mooney, a collection of essays, *Design and Distribution of Late Medieval Manuscripts in England* (2008).

Linda P. Cummins is Associate Professor and Coordinator of Musicology at the University of Alabama, Tuscaloosa. Her most recent publication is "The *Compendium musicale per presbyterum Nicolaum de Capua ordinatum*: A New Text," with Jan Herlinger (*Il saggiatore musicale*, 2008). She has also published the monograph *Debussy and the Fragment* (2006) and "Correr 336, Part 4: A New Compendium of Late Medieval Music Theory" (*Philomusica online*, 2005-06).

Bryan P. Davis is a Professor of English and Director of Institutional Effectiveness and Planning at Georgia Southwestern State University. His interests include the reception of Chaucer and Langland during the fifteenth and sixteenth centuries, as well as modern electronic media as vehicles for teaching and studying the medieval period and its literature. His current research explores scribal handling of the early *Piers Plowman* C-manuscripts and Chaucer in the contemporary English education curriculum.

Martha W. Driver is Distinguished Professor of English and Women's and Gender Studies at Pace University in New York City. A co-founder of the Early Book Society for the study of manuscripts and printing history, she writes about illustration from manuscript to print, book production, and the early history of publishing. In addition to publishing some 45 articles in these areas, she has edited sixteen journals over thirteen years, including *Film & History: Medieval Period in Film* and the *Journal of the Early Book Society*. Her books about pictures (from manuscript miniatures to woodcuts to film) include *The Image in Print: Book Illustration in Late Medieval England* (British Library Publications and University of Toronto), *An Index of Images in English MSS*, fascicle four, with Michael Orr (Brepols), and *The Medieval Hero on Screen* and *Shakespeare and the Middle Ages*, with Sid Ray (McFarland).

Carl James Grindley is Associate Professor of English at The City University of New York and is an adjunct editor of the *Piers Plowman* Electronic Archive. His most recent publications are: "'We're Everyone You Depend On': Filming Shakespeare's Peasants," in Martha Driver and Sid Ray's volume *Shakespeare and the Middle Ages*, and "The Black Death in Filmed Versions of *Romeo and Juliet* and *Twelfth Night*" in Melissa Croteau and Carolyn Jess-Cooke's *Apocalyptic Shakespeare*. Both collections were published by McFarland in 2009.

Joseph J. Gwara is Professor of Spanish at the United States Naval Academy. In 2008, the Bibliographical Society of America awarded him the first annual Katharine F. Pantzer Senior Fellowship in Bibliography and the British Book Trades.

Ralph Hanna is Professor of Palaeography, Faculty of English Language and Literature, at the University of Oxford. His recent publications include editions for the Early English Text Society, *Richard Rolle: Uncollected Verse and Prose, with Related Northern Texts* (o.s. 329, 2007) and *Speculum Vitae: A Reading, Editions I and II* (o.s. 331-2, 2008).

Joni Henry is a PhD candidate at the University of Cambridge researching the production and circulation of saints' lives in the fifteenth century in manuscripts and early printed books. She is supervised by Daniel Wakelin.

Simon Horobin is a Reader in the Faculty of English and Tutor and Fellow in English, Magdalen College, University of Oxford. He has published widely on Middle English literary manuscripts of the fifteenth century.

Cathy Hume is a Teaching Fellow at the University of Leeds. Her book *Love, Marriage, Flirtation: Competing Cultures and Chaucer's Poetry* is forthcoming.

Michael P. Kuczynski teaches at Tulane University, New Orleans in the English Department and Medieval and Early Modern Studies Program. His research for several years has focused on the use of the Psalms in medieval England. He has published a book on this topic, *Prophetic Song: The Psalms as Moral Discourse in Late Medieval England* (Philadelphia: University of Pennsylvania Press, 1995), and is currently completing an edition of a Lollard commentary on the Psalter from Bodleian Library, Oxford, MS Bodley 554. He is also compiling a volume on Middle English religious and secular lyrics for the revision of Wells and Severs, *A Manual of the Writings in Middle English, 1050-1500*.

Helen Marshall is a graduate student at the University of Toronto whose work combines the traditional bibliographical fields of codicology and palaeography with literary analysis. Her conference papers have addressed the manuscripts and texts of early Middle English works including the romances of the Auchinleck manuscript, the *South English Legendary*, and the *Canterbury Tales*.

Linne R. Mooney is Professor in Medieval English Palaeography at the University of York. She works on late-medieval English scribes and currently heads an Arts and Humanities Research Council project to study the scribes who copied works of Geoffrey Chaucer, John Gower, William Langland, John Trevisa and Thomas Hoccleve. As the editor of *Nota Bene*: Brief Notes on Manuscripts and Early Printed Books, she is a regular contributor to JEBS.

Bridget Morris was formerly Senior Lecturer in Scandinavian Studies at the University of Hull. She is the author of several articles and books on St. Birgitta and medieval Swedish literature; she is currently editor-in-chief of the English translation of the entire Birgittine corpus that is being published by Oxford University Press, New York (2006-).

Daniel W. Mosser is Professor of English at Virginia Tech. He is co-editor and co-creator of the Thomas L. Gravell Watermark Archive (www.gravell.org), author of the "Witness Descriptions" on the *Canterbury Tales* Project's digital editions, co-editor of *Puzzles in Paper*, and the author of articles on Middle English manuscripts, fifteenth-century paper stocks, and Chaucer incunabula. His *A Digital Catalogue of the Manuscripts and Pre-1500 Editions of the Canterbury Tales* is nearing publication and will appear on CD and the Web.

Veronica O'Mara is a senior lecturer in the Department of English at the University of Hull. Her research concentrates on medieval religious prose, female literacy, and the relationship between manuscript and print. Her most recent publications are *Four Middle English Sermons Edited from British Library* MS *Harley* 2268, Middle English Texts, 33 (Heidelberg: Universitätsverlag C. Winter, 2002), and with Suzanne Paul, A *Repertorium of Middle English Prose Sermons*, 4 volumes (Turnhout: Brepols, 2007).

Sue Powell holds a Chair in Medieval Texts and Culture at the University of Salford, where she teaches the history of the English language, Chaucer, and medieval Arthurian literature. As review editor for JEBS, she regularly contributes several reviews to each issue. Her essay 'What Caxton did to the Festial" appeared in JEBS 1 (1997). Her research interests are in manuscripts and early printed books, with particular relation to late medieval and Tudor preaching and devotional texts.

Geoff Rector teaches in the English Department at the University of Ottawa. His most recent publications deal with twelfth-century Psalter translations, the architecture and sociabilities of early Anglo-Norman literature, as well as studies of Jordan Fantosme's *Chronicle* and Geffrei Gaimar's *Estoire des Engleis*. He is currently finishing a monograph, *The School of Letters: Pedagogy, Formation, and Sociability in Anglo-Norman Literature* (1100-1215), and has begun work on a new monograph project, *Emergence and Location in Early Anglo-Norman Literature*, that locates early Anglo-Norman literature and the cultural developments of the twelfth-century renaissance in the very particular sociabilities, social contexts, and local geographies of their emergence in high medieval England.

Robert Shaw is currently completing a doctoral thesis at Oriel College, Oxford, on the Celestine monks of France in the Later Middle Ages.

Amy N. Vines is Assistant Professor of English at the University of North Carolina-Greensboro. She is preparing a monograph on literary models of female social and cultural influence in late medieval romance; her most recent publications include a book chapter titled "Lullaby as Lament: Learning to Mourn in Middle English Nativity Lyrics" forthcoming in *Laments for the Lost: Medieval Mourning and Elegy*, edited by Jane Tolmie and M. Jane Toswell (Brepols 2010), and an essay in *Modern Philology*, "A Woman's 'Crafte': Melior as Lover, Teacher, and Patron in the Middle English *Partonope of Blois*" (2007).

Edward Wheatley is the Edward L. Surtz, S.J., Professor of Medieval Literature at Loyola University, Chicago. His book, *Stumbling Blocks Before the Blind: Medieval Constructions of a Disability*, was published in the University of Michigan Press series *Corporealities: Discourses of Disability* in Spring 2010.

Katherine Zieman is Assistant Professor of English at Notre Dame. Her recent book is *Singing the New Song: Literacy and Liturgy in Late Medieval England* (University of Pennsylvania Press, 2008).

Jordan Zweck is a Ph.D. candidate in English at Yale University. She has recently completed a dissertation which traces the circulation and audiences of the Sunday Letter in medieval England, Ireland, and Iceland, exploring the ways in which documentary culture created and shaped communities. Starting in the fall, she will be Assistant Professor of English at the University of Wisconsin at Madison.

Corrigendum for JEBS 12

Fredell, Joel. "Design and Authorship in the Book of Margery Kempe," *Journal of the Early Book Society* 12 (2009): 1-28. The text of note 18 should read as follows:

On the "IHU" as a signal for meditation in Carthusian manuscripts, see Mary Morse, "Mise-en-page," *Studia Mystica* 20 (1999): 15-42; for its appearance in northern devotional manuscripts see John B. Friedman, *Northern English Books, Owners and makers in the Late Middle Ages* (Syracuse 1995), 149.

Breinigsville, PA USA
13 May 2010
237982BV00005B/1/P